FUNCTIONAL INEFFICIENCY

FUNCTIONAL INEFFICIENCY

THE UNEXPECTED BENEFITS OF WASTING TIME AND MONEY

PETER S. WENZ

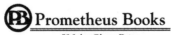 Prometheus Books

59 John Glenn Drive
Amherst, New York 14228

Published 2015 by Prometheus Books

Cover design by Grace M. Conti-Zilsberger
Cover image © Bigstock

Prometheus Books recognizes the following registered trademarks and service marks mentioned within the text: Avastin®, Blackboard®, Campath®, Cardiolite®, Celexa®, Cerezyme®, Chevrolet Sonic®, Chivas Regal®, Clarinex®, Cord Blood Registry℠, Corian®, Detrol®, Diovan®, Energizer Bunny®, Ford Excursion®, Ford Fiesta®, Formica®, Honda Accord®, Honda Civic®, Honda Fit®, iPad®, iPhone®, Jeep Grand Cherokee®, Kenworth®, Lexapro®, Lincoln Navigator®, Mirapex®, Nexium®, Paxil®, Prozac®, Sarafem®, Seroquel®, Tarceva®, Walt Disney World®, Xanax®

Inquiries should be addressed to
Prometheus Books
59 John Glenn Drive
Amherst, New York 14228
VOICE: 716–691–0133 • FAX: 716–691–0137
WWW.PROMETHEUSBOOKS.COM

19 18 17 16 15   5 4 3 2 1

Library of Congress Cataloging-in-Publication Data

Wenz, Peter S.
    Functional inefficiency : the unexpected benefits of wasting time and money / Peter S. Wenz.
        pages cm
    Includes bibliographical references and index.
    ISBN 978-1-63388-040-5 (hardback) — ISBN 978-1-63388-041-2 (e-book)
    1. Unemployment—United States. 2. Technological innovations—Economic aspects—United States. 3. Economic development—United States. 4. United States—Economic policy—21st century. I. Title.

HD5724.W4176 2015
330—dc23
                                                                          2015000804

Printed in the United States of America

*This book is dedicated to the memory of Joyce,
and to Lola,
the great granddaughter whom she knew too briefly.*

CONTENTS

ACKNOWLEDGMENTS

Many people were kind enough to help me with this book. Most of them are members of CIPG, the Central Illinois Philosophy Group, including Jose Arce, Peter Boltuc, Meredith Cargill, Cindy Cochrane, Bernd Estabrook, Bob Kunath, Dick Palmer, Larry Shiner, and Bill Underwood. Special thanks among these thinkers are due to Meredith and Larry for being such pains in the butt. I thank additionally my New York City friend Steve Allen, who tried to keep my figures honest. Any remaining errors are entirely my fault for not having smarter friends.

I want to thank my agent, Grace Feedson, and my editor at Prometheus, Steven L. Mitchell, the former for finding the latter and the latter for exercising good judgment.

Finally, I thank my wife, Grace, who was always available and even seemed happy to assist when I had queries or quandaries to sort through.

CHAPTER 1

INTRODUCTION

How Inefficiency Can Be Beneficial

How can inefficiency be beneficial? Contemporary Americans value efficiency. We assume that efficiency is a good thing, and we take inefficiency to be dysfunctional. In this book I explain how problems of unemployment stemming from increasingly efficient uses of labor lead us nevertheless to tolerate certain inefficiencies that serve the function or are meant to serve the function of reducing unemployment. I identify six categories of social practices that address or are meant to address unemployment, investigating efficiencies and inefficiencies associated with each category, and suggesting ways to promote American economic growth and job creation within environmental limits with less inefficiency. I use four criteria to evaluate each category and its component practices. Do the practices in the category actually reduce unemployment? Do they embody efficiency or inefficiency? Are they environmentally sustainable? And is adoption of the practices culturally acceptable and politically feasible in the current American context? I conclude that *the American economy can grow indefinitely and create an unlimited number of jobs within environmental limits while many inefficiencies that impair human welfare are eliminated.* But to keep unemployment at acceptably low levels, some forms of inefficiency must remain.

The First Opium War (1840–1842) between Britain and China illustrates how, under conditions of increasing labor efficiency, inefficiency can function to forestall or reduce unemployment. In 1839, Chinese Commissioner Lin Tse-hsu addressed an open letter to the young Queen Victoria of England. His concern was that smugglers using British ships were supplying opium to the people of China, resulting in massive addiction. His complaint will sound familiar to twenty-first century Americans concerned about cocaine from Columbia and heroin from Afghanistan.

Commissioner Lin assumed incorrectly that opium was illegal in England, but he was certainly correct about the drug's baleful influence. Opium consumption slows the heart and general metabolism, causes irregularity of basic bodily functions, and leads to loss of body weight. Worst of all, it's addictive, becoming as necessary to the addict as food or water. Withdrawal symptoms are severe, including "extreme restlessness, chills, hot flushes, sneezing, sweating, salivation, running nose . . . , nausea, vomiting, and diarrhea. There are severe cramps in the abdomen, legs, and back; the bones ache; the muscles twitch; and the nerves are on edge. Every symptom is in combat with another. The addict is hungry, but he cannot eat; he is sleepy, but he cannot sleep."[1] Most addicts will lie, cheat, steal, ignore work and family obligations, and violate all other moral norms essential to society's peace and prosperity just to get another dose. It's hard to imagine a more baleful use of resources than to promote such an addiction. This is why Commissioner Lin assumed opium consumption to be illegal in England.

"We are of the opinion," Lin wrote, "that this poisonous article is clandestinely manufactured by artful and depraved people of various tribes under the dominion of your honorable nation. Doubtless you, the honorable sovereign of that nation, have not commanded the manufacture and sale of it." (This was true. The queen had not commanded the manufacture and sale of opium, but neither had she effectively prohibited it.) Lin continued, "To manufacture and sell it, and with it to seduce the simple folk of this land, is to seek one's own livelihood by exposing others to death, to seek one's own advantage by another man's injury. Such acts are bitterly abhorrent to the nature of man and are utterly opposed to the ways of heaven."[2] Commissioner Lin then appealed to the Golden Rule,

> Let us suppose that foreigners came from another country, and brought opium into England, and seduced the people of your country to smoke it. Would not you, the sovereign of the said country, look upon such a procedure with anger, and in your just indignation endeavor to get rid of it? Now we have always heard that Your Highness possesses a most kind and benevolent heart. Surely then you are incapable of doing or causing to be done unto another that which you should not wish another to do unto you.[3]

The commissioner recommended that Queen Victoria destroy the poppy fields and punish manufacturers of opium. His letter, which probably never reached the queen, was intended to solicit cooperation regarding illegal opium traffic, thereby reducing tensions between the two countries and averting war.

For his part, the commissioner was determined to catch and punish those who tried to smuggle opium into China. He had been sent by the Chinese emperor to Canton, the main locus of legitimate trade between China and the rest of the world, to eradicate the illegal traffic. He knew that ships anchored offshore contained huge amounts of opium and demanded that this contraband cargo be given to him for destruction. He wouldn't accept the word of British and American sea captains that they would abandon efforts to move the heroin to the mainland. When the cargo was not turned over to him, he confined all the foreign merchants in Canton's factory district (the area of foreign trading), denying them some of the comforts of life for forty-seven days until they finally relented.

The merchants who owned the opium complained that the seizure of their property was illegal and demanded compensation from the Chinese or from their own governments. But Commissioner Lin didn't think he owed them anything, any more than current drug enforcement agencies feel obligated to compensate manufacturers and smugglers when they confiscate and destroy illegal drugs.

While all of this was taking place, British naval officers in the area appealed to England to send war ships, which arrived the following year. The British were determined to force the Chinese to allow free trade along the Chinese coast. Against international trading rules then and now, the British had no intention of interfering with the illegal opium traffic because that traffic helped Britain sell the enormous quantities of cotton goods that were then pouring out of the recently mechanized and increasingly efficient mills in Lancashire.

The nineteenth-century conflict between Britain and China over opium may be the first indication in history that *labor efficiency often provokes countervailing inefficiency*. Cotton textiles were the foundation of early British industrialization and remained its backbone until about 1840. Textiles are important in every society because there's always a market; everyone needs at least one set of clothing. English manufacturers started to meet this demand in novel ways with James Hargreaves's invention of the spinning jenny in about 1764, which mechanically drew out and twisted fibers into threads. Around the same time, carding and combing machines were developed to prepare thread for spinning. In 1769, Richard Arkwright added nonhuman power to the process by developing a water-powered spinning machine. Cotton worked better in these new machines than either wool or linen, which is why the revolution in textiles was initially confined to cotton. Even in cotton, however, weaving was still done by human power until, after some unsuccessful attempts, power looms took over in Manchester, the center of textile manufacture in England, in the first two decades of the nineteenth century.[4]

Increases in productivity were astounding. Already by 1800, before large-scale introduction of power looms, the production of cotton cloth had increased eight fold over what it had been just twenty years earlier.[5] In spinning, one English worker in 1812 could equal the output of two hundred people in 1770. In weaving, "by 1833, one worker with a child helper could operate four looms that could produce twenty times the output of one hand-loom weaver."[6] Power looms soon replaced hand looms.

As the labor efficiency of production improved, prices declined and demand for inexpensive cotton goods increased at home and abroad. Formerly, India had exported cotton goods to Britain because cotton is native to India and Indians were masters of cotton textile manufacture. As late as 1813, India was still exporting £2 million of cotton goods to Britain, whereas by 1830 the same value of cotton goods was imported by India from Britain.[7] Historian Jack Beeching explains,

> By applying steam power to textile manufacture, and filling their mills with little children who worked until they dropped, Lancashire manufacturers had managed . . . to produce cotton cloth so cheap and yet so good that a native craftsman depending on his spinning wheel and hand loom could hardly hope to compete. . . . British textiles poured into India. The 30,000 looms that had woven the famous Cashmere shawls were slowly reduced to 6,000 and the weavers made destitute.[8]

At first, because cotton doesn't grow in Britain, the British increased the amount of cotton it imported from India. But it was soon much cheaper to import cotton from places closer to home, such as Surinam, Demarara,

Berbice, Grenada, St. Lucia, and the southern United States.[9] This created a problem. British manufacturers depended on exporting their finished textiles to India and elsewhere to keep their factories operating profitably. "By the 1830s, three fourths of British exports were textiles and clothing."[10] But the Indians had just lost a major source of their own earning power owing to reduced exports of raw cotton and cotton textiles to Britain. Where were the Indians to get the money they needed to continue to pay for the extraordinary output of Britain's Lancashire mills?

India needed to create a demand for something else it produced, and Britain was ready to help because profits in textiles hung in the balance. "This explains," historian Tan Chung writes, "why the [British] Indian interests were bent on increasing Indian exports to China to an excess over Britain's demand for China's goods."[11] Why China? China was attractive to Indian and other exporters for some of the same reasons that the United States is an attractive market today. China had then, as it has now, a significant percentage of the world's population and, before 1860 or so, it was among the world's wealthiest societies.[12]

However, the Chinese felt little need to import goods from India or elsewhere, because they were satisfied with their own products. When King George III tried to improve commercial ties with China in 1793, the ageing Emperor Ch'ien Lung replied to the King's letter,

> Our ways have no resemblance to yours, and even were your envoy competent to acquire some rudiments of them, he could not transplant them to your barbarous land. . . . Strange and costly objects do not interest me. As your Ambassador can see for himself, we possess all things. I set no value on strange objects and ingenious [devices], and have no use for your country's manufactures.[13]

A generation later the British found an item that was not produced in China and that the Chinese would find attractive enough to buy from India: opium. Efforts to sell other goods were still unsuccessful. In 1832, the East India Company sent a ship to China with two hundred sample bales of textiles and lost £5,647, whereas that same year a ship selling opium in Amoy, Foochow, and Ch'uan-chou Bay China came back with $330,000 in silver.[14] "As a result [of Indian sales of opium to China], silver began to flow from

China to India as her payment for Indian goods. Indian revenues got replenished in this process."[15] This gave India silver that it could use to pay for British goods, including textiles. Thus, a harmful practice, which we will see below is reasonably called "fundamentally inefficient," was highly functional; it helped to maintain profits and forestall unemployment in England's increasingly labor-efficient textile industry.

*   *   *

This episode in history would have little current significance except that it illustrates a phenomenon of enormous importance today—inefficiency often counterbalances efficiency. Inefficiency (of one sort) maintains employment when efficiency (of another sort) throws people out of work.

Efficiency is a matter of inputs and outputs; the greater the desired output from a given quantity of necessary inputs, the more efficient the operation. So, there are many types of efficiency corresponding to different inputs and outputs. Fuel efficiency in cars, for example, measures how many miles the car will go (desired output) per gallon of gas (needed input). A common measure of efficiency uses human labor hours as inputs and desired product as output. For example, people often say that American agriculture is the most efficient in the world because it takes the full-time work of less than two percent of the American population (input) to grow enough food to feed the nation (output). This is labor efficiency. Other countries use a larger percentage of their populations to grow enough food for everyone, so their agriculture is considered less efficient on this measure. However, labor hours are not the only reasonable input. Because fresh water is in short supply worldwide and is necessary to grow crops, it's reasonable to measure agricultural efficiency with water as the input and crops as the output. On this measure of efficiency, water efficiency, some Israeli agriculture is more efficient than most American agriculture. Another plausible measure of agricultural efficiency emphasizes the importance of arable land because it, too, is in short supply: the more food that results from an acre of land, the more efficient the agriculture. On this accounting, some labor-intensive (less labor-efficient) agricultural methods in other countries are often more efficient than America's more labor-efficient techniques.

Judgments of efficiency are inherently comparative, although the comparison is often implicit. A car that gets 45 mpg is considered fuel efficient because most cars get much less. If most cars got 85 mpg it wouldn't be considered fuel efficient. As we'll see in chapter 7, the American healthcare system is very inefficient, a judgment based on the fact that other advanced industrial countries get better health outcomes with much less per capita spending on healthcare.

Labor efficiency, one of the most important types of efficiency in the modern world, *is both a blessing and a curse.* The curse is *unemployment created by increasingly efficient uses of human labor hours*. Because labor-efficient productivity allows fewer workers to produce the same product, many workers are thrown out of work when there is insufficient demand for an increased supply of that product. For example, if automated production methods enable a soda-bottling company to use only one third the number of workers to bottle the same amount of soda, all workers could be retained if the company had customers for three times as much soda as it was selling previously. In most cases, however, although demand may increase somewhat owing to the lower price of the more efficiently produced soda, demand is not likely to triple. Keeping all workers on the job would therefore result in overproduction. Unemployment stems from increased labor efficiency because overproduction results in unsold product and financial loss.

This was evident early in the Industrial Revolution as skilled workers, displaced by increasingly efficient manufacturing processes in the textile industry, tried in vain to retain their jobs by smashing machines used to improve labor efficiency. Richard Hargreaves's original spinning jenny was destroyed in 1767, and its newer version was destroyed in 1769. In Normandy, France, writes historian William Rosen, there were dozens of such incidents in 1789 alone: "In July, hundreds of spinning jennys were destroyed, along with a French version of Arkwright's water frame. In October, an attorney in Rouen applauded the destruction of 'the machines used in cotton-spinning that have deprived many workers of their jobs.'"[16]

The most notorious machinery-destroying rebellion was at its height in 1811 and 1812 in England. In March 1811, weavers of stockings began smashing efficiency-improving stocking frames, a practice that they continued for weeks. After a summer lull they resumed in the fall, by which time they had destroyed almost one thousand of the twenty-five thousand to twenty-nine thousand such machines in Nottingham, Leicestershire, and Derbyshire. Their commander used the name Ned Ludd in honor of a young stocking maker, Ned Ludham, who had earlier smashed a stocking frame in Leicester. By December 1811, these Luddites were smashing both weaving and spinning machinery.[17] In 1812, the Crown deployed twelve thousand troops to put down the rebellion. Rosen concludes, "The Luddite rebellion failed for the most obvious reason: an enormous disparity in military power." In addition, "the Luddite idea lost the historical battle—'Luddite' is not, in most of the contemporary world, used as anything but an insult." The Luddite idea lost because their opponents had economics on their side. The opponents "produced more wealth, not just for individuals, but for an entire nation."[18]

Increased labor efficiency won the day because it generally improved the lives of people by increasing material wealth. This is the blessing of labor efficiency. According to economic historian Natalie McPherson, increased *labor efficiency—fewer hours of work needed as input for a given product as output*—is the cornerstone of our current material prosperity.

> In 1770, the average European farmed from sunrise to sunset six days a week. This individual ate mostly bread and owned one outfit of clothing. If this person was British he was slightly richer: He probably owned a pair of shoes. Travel to the next village was an occasion to remember for a lifetime. People went to bed when the sun went down because oil lamps were expensive and homemade candles and fat lamps were not bright enough to allow much activity at night. . . .
>
> In industrial societies today we work forty-hour weeks. Our modern closets are full of clothes and shoes. We jet to vacations in sunny spots far away. Our homes are full of electric lights, washing machines, refrigerators, soft beds, and chairs. We have personal computers, television sets, and automobiles. The change in the lifestyle of the average person in the United States in the past 250 years is greater than the change in lifestyle in the preceding 2,000 years. . . . In fact, the standard of living in eighteenth-century England was roughly the same as that in Rome in the first century.[19]

McPherson attributes dramatic changes in our material circumstances to astronomical increases in the average worker's economic output. Machines using nonhuman and nonanimal sources of energy now do much of the work that was formerly done by hand, and our competitive economic system rewards continuous innovation, resulting in products that were unimaginable in previous eras, such as televisions and automobiles.

Journalist Adam Davidson puts the matter this way,

> Productivity, in and of itself, is a remarkably good thing. Only through productivity growth can the average quality of human life improve. Because of higher agricultural productivity, we don't all have to work in the fields to make enough food to eat. Because of higher industrial productivity, few of us need to work in factories to make the products we use. In theory, productivity growth should help nearly everyone in a society. When one person can grow as much food or make as many car parts as 100 used to, prices should fall, which gives everyone in that society more purchasing power; we all become a little richer. . . . As workers become more productive, they should be able to demand higher salaries.[20]

As salaries rise, producers find it profitable to substitute increasingly efficient labor-saving machinery for human labor, because human labor is now more costly. Some people lose their jobs, but the hourly productivity of those who retain their jobs increases again, because these workers are now using more sophisticated machines. This is a virtuous circle of material enrichment. One result, historian William Rosen notes, is that people are now able to earn more quickly the money they need for basic necessities: "A skilled fourth-century weaver in the city of Constantinople might earn enough by working three hours to purchase a pound of bread; by 1800, it would cost a weaver working in Nottingham at least two. But by 1900, it took less than fifteen minutes to earn enough to buy the loaf; and by 2000, five minutes."[21]

In sum, people in industrial countries are richer than their ancestors because industrial and related technological developments make people's labor hours more productive than in the past. People have more powerful tools than ever to appropriate earth's natural resources and alter earth's ecosystems in the course of creating products that people need and want. According to mainstream economic thinking, human needs and wants (which economists seldom differentiate from one another) are for all practical purposes infinite, making scarcity a permanent feature of the human condition. Increased labor efficiency helps to reduce this scarcity and thereby improve human wellbeing (welfare, satisfaction, flourishing) through the provision of increased amounts of material wealth.

*   *   *

However, as we'll see in later chapters, increased material wealth doesn't always improve human wellbeing. In societies that are already wealthy as a result of industrialization, increased material riches may leave most people's quality of life unaffected or degraded. Another kind of efficiency distinct from labor efficiency is needed to discuss this phenomenon—*fundamental efficiency*. Like all types of efficiency, *fundamental efficiency improves with increases in desired output per unit of needed input, but fundamental efficiency is more inclusive because the needed input is human and natural resources generally, and the output is human wellbeing (satisfaction, happiness, welfare, flourishing)*. Economist William Baxter gets at the concept this way,

> The dominant feature of human existence is scarcity—our available resources, our aggregate labors, and our skill in employing both have always been, and will continue for some time to be, inadequate to yield to every man all the tangible and intangible satisfactions he would like to have. Hence, none of those resources, or labors, or skills, should be wasted—that is, employed so as to yield less than they might yield in human satisfactions.[22]

For reasons of endemic scarcity, therefore, resources, labors, and skills (all that people have at their disposal to be productive) should be used as efficiently as possible to produce what people need and want in order to improve human satisfaction. The ultimate goal is human satisfaction, not material wealth, because human satisfactions are intangible as well as tangible and because it would make little sense to produce more material wealth if that wealth didn't contribute to human satisfaction (welfare, wellbeing, flourishing). Nobel Prize-winning economist Paul Krugman puts it this way, "Economics is not about wealth—it's about the pursuit of happiness."[23]

In other words, *the ultimate economic goal is human welfare (wellbeing, satisfac-*

tion, flourishing). The most important kind of efficiency could therefore be called "human-welfare efficiency" or "human-wellbeing efficiency." However, such terms (besides being long and ugly) may give the impression that such efficiency is just one more kind of efficiency on a par with fuel efficiency, water efficiency, and labor efficiency, whereas what I'm trying to get at is something much more central to all human enterprises, the attempt to get as much human good as possible from expenditures of natural resources and human efforts. Because mainstream economic thinking considers the human good to be fundamental to all human economic activity, I call this kind of efficiency "fundamental efficiency."

Fundamental efficiency exists to the extent that human and natural resources are used to make the greatest possible contribution to human welfare under the circumstances. The absence of fundamental efficiency is fundamental inefficiency. *Fundamental inefficiency exists to the extent that the use of human and natural resources fails to maximize human wellbeing.* Failure to maximize employment, production, or profit constitutes fundamental inefficiency only insofar as such failure deprives human beings of the greatest flourishing possible under the circumstances.

It's important to avoid confusing fundamental efficiency and inefficiency with functional efficiency and inefficiency, because the two terms "fundamental" and "functional" sound so much alike. *Fundamental* efficiency and inefficiency refer to efficiency and inefficiency as measured by the most inclusive or overall inputs and outputs; the inputs are all of the human and natural resources at human disposal at any given time, and the output is human welfare or flourishing. Other types of efficiency concern more limited categories of inputs and outputs, such as fuel as input and miles traveled as output, or hours worked as input and cars produced as output. *Functional efficiency and inefficiency*, by contrast, don't refer to a type of efficiency as indicated by certain inputs and outputs. Instead, they *refer in the present work exclusively to the roles that efficiency and inefficiency play in reducing unemployment*. Both efficiency and inefficiency can be functional in this sense. In some circumstances, efficiency can reduce unemployment; in other circumstances, inefficiency can reduce unemployment. I am concerned about the functionality in this sense of both fundamental efficiency and fundamental inefficiency.

In the fundamental sense of efficiency, manufacturing and marketing opium, as the British did in China, was inefficient, because opium addiction impairs rather than promotes human flourishing, and there was no over-riding good that justified damaging people in this way. Intuitively, it seems that addicting millions of people to opium harms humanity much more than humanity was helped by thousands of people getting to keep their jobs under near slave conditions in mechanized textile factories. Nor, in my view, was the fundamental inefficiency of manufacturing and marketing opium ameliorated by the positive result that Indian consumers got cheaper cotton goods. Surely many alternative uses of human and natural resources available to humanity at the time would have better promoted human flourishing. So the practice of manufacturing and marketing opium was fundamentally inefficient.

This is not to say, however, that it was inefficient in any other sense. The poppies may have been grown with great labor efficiency or with the efficient use of water, meaning that more poppies were produced per hour of labor or liter of water than in most other processes. The poppies may have been trans-formed into opium with great labor efficiency or energy efficiency, meaning that more opium was produced from the poppies per hour of human labor or unit of nonhuman energy than in most other processes. Nevertheless, from the most inclusive or overall perspective of human welfare, the entire practice was fundamentally inefficient because human and natural resources were used in ways that unnecessarily impaired rather than improved human welfare. Alternative uses of these resources would have resulted in greater human wellbeing. But raising poppies and manufacturing opium in India for sale in China was nonetheless functional in the context of the nineteenth-century because it helped to reduce unemployment in England.

When discussing the efficiency of a practice or process, the context usually suffices to indicate the kind of efficiency at issue, whether labor efficiency, energy efficiency, water efficiency, or fundamental efficiency. For example, if the issue is the efficiency of electricity generation from a certain kind of power plant, the input is fuel and the output is electricity, unless otherwise indi-cated. Fundamental efficiency—in which the input is all human and natural resources at people's disposal and the output is human flourishing—may or may not be advanced by fuel-efficient electricity generation. The relationship of fuel efficiency or any other kind of efficiency to fundamental efficiency must be established by further discussion.

Fundamental efficiency is the most inclusive measure of efficiency, but as used here it doesn't include all cases and sources of human flourishing. First, limited knowledge about the future makes me reticent to judge what practices or institutions will conduce to human wellbeing thousands, much less hundreds of thousands of years in the future. People today have powers of movement, communication, and productivity that would have been science fiction in past centuries. I can't tell what speculations of current science fiction might become practical realities in the future, or how the employment of new technologies might affect human flourishing. I confine myself for this reason primarily to human practices and welfare in the twenty-first century, with most emphasis on our current situation and the next generation or two.

Second, although human flourishing concerns all human beings, I concentrate in this work on the United States, using examples drawn from other countries primarily to clarify concepts and make comparisons that may be helpful in addressing the American situation.

* * *

As opium addiction in China illustrates, the problem of unemployment created by increasing labor efficiency sometimes makes fundamental inefficiency functional in an otherwise efficiency-oriented economy. Inefficiency is one way of soaking up efficiency's overproduction. In some respects, the goods and services that humans produce with industrial efficiency are like carbon dioxide, something that's generally good until it's overabundant, at which point it becomes a pollutant; CO_2 threatens to warm the planet, increasing storm activity and inundating coastal cities. There are two general approaches to dealing with overabundant CO_2. We can put less carbon dioxide into the air, such as by burning less fossil fuel, and/or we can improve the environmental sink—that is, increase the ability of the environment to absorb or remove CO_2 from the air, such as by planting more trees than we cut down.

In the case of labor efficiency, the extra goods and services that have not yet found a want they can satisfy are like carbon dioxide in excess. Just as carbon dioxide is good in itself, so, generally speaking, are these goods and services, except when they are overabundant. In excess they are like pollution insofar as they create noxious conditions. They reduce profitability and increase unemployment.

The consequences of overproduction can be drastic. Novelist and journalist James Kunstler blames overproduction resulting from increasing labor efficiency for creating the conditions that resulted in the Great Depression. Farmers started using tractors with internal combustion engines instead of horses in the 1920s. When hitched up to accessory machines such as reapers, seed drills, threshers, diskers, and mowers, the tractors enabled farmers to increase their output, which caused prices of agricultural products to drop because demand had not increased commensurate with supply. At the same time, farmers had more expenses because, lacking horses and their excrement, they had to buy more fertilizer.[24] Thus, many farmers became impoverished in the 1920s, and this significantly reduced overall consumer demand because as late as 1930 over 21 percent of the American workforce was engaged in farming.[25]

In addition, greater efficiency in automobile manufacture, which was the backbone of American prosperity in the 1920s according to Kunstler, also resulted in overproduction. An auto industry survey conducted in 1926 revealed that only one-third of auto dealers were making a profit because the market for cars was saturated. Kunstler writes,

> The building boom associated with the new automobile suburbs started fizzling in early 1928. . . . The huge public expenditure in paving streets and building new highways also reached a kind of natural limit in the late twenties; the basic infrastructure for cars was now in place. The slowdown in car and home sales and in road-building affected suppliers down the line: steel makers, tire makers, glassmakers, lumber companies, cement companies. The makers of small consumer products like waffle irons, having adopted the assembly-line methods of Ford, also ran up against the wall of market saturation. American industry had geared up for rates of production that could not be justified by flattened demand.[26]

If it can abet a slide toward depression, overproduction is a serious economic problem that cannot be ignored.

Inefficiency is one way, but not the only way, that our society avoids or absorbs the overabundance that results from increasingly labor-efficient methods of production. As we will see, we avoid overabundance in part by idling workers, such as through incarceration, shorter work weeks, extended educational programs, and early retirement. Some of this idling, besides functioning to reduce unemployment, is fundamentally efficient; it improves human flourishing more than available alternatives. But some is fundamentally inefficient because it unnecessarily degrades human life. In addition, we absorb overproduction, creating sinks for overproduction as if it were a pollutant, in part by meeting some of our needs through inefficient systems, such as inefficient systems in transportation and healthcare. These systems are functional insofar as they combat unemployment but are nevertheless fundamentally inefficient. We also encourage people increasingly to consume goods and services. Some of this consumption is fundamentally efficient and some is not.

Not all inefficiency in our economy functions primarily to forestall or soak up overabundance that leads to unemployment. Many inefficiencies are adopted to increase corporate profits without regard to overabundance or unemployment. The investment company Goldman Sachs, for example, is reported to earn additional profit from its aluminum storage business by retaining aluminum in storage longer than necessary so it can collect additional storage fees. Because international rules require moving three thousand tons of aluminum per day, Goldman Sachs has the aluminum moved from one warehouse to another in the Detroit area, thereby delaying the delivery of aluminum to manufacturers. This practice cost consumers of products containing aluminum an extra $5 billion between 2010 and 2013. It generated employment, as workers were needed to move aluminum from one warehouse to another, but the main goal and function was to increase profit for the company, not to reduce unemployment, much less to improve fundamental efficiency, which it clearly degraded.[27]

Companies sometimes maximize profit at the expense of fundamental efficiency by convincing consumers that their products improve human wellbeing when they really don't. Tobacco companies come to mind in this context. Other inefficiencies may result from companies trying to maximize profit by using campaign contributions to convince politicians to perpetuate monopolies through patent extensions. Pharmaceutical companies may fall into this category. Some companies maximize profits by convincing government officials that the economy functions best when environmental damages are ignored. Campaign contributions by fossil fuel interests may thus promote government policies that are inefficient (when all environmental factors are considered). Still other inefficiencies may result from companies seeking to maximize profit by convincing voters and politicians through public relations efforts and campaign contributions to extend inefficient, government-sponsored projects, such as the production of corn-based ethanol for automotive fuel. In addition, all inefficiencies promoted through campaign contributions may function in part to fulfill the political ambitions of people who want to be or to remain elected officials regardless of the effects on human welfare.

Inefficiencies that serve these purposes may also function to forestall or soak up overabundance and thereby combat unemployment. Because the effect of inefficiency on unemployment is the focus of the present work, I consider in this work inefficiencies primarily insofar as they promote employment or combat unemployment.

One additional word before moving on: functionality is not the same as either intentionality or conscious recognition. My claim is that a great deal of inefficiency in our society serves the function of reducing unemployment. This is not to say that *all* of these inefficiencies were designed intentionally to serve this function, nor is it to say that all inefficient practices are recognized consciously as being inefficient. Consider this: For some people, hitting baseballs serves the functions of relieving tension and abating aggression, but this doesn't mean these people hit baseballs intentionally to relieve tension or abate aggression, nor that they even recognize that the practice serves these purposes. Our actions sometimes have results, both welcome and unwelcome, that we don't intend or even recognize.

✻   ✻   ✻

Mainstream economists look to overall economic growth, not to inefficiency, to lower unemployment in the long run. As the economy grows, more workers are needed and unemployment falls. In addition, because human needs and wants are virtually limitless, economic growth enables more people to have more of the goods and services that they desire. Politicians on all sides compete for votes with alternate means of generating economic growth to create jobs for willing workers and material abundance for society in general.

However, there are two problems with the current economic-growth solution to unemployment. First, it doesn't seem to be working very well. Economist Paul Krugman notes significant deterioration of the unemployment situation between 2007 and 2013. "Back in 2007," he writes, "there were about seven million unemployed Americans—but only a fraction of this total, around 1.2 million, had been out of work more than six months." Five years later, almost 12 million were unemployed, and, worse yet, 4.6 million of them had been jobless for at least six months and more than 3 million were unemployed for a year or more. Because employers tend to shy away from hiring people who have been out of the workforce for more than 6 months or a year, we may be witnessing the creation of "a permanent class of jobless Americans."[28]

In addition to the nearly 12 million Americans who were unemployed in April 2013, another 7.6 million—3 million more than in 2007—were employed only part-time, even though they wanted full-time jobs. If you add these underemployed workers and those who want to work but have become so discouraged that they've stopped looking for work to the officially unemployed, the level of employment shortfall in April 2013 goes from an unemployment rate of 7.6 percent to the discouraging but more realistic rate of 13.8 percent.[29]

Another way to see the problem is to look at labor force participation, the percentage of people 16 years and older who participate in the workforce. In spite of the "economic recovery" after the Great Recession, as the unemployment rate dropped from 10 percent in October 2009[30] to 7.6 percent in April 2013[31] the rate of labor force participation dropped from 65 percent to 63.4 percent.[32] Worse yet, labor force participation declined further between April 2013 and April 2014 even as economic recovery continued. The unemployment rate went from 7.6 percent to 6.3 percent as job growth averaged 190,000 per month. Long-term unemployment dropped by over 900,000. Even so, labor force participation went from 63.4 percent to 62.8 percent. By the end of 2014 the unemployment rate was only 5.6 percent but labor force participation was down yet again, to 62.7 percent.[33] Thus, addressing American unemployment through increased economic growth seems not to be working. The efficient use of human labor may have reached such a point that the economy can't grow fast enough to keep people working and thereby forestall declines in labor force participation.

The second problem with economic growth as a solution to unemployment is that many environmentalists who are as keen as economists to promote human wellbeing find that such growth in advanced industrial societies threatens our physical safety. These environmentalists worry that increased production and consumption of *material goods* jeopardizes human wellbeing in the long run because it degrades the environmental conditions on which human flourishing depends. Christopher Flavin, president of the Worldwatch Institute, explains,

> In a physically constrained world, material growth cannot continue indefinitely, and when that growth is exponential . . . the limits are reached more abruptly and catastrophically than even the best scientists are able to predict. From falling water tables to soaring oil prices and collapsing fisheries, the ecological systems that underpin the global economy are under extraordinary stress.[34]

Alan Durning of the Worldwatch Institute points out that labor-efficient methods of manufacture and consequent increases in consumption are often particularly environmentally ruinous:

> Industrial countries' factories generate most of the world's hazardous chemical wastes. . . . The fossil fuels that power the consumer society are its most ruinous input. Wresting coal, oil, and natural gas from the earth permanently disrupts countless habitats; burning them causes an overwhelming share of the world's air pollution; and refining them generates huge quantities of toxic wastes.[35]

Similarly, labor-efficient fishing techniques deplete fisheries and labor-efficient methods of raising livestock (factory farms) cause air and water pollution. Considerations such as these convince many environmentalists that human wellbeing is best served by curtailing the production of material goods, even if that means curtailing economic growth.[36]

But that's not realistic; it's way outside the mainstream of American economic and political thought. Can you imagine someone running for president saying that because past economic growth has harmed the environment our country should no longer seek economic growth; that we should now cease trying to provide employment for people by growing the economy; that material comforts have reached their limit; that it's only right and proper that the next generation be no more materially comfortable than the present generation? You don't have to be a professional political consultant to know that for now and for the foreseeable future a campaign based on such a no-growth platform would do well only on Comedy Central.

In addition, claims Harvard political economist Benjamin Friedman, societies that favor economic growth promote many commendable habits and values in order to foster that growth: "Thriftiness fosters saving, which enhances our productivity by making capital investment possible. Education likewise increases our individual capabilities as well as our stock of public knowledge."[37] Friedman argues also that for the most part since the Civil War periods of economic growth have been characterized by greater openness, tolerance, mobility, fairness, and democracy than periods of economic stagnation. The growth periods of the Horatio Alger era (1865–1880), Progressive era (1895–1919), and Civil Rights era (1945–1973) correspond with what most people consider progress in our political morality, as our society during these periods became more tolerant, inclusive, fair, and democratic. Friedman quotes historian David Potter: "An economic surplus was available to pay democracy's promissory notes." By contrast, with the exception of the Great Depression, during periods of economic stagnation and consequent economic insecurity, Friedman argues, people moved away from openness, tolerance, mobility, fairness, and democracy, as the Populist era (1880–1895), the Klan era (1920–1929), and the Backlash era (1973–1993) illustrate.[38] Friedman finds the same correlation of economic growth with moral progress in other countries as well. Worldwide, "the evidence suggests that economic growth usually fosters democracy and all this entails . . . , [whereas] the *absence* of democratic freedoms *impedes* economic growth, and that the resulting stagnation in turn makes a society even more intolerant and undemocratic."[39] So, economic growth is not only politically popular, it may also be necessary for the maintenance and advancement of the highest personal and collective moral standards.

This seems to create a dilemma. The increasing labor efficiency with which human beings manipulate and transform nature into products for human use is both good (it gives us consumer goods, lighter workloads, more varied experiences, and less expensive food, while also fostering high moral standards) and bad (it causes unemployment and despoils the earth). It seems that industrial people must choose between a future with economic growth, environmental decline, and more unemployment than we would wish, and a future of economic stagnation, environmental stability, and catastrophic levels of unemployment. Either way, it seems that human wellbeing is threatened. Because the no-growth alternative is politically unacceptable, it seems that we are doomed to environmental decline.

Fortunately, this bleak prospect is not inevitable. Focusing mainly on the United States in the twenty-first century, I hope to show that *our economy can grow indefinitely and provide unlimited numbers of jobs when our infrastructure is altered to be more environmentally friendly and the major growth sectors are in the provision of relatively environmentally benign services*. I am optimistic also about our ability to reduce fundamental inefficiency which, by definition, is bad for human beings because it implies that the human and natural resources at our disposal are not being used to promote maximum human satisfaction (wellbeing, welfare, flourishing). *There is no fixed amount of fundamental inefficiency that our society must maintain in order to keep unemployment at bay*. Although I don't think that we in the United States can eliminate such inefficiency entirely (in this century, at least), I think we can make choices that reduce such inefficiency. We can start by looking at the practices currently intended or tending to forestall or reduce unemployment to see which among them involve fundamental inefficiency.

✳   ✳   ✳

Currently, our society engages in six types of practices that function or are intended to function to reduce unemployment by avoiding and/or offloading overproduction. As we will see in the chapters that follow, fundamental inefficiency is prominent in some of these practices and only marginally present in others.

1. *Manufacture for Export* (chapters 3 through 5): Increase exports of efficiently produced goods. This is what the British were doing at the beginning of the Industrial Revolution with the oversupply of textiles that resulted from its increasingly labor-efficient methods of production. They were attempting to sell their textiles around the world, with much more success in India than in China. Today, corn farmers in my state of Illinois are eager to market corn around the world because efficient methods of agriculture have created an oversupply of corn that can lower its price and jeopardize profits.

   Generally speaking, international trade tends to increase efficiency, as manufacturers able to meet a human need or want in the most efficient way are likely to prevail in international competition by providing products that give customers the greatest welfare at the lowest cost. However, as the case of opium exports to China illustrates, there is no guarantee that international trade will in every instance improve human wellbeing. There are cases of fundamental inefficiency, trade that's inefficient insofar as human time and effort is not being used to maximize human wellbeing, but the trade is still functional insofar as it soaks up overproduction that results from labor efficiencies in the economy.

2. *Inefficient Systems* (chapters 6 and 7): Employ inefficient systems to meet some common needs (a system that requires more goods and services than a clearly available alternate system would require to meet the same human needs), such as a system of personal transportation that relies primarily on automobiles, a system of freight transport that relies primarily on long-haul trucking, and a system of healthcare that contains incentives to provide more care than is often desired, needed, or helpful. These inefficient systems provide many jobs in the automobile industry, in road construction and maintenance, and in healthcare and health insurance that would not exist if the systems were more efficient. So, these systems are functional even though they are inef-

ficient. Their function of providing job opportunities helps to explain their persistence in a society that mostly rewards efficiency.

3. *Consumerism* (chapters 8 and 9): Use human time and effort efficiently to produce an increasing quantity and variety of consumer goods and services for which there is effective demand. This is the mainstay of the current pro-economic-growth approach to maintaining full employment. Consumer demand constitutes about 70 percent of our gross domestic product (GDP)[40] and much of that demand is for radios, computers, cars, phones, toasters, microwaves, television sets, refrigerators, sofas, and a host of other material goods, plus larger houses to store them. We also demand many services, such as hair dressers, party planners, marriage counselors, weight-loss coaches, doctors, lawyers, teachers, and accountants. Insofar as these consumer goods and services improve human wellbeing, all things considered, consumption is efficient as well as job creating.

However, we will see that our consumption of goods and services takes place in the context of consumerism, which tends to degrade human wellbeing. Consumerism is not the same as consumption, and a consumerist orientation or society is not the same as a society with a lot of consumption and consumer items. *Consumerism exists when consumption is kept high by convincing people that they need to consume ever more goods and services whether or not they can afford them.* This is done in part by getting people to compare their own purchases with those of others and convincing them to associate their self-worth with purchases they would not make except for the induced desire to keep up with the Joneses. Such consumption generally detracts from fundamental efficiency. *Compulsory consumption* is similarly inefficient. This takes place when *purchases by the majority make it socially and/or physically difficult for the minority to refrain from similar purchases.* Cell phones fall into this category, as do many purchases made necessary by our inefficient transportation system. Because consumption patterns in the United States are currently suffused with consumerism and compulsory consumption, much of our consumption does not promote human wellbeing; it's functional but fundamentally inefficient.

In general, a good or service detracts from human wellbeing, making its production or provision inefficient, if:

a)   Used as directed it harms people more than it helps. Many people would put cigarettes, some drugs, and even some medical care in this category;

b)   Its use discourages and thereby reduces consumption of some other good or service that would better promote human wellbeing; or

c)   Its use discourages or otherwise reduces noneconomic activity that would promote human wellbeing better, such as pursuing personal relationships or accomplishments.

4. *Idle Workers* (chapters 2 and 10): Withdraw human time and effort from labor-efficient production by idling workers without increasing unemployment. This includes such practices as increased levels of incarceration; denying to convicts employment that competes with free labor; generous family-leave policies with full pay; increased vacation days with full pay; shorter work weeks with full pay; and extended programs of education and training.

If the only basis for human wellbeing were the production of goods and services, all labor-idling practices, because they withdraw human labor power from such productivity, would be inefficient. However, commercial activity is not the only basis for human wellbeing. Commercial activity, according to mainstream economic theory, includes only the production and consumption of (not necessarily material) goods and services that can be sold or traded. The goal of commercial activity is to improve human wellbeing to the greatest extent possible through such pursuits. But most economists recognize that commercial production and consumption are irrelevant to many sources and kinds of human flourishing. Most people who have children, for example, aren't rewarded for their efforts with goods or services that can be traded in the marketplace, notwithstanding the experience of Shirley Temple's family. Prospective parents nevertheless expect their wellbeing to be improved through the meaning and joy that parenthood brings to their lives. Similarly, a good marriage cannot be sold or traded, but contributes greatly to the wellbeing of the marriage partners. In addition, personal accomplishments, such as learning to play the piano or running a marathon, are meaningful to many people and contribute to their welfare outside of any purely commercial considerations.

In sum, idling workers without unemployment would be inefficient if the input were human labor hours and the only output was human wellbeing that results from the consumption of tradable goods and services. However, because overall human wellbeing requires activities that do not result in tradable goods and service, idling workers can be fundamentally efficient if the activities of the idled workers improve human wellbeing more than wellbeing could be improved through devotion of the same time and effort to strictly commercial pursuits. For this reason, we will see, some labor-idling practices do not contribute to fundamental inefficiency, but some do.

5. *Public Goods* (chapters 11 and 12): Use human labor and natural resources to provide public goods—goods that generally increase human wellbeing but that no individual has an incentive to provide because they must be shared with others. National defense is the classic example, but many environmental and social goods fall into this category as well, including clean air and water and functioning systems of banking and education.

Fundamental efficiency may or may not be improved through work that supplies these public goods. For example, although national defense creates many jobs, blowing things up and killing people may be harmful. In many contexts, therefore, expenditures on national defense can be fundamentally inefficient because they provide jobs without improving human wellbeing. Many other public goods, by contrast, such as education and environmental protection, are more likely to improve human wellbeing, so their production and consumption are more likely to be fundamentally efficient.

6. *Services* (chapter 13): Many services as well as goods are included in the category of consumerism. However, services that have little direct environmental impact, such as accounting services, legal advice, management consultation, home-decorating tips, personal physical training,

educational services, and weight-loss counseling deserve additional attention. They support growth in the economy and improved job prospects without exceeding environmental limits, whether or not their purchase is consumerist. Unlimited growth in the provision of goods, by contrast, runs up against environmental limits and therefore cannot be the basis of unlimited economic growth. So long as services meet a consumer demand and promote human wellbeing as well as or better than alternate expenditures of human time and effort, the increasing focus on the provision of services is compatible with fundamental efficiency. Many services meet this criterion of efficiency, but many others do not because they reflect consumerism, which often frustrates human flourishing.

These are not the only ways that our society avoids or soaks up overproduction. Where unions are strong, for example, featherbedding rules embedded in labor contracts enable more people to be employed than the work really demands. Artisanal methods of production, which use more labor hours than industrial methods to produce the same or similar goods, afford employment to Americans catering to some wealthy consumers. Labor-intensive agriculture is like artisanal production in this respect and has the potential of catering to a larger public. However, unlike the six methods outlined above, these three methods of avoiding unemployment are not among the most influential or powerful in our society at this time. Union contracts that allow featherbedding are largely a thing of the past, and compared to the market for mass-produced goods of manufacture and agriculture the market and therefore the job-creating potential is small for artisanal goods from workshops and farms.

The six influential categories outlined above are interrelated and overlapping. We've seen already that most services (category 6) are also consumer items (category 3). Our inefficient transportation system (category 2: inefficient systems) promotes consumerism (category 3) insofar as it requires the purchase of more cars than a more efficient transportation system would require. Although many such car purchases may be compulsory, they are nevertheless a form of consumer goods consumption. Such car purchases provide work for people in the mining, oil, automotive, and other industries, which makes our inefficient transportation system functional. Provision of the public good of higher education (category 5: public goods) is related to idling workers (category 4), because many people withdraw from the labor force or voluntarily reduce their work hours to engage in higher education. In addition, the public good of education (category 5) and the systematic inefficiency of our health-care industry (category 2: inefficient systems) are related to service employment (category 6), because teachers and health insurance employees provide services. In spite of these overlaps and interconnections, I will look at each of these six categories individually, relating them to one another as needed.

＊　＊　＊

As societies become richer through greater access to industrially produced goods—in other words, as they become more like the United States and other advanced industrial countries—they have greater recourse to these six methods of avoiding and/or absorbing overproduction and thereby reducing or at least containing unemployment. But rich societies often differ from one another in their use of these methods. By emphasizing one method of containing unemployment, a society can reduce its reliance on another. For example, western European countries that provide longer vacation and family leave time at full pay idle their workers more than we do in the United States. The United States makes up for its failure to idle workers in these ways by relying more on the job-creating potential of consumerism and of inefficient systems in transportation and healthcare. Another contrast is that Europe makes up for its failure to spend as much as we do on the public good of national defense in part by spending more on some other public goods, including relatively efficient public transportation. Finally, countries differ in their overall use of these six methods of containing unemployment. The lower the total or cumulative use of these six methods in advanced industrial countries, other things being equal, the higher the unemployment. Most European countries may have higher unemployment rates than we have in the United States because their cumulative use of these six methods is less than ours.

The total fundamental inefficiency resulting from the use of these six methods also differs from country to country and from practice to practice.

For example, to the extent that human welfare is promoted by additional time devoted to noncommercial as opposed to commercial pursuits, idling workers may not be fundamentally inefficient. Some countries idle workers in this way more than we do, which lowers their total inefficiency in comparison with us. We idle (potential) workers more than other industrial countries through incarceration, which is fundamentally inefficient. Much of our consumerism detracts from human wellbeing, which contributes to greater overall fundamental inefficiency in our society compared to societies with less consumerism. Some public goods, such as education and transportation, clearly improve overall fundamental efficiency in society, but others that provide jobs at public expense may not be fundamentally efficient, such as military expenditures beyond what society genuinely needs to protect itself. On the other hand, basic scientific and technological research that is part of the military budget may improve human welfare in the long run and be to that extent a fundamentally efficient use of time, effort, and resources. Systematic inefficiencies, by contrast, such as those in US transportation and healthcare, are irredeemably fundamentally inefficient, but functional at this time nevertheless.

I don't claim that the current level of inefficiency in America is unavoidable. It will change with the choices that we make. I do claim, however, that much of it is functional, and that it persists in part because (most of) it performs the function of providing jobs and containing unemployment. It has provided this function for a long time and, environmental limits aside, could continue to do so indefinitely. It's not a phase in the development of our society that will inevitably be overcome. There is no automatic tendency within our free market system to extrude such inefficiency; people are used to it, and so long as it functions to contain unemployment, much of it remains politically popular.

Again, this doesn't mean that such inefficiency is good, all things considered. By definition, what I have identified as fundamental inefficiencies are uses of time, effort, and resources that fail to promote human wellbeing as well as available alternatives. In addition, there are environmental limits to some of our inefficient practices. Recognition of these limits is already provoking rules of international trade that will constrain our use of fossil fuels, for example, and this will reduce the practicality of our fossil-fuel intensive inefficient transportation system. It's therefore reasonable to investigate the inefficiencies in our use of the six methods of containing unemployment. We should try to eliminate as much fundamental inefficiency as possible while retaining as much of the sum total of the six unemployment-reducing practices as is necessary to keep unemployment at acceptably low levels.

In this book I evaluate these six methods and their specific implementations on the basis of the four criteria mentioned at the start: *efficiency/inefficiency, job-creating potential, environmental sustainability, and political acceptability*. The goal is to find politically acceptable alternatives to current job-sustaining inefficiencies, alternatives that will allow the economy to grow, employment to expand, and humans to flourish within environmental limits. I believe that our economy can grow indefinitely and thereby supply an unending variety of good jobs in environment-friendly service employment. I believe also that we can eliminate much of the fundamental inefficiency that currently functions to forestall or reduce unemployment. But I don't believe that we can in the foreseeable future eliminate all fundamental inefficiency in our society. Some fundamental inefficiency is too important in the fight against unemployment and too popular in our culture to make its complete elimination politically acceptable.

CHAPTER 2
IDLING WORKERS I
CONVICTS AND WOMEN

One way of reducing unemployment is to idle workers. The modern problem of unemployment results primarily from the increased productive capacity of most workers. With most workers producing more, more goods and services become available for sale. But there is often insufficient demand for this increased volume of goods and services, so some people are thrown out of work (become unemployed). If more workers are idled (become unproductive because they're not working or less productive because they're working less) the volume of goods and services may be reduced sufficiently so that there is enough demand for the work products of all who want to work. Unemployment can thus be reduced.

This may seem paradoxical, because unemployment is one way of idling workers; people are idle (in their capacity as workers) when they are unemployed. How can idling workers be one of this book's six strategies for soaking up our increased productive capacity in order to contain or reduce unemployment when unemployment is itself one way of idling workers? If idling workers is desirable, why object to unemployment in the first place?

The answer is that unemployment is much worse for human wellbeing than most other forms of worker idling, such as a shorter workday, a shorter work week, or more vacation days. President Franklin Roosevelt said in one of his "Fireside Chat" broadcasts in 1934,

"Demoralization caused by vast unemployment is our greatest extravagance. Morally, it is the greatest menace to our social order."[1] Economist Joseph Stiglitz agrees; social order is disrupted by unemployment. "Those without jobs lose a sense of worth; they are more likely to get divorced; their children are more likely to have their education interrupted."[2] Sociologist James Russell explains these phenomena by noting that unemployment tends to induce a state of anomie, "a condition that results from loss of reference points in life."[3] Most people thrive when they have predictable routines. Unemployment disrupts reference points that structure such routines, leaving a majority of the unemployed in a state of stressful uncertainty.

As unemployment increases, people who still have work fear for their jobs, while unemployed people are plagued by uncertainty about the duration of their unemployment, about the financial impact of reduced income during unemployment, about the type of job they will get next, about the location of that job, and about how much income they will eventually be able to earn. Such fear, uncertainty, and stress, combined with a sense of being helpless and unworthy, reduces the overall wellbeing of those who are unemployed.

DW Gibson provides several illustrations in *Not Working: People Talk about Losing a Job and Finding Their Way in Today's Changing Economy*. Wendy, for example, is a bright thirty-three-year-old woman with a master's in Arts Management who worked in Omaha as a fundraiser for a museum. In September 2008, after she had worked there for two-and-a-half years, the museum hired an executive consultant to help them deal with reduced revenue stemming from donors no longer fulfilling their pledges because the donors were themselves losing funding. It was the start of the Great Recession. Ultimately, Wendy told Gibson, "We went from a staff of 79 to 40."

> Over the course of four months, it was like walking on eggshells every day, and you never knew who it was gonna be. Job security didn't exist anymore. It lasted so long—it was so belabored. It was just that feeling, you know, a constant . . . in the pit of your stomach . . . it's just like "I don't know what to do, I don't know if I should be looking for another job because I really like this job, but any minute this job could go away."[4]

Wendy was finally "let go" on January 8, 2010. During the following eight months, she had several interviews but no job offers. She thought,

> I must have done something wrong . . . it's my fault.
> I believe it doesn't matter how confident you are, how old you are, what class you're in, when you get laid off, that's going to get into your mind, at

some point. Even if it's only for five seconds, there will be a moment of . . . it's my fault.[5]

By September 2010 she was so financially stressed that she moved in with her parents. But she soon got another job in her field, which made her ecstatic. However, several months later her new employer experienced the same financial problems as her old employer and she again joined the ranks of the unemployed. Wendy told Gibson,

> I have all of these things in my head like what did I do wrong, how did I fail? In my mind, I'm like, panicking. Like, "No. You're wrong. You're wrong. You've got the wrong person." Or "this isn't the position you want to cut, because I'm doing this, this and this. . . ."
>
> And I thought, "God, I have to start telling people, and what am I going to say?" And they're going to say, "Again? Again you lost your job?" I was ashamed, and I was sad, and I was humiliated. I remember I was crying and crying and crying and crying to my parents, and then I just kept saying, "I am so embarrassed. I am so embarrassed. . . ."
>
> And then I stayed in bed the following week. I got really, really sad. . . . And those were the days that I was humiliated and really just felt like a loser.[6]

Such devastation is common among the unemployed. Economist Richard Layard finds that unemployment reduces average happiness more than divorce and has three times the negative effect on happiness as a one-third reduction in family income.[7] Layard explains,

> Some people think that the main evil is not unemployment but nonemployment. In other words, it is as bad to be "out of the labour force" and not looking for work as to be unemployed: you are not looking for work because you are discouraged. The data totally refute this. Moves between work and being "out of the labour force" involve much smaller changes in happiness than moves between work and unemployment.[8]

The German study on which Layard relies shows that overall satisfaction fell for employed men from 7.4 to 7.1 on a 10-point scale between 1984 and 1989, and that average satisfaction levels for men out of the labor force were one-half point lower than those for men who were employed. But the unemployed scored between 1.5 and 2.0 points lower than the employed on that scale. In other words, the gap between the satisfaction of the employed and the unemployed was three to four times the gap in satisfaction between the employed and those who were voluntarily out of the labor force as "discouraged workers." The study concludes that "the adverse effect of unemployment is much stronger than the effect of nonparticipation."[9]

Layard found also that unemployment "hurts as much after one or two years of unemployment as it does at the beginning. In that sense you do not habituate to it. . . . And even when you are back at work, you still feel its effects as a psychological scar."[10]

The negative effects of unemployment are physical as well as psychological. Medical indicators of reduced wellbeing among the unemployed include increases in: suicides, strokes, heart and renal disease, deaths from cardiovascular and renal disease, deaths from cirrhosis of the liver, hospital admissions, state prison admissions, and homicides.[11] Increased unemployment between 2008 and 2010 during the Great Recession coincided with increased suicides in the United States, Benedict Carey reports in the *New York Times*. According to recent research,

> In 2008, the [suicide] rate began increasing by an average of 0.51 deaths per 100,000 people a year. Without the increase in the rate, the total deaths from suicide each year in the United States would have been lower by about 1,500. . . .
>
> The research team linked the suicide rate to unemployment, using numbers from the Centers for Disease Control and Prevention and from the Bureau of Labor Statistics.
>
> Every rise of 1 percent in unemployment was accompanied by an increase in the suicide rate of roughly 1 percent. . . . A similar correlation has been found in some European countries since the recession.[12]

In sum, when economic pressures require idling workers, human wellbeing is advanced when workers are idled in ways that do not involve unemployment. In this chapter we explore two episodes in American history when idling was pursued to relieve or avoid unemployment. The first concerns convicts and the second concerns women. In both cases, idling workers may have avoided some unemployment, but the overall strategy was certainly fundamentally inefficient. These are two cases of functional inefficiency.

*　　*　　*

In nineteenth-century America few people doubted that prisoners should work. Much of the work for the average citizen, whether agricultural or industrial, included hard physical labor six days a week. If prisoners didn't work, they would be among the privileged few exempt from such labor. They would be at leisure while honest, law-abiding citizens would be taxed to provide their support. This would create a perverse incentive to crime. If you get away with your crime, you get the fruits of your crime. If you don't get away with it, you get a vacation from the kind of hard labor that almost everyone else had to endure. It was essential, therefore, that prisoners endure hard labor just so they were not advantaged relative to most other people in society.

Prison labor was necessary also to finance the prisons. Why should society pay for able-bodied men to sit in leisure? The public simply wouldn't stand for any such proposal. An American politician who proposed complete taxpayer funding of prisons, as they already had in England, would be ridiculed and voted out of office. So, if prisoners were to have humane conditions, they needed to generate all or most of the revenue needed to make the prison habitable and its food edible.

Further, hard labor was believed to instill discipline in prisoners. Discipline would help inmates when they got out of prison resist the temptation to break the law. Hard labor would also teach prisoners skills that they could use after their release to make an honest living. Finally, hard labor in a realistic manufacturing setting would inculcate in prisoners the habits and dispositions of cooperative, productive interaction with coworkers needed for them to assimilate to an increasingly industrialized society. Again, such assimilation would discourage recidivism.

Zebulon Brockway, one of the chief prison reformers of the nineteenth century, explained to the National Prison Congress in Cincinnati in 1870,

It is true that the reformation of prisoners during their imprisonment is indispensable, for to return to society discharged prisoners unreformed is to poison it with the worst elements possible; and to retain them in prison indefinitely, while affording at the same time protection from their evil influence, would impose a burden impossible to be born. A fundamental condition of success in this respect is the financial independence of the organization and its institutions. The importance of this feature cannot well be too prominent. It is too much to expect in our day that citizens generally will vote taxes upon themselves not only to provide suitable institutions for the reformatory treatment of criminals, but to support them in unproductive industry, and to supply them with the indispensables of reformatory progress, viz.; good diet, good clothes, good quarters, entertaining educational agencies, and the pure personal friendship of a refined religious instructor. If these are supplied regularly to prisoners, it must come through their own exertions.[13]

Brockway spoke from successful experience. He had been warden of a municipal prison in Detroit, which he turned into a profit-generating enterprise in the 1860s. The Detroit prison registered losses the first two years of the program but generated a profit of $2,011.80 in the third year. "From this time on," Brockway recalls in his memoir, "an annual profit was derived to the city from this prison establishment: the fourth year, $10,097.27; fifth year, $20,108.32; and, when ten years had passed, the tenth year showed a profit of $34,303.90, and the whole period from the very beginning a balance profit of $103,004.50."[14] Brockway had similar success in New York State prisons in Rochester and Elmira.

Success at lowering or eliminating taxpayer subsidy of prisons made the contract system of prison employment popular, especially in northern states, during the nineteenth century. The contract system worked this way: An entrepreneur outside the prison system would contract for prison labor that would take place in the prison. The outside contractor would make the capital investment and usually place manufacturing equipment in the prison. The contractor would also hire non-convict laborers to train and supervise prisoners at work. The state retained responsibility for security, housing, healthcare, and food, but the contractor paid the state for convict labor, thereby offsetting much (in Brockway's case, more than all) of that cost. These prisons resembled the factories of that era. When Charles Dickens visited them in the 1840s he wrote that he found it "difficult at first to convince myself that I was really in a jail: a place of ignominious punishment and endurance."[15]

*   *   *

Today, relatively few prisoners are engaged in gainful production, in spite of the advantages of prison occupations recognized in the nineteenth century. Consequently, taxpayers foot the bill for prisons. What happened? What went wrong? Why are prisoners largely idle today? The reason is that prison labor is generally bad for free labor. Historian Glen Gildemeister gives this example of convict labor undercutting free labor:

> Auburn (New York) boot and shoe contractor Charles E. Morse testified in 1871 that he paid $.45 per day for prisoners, a mean of $3.00 per day to workers in his outside shop. Morse estimated that his convict labor produced about half what outside workers would accomplish. Morse also paid his ten instructors at the Auburn Prison $3.00 per day, his foremen $8.00 per day. Even allowing for fifty per cent lower productivity and increased costs of supervision, Morse enjoyed a considerable advantage inside the prison.[16]

The economics of his situation led Morse to prefer convict labor to free labor, which caused unemployment outside the prison.

Hatters were hit by prison competition about as hard as any free laborers. In 1882 the New Jersey Bureau of Statistics of Labor and Industry found that the daily wage of pouncers, sizers, and shapers was $1.84 per day, almost four times the rate of prison labor. Consequently, noted the Fur and Wool Hat Manufacturers Association, prison-made hats sold for "$1.00 to $2.00 per dozen less than goods of similar qualities would *cost* regular manufacturers."[17] As a result, free laborers in these categories were unemployed an average of 128.6 days per year.

The influence of convict labor is evident in what happened two years later. Following free-labor agitation, hat manufacturing was (nearly) abolished in the prisons of New York, New Jersey, Connecticut, and Rhode Island. The wages of hatters began a steady rise, even though the country was in a mild recession. Equally significant, the average number of days per year that hatters were unemployed fell 70 percent to only forty-four days a year.[18]

Coopers experienced similar problems, compounded by technological advances in manufacturing. Making barrels was traditionally a well-paid craft. Owing to the skill required to make barrels that don't leak, competition from prison labor was insignificant until the industry became increasingly mechanized between 1875 and 1895. Steam-driven machinery was increasingly used to break down the processes of barrel making into a large number of small steps that people could learn fairly easily and perform quickly. The result was greater industrial efficiency—barrels could be made faster and at less cost—which put coopers' high wages in jeopardy because now a larger pool of less-skilled workers could compete with them. Worse yet for the coopers, low-skilled prison labor joined the competition. As a result, while the need for barrels in the Chicago area increased greatly due to the growing meat packing industry, the annual earnings of free coopers declined from $613 in 1875 to $432 in 1885, as prisoners in Joliet State Prison in Illinois and the Michigan City Indiana penitentiary nearly quadrupled production.

The iron molders had similar problems competing with prison labor, exacerbated by the use of prison labor to break strikes. Just before the Civil War, historian Rebecca McLennan explains,

> an iron-molding contractor by the name of I. G. Johnson locked Local 11 of the Union of Iron Molders out of his Spuyten Duyvil factory and moved his operation *in toto* to Sing Sing prison. That a Sing Sing laborer cost forty cents a day, against a free iron molder's $3 daily wage, no doubt attracted the industrialist; but equally attractive to Johnson was the possibility that he could use convict labor to break the union—which is what he proceeded to do, in 1862–63. In the months that followed the Johnson action, the iron molders urgently petitioned the legislature for relief.[19]

When the molders union regrouped and faced the John S. Perry Stove Company in 1877, results were similar. Perry transferred his operations as much as possible to Sing Sing where, by 1879, 80 percent of Sing Sing's 1,253 inmates were making stoves for Perry's company. The strike was broken.

Perry's partner, Mr. Dickey, testified before a Connecticut Special Commission in 1880 that independent, blind evaluations of stoves made by free labor in Albany, New York, compared to those made at Sing Sing indicated the superiority of convict labor.

Legislation aimed at limiting the possibilities for gainful employment of prisoners was subsequently passed in New York and other states in response to the demands of free labor. In 1886, New York passed by popular referendum a total ban on contract labor in prisons.[20] In the 1890s, Pennsylvania Democrats passed a law limiting convicts to eight hours of work per day when free labor had longer hours. Not to be outdone, when Republicans regained a legislative majority they limited the number of prisoners who could work in any given industry, disallowed the prison manufacture of products that free laborers were making in the state, and outlawed the use of power machinery in prisons. This final provision required that convict labor be relatively inefficient, as power machinery was then as it is now necessary for maximum industrial efficiency. According to historian Blake McKelvey, "This crippled the industry in the Eastern as well as in the Western penitentiary. . . . The act made a farce of prison labor in Pennsylvania for the next thirty years and did more than any other factor to degrade the two great penitentiaries of the Keystone State from the first rank of American prisons."[21]

Thus, convicts were increasingly deprived of work, which they had the time and in most cases the inclination to perform. When they were allowed to work, they were deprived of the most efficient means of production. This was certainly an exercise in fundamental inefficiency, as it reduced people's ability to meet humanity's supposedly unlimited wants and needs.

Lack of work also caused disciplinary problems in prisons, whether idleness was due to economic recession or restrictive legislation. The United States' economy experienced recession after the "panic" of 1873. Many firms with prison contracts went bankrupt and even two years later most prisoners at Sing Sing and Auburn had no work. Rebecca McLennan writes, "For almost as long as the cellular prison had existed, productive labor had been the object around which institutional discipline in general was organized."[22] Deprived of work, prisoners at Auburn took to fighting with knives and those at Sing Sing engaged in protests and attempted escapes.

When legislation deprived prisoners of work in the 1890s, one warden told a meeting of the National Prison Association in 1894,

> I can think of nothing so near chaos as a prison with fifteen hundred men without labor. . . . It needs no argument to demonstrate that the worst thing in the world for a man who has the ability to work is *enforced idleness*. . . . In penal institutions especially it has been shown time and again, that it leads to habits of immorality, to disorder, and riot, and in a large number of cases mental derangement and physical ruin.[23]

Besides impairing prison discipline, another warden claimed, idleness deprives convicts of the means of self-improvement essential for rehabilitation:

> So fraught with evil would this be that I cannot conceive that any intelligent man, having the good of his kind heart, could give it a moment's serious consideration. Idleness is the prolific cause of mischief and crime; in no place is this truth more shockingly demonstrated than inside prison walls. Language would fail to describe the horrors of a prison in which men have nothing to do. The fearful sights and sounds of which we read, in some prisons in South America and Mexico, would be reproduced.[24]

So prisoner idleness is very harmful. But so, it seems, is prisoner productivity. Free labor was correct when complaining that competition with convict labor reduced their incomes and increased their unemployment. An alternative way of giving work to prisoners was needed, and this inspired the state-use system. Convicts can produce what the state, and perhaps what municipalities and other smaller units of government need. Alternatively, convicts can provide services to the state, such as constructing public buildings, repairing roads, maintaining parks, etc. Either way, prisoners are employed, but do not compete with free labor by offering goods or services for sale on the free market. States save money by having convicts do what the taxpayers would otherwise have to pay private parties to produce or perform. Before long New York State's prisoners were making "desks and chairs for the Executive Mansion in Albany . . . , brooms and mattresses for public hospitals . . . , trash carts for the New York City sanitation department, uniforms for the National Guard . . . , wooden ornaments for various departments . . . , and boots and striped uniforms for the state's penal institutions."[25] Sing Sing's print shop printed up the reports of various state agencies and was preparing to print textbooks for public schools.

From its beginning in 1897, the state-use system met the same opposition from organized labor as the contract system and all other systems of convict labor. When the skilled printers' and bookbinders' unions heard that the State Prison Commission may recommend a printing facility at Sing Sing they immediately drafted legislation to limit the scope of Sing Sing's printing to documents for use within the prison. The unions adamantly opposed the prison printing school textbooks of any kind. After meeting with the unions in March 1897, the Commission declared that printing facilities in the prison would be impractical.

In the same month a powerful New York State senator, John Francis Ahearn said, "The extension of convict employment to new industries, including the manufacture of blankets, cloth, woolens, shirts, stockings, ties, woodenware, the printing of books, reports and documents, will eventually take the State and the cities . . . out of the open market as purchasers of supplies . . . , [which] will deprive honest labor of employment in the ever-narrowing channels of legitimate trade."[26] This view of Senator Ahearn reflected the perspective of manufacturers as well as free labor in the fields where convict labor threatened to reduce the demand for goods on the open market. In fact, the state-use system actually harmed some of the state's manufacturers and free workers more than the old contract system, because goods produced under contract could be sold out of state, thereby reducing competition with the state's manufacturers and free laborers. Under state use, by contrast, all the convict-made goods were sold within the state, maximizing the negative impact on the state's free citizens.

The movement against prison-made goods continued in the new century. President Theodore Roosevelt signed an executive order excluding convict labor from federal projects. The result of all this opposition was that New York was unable to provide sufficient work for its prisoners. One prison administrator said, "Every industry we tried to start seemed to conflict with somebody. I couldn't find work for our people, and they were getting crazy."[27] Consequently, whereas prison labor had supplied between two-thirds and three-fourths of prison expenses under the contract system, it supplied only about one quarter during the fifteen years following the move to state use in 1897.

Depriving convicts of meaningful labor was certainly *financially inefficient*; it reduced the monetary worth of the prisons' output in relation to every dollar of taxpayer input used to support the prisons. In was also *productively inefficient*; it reduced the goods and services produced (output) by available able-bodied Americans (input). Today, productive inefficiency is not a problem because, as we've seen, labor-hour efficiency is so great that it threatens us with endemic unemployment because we don't need all available able-bodied Americans to be productive in order to meet society's material needs and wants. In the nineteenth century, by contrast, most Americans still worked on farms and labor productivity in the production of goods was so much lower than it is today that failure to maximize the productivity of available able-bodied Americans deprived society of genuinely helpful material goods. In the nineteenth-century context, therefore, productive inefficiency implied *fundamental inefficiency*; human and natural resources weren't being used to provide as much human wellbeing as possible. The practice of excluding convicts from meaningful work was fundamentally inefficient also because it created stress among convicts and discipline problems in the prisons; human wellbeing was degraded.

*   *   *

Today, only a small fraction of convicts in the United States are employed. In Illinois, for example, the Department of Corrections (DOC) has a partnership with Lutheran Social Services of Illinois to have inmates in eighteen prisons around the state make prefabricated walls and roof trusses for Habitat for Humanity houses. By all accounts it's an excellent program that has helped to provide literally hundreds of homes for poor people since its inception in 1995. However, it employs only about one percent of Illinois's approximately 45,500 inmates.[28]

Idling convicts is still financially inefficient. In 2012 each of Illinois's 45,500 prisoners cost taxpayers an average of $38,268 per year, according to the Vera Institute of Justice. Annual costs per inmate vary in other states, from a low of $14,600 in Kentucky to a high of over $60,000 in New York State.[29] A breakdown of California's annual costs of $47,102 for each prison inmate in 2008–2009 reveals that security cost $19,663, inmate healthcare cost $8,768, administration cost $3,493, inmate support (food, activities, clothing, etc.) cost $2,562, and rehabilitation programs cost $1,612.[30] The Center for Economic and Policy Research estimated that incarceration costs governments at all three levels (municipal, state, and federal) about $75 billion per year.[31]

Consider what could be done with the money saved if prisons today were as self-supporting as were Zebulon Brockway's prisons in the nineteenth century. The cost of each prison inmate in California is nearly the median family income in the United States and about the median starting salary of school teachers. Imagine how many more families could be supported and how school class sizes could be reduced through the funding of more teachers if prisons were self-supporting.

But there's functionality here. Even though the function of combating unemployment is not recognized or acknowledged today as it was in the nineteenth century, it's as true today as it was then that depriving convicts of meaningful labor reduces unemployment among the general population by avoiding prisoners competing for jobs held by others. Unemployment is reduced overall because convicts who are deprived of work are not considered unemployed; they are simply out of the workforce.

The United States increases the unemployment-reducing potential of its criminal justice system by incarcerating more people than are incarcerated in other developed countries. The total number of individuals incarcerated in the United States at any one time in 2012 was nearly 2.4 million.[32] This represents 753 inmates for every 100,000 of population, an enormous number by historical and international norms. In 1980 about 220 people per 100,000 were incarcerated in the United States, before state spending on prisons increased six times faster than state spending on higher education in response to the War on Drugs.[33] In other countries incarceration rates remain low: 197 per 100,000 in New Zealand, 153 per 100,000 in England and Wales, and 134 per 100,000 in Australia. If the rate of incarceration in the United States equaled the average rate in these other English-speaking countries, we would have only half a million people incarcerated instead of

2.4 million. We'd have even fewer people in prison if we were more like much of western Europe, where rates of incarceration per 100,000 of population are 104 in Portugal, 99 in Austria, 96 in France, 94 in Belgium, 90 in Germany, and 66 in Denmark.[34]

Some people claim that high incarceration rates in the United States are justified because the War on Drugs improves human welfare by curtailing harmful drug addiction. Others maintain, to the contrary, that the War on Drugs is a cure that's worse than the disease. Incarceration degrades the skills and reduces the job prospects of inmates after release; it deprives many children of a parent, thereby impairing the life chances of the next generation; and it disrupts community life. According to this view, any incarceration beyond what is needed to protect innocent people is fundamentally inefficient insofar as other uses of human and natural resources would better promote human flourishing. I'd say that our high rate of incarceration is arguably, but not certainly, fundamentally inefficient.

I'm more certain that our high rate of incarceration functions to reduce unemployment. It sequesters workers as effectively as planting trees sequesters carbon dioxide. In addition, the expansion of the corrections system has created hundreds of thousands of jobs. Running prisons and jails now employs nearly half a million people, and 88,500 more work as probation officers and correctional treatment specialists. Still others serve the correctional system in such varied areas as landscaping, architecture, and computer services.[35] If we incarcerated only half a million instead of nearly 2.4 million people in the United States, most of these jobs would disappear. As we will see in chapter 13, the privatized prison industry is well aware of this.

In sum, the history of convict labor from the nineteenth century to the present War on Drugs illustrates well the claim that society sometimes adopts practices that are arguably or certainly fundamentally inefficient but functional insofar as they protect or create jobs and reduce unemployment.

*   *   *

Another illustration of the same phenomenon, another example of functional inefficiency, was provided in the aftermath of World War II when women were fired from factory jobs. These were the jobs that women had been encouraged to take during the war to boost production to meet wartime needs.

Even before the United States entered World War II, President Franklin Delano Roosevelt began preparing the public for the need to improve the efficient production of war materials. In December 1940 he gave his famous "Arsenal of Democracy" speech:

> Guns, planes, and ships have to be built in the factories and arsenals of America. . . . Manufacturers of watches, of farm implements, linotypes, cash registers, automobiles, sewing machines, lawn mowers, and locomotives are now making fuses, bomb-packing crates, telescope mounts, shells, pistols, and tanks. . . . But all of our present efforts are not enough. We must have more ships, more guns, more planes—more of everything. This can only be accomplished if we discard the notion of "business as usual." . . . We must be the great arsenal of democracy.[36]

Part of the deviation from "business as usual" was the employment of women in factories and shipyards. Chairman of the War Manpower Commission Paul McNutt wrote in 1943, "Under modern conditions of war, every person will have to serve where he can best serve the country. War manpower means everyone—women as well as men in the right job."[37] In 1939, only two percent of shipyard workers were female; five years later between ten and twenty percent were female.[38]

Women didn't just show up for new work opportunities; they were recruited. The War Advertising Council for the War Manpower Commission put out booklets that included sample advertisements like this: "There is a war job you can do and earn money doing it. You need no experience; you're taught the job you want to do by your employer or given a government training course, FREE. Woman-power can produce goods of war . . . ; use it . . . ; speed the victory."[39] Other ads were designed to give women confidence that they could do work that had previously been reserved for men. Attempting to attract women to the aircraft industry, the *Boeing News* "compared spot-welding to sewing, stamping and piling parts in the heat treat department to cutting cookies, and ordering parts from the parts store to shopping at a bargain counter."[40] A welding instructor in shipbuilding claimed, "The best prerequisite for a course in welding is a deft hand, and the hand that formerly did needlework, measured flour or rocked the cradle is usually better at welding than a man's hand."[41]

The financial advantages of factory work loomed large for many women. Because women were traditionally so poorly paid, the percentage increase in their pay when they switched from traditional female occupations to war work was impressive. For example, waitresses earned an average of about $14 per week, whereas the same women earned an average of about $37 per week in war-related factory work.[42] One third of the women at the Willow Run Bomber Plant experienced a pay increase of at least 100 percent, but only one ninth of the men experienced a comparable increase.[43]

Two stereotypes about these women workers should be dispelled. First, people often imagine that the majority of women industrial workers were the wives of soldiers. If fact, however, only ten percent of these women workers were married to soldiers.[44] Second, people often think that gainful employment for most of these women was an aberration from a domestic life that didn't include working outside the home. In fact, however, before the war the American workforce included 11.5 million women (many unmarried), joined by another 6.5 million during the war. In short, most women workers, whether married or single, needed to work whether there was a war or not. The big change brought about by the war was the opportunity to engage in higher-paid work formerly reserved for men. Some 6.5 million women took war-related factory jobs that were unavailable to women but for the war.[45]

Systematic studies during the war showed that women performed their factory work as well as men, or better, at many or most tasks. In 1943 W. F. Weher reported on the experience at Western Electric: "Women are just about the same as men in factories. . . . When first starting to work, women are sometimes afraid of machinery, but once trained they follow instructions more scrupulously than men."[46] Women were found to be especially good at detailed and repetitive work, often displaying greater stamina than men. The only areas where they were generally inferior were in brute physical strength, which was required for some, but not a large percentage of jobs, and in bench work using a hammer and chisel. Even with these liabilities, however, a study done in New York in 1943 to assess problems associated with replacing men with women confirmed the value of women in the workplace. The study included two hundred firms, mostly in manufacturing. Eighty-eight percent of the businesses reported that women's productivity was "equal or greater than men's on all or some jobs."[47] In 1944, of 140 executives commenting to the National Industrial Conference Board on the efficiency of women in production, nearly 60 percent claimed that the productivity of women in jobs formerly held by men was greater than that of the men they had replaced.[48]

What is more, women made outstanding contributions as on-the-job inventors, reports historian Chester Gregory, who gives these two examples:

> Two women shipfitter trainees invented a device that cut the time on their job 60 percent. The invention was a stop gauge that performed a cutting operation on a shearing machine in the plate shop which proved to be automatic and more accurate. A woman working in a sand-mill department of a steel foundry made a suggestion that resulted in an ingenious device that cut down the time involved in communicating test results. It was a clock-like device placed about the door of each testing room that enabled the mill operator to see at a glance what the moisture content was.[49]

Many other efficiency-promoting inventions by women in the workplace were based on women's experiences in gender-stereotyped pursuits. Laurance Hammon reported in 1943,

> Grey-haired Mrs. Cora Kepner helps make rubber life rafts at the Goodrich plant in Akron. . . . Putting on the "abrasion strips" was a slow hand job. Mrs. Kepner observed it was something like handling pastry and she suggested using giant rolling pins. . . . It works fine, as have forty-four other suggestions she has made. . . .
>
> In the same plant, Mrs. Carrie Syler is one of thousands of women who make barrage balloons. . . . The work made Mrs. Syler think of her home dressmaking experience. She always used pinking shears to scallop the raw edges of seams. . . . Why not try them on the balloons? It is standard practice now.
>
> Threading wires through flexible tubing . . . was a slow job with considerable spoilage of tubing. Mrs. Quincy Smith remarked, "If I had a thing like this to do at home, I'd use a tape needle." She proceeded to improvise one. . . . It saved 4,992 man-hours of labor this year.[50]

*   *   *

Many men saw women, even those who helped to improve efficiency, as threats to their jobs. But it was improved manufacturing efficiency, only some of it introduced by women, more than the number of women in the factories that threatened men's jobs. The nature of much factory work changed during the war in order to generate efficiencies that would result in greater productivity. For example, ships that had previously been held together by rivets came to be welded during the war. Time was saved by having major components of the ships constructed in separate subassemblies that were eventually welded together to form the ship. One result was that welders, who require relatively little training, could replace master craftsmen. The union's lengthy apprentice-ship system was replaced by much shorter training for more specific tasks.[51] Historian Karen Anderson gives two striking examples of increased efficiency:

> At the Willow Run Bomber Plant . . . the number of worker hours per bomber was reduced from a 1941 industry average of 200,000 per ship to less than 18,000 by 1945. Approximately 29 percent of the plant's work force was women. Boeing Aircraft in Seattle increased its monthly output four times between 1942 and 1944 and decreased the cost of its B-17 despite its large numbers of inexperienced workers, continuous changes in airplane design, and greater overhead caused by higher wages. At the same time, its labor force remained the same size. In both cases a program of simplification of individual jobs accounted for improvement in output per worker.[52]

In short, efficiencies were created in large part by de-skilling the manufac-turing process. Instead of relying on master craftsmen to produce a product, production was broken down into many tasks that less accomplished indi-viduals could perform as a group much faster and cheaper than could master craftsmen.

As we saw earlier, nineteenth-century coopers experienced the same problem of de-skilling. Breaking down the process of making something, whether a cooper's container or a whole ship, into smaller tasks that can be learned quickly, jeopardizes the relatively high pay of skilled craftsmen, whether coopers or shipbuilders. The great skill of journeymen is no longer needed when less skilled people can produce items more quickly and cheaply because a greater division of labor improves efficiency. So, just as coopers in the nineteenth century were jeopardized more by increasingly efficient production method than by competition from convict labor, journeymen shipbuilders were jeopardized by new, efficient production methods more than by competition from newly hired female colleagues.

As women were still being recruited for war-related factory work in 1942, Brigadier General Frank McSherry looked forward to women's continued work in factories: "Many of the jobs on which women are now working are being done better by them than by men, and it's not hard to figure that there'll be plenty of work for women as well as men in the aircraft plants . . . after the war is over."[53] In 1943 Senator Harry Truman, the future president, said while chairing the Senate War Investigating Committee, "The last war put the women into offices and they never left them. This war has put them into factories. Let no one imagine that women will permit themselves to be shunted out of these jobs which they have demonstrated so well their capacity to do."[54] Also in 1943, the industrialist Henry Kaiser told the *New York Times* that he planned to employ women after the war—"the ones who consider welding a better postwar achievement than wielding a typewriter or a broom. . . . I'm one who believes that 50 percent of women now in war work will stay in industry after the war. Do you think women are not going to demand the right to stay in industry?"[55] Kaiser backed up this speculation with a 1944 study of worker sentiment in three Kaiser shipyards. The study found that 53 percent of the women surveyed intended to continue an industrial job after the war.[56]

Yet an article that faithfully reported the study's statistics selected only one worker quote, and it left the impression that women did not want factory work after the war, the impression that the journal obviously wanted to convey. Mrs. Fern Webster, a welder at Oregon Ship, was quoted as saying, "I intend to return to my home. I believe a woman who has an able-bodied husband should not work after the war is over. There will be plenty of returning soldiers to fill all the jobs which will be available."[57] In the same vein, *The Ladies Home Journal* conducted a study to reinforce its view that "women want marriage and homemaking, not factory jobs; that they work in industry only because they have to or for an emergency." But its own survey results showed that more than half the women surveyed said they didn't plan to stop working at war's end and 79 percent said they enjoyed working more than staying home.[58]

Women's personal and commercial aspirations, however, were beside the point. No matter what women may have wanted, the general belief among economists was that there would at war's end be too few jobs for both men and women, so women must give way to allow for gainful employment among men. The 1944 report on War and Postwar Adjustment Policies, summarized by Bernard Baruch and John Hancock, was very clear on this point. It related the idling of women explicitly to worries about employment prospects for men and the possibility of unemployment-induced economic depression after the war:

> As one indication of the size of the job, about 50 billion dollars of the current annual production represents strictly war goods—that is, things which, when peace comes, we will stop making. This gap must be filled in large part by civilian production and services, if we are to keep the needed volume of employment. The demobilization of the armed forces will come gradually. Their absorption by industry will be aided materially by several factors, the weight of which is not now clear, such as: the giving up of war jobs by many women.[59]

Women giving up their highly paid war jobs is the *first possibility mentioned*. Similarly, Robert Moses, most famous for city planning in the New York City metropolitan area, prepared a report for Portland, Oregon. This report, *Portland Improvement*, discusses strategies for avoiding massive unemployment and a resumption of depression conditions in the Portland area when the war ended. Moses expected an economic slump even if "all women in industry retire gracefully, if at least half of the newcomers go back to their homes or elsewhere and if business revives and expands in answer to insistent unsatisfied consumer demands."[60] Again, women giving up their jobs was being counted upon to protect men from unemployment.

* * *

When the war did come to an end, the women of Seattle Local 104 of the International Brotherhood of Boilermakers and Iron Shipbuilders were treated to a patronizing editorial by the union's business agent, A. F. O'Neill, in the *104 Reporter*. O'Neill wrote,

> Our hats are off to the women. Yours is a job all well done. We have never heard you complain, after going home from your eight-hour shift in the shipyards, about doing your household work and raising your family. You have made mere man ashamed of himself when it came to sacrifices. Your record for loyalty to your employers, your job and your Union can never be questioned. . . .
>
> Now we are faced with cutbacks in shipbuilding, and you are being taken off the production team. You are being benched. Competition for playing positions on the team is great. We know some of you don't like it, but the majority feel theirs is a rest well earned. They feel they have fulfilled their part in winning the war. You have more than done your part. Let the lowly male species do the work (they don't know any better), and you see that he provides the American standard of living to which you are entitled.[61]

Many women were perfectly happy to give up their jobs after they felt they had done their patriotic duty. Yet, the assumption that most working women would stay home after the war was completely unrealistic. Women had been increasing their representation in the workforce by about six percent per decade since the beginning of the twentieth century.[62] As noted earlier, 11.5 million American women worked outside the home before the war, mostly out of economic necessity. This included more than half of the women who did factory work during the war. Little wonder, then, that more than half of such workers responded in surveys that they expected to continue working outside the home after the war. Their preference for continuing factory work after the war is accounted for in part by the higher wages they earned in factories compared to wages common in traditionally female jobs. For example, in and around Portland, Oregon, a shipyard worker who earned $1.20 an hour could earn only $.71 an hour in cannery work. In Seattle, Washington, a woman who had been making $1.20 an hour as a welder during the war was offered non-factory work at only $.92 an hour. Women in Baltimore who continued to work in the factories that had employed them during the war averaged $44 per week, whereas those with other employment averaged only $31 per week.[63]

Particularly ironic is the fact that many men returning from the war preferred clerical to manual work. Many of these men had worked in factories before the war but had been taught clerical skills during the war so they could perform clerical duties for the military. A large number said they preferred clerical work after the war because factory work was too monotonous or confining. Historian Karen Anderson explains,

> At the same time, women workers continued to hope that they could utilize the skills they had developed in war industries. As a result, the Detroit applications for clerical and service work in July 1946 included 2,770 women and 3,572 veterans, while the applicants for semiskilled and unskilled work included 8,137 women and 4,531 veterans. Moreover, the veterans proved as obdurate as the women regarding their occupational preferences; 35 percent of them refused jobs offered them.[64]

But within a year or so the United States Employment Service (USES) had for the most part successfully reestablished traditional patterns of employment among both men and women. Lower-paid clerical positions went to women and higher-paid factory work went to men. With so much factory work dependent upon war contracts that came to an end, and with increasingly efficient methods of production introduced during the war, it was feared that not enough high-paid factory work remained to accommodate both the women who had worked in factories for the first time during the war and returning soldiers who needed well-compensated work because they were expected to support a family on a single salary. In short, with the return of peace the specter of unemployment reappeared, the specter that haunts industrial societies because industry is so productive that consumer demand is often insufficient to keep everyone employed.

Was the policy of denying women continued opportunities of employment in most factory jobs inefficient? It seems that it was fundamentally inefficient because it didn't actually expand the sum total of job opportunities. It just reallocated them from many willing, skilled workers to other workers less skilled and in many cases less willing. This probably had some negative effect on labor-hour efficiency, which is the cornerstone of modern affluence. Such efficiency was particularly important in the aftermath of World War II.

During the war many people had forgone consumption because they bought war bonds instead of products, and many products they desired were rationed or unavailable. The result was enormous pent-up consumer demand by war's end, so there may have been enough factory work for everyone who wanted it. In that case, allowing all skilled, willing workers, regardless of gender, to remain maximally productive would have been an excellent way of using human and natural resources to promote human welfare through the production of goods that people needed and wanted. The policy of excluding women from most factory work was thus probably fundamentally inefficient.

Injustice tends also to impair human welfare. Juliet Gattuso, an employee at Grumman in New York, complained in a letter to President Truman after she was laid off in 1945:

> I happen to be a widow with a mother and son to support. . . . I would like to know why after serving a company in good faith for most of three and a half years, it is now impossible to obtain employment with them. I am a lathe hand and was classified as skilled labor, but simply because I happen to be a woman I am not wanted.[65]

It does seem that Mrs. Gattuso, like thousands of other women, was treated unjustly.

A major argument in favor of firing women from most factory jobs was the felt need after the war to reestablish traditional gender roles and thereby avoid social disruption that could have reduced wellbeing. This argument seems weak in light of the alteration of traditional gender roles that has taken place since the 1970s, alterations that most people consider to have more positive than negative effects on human welfare. It's not obvious why the change would have had more negative effects on human wellbeing if it had taken place three decades earlier.

In sum, the nineteenth-century denial of work to convicts to reduce unemployment among other workers seems clearly to have been fundamentally inefficient. Current sequestering of potential workers in the War on Drugs, which serves the unacknowledged function of reducing unemployment, is certainly financially inefficient and may also be fundamentally inefficient. Its fundamental inefficiency depends on whether the War on Drugs benefits human welfare enough to outweigh the negative effects of incarcerating five times as many people per 100,000 of the population as are incarcerated in other English-speaking countries. Finally, the denial of most factory work to women after World War II, done explicitly to avoid unemployment (among returning soldiers) seems most likely to have been labor-hour inefficient and, given the pent up consumer demand at the time, fundamentally inefficient.

In chapter 10 we'll look at several current practices that involve idling workers, practices that function, but only sometimes intentionally, to reduce unemployment. These practices include reducing the number of hours in a week of full-time employment, adding vacation days, allowing for longer periods of education and training, and granting more family leaves and early retirements. We will find that some of these practices are fundamentally efficient whereas others are fundamentally inefficient in the American context.

CHAPTER 3
MANUFACTURING FOR INTERNATIONAL MARKETS

One response to persistent unemployment in the United States is to encourage companies to manufacture items for export. Global sales may allow companies to retain their workforce even as workers become more efficient and productive. The extra productivity of increasingly efficient methods of manufacture isn't overproduction and doesn't cause job loss if the resulting products can be sold for a profit overseas. However, as we'll see in this chapter, the way that American companies can best compete for global market share is to employ ever fewer people in manufacturing, making manufacture for export a poor response to our unemployment problem.

Manufacture for export was already well underway in the middle of the nineteenth century. Writing in 1848, several years after the First Opium War, Karl Marx and Friedrich Engels knew that international trade was needed to absorb the plethora of goods created by the Industrial Revolution. They wrote in *The Communist Manifesto*, "The bourgeoisie, during its rule of scarce one hundred years, has created more massive and more colossal productive forces than have all preceding generations together."[1] Continued profitability, they realized, depended on increasing demand for products beyond the upper limit of domestic markets. "The need of a constantly expanding market for its products chases the bourgeoisie over the whole surface of the globe."[2] Marx and Engels go on to describe what we now call globalization:

> The bourgeoisie has through its exploitation of the world market given a cosmopolitan character to production and consumption in every country. . . .
> It has drawn from under the feet of industry the national ground on which it stood. All old-established national industries have been destroyed or are daily being destroyed. They are dislodged by new industries . . . , industries that no longer work up indigenous raw material, but raw material drawn

from the remote zones, industries whose products are consumed not only at home, but in every quarter of the globe. In place of the old wants, satisfied by the productions of the country, we find new wants, requiring for their satisfaction the products of distant lands and climes. In place of the old local and national seclusion and self-sufficiency, we have intercourse in every direction, universal inter-dependence of nations.[3]

Adopting this global vision at the end of the nineteenth century, Americans saw in China an important market for its overproduction. This was an argument given by Indiana Republican Senator Albert Beveridge for annexing the Philippines after the Spanish-American War:

Our largest trade must henceforth be with Asia. The Pacific is our ocean. More and more Europe will manufacture the most it needs, secure from its colonies the most it consumes. Where shall we turn for consumers of our surplus? Geography answers the question. China is our natural customer. She is nearer to us than to England, Germany, or Russia, the commercial powers of the present and the future. . . . The Philippines gives us a base at the door of all the East. . . . The Philippines command the commercial situation of the entire East.[4]

Arguments similar to this one were given for the Marshall Plan after World War II. The plan, which helped Europeans reestablish healthy economies through American investment, had several motivations. It was motivated in part by the simple humanitarian concern for the welfare of Europeans, who continued to suffer from desperate economic conditions two years after the war. Another reason for the plan was concern that communism would become so popular as to take over western Europe if the economic crisis there continued. But many in the United States thought that the plan's most important effect would be to provide markets for American goods and thereby forestall recession in our own country. Freda Kirchwey, for example, wrote in *The Nation*, "The Marshall Plan, put simply, is an attempt to reestablish the capacity of the world, starting with our best customers, to buy American goods. Our own economy will slump, our prosperity will disappear overnight, if the huge output of American factories, whose capacity to produce

. . . increased 50 percent during the war, cannot find overflow markets outside the United States."[5] Some business leaders agreed with this assessment. The chairman of Johns Manville Corporation told the Academy of Political Science that "a restored Europe will buy far more American goods than is now possible and will help to prevent a depression and unemployment in the United States."[6] This was an official government view as well. President Truman reported to Congress, "Considered in terms of our own economy, European recovery is essential."[7]

Increasing exports to create manufacturing jobs in the United States continues to be popular. In February 2012, for example, President Obama said, "Two years ago, I set a goal of doubling U.S. exports over five years. Today, we're on track to meet that goal—ahead of schedule. But we need to do more, which is why I'm pleased to announce several steps that will help more American businesses sell their products around the world, create jobs right here at home, and help us build an economy that lasts."[8] The following month, the *Miami Herald* reported, US Commerce Secretary John Bryson visited Miami to meet with local business leaders in hopes that they could, in the words of Miami-Dade County Mayor Carlos Gimenez, "work together to expand exports and create jobs."[9] DemeTech Corporation, which is based in the Miami area and makes surgical sutures and blades, had already been part of a Commerce Department trade mission designed to increase exports to Saudi Arabia. Another Miami-based firm, Target Engineering, was about to join a similar Commerce Department mission to India.[10]

It's no surprise that, from the early days of the Industrial Revolution to our own time, industrial countries have sought overseas markets for their manufactured goods. Historian William Rosen notes, "From 1700 to 2000, the world's population has increased twelvefold—but its production of goods and services a hundredfold."[11] There would be massive unemployment unless new markets could be found to purchase the products of this increasingly abundant output. For this reason President Obama promotes production for export. So, the answer to one of our four questions is affirmative. *Selling manufactured goods overseas to reduce unemployment is popular in the United States and therefore politically acceptable.* Three questions remain: Does international trade in manufactured goods promote fundamental efficiency? Can the United States realistically keep people working by producing goods for export? Is a continuous global increase of manufactured goods for export environmentally sustainable?

✳   ✳   ✳

Most mainstream economists give a positive answer to our second question. *Increased global trade improves efficiency in manufacturing, and thereby fundamental efficiency, where the inputs are human and natural resources and the outputs are material goods that improve human welfare.* Even if one country can produce everything better than anything can be produced elsewhere, the production-gifted country can still benefit from trade with its production-challenged counterparts. This is "the theory of comparative advantage." Globalization enthusiast Johan Norberg offers this simplified example to illustrate the general point of the theory:

> Imagine . . . two people . . . stranded on a desert island, where each needs to eat a fish and a loaf of bread every day in order to survive. To achieve this, Julia has to spend two hours baking and one hour fishing. John needs two and one-half hours to bake and five hours to fish. So . . . Julia is best at both jobs. But she still gains by swapping with John, because then she can devote her time to what she is absolutely best at—fishing. She can then catch three fish in the same three hours, while John in the course of his same seven and one-half hours can bake three loaves. They then exchange the surplus, getting one and a half each. Thus without working an iota harder or a minute longer, John and Julia have increased their daily output from two fish and two loaves to three fish and three loaves. They can opt for this higher output level and have a better meal, or they can each work a bit less and make do with the old quantities. . . . If they were able to trade with other islands in the vicinity, they would be able to trade off their surplus for clothing or tools that represented someone else's comparative advantage.[12]

The same logic works for trade among nations, Norberg contends. Suppose, for example, that the United States makes both cars and boats more efficiently than Mexico. By the logic of comparative advantage, if we make cars better than we make boats and Mexico makes boats better than they

make cars, both countries might be enriched if the United States were to concentrate on making cars for both countries and Mexico were to concentrate
on making boats for both countries. Such examples, Norberg claims, "expose
the hollowness of the argument that countries should be self-sufficient and
produce for their own populations. Under free trade, producing for others *is*
producing for yourself. It is by producing and exporting what we are best at
that we are able to import what we need."[13]

Such trade enriches countries at different levels of industrial development
as well. Philosopher Peter Singer points out that global trade should be particularly helpful to people in poor countries that have low labor costs: "They
should be able to produce goods more cheaply than countries with high labor
costs. Hence we can expect the demand for labor in those countries to rise, and
once the supply of labor begins to tighten, wages should rise too. Thus a free
market should have the effect not only of making the world as a whole more
prosperous, but more specifically, of assisting the poorest nations."[14]

China is an excellent example of this phenomenon. Its economy has grown
enormously since the 1970s and is currently the largest in the world, owing in
part to low labor costs. But now wages are increasing, especially in Guangdong
province, where the government located three of its first four "special economic zones." The province's special tax rates and exemptions from import
duties helped to make it the center of China's consumer export industry by
attracting investors from Taiwan and Hong Kong. However, there were problems. According to Alexandra Harney, writing in *Far Eastern Economic Review*,
"local officials often looked the other way when factories violated labor and
environmental laws to keep investors happy. . . . [This] brought serious social
and environmental problems."[15]

The province's increased prosperity is helping to solve these problems.
Laborers are no longer willing to accept poor wages and unsafe working
conditions. "Labor protests and strikes are now common in Guangdong,"
Harney reports. "Factories in Guangdong have been struggling to find staff
for five years, driving up wages at double-digit rates."[16] In addition, a new
law requires employers to provide pensions and to grant collective bargaining
rights.[17] Leaders in Beijing and Guangdong want to move away from pol-
luting, labor-intensive light industry to cleaner high-tech manufacturing and

service businesses that generate more revenue per hour of work and justify higher wages.[18] Light manufacture for export is moving to India and to less prosperous areas in China,[19] such as "the northern city of Tianjin as well as the eastern cities of Ningbo, Wenzhou and Nanjing. . . . As these areas develop, wages have started to rise. In Wuhan, in Hubei province, the urban minimum wage has nearly tripled since 1995."[20] The younger generation of workers, many of whom were born after the one-child policy was instituted in 1979, also tends to be more assertive than their older peers and are more willing to blow the whistle on employers who violate standards designed to protect workers and the environment. In sum, Harney concludes, "China's manufacturing sector and industrialized areas will begin to more closely resemble those of more developed countries."[21]

These events illustrate perfectly what Peter Singer had in mind. Development economist Jeffrey Sachs reports the same trajectory at an earlier point in its arc in Bangladesh. While in Bangladesh, Sachs noticed that an English-language newspaper contained stories of women who were thrilled to have left their rural villages to work for low wages in apparel factories under conditions that many people in advanced industrial societies might find appalling. However, for these women it was an enormous step up. They were escaping chronic hunger and domineering patriarchy. They could make their own decisions about marriage and children and were even saving money to afford an education. "These Bangladeshi women share the experience of many generations of immigrants to New York City's garment district and a hundred other places where their migration to toil in garment factories was a step on the path to a future of urban affluence in succeeding generations."[22]

Evidence that Bangladeshi women are starting to climb the ladder of material wealth is contained in Sachs's report on the work of the Bangladeshi Rural Advancement Committee (BRAC). With BRAC's help, women who live about an hour outside the city of Dhaka are engaged in small-scale food processing and trade, selling their wares within their village and on the road to Dhaka. They were able to start these businesses with BRAC's microfinancing, similar to that of the more famous Grameen Bank, which lends small amounts of money, usually just a few hundred dollars, to a group of (usually) women who have sensible business plans. Default rates are very low.[23]

Perhaps even more remarkable is the fertility rate among these women and their attitudes about family size. As women gain more independence through their own sources of income, they can more readily resist pressures to have more children than they really want. In a meeting that Sachs attended with some microfinanced entrepreneurs, it was discovered that on average each woman had fewer than two children, and almost all the women considered two children to be ideal. Along with improved public health measures, the extra nutrition and attention that each child receives in a smaller family has already "dramatically reduced rates of child mortality." Another effect of smaller families is that more can be spent to educate each child, resulting in greater literacy among girls and young women, which further empowers women to control the size of their families. Sachs summarizes, "With fewer children, a poor household can invest more in the health and education of each child, thereby equipping the next generation with the health, nutrition, and education that can lift Bangladesh's living standards in future years."[24]

New York Times columnist Thomas Friedman believes that global trade will improve living standards dramatically throughout the world because people around the world will demand it. Now that they see through worldwide media how comfortable and exciting life is in developed countries, they will settle for nothing less.[25] He writes, "Globalization emerges from below, from street level, from people's very souls and from their deepest aspirations . . . , [from] the basic human desire for a better life—a life with more choices as to what to eat, what to wear, where to live, where to travel, how to work, what to read, what to write and what to learn."[26] He notes that there has been considerable success so far and more success is on the horizon. "In relatively short periods of time, countries that have been the most open to globalization, like Taiwan, Singapore, Israel, Chile and Sweden, have achieved standards of living comparable to those in America and Japan, while the ranks of the middle class in countries like Thailand, Brazil, India and Korea have swelled, due partly to globalization."[27]

Friedman believes that any country can become rich. He quotes Harvard University Business School professor Michael Porter, "A nation's wealth is [now] principally of its own collective choosing. Location, natural resources and even military might are no longer decisive. Instead, how a nation and its citizens choose to organize and manage the economy, the institutions they put in place and the types of investments they individually and collectively choose to make will determine national prosperity."[28] Friedman goes even farther, writing,

> The ideal country in a flat [globalized] world is one with *no natural resources*, because countries with no natural resources tend to dig inside themselves. They try to tap the energy, entrepreneurship, creativity, and intelligence of their own people—men and women—rather than drill an oil well. Taiwan is a barren rock in a typhoon-laden sea, with virtually no natural resources—nothing but the energy, ambition, and talent of its own people—and today it has the third-largest financial reserves in the world. The success of Hong Kong, Japan, South Korea, and coastal China can all be traced to a similar [embrace of global trade].[29]

Friedman claims that in the long run global trade will improve job prospects for American workers just as did the Marshall Plan. In the short run, he recognizes, many Americans lose manufacturing and service jobs as employers hire cheaper labor overseas. However, such loses will be reversed in the long run so long as the economic pie keeps growing, which it will if people remain creative and entrepreneurial, altering products, inventing new products, and making both altered and new products necessary for millions of consumers. Friedman is his own exhibit A:

> I like going to coffee shops occasionally, but now that Starbucks is here, I *need* my coffee, and that new need has spawned a whole new industry. I always wanted to be able to search for things, but once Google was created, I *must* have my search engine. So a whole new industry has been built up around search, and Google is hiring Ph.D.'s by the bushel—before Yahoo! or Microsoft hires them. People are always assuming that everything that is going to be invented must have been invented already. *But it hasn't.*[30]

As Mark Andreessen, co-founder of Netscape, put it, "If you believe human wants and needs are infinite, then there are infinite industries to be created, infinite businesses to be started, and infinite jobs to be done. . . . If you look over the sweep of history, every time we had more trade, more communications, we had a big upswing in economic activity and standard of living."[31] As we saw in chapter 1, this is the general trend of the last 250 years. Over several generations technological change has drastically reduced job opportunities in agriculture, as the percentage of people working the land went from ninety percent to only two percent.[32] But this has freed up labor to create many products that most of us, like Friedman, now consider necessities. Producing these necessities creates jobs.

When huge countries such as India and China become more like the United States, Japan, and western Europe, the whole process of worldwide enrichment goes farther and faster. Friedman notes, *"The Indians and Chinese are not racing us to the bottom. They are racing us to the top—and that is a good thing!* They want higher standards of living, not sweatshops; they want brand names, not junk; they want to trade their motor scooters for cars and their pens and pencils for computers."[33] The Indian conglomerate Tata has designed an inexpensive car to meet the increasing demands of Indian consumers.[34] Elizabeth Economy, senior fellow at the Council on Foreign Relations writes in *Foreign Affairs*, "Chinese developers are laying more than 52,700 miles of new highways throughout the country. Some 14,000 new cars hit China's roads each day. By 2020 China is expected to have 130 million cars, and by 2050—or perhaps as early as 2040—it is expected to have even more cars than the United States."[35]

In sum, as the Indians, Chinese, and eventually even the Bangladeshis and others in the third world have standards of living more like our own, trade enthusiasts contend, our trade relationships with them will become more like the relations we have with western Europe and Japan, whose economic recovery after World War II has created so many job opportunities in the United States. Thus, manufacturing for export and increased global trade, conducted almost completely by the private sector, seem good ways to employ people while raising standards of living and improving human wellbeing around the globe. If the goal of economic activity is to improve net human wellbeing worldwide, global trade and manufacture for export would seem to be efficient uses of human and natural resources.

Drawbacks associated with consumerism characterize increased commercial prosperity in already wealthy countries, and those will be considered in chapters 8 and 9. But the benefits of generalized material enrichment (within environmental limits) for the majority of humanity (who are relatively poor) are not affected by these drawbacks. So the second of our four questions is answered in the affirmative. International trade in manufactured goods tends to promote fundamental efficiency. It achieves such efficiency, however, only when the benefits of economic growth enrich the poor. It is not fundamentally efficient when it helps only people who are already wealthy.

*   *   *

Two of our four questions remain. Will international trade in manufactured goods reduce unemployment in the United States? And is such manufacturing environmentally sustainable? The answer to the first question is generally negative. Owing to increasingly labor-efficient methods of manufacture, Americans will not lower unemployment by manufacturing for export. Prospects are dim in the near term in part because American workers are competing with much cheaper labor in the third world. Environmental limits preclude the possibility that most people in the third world will eventually live as Americans do now so that American workers can compete globally on a level playing field. So the answers to both our third and fourth questions are negative. The present chapter explains why manufacturing for export won't create enough jobs in the United States to make a meaningful dent in unemployment. The two chapters that follow explain why environmental limits preclude the possibility of the entire world living as Americans do today.

China has become the workplace of the world in many product areas, so let's look at the prospects for American workers finding jobs in the near future manufacturing products for export when faced with competition from China. In 2004, Ted Fishman explored this issue in the *New York Times Magazine*. He visited the Wanfeng automobile factory outside Shanghai, which was producing 60,000 vehicles a year that resemble Jeep Grand Cherokees, many with such luxury features as leather seats and DVD video systems. Instead of the computer-guided robot assembly machines that fill factory floors in the United States, Europe, and Japan, Fishman found "hundreds of young men, newly arrived from China's expanding technical schools, manning the assembly lines with little more than large electric drills, wrenches and rubber mallets. Engines and body panels that would, in a Western, Korean or Japanese factory, move from station to station on automatic conveyors are hauled by hand and hand truck here."[36] Precisely by substituting labor for expensive machinery, Fishman thinks, the Chinese manufacturer saves money. "It's using highly skilled workers who cost at most a few hundred dollars a month—whose yearly pay, in other words, is less than the monthly pay of new hires in Detroit." As a result, Wanfeng "can sell hand-made luxury versions of the Jeep . . . for $8,000 to $10,000."[37]

The abundance of skilled workers not only gives the Chinese a price advantage, but also a flexibility advantage. In 2012 Charles Duhigg and Keith Bradsher reported in the *New York Times* that Foxconn Industry, the company that assembles iPhones in China, employs 230,000 people at a single facility, where over a quarter of the workforce lives in company barracks, making them available at all times on short notice. Jennifer Rigoni, who managed supply for Apple until 2010, said of Foxconn, "They could hire 3,000 people over-night. What U.S. plant can find 3,000 people overnight and convince them to live in dorms?"[38]

Living and working conditions in China are often poor, which reduces costs and gives Chinese workers a competitive advantage. The *New York Times* reports that the dorms at such facilities as Foxconn's can be overcrowded, with up to twenty people sharing a three-bedroom apartment. Workers are some-times forced to stand up while working so much overtime that their legs swell up and they can hardly walk. Many workers are underage. "Bleak working conditions have been documented at factories manufacturing products for Dell, Hewlett-Packard, I.B.M., Lenovo, Motorola, Nokia, Sony, Toshiba and others." Health and safety standards are often disregarded. For example, 137 people were injured at an Apple plant in eastern China when workers were required to use a poisonous chemical to clean iPhones. In 2011, "two explosions at iPad factories, including in Chengdu, killed four people and injured 77. Before those blasts, Apple had been alerted to hazardous conditions inside the Chengdu plant."[39]

Apple does have a code of conduct for its suppliers, but Apple's own reports indicate that most of its suppliers have violated at least one aspect of this code of conduct since 2007. Although the company claims to have worked assiduously over a four-year period to rectify problems of compliance with its code of conduct, one executive commented, "If half of iPhones were malfunctioning, do you think Apple would let it go on for four years?"[40]

Even if they had better living conditions, Chinese workers would still have the advantage of their willingness to live in company-owned housing near the factory. This advantage was evident at Foxconn when Steve Jobs, as head of Apple, insisted just weeks before the scheduled release of the iPhone that the phone's screen be switched to scratch-resistant glass. A former Apple executive told the *Times* that when the new screens arrived at Foxconn near midnight, eight thousand workers were roused from their beds and within half an hour began twelve-hour shifts. Within four days the plant was turning out more than ten thousand iPhones a day.[41]

Chinese workers and factories benefit also from increasing technological sophistication. China initially made its mark in international trade in the late twentieth century by manufacturing toys, shoes, shirts, and jackets. It has since moved up the technological ladder to make cars and consumer electronics, such as TVs, DVD players, and cell phones. It's now developing expertise in biotechnology and high-tech computer manufacturing.[42] To further this trajectory, the Chinese are turning out engineers at an impressive rate—325,000 in 2004, five times the American number—and are giving solid technical educations to millions of their young people. China has more than 17 million university- and advanced-vocational students, most of them in science and engineering.[43] Thus, when Apple was gearing up to produce its iPhone, it estimated that it would need 8,700 industrial engineers to oversee the work of 200,000 assembly-line workers. They calculated that it could take as long as nine months to find the needed engineers in the United States, whereas in China it took only fifteen days.[44]

Material supplies are also readily available in China as a result of so many industries finding it cost-effective and convenient to locate there. A former high-ranking Apple executive said, "The entire supply chain is in China now. You need a thousand rubber gaskets? That's the factory next door. You need a million screws? That factory is a block away. You need that screw made a little bit different? It will take three hours."[45]

Not only are there abundant, inexpensive, flexible workers in China, and material supplies flexibly produced in great proximity, for many products the customers are also in Asia. Corning Glass, which produces glass for iPhones, increased its workforce in the United States to fulfill its contracts with Apple. But when orders came flooding in from other countries trying to imitate Apple's design, the company decided to open factories in Asia instead of building more factories in the United States. James Flaws, Corning's vice president and chief financial officer said, "Our customers are in Taiwan, Korea, Japan and China. We could make the glass here, and then ship it by boat, but that takes 35 days. Or, we could ship it by air, but that's 10 times as expensive. So we build our glass factories next door to assembly factories, and those are overseas." He concludes, "The consumer electronics business has become an Asian business. . . . Asia has become what the U.S. was for the last 40 years."[46]

*   *   *

How, then, can American manufacturers compete? They can hold down costs by using high-tech machinery instead of human labor as much as possible and by giving low pay to the relatively few workers that they do hire. Ted Fishman, who visited the Wanfeng auto plant in Shanghai, traveled to Wisconsin, which had lost 90,000 manufacturing jobs in the early 2000s, to investigate a metal casting factory owned by Signicast Corporation. Metal castings are used directly or indirectly in 90 percent of all manufactured goods and capital equipment, and the United States still had the world's largest metal casting industry (as measured by the dollar value of its products) in 2004, with nearly 3,000 relatively small factories, mostly in the Midwest. But China was moving up fast. In the mid-2000s, metal casting imports from China were growing by seven to ten percent a year. By volume, China's metal casting industry was already the largest in the world by 2004.[47]

Growth of the Chinese metal casting industry was similar to growth in other industries. The Chinese compete successfully with high quality and a low price that has come to be called the "China price." In November 2003, the Federal Reserve Bank in Chicago noted that "auto-makers [who use a lot of metal castings] have reportedly been asking suppliers for the 'China price' on their purchases," and some large metal casting customers have suggested that their suppliers relocate their facilities to China, or find subcontractors in China. As a result, 140 American metal casting foundries went out of business in 2002 alone.[48]

So how does Signicast Corporation compete? Signicast uses a great deal of automation. Fishman writes, "Robots fill its factory, moving everything from thumb-size precision parts to the boxes in the warehouse. Workers are scarce. Walking through the plant is a lesson in how the hardware business has become a software business. The whole plant seems to be run by smart ghosts."[49] In short, one way for Americans to compete successfully is to do just the opposite of what the Chinese are doing—replace workers with expensive, sophisticated machines in order to reduce labor costs. Signicast stays competitive by employing very few people, which indicates the severe limitations of an American job-growth strategy that relies on manufacturing for export. In 2012, the dollar value of American manufacture was about the same as China's, but the United States accomplished this parity with only one-tenth the number of workers in manufacturing.[50]

There is nothing unique about car manufacture and metal castings. The replacement of people with machines pervades American industry, provoking a joke among manufacturers of cotton textiles. "A modern textile mill employs only a man and a dog. The man is there to feed the dog, and the dog is there to keep the man away from the machines."[51]

Recent developments have only reinforced the strategy of retaining or regaining manufacturing output in wealthy industrial countries by replacing labor with machines. In general, notes the British *Economist* magazine, "As the number of people directly employed in making things declines, the cost of labour as a proportion of the total cost of production will diminish too. This will encourage makers to move some of the work back to rich countries."[52] For example, Royal Philips Electronics makes high-end electric razors in Drachten, the Netherlands. "The assembly line," writes John Markoff in the *New York Times*,

> is made up of dozens of glass cages housing robots made by Adept Technology
> that snake around the factory floor for more than 100 yards. Video cameras

atop the cages guide the robot arms almost unerringly to pick up the parts they assemble. The arms bend wires with millimetric accuracy, set tooth-pick-thin spindles in tiny holes, grab miniature plastic gears and set them in housings, and snap pieces of plastic into place.[53]

The next generation of robots promises to be more flexible than current models. Typical robots in automobile manufacture, for example, perform one task each. At the Tesla assembly plant in Fremont, California, by contrast, a single robotic arm may be able to do four different tasks, such as welding, riveting, bonding, and installing a component.[54] Increased robotic flexibility means even less need for human intervention. Already in Japan a maker of smarter and more dexterous robots, FANUC, "has automated some of its production lines to the point where they can run unsupervised for several weeks. Many other factories use processes such as laser cutting and injection moulding that operate without any human intervention."[55]

Pharmaceutical manufacture may soon be transformed also to require fewer workers. Currently, making drugs involves gathering materials from around the world, processing them into desired chemical compounds, trans-forming those compounds into pills, creams, or liquids, and then shipping the finished products around the world. But a pilot production line resulting from collaboration between MIT and Novartis reduces the number of discreet operations from twenty-two to thirteen, reduces the time for processing from three hundred hours to forty hours, and allows each and every pill, not just samples from a large batch, to be tested for quality. The company expects this simplified process to be commercially operational before 2020.[56]

Additive manufacturing, often called 3D printing, is also likely to reduce the need for human labor in manufacturing. The fabricating unit is like a two-dimensional printer except that it passes over the same areas many times, depositing some material each time, to produce three-dimensional objects. Items with moving parts, including guns, can be manufactured this way.[57] All anyone needs is the proper 3D printer, the (usually plastic) material to be deposited by the machine, and a downloadable program. Material as well as labor can be saved this way because additive manufacture is additive; mate-rial is added to material until the object is finished. There is no need to trim down a larger piece of matter to conform to the size and shape of the desired object or part. Products can more easily be altered with additive manufacture because alteration requires merely changing the computer program rather than designing and manufacturing new molds and production processes. In this way, it's easier and cheaper for producers to keep up with emerging consumer preferences. Individualized versions of products can also be made simply by altering the program, allowing products more easily to reflect a particular consumer's taste. Innovation can be faster and easier, too, because a prototype can be made quickly and shared with collaborators around the world simply by sharing the manufacturing program. "This means," according to an official of the Silicon Valley software company Autodesk, "the factory of the future could be me, sitting in my home office."[58]

At present such printers make one item or a small batch of items at a time. In the future, however, several or many 3D printers may be configured in an assembly line, like the machines at the new Novartis plant, allowing additive manufacture to produce quickly larger batches of items, including items that are larger than any individual 3D printer can accommodate. The flexibility of altering and customizing products would be retained because alterations will still require nothing more than tweaking the appropriate computer programs.[59]

The prospects for additional American manufacturing jobs diminish as US manufacturers employ such innovations. Thus, the United States competes with China in the manufacture of solar panels. The American solar panel manufacturer Flextronics in Milpas, California, just south of San Francisco, claims to be "Bringing Jobs & Manufacturing Back to California," but look inside the plant and you'll find a lot of robots and very few workers.[60]

However, all is not lost. These more efficient, computer-guided manufacturing methods need increasing numbers of technically trained workers, even if many are not on the factory floor. Such workers include product engineers and designers as well as people who design, operate, and service the nearly worker-free assembly lines. By 2012, for example, the robotics industry itself employed about 150,000 people worldwide.[61] Many jobs related to high-tech manufacture are in research and development. Although manufacturing constitutes only 11 percent of the US GDP, 68 percent of American R & D is devoted to manufacturing. And in addition to technical jobs in IT and engineering, factories of the future will still need people working in accounting, marketing, customer relations, cooking, and cleaning. MIT president Susan Hockfield calls this "a huge supply chain in which there are lots of jobs and large economic benefits."[62]

Still, I don't think we should be optimistic about job prospects in manufacturing, because the situation in manufacturing resembles historical developments in agriculture. In 1800, 90 percent of Americans were farmers;[63] in 1900, 40 percent were farmers; and by 2012 only 2 percent were farmers.[64] But many more workers than this two percent are needed to put food on our tables. Our current food abundance is the result of mechanized agriculture that uses large pieces of machinery and many chemical inputs, all of which must be manufactured and transported. The basic metals for farm equipment must be mined. The fuel used in agricultural machinery is petroleum based, which requires oil drilling and refining. Much of the fertilizer used on modern farms is also petroleum based. New types of seeds and herbicides are in constant development and dissemination. All the companies involved need accountants, marketing specialists, customer services representatives, and so forth. So far, this sounds good for job prospects. But wait. At the end of the day Americans spend relatively little on food, suggesting that the total of agriculture and agriculture-related jobs is down. As a share of personal income, expenditures for food have gone from about 24 percent in the 1930s to under 10 percent by 2008.[65] This suggests that the total American work effort needed to put food on the American table has been decreasing despite the great variety of jobs involved. All told, Americans have lost many more jobs than they've gained. If the situation were otherwise, if more total jobs were involved in getting food on our tables (as a result of needed mining, oil refining, implement manufacture, and the like) food costs would rise, defeating a major purpose of mechanizing agriculture in the first place.

A similar situation exists and similar reasoning applies to the total work effort needed in manufacturing as IT, robotics, 3D printing, etc. take over. Manufactured products made in the United States and other wealthy industrial countries are much cheaper than they would be without high-tech methods. Net savings are primarily in labor costs. So, in spite of the fact that high-tech methods require a lot of R & D, engineers, IT specialists, and other highly trained professionals, total job opportunities in manufacturing and related to manufacturing must be vastly fewer and diminishing with the advent of high-tech manufacturing just as total agriculture and agriculture-related jobs have diminished with increasingly mechanized agriculture. If total job opportunities related to manufacturing a given item weren't reduced, high-tech manufacturing processes would make the item more expensive and would be abandoned.

So this is what we see. As a result of recent success, Apple added 8,000 jobs in 2011.[66] But this employment gain is modest. In electronics most of the work that stays in the United States requires relatively few additional workers even when sales increase dramatically. Jean-Louis Gassee, a former head of Apple's product development and marketing, observed, "If you scale up from selling one million phones to 30 million phones, you don't really need more programmers. All these new companies—Facebook, Google, Twitter—benefit from this. They grow, but they don't really need to hire much." Apple's recently built $500 million North Carolina data center employs only one hundred people.[67]

✳   ✳   ✳

Manufacturing jobs in the United States under present conditions of global competition are not only fewer; they often don't pay well either. Adam Davidson reports in the *Atlantic* on Standard Motor Products, which makes replacement parts for cars. They manufacture fuel injectors in the United States because fuel injectors must be constructed to extremely high levels of precision in order to function properly, and manufacturing in the United States makes it easier to control quality.

> Based on the car's speed, ambient temperature, and a dozen other variables, the computer tells a fuel injector to squirt a precise amount of gasoline (anywhere from one to 100 10,000ths of an ounce) at the instant that the piston is in the right position (and anywhere from 10 to 200 times a second). For this to work, the injector must be perfectly constructed. When squirting gas, the syringe moves forward and back a total distance of 70 microns—about the width of a human hair—and a microscopic imperfection in the

metal, or even a speck of dust, will block the movement and disable the injector.[68]

Where does this leave the American worker? Standard attains the precision it needs on fuel injectors by using a very expensive machine that's run by a computer. The machine does the work under control of the computer, but a human operator is needed who understands the machine, the computer, the computer's language, and a good deal of math in order to know how to make adjustments when necessary. When the machine's cutting tool wears down, for example, the worker needs to get the computer to move the tool a few microns closer. Such adjustments may be needed ten or twenty times an hour, but with that one skilled worker's assistance, the machine can put out a lot of fuel injectors.[69]

A worker who does this job and was interviewed by Davidson at the Standard plant in Greenville, South Carolina, Luke Hutchins, became qualified by completing the Machine Tool Technology program at Spartanburg Community College. He also had five years of experience after graduation before being hired by Standard and still needed one month of on-the-job training. Yet, he makes only about $20 an hour, compared to the $13 an hour that is typical for unskilled workers at the plant.[70] Because he has three twelve-hour shifts per week, he makes about $36,000 a year. He's not poor, but he could hardly raise a family at a middle class standard of living on that amount of income.

It's important that wage earners make enough money to support a family on a single income because in 2011 more than a quarter of all US households were headed by single women with children,[71] and another eight percent were headed by single men with children.[72] If a single paycheck doesn't support a middle-class family, between one quarter and one third of American children will fall below middle-class status for this reason alone.

Unfortunately, as we just saw, in our globalized world substituting manufacturing jobs for service work doesn't automatically increase paychecks to the middle-class level. Automobile manufacture illustrates the problem as well. It had long been thought that subcompact cars could not be manufactured in the United States because profit margins on such vehicles are too low and labor costs here are too high. For this reason, Ford builds its Fiesta in Mexico and Honda makes its Fit in such countries as China and Brazil. GM addressed the economic issue when it decided it could build its new subcompact, the Chevrolet Sonic, in the United States by redesigning its plant to require fewer workers and rewriting the labor contract to allow for a less expensive workforce. The plant uses 25 percent fewer workers than it had used previously, and a special agreement with the United Auto Workers (U.A.W.) allows GM to pay some entry level workers only $14 an hour, compared to the ordinary entry-level pay of $28 an hour.[73] Thus, the low pay at Standard Motor Products and at GM removes one of the most attractive features of employment in manufacturing in the generation following World War II—middle-class salaries.

The scarcity of jobs that pay good incomes is partly a result of the increasing use of capital to augment the productive power of each worker, according to MIT management theorists Erik Brynjolfsson and Andrew McAfee:

> If the technology decreases the relative importance of human labor in a particular production process, the owners of capital equipment will be able to capture a bigger share of income from the goods and services produced. . . .
>
> In particular, if technology replaces labor, you might expect that the shares of income earned by equipment owners would rise relative to laborers—the classic bargaining battle between capital and labor. . . . Since the recession ended, real spending on equipment and software has soared by 26% while payrolls have remained essentially flat.[74]

Another factor keeping the American working wage down is, again, competition from China. The sheer number of Chinese workers, including the highly educated, the skilled, and the unskilled, is daunting. Sandra Polaski, a former State Department special representative for international labor affairs who later worked for the Carnegie Endowment for International Peace, wrote, "If *all* U.S. jobs were moved to China, there would still be surplus labor in China."[75] Fishman adds, "That fact highlights what is most sobering about China's booming economy; it can force down the value of work in any job that is at all transferable."[76] Thus, the increasing use of high-tech methods in manufacturing and competition from millions of low-wage workers in China and other third world countries combine to reduce the number of manufacturing jobs in the United States and to reduce the pay of those that remain.

As if this weren't bad enough, as more companies relocate to China, or manufacture through Chinese subsidiaries, more technological sophistication is transferred to China.[77] So, as wages are going up in China, Chinese manufacturers are turning increasingly to high-tech production methods. Foxconn, the Chinese company that manufactures iPhones for Apple, plans to start using a million robots in the next few years.[78] According to the French journal *Le Point*, the company will thereby displace 500,000 workers,[79] which should help to keep labor costs low in China. In addition, the use of high-tech manufacturing methods may undercut one of the remaining reasons for keeping jobs in the United States, the need for very high levels of precision in such products as fuel injectors. Robots can be as precise in China as in the United States.

Consumers definitely gain from American workers earning less. The Sonic sedan has a base price under $14,000. Apple and other electronics makers use Chinese factories to produce goods at low cost for American consumers. In 2004, 12 percent of China's exports went to Walmart, thereby placing enormous downward pressure on the price of a host of items on the shelves of most American retail stores, not just Walmart—as most American retailers must compete with Walmart's prices. The American factory worker's loss is the American consumer's gain.[80] But that kind of gain, which is real and important, is not going to improve the prospects of American employment in manufacture for export, which is the topic at hand.

*   *   *

The situation of American workers is not unique. The US Bureau of Labor Statistics released a report in 2009 showing that almost all other advanced industrial countries lost manufacturing jobs in the preceding forty years. While employment in the manufacturing sector has fallen in the United States from 26.4 percent of jobs in 1970 to 10.9 percent of jobs in 2008, in Britain the reduction was from 33.9 percent of jobs in 1971 to 12 percent of jobs in 2008. Sweden went from about 25 percent to 16 percent, Germany from nearly 40 percent to 25 percent, Canada from 22 percent to 10.5 percent, Australia from 24.5 percent to 10 percent, and France from 25 percent to 15 percent. The trend lines are all down.[81] And the slide continues. By 2013 only 8.7 percent of American workers were engaged in manufacturing.[82]

Because the US population has been growing, the number of manufacturing jobs increased for a generation even as the percentage of the workforce in manufacturing declined. But then in the late 1990s the bottom really dropped out of the American manufacturing labor market. Adam Davidson writes, "In the 10 years ending in 2009, factories shed workers so fast that they erased almost all the gains of the previous 70 years; roughly one out of every three manufacturing jobs—about 6 million in total—disappeared. About as many people work in manufacturing now as did at the end of the Depression, even though the American population is more than twice as large today."[83]

In sum, so long as American factory workers are competing with low-wage workers in poorer countries such as China, India, Mexico, Indonesia, and Bangladesh, international trade in manufactured goods will not lead to increased employment in the United States, much less in manufacturing jobs that pay well. Our best efforts at producing competitively for export are needed simply to reduce the loss of jobs that result from increased imports from around the globe. And these efforts tend to include lowering wages for American factory workers to make more American products price competitive, thereby depriving American workers of a major benefit of manufacturing work in previous generations—a middle class lifestyle.

Optimists claim, however, that this lamentable situation will not persist indefinitely if we remain conscientious about pursuing international trade. Our trade relations are good with western Europe even though they had much lower wages after World War II than we did, because the Marshall Plan enabled Europeans to improve their standard of living to the American level, putting competition with them on a level playing field. As we have seen, living standards in many other parts of the world are starting to improve as international trade enriches people generally. Optimists look forward to a time during this century when all human beings will be as wealthy as Americans so that we can compete with everyone on a level playing field.

New York Times columnist Tom Friedman puts it this way, "'Americans' are popping up all over now—from Doha to Dalian and from Calcutta to Casablanca to Cairo, moving into American-style living spaces, buying

American-style cars, eating American-style fast food, and creating American levels of garbage."[84] He notes that in Shenzhen, where Foxconn Industry has that enormous factory that assembles iPhones, "a single Sam's Club, part of the Walmart family of stores, sold roughly 1,100 air-conditioners in one hot weekend in 2006."[85]

The question remains: Can this improvement in the standard of living in developing countries continue to such an extent that standards of living worldwide rise to the American level so that American workers can compete with workers elsewhere on a level playing field? Or are there environmental limits that preclude the possibility of everyone in the world sharing America's level of affluence? If such environmental limits exist, the goal of reversing losses in American manufacturing jobs through manufacture for global trade would be as unattainable in the foreseeable future (later in this century) as it is today. We turn to this topic next.

CHAPTER 4

ENVIRONMENTAL LIMITS

FOOD AND WATER

merican workers are hampered in their efforts to maintain markets for their manufactured goods by competition from workers in poor countries where labor is very inexpensive. One proposal is to duplicate the American standard of living in the rest of the world so as to level the playing field of international competition, just as the field was leveled for American workers in relation to workers in western Europe through the material enrichment of European workers after World War II. When everyone in the world is as wealthy as Americans, American workers will not be competing with less expensive labor elsewhere. As we saw in the last chapter, global trade is already lifting hundreds of millions of people out of material poverty. As they approach the American standard of living, according to this approach, private enterprise will be able to make money selling globally goods made with American labor, and more Americans will have good jobs in manufacturing. Unfortunately, as the present chapter shows, this solution to declining opportunities in the United States for jobs in manufacturing is not viable. The earth couldn't possibly sustain material consumption at anything like the American level for everyone.

According to *New York Times* columnist Thomas Friedman, everyone on earth would like to adopt America's earth-consuming habits. He writes, "The Great Chinese Dream, like the Great Indian Dream, the Great Russian Dream, and the Great American Dream, is built around a high-energy, high-electricity, high-bent-metal lifestyle."[1] As we saw in the last chapter, China is having major success fulfilling such dreams. Air-conditioners are flying off the shelves at a Beijing-area Sam's Club. Moises Naim points out in the journal

Foreign Policy that meat consumption in China has more than doubled since the mid-1980s, again making it more like the United States. And as more Chinese join the middle class "they also buy more clothes, refrigerators, toys, medicines, and, eventually, cars and homes."[2] Friedman reports that in 2004 Beijing was adding 30,000 new cars to its roads every month, a thousand cars a day. Naim writes that "in 2005 China added as much electricity genera-tion as Britain produces in a year. In 2006, it added as much as France's total supply. Yet, millions in China still lack reliable access to electricity." And China is not alone, according to Naim: "In India, more than 400 million don't have power. The demand in India will grow fivefold in the next 25 years."[3] In addition, as more people in the world become affluent, the World Tourism Organization estimates, the number of outbound tourists will nearly double, reaching a total of 1.6 billion by 2020.[4]

This is only the tip of the iceberg. Friedman claims that "in India and China some 200 million people have emerged from poverty in the last thirty years, most of them moving from low-impact village life to middle-class life in urban areas. But, as economists point out, there are still 200 million behind them, and another 200 million behind them . . . all waiting their turn. . . . They will not deny themselves an American style of life."[5]

Yet it's hard to see how the earth can accommodate such a proliferation of affluence. According to Lester Brown, president of the Earth Policy Institute,

> Demands of the expanding economy, *as now structured*, are surpassing the sustainable yield of ecosystems. Easily a third of the world's cropland is losing topsoil at a rate that is undermining its long-term productivity. Fully 50 percent of the world's rangeland is overgrazed and deteriorating into desert. . . . The overpumping of aquifers . . . has led to falling water tables as pumping exceeds aquifer recharge from precipitation. . . . Economic demands on forests are also excessive. Trees are being cut or burned faster than they can regenerate or be planted. . . . The human demand for animal protein has . . . begun to exceed the sustainable yield of oceanic fisheries.[6]

Finally, "burning vast quantities of artificially cheap fossil fuels . . . is desta-bilizing the climate." We are in jeopardy of "more intense heat waves, more destructive storms, melting ice caps, and a rising sea level that will shrink the land area even as population continues to grow."[7] It's hard to see how we can continue the present course of general human material enrichment—increasingly providing first-world standards of living to people in the more populous third world—without environmental catastrophe.

Geographer Jared Diamond offers some numbers to illustrate the point. All life involves extracting resources and excreting waste. In species other than humans, each member of the species extracts and excretes roughly similar amounts. In humans, by contrast, some people extract and excrete (in the form of pollution generated by their activities) much more than others, which is where the numbers come in. The average American consumes (draws resources from the earth and returns waste to the earth) 32 times as much as the average person in Kenya, one of the world's poorer nations. Although China has made great strides toward affluence, Diamond claims that in 2007 the average American still consumed 11 times as much as the average Chinese. Diamond invites us to imagine China alone increasing its consumption to the American level of 2007:

> Let's . . . make things easy by imagining that nothing else happens to increase world consumption—that is, no other country increases its consumption, all national populations (including China's) remain unchanged and immigration ceases. China's catching up alone would roughly double world consumption rates. Oil consumption would increase by 106 percent, for instance, and world metal consumption by 94 percent.
>
> If India as well as China were to catch up, world consumption rates would triple. If the whole developing world were suddenly to catch up, world rates would increase elevenfold. It would be as if the world population ballooned to 72 billion people (retaining . . . consumption rates [like those in China in 2007]).[8]

Diamond says that he has never "met anyone crazy enough to claim that we could support 72 billion."[9] It's physically impossible for everyone in the world to share the American lifestyle of 2007, much less the current American lifestyle. Yet, this is the promise of globalization and the best prospect for reducing American unemployment through manufacturing goods for export on a level playing field, that is, to a global community as materially affluent as our own society. So this is the thought experiment examined in the present chapter: Curtail unemployment by creating additional American jobs in manufacturing by encouraging (mostly private-sector profit-oriented enterprises) to meet worldwide consumer demand for manufactured goods, thereby increasing greatly the world's economy, so that everyone can enjoy the American level of material affluence.

Our conclusion in this chapter is that *environmental limits preclude everyone in the world living the way that Americans live presently, so the world's economy cannot increase in this way, nor can American unemployment be addressed by such means.* This conclusion doesn't imply that the world is likely to experience environmental ruin, that we will have to abandon economic growth as a goal, or that American unemployment must remain the problem that it is today. In later chapters we'll see that *the best prospects for reducing unemployment in the United States involve such strategies as increasing emphasis on providing services instead of goods in the economy; greater emphasis on public investment in pubic goods rather than private investment in consumer items; pricing goods so that they reflect the full cost of manufacture; and providing more Americans with time off of work that doesn't constitute unemployment.* These strategies can reduce unemployment and environmental damage while contributing to economic growth and human wellbeing.

❋   ❋   ❋

In the light of exaggerated claims of looming catastrophe made by environmentalists in the past, it's tempting to dismiss current worries about environmental limits. Environmentalist Paul Ehrlich, for example, announced in his 1968 book *The Population Bomb*, "The battle to feed all of humanity is over. In the 1970s the world will undergo famines—hundreds of millions of people are going to starve to death in spite of any crash programs embarked upon now. At this late date nothing can prevent a substantial increase in the world death rate."[10] Well, there actually were famines in the 1970s among people in poor third world countries, and there have been additional famines since then. But we now know that from the 1960s through the present, when people starve to death or die of diseases related to malnutrition, the causes are political and social. Enough food existed all along to feed everyone adequately. In fact, per capita food production was already increasing worldwide when Ehrlich's book was published. Bjorn Lomborg reports in *The Skeptical Environmentalist* that even though global population doubled between 1961 and the late 1990s, per capita calorie intake increased 24 percent on a global basis. As a result, fewer people are starving today, both as a percentage of world population and in absolute numbers than in the 1960s.[11] Lomborg attributes this success to the Green Revolution, which contains four main elements: high-yield crops, irrigation and controlled water supply, fertilizers and pesticides, and improved agricultural management.[12]

Ehrlich claimed that pollution was depriving people of food even in the United States. He pointed out that between 1955 and 1968 Lake Erie essentially died. Whereas in 1955 the lake supported commercial fishing, with 75 million pounds of fish taken that year alone, by 1968 the lake was so polluted that no one would dare eat its fish.[13] Ehrlich didn't mention the possibility that the lake might come to life again, but that's what actually happened. Largely as a result of the 1972 amendments to the Clean Water Act, Lake Erie's water quality has long since improved. The lake is alive and fishing is again possible there.

Ehrlich even thought we could run out of oxygen. "We are . . . removing many terrestrial areas from oxygen production by paving them. We are also depleting the world's supply of oxygen by burning (oxidizing) vast quantities of fossil fuels and by clearing iron-rich tropical soils in which the iron is then oxidized. When the rate of oxygen consumption exceeds the rate at which it is produced, then the oxygen content of the atmosphere will decrease." To be fair, Ehrlich didn't predict that we would actually run out of oxygen. He expected oxygen depletion to be very slow, writing, "I suspect that other ecological catastrophes accompanying poisoning of the sea and clearing plants from the land would lead to mankind's extinction long before he has to start worrying about running out of oxygen."[14] Well, that's a relief!

Whereas Ehrlich concentrated on problems associated with population growth, the Club of Rome, Donella Meadows and company, issued a warning in the early 1970s about continued exponential economic growth. Among their many projections was the exhaustion of petroleum supplies in the 1990s. Yet it turned out that the 1990s was the heyday of the gas-guzzling SUV. The

Club of Rome did acknowledge that if five times known reserves were discovered, oil could last for an additional thirty years,[15] but I don't think any expert today expects us to run out of oil in the 2020s, as this prediction suggests, or at any other time in the foreseeable future.[16]

Professor of Business Administration Julian Simon explains why, in general, resource limits don't impede economic growth. As a natural resource like oil becomes scarce, its price tends to rise, so people use less of it, figure out ways to increase supplies, and/or find alternatives. Using copper as his example, Simon writes that when supplies are short and the price rises, people may

> invent better ways of obtaining copper from a given lode, say a better digging tool, or they may develop new materials to substitute for copper, perhaps iron. . . .
>
> This sequence of events explains how it can be that people have been using cooking pots for thousands of years, as well as using copper for many other purposes, and yet the cost of a pot today is vastly cheaper by any measure than it was 100 or 1,000 or 10,000 years ago.[17]

The title of a *New York Times* article in 2012 illustrates this process with respect to oil and natural gas: "U.S. Inches toward Goal of Energy Independence: Friendly Policies Help Oil and Gas Industry Lift Output as Consumption Falls."[18] Higher gasoline prices had reduced consumption of oil, and newer technologies for extraction increased supplies of oil and natural gas. In the following few years, increased extraction made so much oil available as to reduce its price.

Warnings of limits to growth often cite China, where environmental deterioration owing to rapid economic growth is evident. Elizabeth Economy writes in *Foreign Affairs*,

> The coal that has powered China's economic growth . . . is also choking its people. Coal provides about 70 percent of China's energy needs. . . . This reliance on coal is devastating China's environment. The country is home to 16 of the world's 20 most polluted cities. . . . As much as 90 percent of China's sulfur dioxide emissions and 50 percent of its particulate emissions are the result of coal use. Particulates are responsible for respiratory prob-

lems among the population, and acid rain, which is caused by sulfur dioxide emissions, falls on one-quarter of China's territory and on one-third of its agricultural land, diminishing agricultural output and eroding buildings.[19]

Evidence of severe health consequences resulting from coal-related pollution was revealed in a study published in 2013. Reporter Edward Wong writes in the *New York Times*,

> Southern Chinese on average have lived at least five years longer than their northern counterparts in recent decades because of the destructive health effects of pollution from the widespread use of coal in the north. . . . Researchers project that the 500 million Chinese who live north of the Huai River will lose 2.5 billion years of life expectancy because of outdoor air pollution.[20]

Serious as such problems are, however, they seem to be the kinds of problems associated with transitions to affluence, not with affluence itself. American cities and waterways were once more polluted than they are at present. As we became wealthier we were able to clean them up. As China's per capita income grows, its increasingly middle-class urban populations will also demand a cleanup. They will demand air quality comparable to that in rich countries just as they demand the same consumer goods enjoyed in those countries. Their improved incomes will enable them to buy not only cars and home appliances, but also public goods, such as clean air, through higher electricity rates that result from installation of cleaner power-generating technologies. This is what Americans, Japanese, and western Europeans have done. There's no reason to think that China, or any other country that becomes affluent through efficient production and world trade, can't or won't do the same. China is already imposing tougher environmental standards in its most economically prosperous but increasingly polluted provinces.[21] What is more, it planned in 2013, shortly after acknowledging the baleful health effects of particulate pollution from burning coal, to reduce air pollution nationwide by limiting coal burning and taking some high-polluting vehicles off the road.[22]

In sum, whether it's mass starvation owing to lack of food, depletion of oxygen, pollution of land, air, and water, or diminished supplies of critical industrial inputs such as petroleum, copper, and tin, environmentalist doom-sayers seem repeatedly to be wrong, which undercuts warnings of doom today.

For this reason, there will be no prognostications of doom in this book. What there is, instead, is an account of why we won't, because environmental limitations indicate that we can't, attain a worldwide level of material affluence similar to the current American standard of living. Although some forward thinking will be necessary regarding climate change, in large part doom will be avoided because, as Julian Simon correctly notes, people change behaviors as shortages become manifest and prices increase.

But there are still reasons to understand environmental limits. First, people and countries that anticipate the kinds of market changes Simon had in mind generally do better economically than people and countries that don't. Early understanding facilitates agile adaptation. Second, an application of this first point is recognition that we can't meaningfully reduce unemployment in the United States by promoting manufactured goods for export on the theory that eventually we'll be competing on a level playing field as people world-wide live as we do now. Because environmental limits preclude that possi-bility, we must adapt by finding other ways of growing our economy and reducing unemployment. I discuss such other approaches in later chapters.

I find limits to worldwide material affluence on the current American model in three interrelated restraining factors—water, food, and climate change. Although there are many varieties of food, some of which can be substituted for one another in the human diet, there is no substitute for food itself. The production of food requires fresh water. Nothing can substitute for the use of fresh water in land-based food production. Finally, greenhouse gases in the atmosphere that cause climate change cannot be cleaned up the way that air quality has been improved in so many urban settings in indus-trial countries. Once they are in the atmosphere, greenhouse gases remain there for hundreds of years. Climate changes that result from their presence in the atmosphere threaten food production on land, partly by reducing fresh water available for agriculture. When the principal among these gases, carbon dioxide, is absorbed by the oceans, it jeopardizes food production in the sea.

*   *   *

Consider water first. Dedicated environmentalists are not the only people worried about water supplies in the near future. The United States Department of State commissioned a study of water shortages that are likely to occur in the next ten to thirty years to assess their severity and their impact on US foreign policy. They write,

> Our Bottom Line: During the next 10 years, many countries important to the United States will experience water problems—shortages, poor water quality, or floods—that will risk instability and state failure, increase regional tensions, and distract them from working with the United States on important US policy objectives. Between now and 2040, fresh water availability will not keep up with demand absent more effective management of water resources. Water problems will hinder the ability of key countries to produce food and generate energy, posing a risk to global food markets and hobbling economic growth.[23]

What is the basis for this sober assessment? Seventy percent of the earth's surface is covered by ocean water, life is presumed to have started in the sea, and the salt content of human beings is similar to that in the oceans. Nevertheless, ocean water cannot be consumed directly by human beings and is unhelpful for raising green plants on land, the foundation of the land-based food chain leading to human nutrition. So, land-based food for human beings depends on available supplies of fresh water, which constitute only 2.5 percent of all the water in the world. However, two-thirds of that 2.5 percent of water is unavailable to grow crops. Journalist Steven Solomon notes that this water is

> locked away from man's use in ice caps and glaciers. All but a few drops of the remaining one-third is also inaccessible, or prohibitively expensive to extract, because it lies in rocky, underground aquifers—in effect, isolated underground lakes—many a half mile or more deep inside Earth's bowels. Such aquifers hold up to an estimated 100 times more liquid freshwater than exists on the surface. In all, less than three-tenths of one percent of total freshwater is in liquid form on the surface.[24]

The surface water used most by civilizations through the ages has been river and stream water, and it amounts to only six-thousandths of 1 percent of fresh water.

Population increase alone would strain supplies of fresh water for agriculture. There are presently more than seven billion people in the world, and the United Nations currently projects the human population to peak by the end of this century at more than ten billion, about a billion more than in previous projections.[25] However, accompanying dramatic population increases in the past three centuries has been equally dramatic increases in the supply of available fresh water. The Industrial Revolution and related ingenuity that enabled people to increase energy use also enabled people to tap additional supplies of fresh water, resulting in fresh water use increasing twice as fast as the human population between 1700 and 2000. In the twentieth century, total fresh water use increased nine fold, compared to a thirteen-fold increase in total energy use.[26]

The bad news is that this trend cannot continue; it's not sustainable. We cannot continue the current trajectory of exponential increases in per capita water use, Solomon explains,

> About half the renewable global runoff accessible to the most populated parts of the planet is being used. Simple math, and the physical limits of nature, dictates that past trends cannot be sustained. Throughout history the ceiling of man's capacity to extract greater water supply from nature had been bounded only by his own technological limitations. Now, however, an additional, external obstacle has arisen to impose the critical constraint— the depletion of the renewable, accessible freshwater ecological system upon which all human civilization ultimately depends.[27]

Consider India, home to nearly 20 percent of the human population. In the 1960s India had difficulty growing enough food to feed its population. Under (I believe) well-meaning pressure from the United States (as a condition for temporary food aid in 1966), India started using the so-called "miracle seeds" of the Green Revolution, high-yield varieties (HYVs) of wheat and rice that had been developed by Norman Borlaug.[28] These varieties produced more wheat and rice per acre, and Indian production of cereals more than doubled between 1968 and 1998.[29] Borlaug received the Nobel Peace Prize in 1970 for his work. The Green Revolution, according to environmental optimist Bjorn Lomborg, helped increase per capita food availability during the twentieth century even as world population soared.

However, as Indian physicist and environmental activist Vandana Shiva points out, "The Green Revolution increased the need for irrigation water at two levels. Firstly, the shift from water prudent crops such as millets and oilseeds to monocultures and multicropping such [cereals] as wheat and rice increased the demand for water inputs throughout the year."[30] Second, "Green Revolution varieties [of wheat and rice] need much more water than indigenous varieties. Thus, while indigenous wheat varieties need 12 inches of irrigation, the HYVs require at least 36 inches."[31]

One result has been an enormous increase of water wells in India to meet the irrigation needs of the Green Revolution's HYVs. Whereas in 1975 India had about 800,000 wells, most of them shallow, it had by the end of the century over about 22 million water wells of increasing depth, and was adding about 1 million wells per year. The depth of wells was increasing because water tables were falling. Steven Solomon writes,

> In India's breadbaskets of Punjab and Haryana, for example, the water tables are falling over three feet per year; monitored wells in the western state of Gujarat show a fall in the water table from 50 feet to over 1,300 feet in thirty years. Southern India, an altogether separate geographic zone, is already effectively dry. As a nation, it amounts to a slow-motion act of hydrological suicide.
>
> In the twenty-first century, India relies on groundwater mining for more than half its irrigation water. . . . By some estimates, water is being mined twice as fast as natural recharge. Food produced from depleting groundwater is tantamount to an unsustainable food bubble—it will burst when the waters tap out.[32]

The effects of insufficient water and the diversion of agricultural land to non-agricultural uses, which is common among increasingly industrial and affluent societies, are already beginning to show. After being food self-sufficient for decades, India began importing wheat in 2006.[33]

Pakistan, home to about 170 million people, with a population increase of 3 million per year, has the same problems as India. It, too, is mining its underground water at unsustainable rates, resulting in the fall of the water table near Islamabad of between one and two meters *per year* between 1982 and 2000. In Yemen, the water table is falling about two meters a year. In Mexico, whose population of 110 million is expected to be over 130 million by 2050, the water table under the agricultural state of Guanajuato is falling by two meters or more a year. Wells in the state of Sonora that used to pump water from a depth of 10 meters now have to go down more than 120 meters to find water. As a whole, more than half of the water extracted from wells in Mexico is from aquifers that are being over-pumped. Iran, too, a country of 71 million people, reports Lester Brown, "is overpumping its aquifers by an average of 5 billion tons of water per year; the water equivalent of one third of its annual rain harvest. Under the small but agriculturally rich Chenaran Plain in northeastern Iran, the water table was falling by 2.8 meters a year in the late 1990s."[34] By 2014, what had been Iran's largest lake, Lake Urmia in northwestern Iran, was losing water volume so fast that large areas were completely dry where cruise ships had sailed only a decade earlier on water that was 30 feet deep.[35]

Similar problems plague China. Like India, China contains about one fifth of humanity, so its ability to feed itself is an important measure of sustainability. It is already unable to do so, because Chinese wheat production fell 15 percent between 1997 and 2007, owing largely to shortages of fresh water.[36] The Chinese breadbasket, which produces about half of China's wheat and a third of its corn, is a northern plain in the Yellow River basin. Rainfall is inadequate for agriculture, resulting in extractions from the Yellow River that caused it to run dry before it reached the sea most years in the 1990s. The river reaches the sea now because wells extract increasing amounts of water from a deep "fossil aquifer," an aquifer that was created under geological and climatic conditions that no longer obtain. This is not a renewable resource.

In general, the Chinese don't have a history of wasting water, using on average only one-third the world average, and in the dry north only one-tenth.[37] However, as the country becomes more affluent, its citizens increasingly imitate the water intensive habits of more advanced industrial societies.

Affluent Chinese take more frequent and longer showers, use washing machines and dishwashers, and grow lawns that have to be watered. Accordingly, Elizabeth Economy reports, "Water consumption in Chinese cities jumped by 6.6 percent during 2004–5."[38]

Draining water reserves produces subsidence. "Some of China's wealthiest cities are sinking—in the case of Shanghai and Tianjin, by more than six feet during the past decade and a half. In Beijing, subsidence has destroyed factories, buildings, and underground pipelines and is threatening the city's main international airport."[39] The buildings, factories, and airport can all be rebuilt, but the underground reservoirs cannot be refilled.

The Chinese are building a system to divert water from the water-rich south to the parched north. However, the long-term effectiveness of this system is uncertain. The system was originally designed to have three branches—east, west, and central. Much of it was supposed to be completed in time for the Beijing Olympics in 2008, but the eastern route was later projected to be completed no sooner than 2013 and the middle route no sooner than 2014. The western route is so difficult, averaging an altitude of 10,000 to 13,000 feet across the Tibetan plain, that plans to start building it have been canceled indefinitely. Edward Wong reports for the *New York Times*, "Some Chinese scientists say the diversion could destroy the ecology of the southern rivers, making them as useless as the Yellow River. The government has neglected to do proper impact studies, they say. There are precedents in the United States. Lakes in California were damaged and destroyed when the Owens River was diverted in the early 20th century to build Los Angeles."[40] Even a former official of the Beijing government responsible for environmental and water management agreed that the project "carries huge risks."[41] One risk is that the water flow in the Han River, one of the major southern rivers to be tapped, is insufficient for the amount of diversion that the plan calls for. Measurements of the Han's flow rely on data from the 1950s to the 1990s, whereas the water flow has dropped considerably since then, partly owing to prolonged droughts. Chinese officials have not altered their plans in the light of this newer information.[42] Longer-range problems associated with this diversion system and with the general availability of water for agriculture relate to global warming and are considered in the next chapter.

* * *

Another water-related problem afflicting increased affluence in China and elsewhere is the different food choices that affluent people make. Diets tend to change from grains, fruits, and vegetables to a greater concentration on meat, eggs, and dairy products. But raising grain-fed livestock for meat and animal products, which is the cost-effective industrial method in the United States, is an inefficient way to feed people, as more land and water are needed to feed each person. The livestock use most of the grain that they consume to grow inedible parts of their bodies and to maintain their own metabolisms. World-watch researcher Gary Gardner reports that "2 kilos of grain are required to produce a kilo of chicken or fish, 4 kilos go into a kilo of pork, and 7 kilos are needed for a kilo of feedlot-raised beef."[43] It is much more efficient to use the land to grow grains and other crops to feed people directly, without the intermediary of livestock. When grain is used instead to feed animals that are in turn used to feed people, more grain is needed to feed each person. This accounts for the fact that Japan, South Korea, and Taiwan, which had pro-duced just about all the grain that they consumed, became major importers of grain within thirty years of industrialization. According to Lester Brown, "In 1994, Japan imported 72 percent of the grain it consumed . . . , South Korea . . . 66 percent, and . . . Taiwan 76 percent."[44]

The need for more grain to feed each person grain-fed meat means that each person's nutrition requires more water. Brown writes, "It takes 1,000 tons of water to produce one ton of grain."[45] Because of this, grain is often con-sidered "virtual water." Countries that lack sufficient water to grow their own grain make up for their water deficiency by importing grain. One way of mea-suring a country's decreasing water sufficiency, therefore, is to look at trends in its balance of grain imports and exports. India and China are now joining South Korea, Taiwan, and Japan as major grain importers largely because of their increased consumption of meat.

In addition to requiring more grain per person, meat eating increases the use of water because livestock need water to live. As a result, Worldwatch researchers Alan Durning and Holly Brough report, "More than 3,000 liters of water are used to produce a kilogram of American beef."[46] Tim Lang, a professor of food policy, writes in the journal *Ecologist*, "One kg of grain-fed beef takes 15 cubic metres of water and 1kg of grass-fed lamb needs 10 cubic metres, while 1kg of cereals needs only" three or four *tenths* of a cubic meter.[47] According to the United Nations Commission on Sustainable Development, "it takes 550 liters of water to produce enough flour for one loaf of bread in developing countries . . . but up to 7,000 liters of water to produce 100 grams [less than a quarter pound] of beef."[48] In the light of China's water shortages, it is simply unrealistic that they would be able to consume meat produced in the cost-effective American manner like Americans and Europeans. Yet the vision of global affluence on the American model needed to spark enough international trade to keep Americans employed in manufacturing for export assumes that eventually the Chinese will live the way that Americans live at present. And as the Chinese become richer they are, as we've seen, eating more meat.[49]

Industrialization leads to increased grain imports not only because of increased meat eating and consequent water shortages, but also because land is taken out of agricultural production and much of the land that remains in agriculture becomes polluted. For all of these reasons, Elizabeth Economy expects China increasingly to depend on other countries for its food:

> In the past half century . . . forests and farmland have had to make way
> for industry and sprawling cities, resulting in diminishing crop yields. . . .
> The Gobi Desert, which now engulfs much of western and northern China,
> is spreading by about 1,900 square miles annually. . . . Meanwhile . . . , as
> much as ten percent of China's farmland is believed to be polluted, and every
> year 12 million tons of grain are contaminated with heavy metals absorbed
> from the soil.[50]

Increased water-intensive meat consumption contributes to China's resulting food insufficiency.

*   *   *

Another water-intensive aspect of American affluence that cannot be transferred to all the world's poor is high-volume textile consumption. The Industrial Revolution began when improved efficiencies led to lower prices, increased demand, and greater profit in cotton textiles. Cotton is still the basis of half the world's textiles.[51] As we've seen, poor people in Bangladesh currently rely on textile manufacture to gain a foothold on the ladder of material enrichment that leads, according to the scenario we're investigating, to the American standard of living.

Because textile manufacture is labor intensive, low labor costs in China, Bangladesh, and other third world countries have reduced the cost of clothing in the United States. In the fifteen years following the early 1990s, the cost of many clothing items went down considerably. The price of Liz & Company Capri pants, for example, went down by one third and Lacoste™ polo shirts became cheaper by nearly one quarter of their previous price.[52] More generally, the consumer price index (CPI) for apparel went from 127 in 1991 to 117.9 in 2006. Corresponding to the price decline, purchases are up, sociologist Juliet Schor reports. "In 1991 Americans bought an average of thirty-four dresses, pairs of pants, sweaters, shirts, underwear, and other items. In 1996 that number had risen to forty-one. By 2007 per-person consumption had soared to sixty-seven items. American consumers were purchasing a new piece of clothing every 5.4 days."[53]

Many of these purchases reflect the desire to be fashionable, another common aspect of consumer-oriented, rich industrial societies. "By all accounts," Schor writes, "fashion is a social, rather than a functional, dynamic. In a fashion-driven world, a piece of apparel . . . can lose its appeal because it is no longer stylish or because it has become too widely available."[54] Journalist Elizabeth Cline writes, "For many consumers, part of the appeal of cheap fashion is that it allows them to get rid of their purchases when newer, more with-it items come along."[55] This is part of the consumer-oriented strategy of avoiding unemployment by providing jobs in manufacturing. The deliberate destruction of useful items is necessary to create enough demand to keep people working as manufacturing processes require ever fewer workers. When all textiles are considered, including sheets and towels, Cline reports, "Every year, Americans throw away 12.7 million tons, or 68 pounds of textiles per person . . . , 1.6 million tons [of which] could be recycled or reused."

As with meat eating, universal adoption of this aspect of the American way of life would be environmentally ruinous. Consider the implications for the use of water. Using current methods of production, it takes two-and-a-half tons of water to produce just one pound of cotton fiber. In rainy areas, forty-four pounds of topsoil are also expended for each pound of cotton.[56] If Americans discard sixty-eight pounds of textiles per person each year and half of this is composed of cotton fiber, each American is responsible for the use of 85 million tons of water each year and thirty-three pounds of irreplaceable topsoil just to keep up with fashions in cheap clothing. Other untoward environmental consequences attend the short-term use of textiles made from wool and from artificial fibers based on petro-chemicals, but water is the focus in this chapter.

Increased water demands that attend adoption of meat eating and textile consumption on the American model would be particularly difficult in areas where population growth already makes water resources and grain production insufficient, necessitating increased importation of grain. North Africa and the Middle East contain countries with some of the world's largest population increases and yet some of the world's greatest aridity. Egypt, for example, with a population of 68 million in 2000, imported 40 percent of its grain that year, and its population is projected nearly to double by 2050.

*   *   *

Raising livestock by having them graze on grass rather than eat grain may seem to be an efficient way of getting people the nutrition that they need in a form that increasingly affluent people prefer. And most meat in the world is raised on range land where livestock eat grasses of one variety or another, not in feedlots where they eat grain. This can be an efficient way of feeding people if the land is not suitable for growing crops that people can eat directly, and if the land in its undeveloped state is not providing essential ecological services. But if too many animals are put on the range, overgrazing can kill the grass, rains can wash away the exposed topsoil, and desertification can result. This is what is happening in many countries, including China, whose continued ability to supply meat is therefore in jeopardy. Lester Brown reports,

> In northwestern China, the buildup in livestock since the economic reforms
> in 1978 is destroying vast areas of grassland. Since then, livestock numbers

have increased dramatically. In Gonge County, for example, in eastern Qinghai Province, the number of sheep that the local grasslands can support is estimated at 3.7 million, but by the end of 1998, the region's flock had reached 5.5 million—far beyond its carrying capacity. The result is fast-deteriorating grassland, desertification, and in some locations the creation of sand dunes.[57]

China and India, representing almost 40 percent of the world's population, are not the only countries whose water and food consumption are unsustainable. In 1950 Africa had 238 million people and 273 million livestock, but half a century later the human population had grown to 794 million and the livestock to 680 million. In many places the livestock exceeds the land's carrying capacity by half or more.[58]

*   *   *

Where are all the grain, meat, and other food supposed to come from in the future? Some people look to the United States, because it has long been one of the world's most agriculturally productive nations and a major exporter of grains, fruits, vegetables, and meat. In 2013, for example, China's largest pork producer agreed to buy the American firm Smithfield Foods, a major producer of pork and owner of the Armour® brand, for $4.7 billion. "Meat consumption in China has exploded over the past decade because of a growing middle class and a shift in diet from rice and vegetables to more protein."[59] In 2012, American producers exported $866 million worth of pork products to China, which constituted only 14 percent of all US pork exports that year. Purchase of Smithfield Foods is intended to increase pork exports to China.

But much of US agricultural productivity, especially of wheat, fruits, vegetables, and livestock, has been in southwestern states that lack adequate water to sustain current levels of productivity, much less increase productivity to meet increasing world demand as population increases, manufacturing processes pollute more land, desertification expands, and more countries become prosperous enough to eat more meat, eggs, and dairy products.

Much of the wheat grown in the American southwest depends on irrigation from the Ogallala aquifer, a source of fossil water (the aquifer doesn't replenish). According to environmentalist Marc Reisner, who considers the Ogallala the greatest aquifer in the world, the aquifer will possibly support agriculture as we know it for some decades, but will certainly be exhausted for all practical purposes before the end of this century. Writing in the mid-1980s, Reisner notes that in the twenty years after World War II the high plains east of the Rocky Mountains and west of the hundredth meridian (which runs through the middle of Kansas and Nebraska) turned from brown to green as a result of irrigation:

> In 1914, there were 139 irrigation wells in all of West Texas. In 1937, there were 1,166. In 1954, there were 27,983. In 1971, there were 66,144. Nebraska irrigated fewer than a million acres in 1959. In 1977, it irrigated nearly seven million acres; the difference was almost entirely pumping from the Ogallala. . . . The overdraft from the Ogallala region in 1975 was about fourteen million acre-feet a year, the flow of the Colorado River. . . . The Colorado is not a big river, but it would be big enough to empty Lake Huron in a reasonably short time.[60]

Reisner concludes, "It is a dead certainty that the Ogallala will begin to give out relatively soon; the only question is when."

❋   ❋   ❋

Salination, an increase in water's salt content, also threatens the future of agriculture because irrigation, on which most of the world's land-based food production depends, tends to make water too saline for agricultural use. This occurs in two interrelated ways. First, most irrigation systems store water in artificial lakes that are exposed to the sun. As water evaporates from the lake, salts are left behind in increased concentrations. In 1980, Reisner writes, "of the 120 million acre-feet of water applied to irrigated American crops . . . , ninety million acre-feet were lost to evaporation and transpiration by plants. The remaining thirty million acre-feet contained virtually all of the salts,"[61] which were left on the land. Second, water tends to pick up salts when it travels through soil. Owing to severe water shortages, many irrigation systems use the same water several times. Water is pumped from a river to irrigate crops, and then that water travels through the soil picking up salts as it flows back to the same river from which it can be pumped again to irrigate more crops downstream. Reisner tells us that "on rivers like the Colorado and the Platte, the same water may be used eighteen times over. It also spends a good deal of its time in reservoirs which, in desert country, may lose eight to twelve feet off of their surface to the sun every year. The process continues—salts are picked up, fresh water evaporates, more salts are picked up, more fresh water evaporates."[62] Salination is believed to be a major reason for the decline of the Sumerian civilization in the second millennium BCE.[63]

Irrigation in areas of poor drainage also causes salination. Irrigation typically delivers more water to the land than would fall on it as rain. If impervious rock prevents drainage of this extra water the water table can rise to the point of reaching the roots of the plants. This water is harmful to plants if salts have dissolved in it while it was trapped in the soil, making it too saline for the crops. This source of salination applies to many places in the American West.[64]

Some people might think that desalination could solve problems of water shortages that threaten agricultural yields. Sea water is for all practical purposes inexhaustible, so if the salt were taken out of this water to convert it to fresh water there would be plenty of fresh water for agriculture and for all other purposes.

Unfortunately, the cost of desalination is prohibitive for this purpose. In 2013 the San Diego County Water Authority agreed to pay $2,000 per acre foot of water to be produced starting in 2016 by a new, state-of-the-art desalination plant in Carlsbad, California.[65] (An acre-foot is the amount of water needed to fill an acre-size tub to the depth of one foot.) Could water produced in this way give California the agricultural as well as the municipal water it needs?

According to a California Water Plan Update in 2005, farmers in California's Central Valley paid between $2 and $30 an acre foot for water in this agriculturally important inland basin,[66] which extends nearly five hundred miles from northwest to southeast and varies in width from sixty to one hundred miles.[67] The Central Valley Project supplies about seven million acre-feet of water to farmers each year at these prices. Using desalinated water that costs $2,000 per acre-foot would alter drastically the price of food.

As of 2005, California used 36.8 million acre-feet of fresh water per year,[68] approximately 80 percent of which was for agriculture, making the agricultural component almost 29.5 million acre-feet per year. At $2,000 per acre-foot, the total cost of water *alone* for California agriculture would be almost $59 billion. Yet total gross receipts for California agriculture were only $43.5 billion in 2011, up from $38 billion in 2010. Thus, even the newest, most efficient, state-of-art desalination plants would have to charge California agriculture considerably more than all the gross receipts from California agriculture. There would be no money at all to pay for other inputs, such as seeds, fertilizers, pesticides, and herbicides, much less for farm equipment, farm workers, or profits. And the $2,000 figure is unrealistically low because it requires delivery of water simply from Carlsbad to San Diego, both of which are at sea level. Most California farms are located in valleys inland, like the Central Valley, so the water would have to be pumped longer distances over mountains that tower above the valley floor. Besides considerations of cost, there's no realistic scenario for generating the energy to do all this desalination, which is very energy intensive, and transporting the resulting fresh water to where it's needed. Worse yet, given anything like the current mix of energy sources in the United States, use of this energy would contribute enormously to global warming, which reduces agricultural yields, a topic considered in the next chapter.

Of course, some water from rain and rivers will continue to be available in California, even if it's far from sufficient to support current agricultural needs, so California agriculture will never depend completely on desalinated water. Nevertheless, any significant proportion of water used in agriculture that costs more than $2,000 an acre-foot would make California agriculture very different than it is today and raise the price of food considerably. Such price increases would impair the consumerism that the manufacture-your-way-out-of-unemployment scenario relies on. People can't afford innumerable, inessential goods and services if they have to spend a large share of their income on food, so consumerism thrives in advanced industrial economies only to the extent that food is cheap. The more consumer-oriented the society, the less it pays for food. Thus, the US Department of Agriculture reports that in 2009 food constituted only 6.9 percent of American household consumption expenditures. The figure for Canada was 9.2 percent and for Germany 11.4, whereas for Algeria it was 43.9 and for Pakistan 45.7.[69] If the increasing cost of water requires us to pay a larger share of our income for food, rather than other countries becoming more like consumer-oriented Americans, Americans will become more like people in other countries where inessential goods and services have a much smaller market.

Worldwide, desalination costs may be lower. *McClatchy* special correspondent Joel Greenberg reported in 2014 that an Israeli company was able to produce desalinated water for about one-third the cost in California. However, the figure of $650 per acre-foot didn't include any accounting for damage to climate resulting from the use of fossil fuels at this desalination facility, or for the environmental damage that can be expected from introducing highly concentrated saline water and chemicals back into the Mediterranean Sea.[70] What is more, desalinated water at $650 per acre-foot would still revolutionize world grain markets. It takes 1,000 tons of water to produce 1 ton of grain. Translating this into acre-feet of water, it takes .77 acre-feet of water to produce 1 ton of grain. If water costs $650 an acre-foot and there are 2,000 pounds in a ton, the water to produce a pound of grain would cost about $.25. Yet the price of wheat on world markets in 2013 was less than $.15 a pound.[71] The cost of water to produce grain would thus be almost twice the price of the product, and there would be no money for workers' wages, for seeds, for fertilizer, for profits, for pesticides, etc. Again, rather than a reduction in the cost of food around the world so that our manufactured goods would find markets there, the cost of food would increase resulting in a shrinking of the world market for consumer-oriented items of American manufacture.

In sum, as a result of over-pumping of water from fossil aquifers, over-commitment of water from rivers, streams, and natural lakes, and salination and other forms of water pollution, no country, not even the United States, can be expected to supply the world with the food that it needs. Jeneen Interlandi summarized the world water situation this way in *Newsweek*:

> Everyone agrees that we are in the midst of a global freshwater crisis. Around the world, rivers, lakes, and aquifers are dwindling faster than Mother Nature can possibly replenish them; industrial and household chemicals are rapidly polluting what's left. Meanwhile, global population is ticking skyward.

Goldman Sachs estimates that global water consumption is doubling every 20 years, and the United States expects demand to outstrip supply by more than 30 percent come 2040.[72]

These facts suggest that if global development continues on its present path, many people around the world will lack food as a result of insufficient water for agricultural crops. Limits to increased worldwide affluence imposed by water shortages alone eliminate the possibility of everyone in the world living as Americans do today so that Americans can be employed increasingly in manufacture for export. But that's not all; global warming imposes additional limits, a topic explored in the next chapter.

CHAPTER 5
ENVIRONMENTAL LIMITS
FOOD AND WARMING

G lobal warming exacerbates problems of food and water availability in the United States and around the world, and increasing imitation of the American lifestyle among billions of people in third world countries exacerbates global warming. Therefore, we can't reduce American unemployment by manufacturing increasing quantities of goods for export because this strategy presupposes billions of middle-class customers around the world, which presupposes in turn a level and type of global material affluence that would catalyze such a level of climate change as to deprive people of the food and water that they need to survive. People around the world can't eat meat as we do, eat farm-raised fish as we do, pay as little as we do for food in general, drive cars as we do, use air-conditioning as we do, use as much per capita fossil fuel energy as we do, or adopt many other aspects of the current American lifestyle. Global warming and its implications for the availability of food and water thus reinforce the message of the last chapter. There are severe environmental limits to growth in material consumption, and this limits job opportunities in manufacturing material goods to be consumed.

The Intergovernmental Panel on Climate Change (IPCC) issued a sobering report in 2007 regarding increasing concentrations of CO_2 in the atmosphere. The preindustrial concentration of 280 parts per million (ppm) had risen to 384 ppm. This is significant because the total difference in CO_2 concentration between glacial periods and warmer interglacial periods during the last 800,000 years is only 100 ppm. The general fluctuation was between a low of 180 ppm during glacial periods and a high of 280 ppm during interglacial periods. Worse yet, the IPCC projects an increase of another 100 ppm in the next fifty years if current trends continue.[1] Exceeding the pace suggested by this projection, CO_2 concentrations reached 400 ppm in 2013.[2] The IPCC expects a concentration of 450 ppm eventually to raise average global temperatures about 2 degrees Celsius (3.2 degrees Fahrenheit). The IPCC report in 2014 confirms these finding with more recent evidence. Some regions are expected to get drier, and many regions will experience more intense storms—hurricanes, typhoons, and cyclones—because greater warmth means more energy from heat is available to feed the storms. Much of the fresh water now stored in glaciers will melt, with the expectation that melting in Greenland and Antarctica will raise sea levels considerably over the next several centuries.[3]

After the Great Recession took hold in 2008, Americans increasingly became skeptical about the existence, importance, and cause of global warming, according the Pew Research Center for People & the Press. In April 2008, 71 percent of Americans thought that there was solid evidence that the earth was warming, whereas in October 2009, only 57 percent thought so. In the earlier poll 44 percent thought that global warming was a serious problem, whereas in the later poll only 35 percent held this opinion. In the earlier poll, 47 percent thought that there was solid evidence that human activity was a major cause of warming, whereas only 36 percent shared this opinion by October 2009.[4] Four years later, according to a poll by the Pew Research Center, amidst evidence of economic recovery, still only 44 percent of Americans thought that human activity was responsible for climate change.[5]

Unfortunately, warming exists whether people believe it or not. The National Climatic Data Center of the National Atmospheric and Oceanic Administration report that worldwide, 2014 was the warmest year on record in both the atmosphere and the oceans.[6] Orrin Pilkey and Rob Young point out in *USA Today* that even people who question the accuracy of such temperature measurements over the last century and a quarter can't deny that the earth is getting warmer, as there is clear evidence in the ice. "Studies from both hemispheres indicate that 95% of the world's alpine glaciers, excluding Antarctica, are retreating. Glacier National Park in Montana is down to 26 named glaciers from 150 in 1850, and if this trend continues, the park is expected to be ice-free by 2020." Buildings are sinking and roads are crumbling in northern latitudes because they are built on permafrost that is thawing.[7] There is really no doubt that the earth is warming.

There's no doubt either that greenhouse gases are the major cause of this warming. When global warming critics had to accept the fact that the earth was warming, their first reaction was to claim that curtailing emissions of greenhouse gases was still unjustified because the warming could be caused by any number of things, such as sunspot activity or some long-cycle climate pattern of unknown origin. The Global Climate Coalition, a group representing industries whose activities emit greenhouse gases, hired scientists to find other causes of warming so that carbon dioxide would be off the hook. However, the Global Climate Coalition's own scientists concluded in 1995, "The scientific basis for the Greenhouse Effect and the potential impact of human emissions of greenhouse gases such as CO_2 on climate is well established and cannot be denied."[8] They unequivocally rejected the arguments of contrarians who hold the opposite view, writing, "The contrarian theories raise interesting questions about our total understanding of climate processes, but they do not offer convincing arguments against the conventional model of greenhouse gas emission-induced climate change."[9] The Global Climate Coalition did not include these statements in its 1996 primer on climate change, but their presence in the draft submitted by scientists in late 1995 came to light in 2009. In sum, by 1996 the rejection of global warming and of carbon dioxide emissions as a major cause was simply unscientific. So let's look at the way global warming interacts with the availability of fresh water for agriculture, with the availability of seafood, with the availability of cheap food, and with increased affluence.

*　*　*

Texas is one area that is expected to become drier as a result of global warming, reducing the availability of surface water and of water from aquifers that normally recharge regularly (as opposed to fossil aquifers like the Ogallala that don't recharge). In 2011, the worst drought in recorded history in Texas resulted in dry wells and shrinking lakes. In addition to a lack of rainfall, many towns experienced record high temperatures. For example, the town of Robert Lee and some others had more than one hundred days in 2011 when the temperature went over one hundred degrees. Climate scientist Katharine Hayhoe of Texas Tech University said, "What climate change is doing is it's increasing our temperatures, and higher temperatures mean faster evaporation. So you need more water to provide the same amount of irrigation for crops if temperatures are higher. And that's what we see happening here in Texas and in many places around the world."[10] In addition, an expected population increase of 82 percent in the next fifty years is expected to increase the state's water need from its current eighteen million acre-feet to twenty-two million acre-feet. Already, to meet the current shortfall of water, says Andrew Sanson, director of the River System Institute at Texas State University, Texas has "given permission for more water to be withdrawn from many of our rivers than is actually in them today."[11] By 2014 inadequate water supplies to meet expectations was sparking legal battles.[12] According to the state's climatologist John Neilson-Gammon, climate change projections suggest continued dry conditions in the future.[13]

Texas is not the only agricultural state that lacks sufficient water. By 2013 wells were running dry in Kansas.[14] The following year federal authorities for the first time responded to drought in the Colorado River basin by decreasing the amount of water sent from Lake Powell to Lake Mead 180 miles downstream.[15]

California has always been water challenged. Marc Reisner writes in *Cadillac Desert* that most of California "is, by strict definition, a semidesert. Los Angeles is drier than Beirut; Sacramento is as dry as the Sahel; San Francisco is just slightly rainier than Chihuahua. About 65 percent of the state receives under twenty inches of precipitation a year."[16] The green golf courses, fancy pools, and opulent gardens of the rich and famous do not use most of the state's meager supplies of water. Neither do the tens of millions of other people watering their lawns, washing their cars, and meeting their daily needs. Agriculture uses 80 percent of the water consumed in the state to produce, through irrigation, one third of all the table food grown in the United States.

Water is procured largely by damming rivers to create artificial lakes and by diverting water from the wetter northern parts of the state to the Central Valley and other agricultural regions. River water, including much of the water in the artificial lakes, is fed to a significant extent during the growing season by snow melting in the mountains.

Global warming threatens California agriculture in three ways. First, as in Texas, a warmer climate causes irrigation water to evaporate more quickly, so more water is needed to grow the same crops. Second, in a warmer climate the water held in artificial lakes behind dams evaporates more quickly, leaving less water available for irrigation. And third, a warmer climate is expected to produce less snow in the mountains, creating water shortages during the critical months of the growing season. According to Steven Chu, Nobel-prize-winning physicist and the first Secretary of Energy in the Obama administration, "We're looking at a scenario where there's no more agriculture in California" by the end of this century if, as could happen in a worst case situation, 90 percent of the Sierra snowpack disappears, thereby eliminating the state's natural water storage system.[17] This warning in 2009 proved prescient as the California snow pack was smaller than average in 2012 through 2014. In 2014, the April 1 survey showed a snow pack just 32 percent of what is normal for that date, and on May 1 it was only 18 percent of normal for the date.[18]

The melting of glaciers will similarly impair European agriculture. According to the *Guardian* newspaper, most glaciers in the European Alps have been retreating for the last 150 years, but the pace has accelerated notably since the 1980s. This is a disturbing development because glacial melt during the summer plays a role in European agriculture similar to snow melt in California. In fact, the Swiss Alps are often called "Europe's water tower." As Matthias Huss, glaciologist and senior lecturer at the Department of Geosciences at the University of Fribourg explains, glaciers "release water exactly when we need it, while storing it in periods when we need it less."[19] They store water in Europe's cold and wet winter months and then release it from May to September during the dry and hot months when crops are growing. Glaciers also balance water needs between hot and cold years. Cold years tend to be wet, so glaciers store more water than usual, which is then released during unusually hot and dry years when water is needed most.

Hydrologist David Volken of Switzerland's Federal Office for the Environment expects glacial runoff in Europe to increase during the first half of this century and then to drop off rapidly. He adds, "Because of the warming climate, snow melt will happen about a month earlier and rainfall will decrease 10 to 15 percent in summer." As a result, "There'll be more runoff in winter and less in summer. During hot summers, less water will be available in the future."[20] Glaciologist Huss agrees. He estimates that by the end of this century glaciers will contribute between 55 and 85 percent less water to Europe's lakes, rivers, and streams. "Even if the climate could be sta-bilized at the current level," he claims, "we'd witness drastic glacier retreat and their storage ability would either drop extremely or be lost totally."[21]

Europe and California are not the only areas that are vulnerable to decreasing water availability as a result of melting glaciers. Currently, Himalayan gla-ciers play the same agricultural role in South Asia, Southeastern Asia, and East Asia as Alpine glaciers play in Europe, and like the Alpine glaciers, the Himalaya's glaciers are retreating.[22] When the glaciers are gone, as they will be if trends continue, China's south to north water diversion system, even if it works in the short run, will provide no help to water-starved northern China because, without the glaciers, the south will itself run dry. Should this occur, the impact on world food supply will be drastic because Himalayan gla-ciers are fundamental to much of the agriculture not only in China, but also in India, Pakistan, Vietnam, Thailand, and Cambodia. Taken together, these countries are currently home to over 40 percent of all human beings.

*   *   *

Current attempts to address water shortage problems with deeper wells not only fail to address long-term issues of water shortage but also exacer-bate the problem by contributing to global warming. Unless and until the world's energy infrastructure replaces heavy reliance on fossil fuels with reli-ance instead on renewable sources of energy, the energy used to pump water will come primarily from fossil fuels that exacerbate global warming. Reisner puts it this way, "As anyone knows who has ever carried a full pail up five flights of steps, water is one of the heaviest substances on earth; pumping it a hundred or two hundred feet out of the ground consumes a lot of energy."[23] The World Bank reported in 2010 that as a result of lowered water tables, some wells around Beijing were pumping water for the city from a depth of more than three thousand feet.[24] China's water diversion system, which pumps water from its southern watershed to its northern plains also requires enor-mous amounts of (at this point, fossil fuel) energy. In sum, like desalination, discussed in the last chapter, deep wells and water diversion systems threaten to exacerbate problems of global warming.

But suppose the world were to switch to renewable forms of energy, perhaps along a path indicated below in chapter 11. Fossil fuels are used now because they are cheap to use, and they are cheap to use because many costs to society, costs associated with water contamination, particulate air pollution, and global warming, aren't built into the market price. Fossil fuel energy is thus highly subsidized because end users don't pay for such externalities. Take away these subsidies and the cost of desalination goes up, too, because at present, Solomon notes, "A third to a half of desalination costs are energy, mainly fossil fuels." For this reason, Solomon maintains,

> any large-scale takeoff of desal [desalination] seems to be contingent upon a cost breakthrough in some renewable energy source. Likewise, the amount of weighty water that can be lifted from deep aquifers, or transported great distances through interriver basin pipelines like China's South-to-North Water Diversion Project is limited chiefly by the expenditure of energy for pumping such a heavy, hard to manage liquid.[25]

Renewable energy will remove the specter of catastrophic global warming from desalination, deeper wells, and massive water diversion projects. In addition, I will argue in a later chapter, renewable energy, all things considered, is actually cheaper than most fossil fuel energy because it has fewer costly externalities. However, it still won't be any cheaper to end users than highly subsidized fossil-fuel energy is today. So the cost of desalination for agriculture will remain overwhelmingly impractical owing to expenses, much of it related to energy, out of all proportion to the value of agricultural products. Again, free-market agriculture and our current consumer society couldn't exist in anything like their current forms if a significant proportion of water for agriculture had to be obtained through desalination.

*   *   *

Here's the summary so far of relationships among food, water, and warming. Global warming exacerbates problems of water scarcity and therefore of food availability. In a hotter world the land is dryer so more irrigation water is needed to grow crops, but more water evaporates behind irrigation dams before it can reach those crops. In addition, decreased rainfall is expected in some of the world's great breadbaskets, including the American Midwest. Reduced seasonal snow packs and retreating glaciers will diminish the availability of water for irrigation from snow and ice that melt during the growing season in agriculturally important regions in California, Europe, and Asia.

Beyond these problems of water availability, global warming threatens world food supplies because some of the most important crops grow poorly in hotter weather. David Battisti and Rosamond Naylor report in the journal *Science* that according to the most respected models of climate change it is more than 90 percent probable that the hottest seasons on record (between 1900 and 2006) will be the normal temperatures by the end of this century in the tropics and subtropics. It is most probable that the same will occur in many parts of the temperate zone as well. To judge the effect of such heat on agriculture, the authors looked at agricultural production during some extraordinarily hot summers in the past. In 2003, when the summer was unusually hot in western Europe, "Record high daytime and nighttime temperatures over most of the summer growing season reduced leaf and grain-filling development of key crops such as maize, fruit trees, and vineyards . . . and resulted in reduced soil moisture and increased water consumption in agriculture." The bottom line was reduced yields. "Italy experienced a record drop in maize yields of 36% from a year earlier, whereas in France maize and fodder production fell by 30%, fruit harvests declined by 25%, and wheat harvests (which had nearly reached maturity by the time the heat set in) declined by 21%."[26]

In 1972 temperatures ranged from two to four degrees Celsius above normal in southeast Ukraine and southwest Russia, the breadbasket of the former Soviet Union, "causing a 13% decline in grain production from a year earlier for the USSR as a whole. Such high summer temperatures in the region will likely be the norm in 2050 and well below the median of projected summer temperatures by the end of the century." Although drought was cited as a major factor at the time, the authors point out that "fully one-third of summers in this area over the past 100 years were drier than in 1972."[27] What made 1972 special was heat, not drought. Whereas the resulting 13 percent decline in grain production may not seem significant in the abstract, its concrete effects were enormous and global. Wheat, the crop most affected by the heat, more than tripled in price on international markets in constant dollars between the winter of 1972 and the winter of 1974.

The good news about 1972 and 2003 was that higher prices enabled heat-stressed regions to import the extra grain they needed. When such high temperatures become the norm around the world, there will be no place from which to import the needed grain, as reductions in crop yields will be expected globally, according to an IPCC document leaked in 2013.[28] Yet, we are imagining in our Marshall Plan-inspired thought experiment that as people become more affluent they will live increasingly the way that Americans live at present. But worldwide adoption of the American lifestyle would require more per capita agricultural production (to feed much larger herds of livestock) even as the human population increases and agricultural production declines.

*   *   *

Rising seas that result from global warming also threaten human wellbeing by reducing the availability of farmland on coastal plains and by threatening to inundate major cities, including not only especially low-lying cities such as New Orleans and Galveston, but many other cities, such as London, New York, Miami, and Shanghai.[29]

If all the ice in Greenland and Antarctica were to melt, sea levels would rise 220 feet. Fortunately, no one expects this to happen.[30] However, the IPCC reports that almost certainly, "Due to sea level rise projected throughout the 21st century and beyond, coastal systems and low-lying areas will increasingly experience adverse impacts such as submergence, coastal flooding, and coastal erosion."[31] These effects will not appear immediately, but will emerge over the coming decades and centuries, with disastrous effects. Ralph Keeling, who runs an atmospheric monitoring program at Scripps Institution of Oceanography, told a reporter for the *New York Times*, "It takes a long time to melt ice, but we're doing it. It's scary." Geochemist Mark Pagani said, "I feel like the time to do something was yesterday." Climate scientist Maureen Raymo adds, "It feels like the inevitable march toward disaster."[32]

This doesn't mean it's futile to combat global warming. We still need to give up fossil fuels in exchange for renewable sources of energy because the warmer the world gets the harder it will be to feed everyone, the harder it will be to meet people's needs for fresh water, the more people's lives will be disrupted by higher sea levels, and the longer the time of such disruption. A CO_2 concentration of 450 ppm is better than one of 550 ppm. Some disasters are worse than others.[33] One enormous danger for humanity is that significant global warming increases the chances of rampant global warming resulting from the thawing of permafrost in higher latitudes, such as in Alaska and Siberia. Such thawing would release billions of tons of carbon that would quickly convert to the much more potent greenhouse gas methane.[34] At that point we could spiral toward a world that we would find hard to recognize. Sea levels could rise far beyond what are currently projected.

In any case, the disaster won't be for the earth itself. The sea has been very high in the past without the earth seeming any the worse for the wear. Environmentalists who declare that we must curtail global warming in order to save the earth may be making the common mistake of considering what's disastrous for those they care about to be disastrous for a greater whole (the way that any tax increase harmful to a particular industry is often considered by that industry to be bad for the economy in general.) In the case of global warming and rising sea levels, the disaster will be primarily for human beings. Imagine having to abandon New York, London, and Shanghai. A lot of coastal cropland will be lost as well. The Pliocene ocean encroached ninety miles inland in North America.[35]

*   *   *

Increased reliance on seafood can't replace cropland reductions due to rising seas in a warmer world. Increased CO_2 emissions threaten food from the sea, and methods used to keep food inexpensive, whether from land or sea, are reducing the potential of the sea to feed people. According to Nick Nuttall of the United Nations Environment Programme (UNEP), fish is the primary source of protein for 20 percent of the human population.[36] But the availability of seafood will diminish unless three problems are properly addressed—acidification (which increases with greater concentrations of CO_2 in the atmosphere), dead zones, and overfishing.

Dead zones exist where there is insufficient oxygen to support marine life of any kind. This problem results primarily from nitrogen fertilizers in land-based agriculture and from nitrogen-containing effluent from large livestock facilities. When such nitrogen is washed into the sea it promotes the excessive growth of algae, particularly during the summer months. When the algae die and sink, they decompose, and the process of decomposition uses oxygen, thereby depleting the water of its oxygen content. Without oxygen other marine life cannot live, so some of the previously most productive areas of oceans and bays have lost their marine life, and people have lost significant sources of food.

According to a report in the journal *Science* there were more than four hundred such dead zones in 2008, which is more than double the number reported by the United Nations just two years earlier.[37] By 2011, 530 dead zones and an additional 228 sites of eutrophication (areas with excessive organic matter that tend to create additional dead zones) were identified by researchers at the World Resources Institute (WRI) and the Virginia Institute of Marine Science (VIMS). Together these zones covered an area of 95,000 square miles, which is about the size of New Zealand. The largest such zone in the United States, covering 8,500 square miles, about the size of New Jersey, is near the mouth of the Mississippi River. Professor Bob Diaz of VIMS writes, "Over the last 50 years, problems related to over-fertilization of the sea and low dissolved oxygen have expanded to the point where large areas devoid of fish, shrimp, and crabs are common occurrences."[38] Some of the world's most high-valued fish are threatened by the growth of these dead zones, including blue marlin and tuna.[39] The IPCC expects exacerbation of this problem,[40] which is caused primarily by the artificial nitrogen fertilizers used in the kind of "efficient" land-based agriculture that keeps food prices low in the United States. Worldwide adoption of such agricultural techniques, giving more people cheap food so they have increased discretionary income for consumer items, would further diminish food availability from the sea.

Acidification is the process of the oceans becoming more acid as a result of increased concentrations of dissolved carbon dioxide, the same gas that is the principal cause of global warming in the atmosphere. From the perspective of climate change, oceans absorbing CO_2 is a good thing because it reduces concentrations in the air. However, as a result of such absorption the ocean's acidity, which had remained stable for twenty million years, increased by 30 percent in the last 250 years. According to the Natural Resources Defense Council, if this trend continues the oceans' acidity will have more than doubled by 2100. This is troubling because many forms of sea life are organisms with shells, and increased acidity tends to dissolve shells, as if the creatures suffered from osteoporosis. Not only will such culinary favorites as lobster and mussels be affected, but the small organisms at the base of the oceans' food chains will also be affected, such as the nearly unpronounceable pteropods and coccolithophores. As the base declines so will all the organisms that depend on the base, devastating sea life as we know it. Sea life as we know it could also be devastated by the effect of acidification on coral reefs, which are habitat and nursery to many forms of marine life. They are composed of the same material as sea shells and are therefore also in jeopardy from increased acidity.[41] Between 1992 and 2000 the share of the world's coral reefs in jeopardy rose from 10 percent to 27 percent.[42] The only viable solution to this problem seems to be reduced release of carbon dioxide into the atmosphere.

Overfishing is another problem that threatens to reduce food supplies from the sea. "Efficient" fishing techniques introduced in the twentieth century enable fishing vessels to take an increasing percentage of fish in a given area in ever-shorter time periods, leaving insufficient numbers of fish in the ocean for the natural regeneration of fish stocks through spawning and maturation. One of these efficient techniques is the use of larger fishing nets capable of pulling in more fish. Because some of the target species, such as cod, are bottom dwellers, cod fishing uses nets that scrape the bottom in coastal waters, thereby disrupting marine habitat needed for the spawning of many species. In addition, the use of sonar and radar to detect populations of targeted fish make it possible for more fish to be tracked and caught. Larger fishing vessels also enable the catch to increase. The advent of freezer-factory ships—where fish are caught, processed, and frozen while the ship is out to sea—encouraged the use of larger ships and longer voyages, thereby making it commercially viable for ships from almost any distance to fish in productive waters. This, too, increases the catch in areas where fish are abundant.[43]

More than a decade ago the Secretary General of the 2002 World Summit on Sustainable Development, Nitin Desai, declared, "Overfishing cannot continue. The depletion of fisheries poses a major threat to the food supply of millions of people."[44] One result has been rising international tensions, such as between India and Sri Lanka, who dispute one another's right to fish in various parts of the sea that separates them.[45]

According to the United Nations Food and Agriculture Organization (FAO) more than 70 percent of the world's fish species are either fully exploited or already overfished. During the 1990s, the commercial fishing populations of cod, hake, haddock, and flounder fell by as much as 95 percent.[46]

The cod population of the Grand Banks near Newfoundland, Canada, collapsed in the 1990s. Between 1962 and 1992 the biomass of northern cod dropped 93 percent.[47] For years, efficient fishing methods enabled the catch of cod on the Grand Banks to remain high in spite of diminishing stocks caused by overfishing. But eventually the catch diminished so drastically that the Canadian government imposed a cod fishery moratorium in 1992, and 20 years later the recovery of the cod population was still in doubt.[48] In 2013, in order to avoid a total collapse of the cod population in New England's waters, the New England Fishery Management Council recommended drastic cuts for three years in the catch allowed in the Gulf of Maine and on Georges Banks.[49]

One result of the diminished cod population is increased stocks of shellfish, such as shrimp and crab, because shellfish are mainstays of the cod diet. With the predator gone, the prey multiply. So commercial fishing in the area now harvests primarily shellfish instead of cod.[50] But as we have seen, increased concentrations of carbon dioxide in the atmosphere adds CO_2 to the oceans, which makes the oceans more acidic, and acid tends to degrade shellfish populations by eating away at their shells. In a world of ten billion consumers emitting CO_2 in the way that Americans do at present, the ocean will almost certainly become too acidic for the continued growth and harvest of shellfish.

Aquaculture is an increasingly popular method of getting food from the sea, accounting now for at least one third of the fish consumed worldwide.[51] Instead of roaming the oceans to find fish, the fish are raised in captivity, similar to the way we raise chickens, hogs, and cattle. Salmon is the most popular fish raised in this way. Just as agriculture on land increased enormously the production of food for human consumption, it might seem that a similar approach to food production in the sea would also increase the availability of food for people.

Unfortunately, just the opposite is the case. One problem is that fish raised in captivity have to be fed, just as do birds and mammals raised in captivity on land. In the case of aquaculture, the feed is for the most part also drawn from the sea. Like other animals, salmon use most of what they eat for their own body's maintenance, not for growth, so it takes about four pounds of wild-caught fish (salmon are carnivorous) to produce one pound of salmon. In short, about the same level of inefficiency characterizes salmon production and consumption as the production and consumption of pork. For this reason alone, feeding a world of ten billion people at a per capita level of farmed fish currently common in the United States, Europe, or Japan is not likely to be sustainable.

But the situation is actually worse because the forage fish used to make the feed given to farmed fish are in danger of overexploitation, making their populations vulnerable to collapse. Forage fish are medium-sized species such as anchovies, herring, menhaden, and sardines that transmit organic energy from the bottom of the ocean's food chain (plankton) toward the top (for example, salmon, penguins, and humpback whales). They constitute most of the vertebrate biomass of marine ecosystems.[52] They are nevertheless in danger of overexploitation because they now constitute 37 percent by weight of all fish harvested worldwide, whereas fifty years ago they constituted only 8 percent.[53] This increased catch is a result and a sign of the declining catch of wild species that people prefer to eat, such as cod, tuna, and salmon. Even today, people directly eat only 10 percent of the forage fish catch, the rest being processed into feed for fish farms and livestock, as well as nutritional supplements for people.[54] Decline in forage fish populations would therefore affect the availability of meat as well as farmed fish.

The Lenfest Forage Fish Task Force, a team of thirteen preeminent scientists, concluded in 2012 that many forage fish populations are in danger of collapse because their populations naturally fluctuate greatly, yet even when their populations remain small they swim as schools, making them easy to catch. In fact, the report notes, "several forage fish populations collapsed in the 20th century."[55] The task force recommends doubling the percentage of the unfished biomass that should be left in the sea—from 20 percent to 40 percent—to assure sustainable yields. But the task force has no enforcement authority, and much of the catch is in international waters. With the increase in fish farming, the expanding use of forage fish in meat production, and the increasing percentage of human beings who eat more farmed fish and meat as they become more affluent, it's hard to believe that forage fish will survive in sufficient numbers in decades to come to play their current role in the production of food for human beings.

To make matters worse, fish farming also harms wild fish stocks and other marine life because of the concentrated waste associated with concentrated and stationary fish populations; because of its destruction of nearby coastal wetlands; because antibiotics used on the farms escape into nearby waters where they can catalyze development of antibiotic-resistant microorganisms; and because cultivated species can escape and jeopardize the fitness of wild species through interbreeding. These are all externalities, negative consequences that current consumers of fish from aquaculture don't pay for.[56] Thus, in its total impact, unlike agriculture on land, aquaculture reduces rather than increases the availability of food for human consumption.

* * *

The American lifestyle, as already noted, is supported in large part by inexpensive food. When food is cheap people have additional money to spend on cars, larger houses, and a host of other consumer items. We pay so little for food in the United States in part because our agriculture makes good use of irrigation and of ammonium nitrate fertilizer. We have seen already that the irrigation component of the system is in great jeopardy, which increases with global warming, and the ammonium nitrate fertilizer component creates dead zones in the sea, which reduces the availability of seafood for human consumption. In addition, Ed Hamer and Mark Anslow note in the British journal *Ecologist*, the fertilizer component, which "is indispensable to conventional farming," exacerbates global warming, thereby further jeopardizing irrigation in many parts of the world. Such fertilizer "produces vast quantities of nitrous oxide—a greenhouse gas with a global warming potential some 320 times greater than that of CO_2. In fact, the production of . . . ammonium nitrate . . . was responsible for around 10 percent of all industrial greenhouse gas emissions in Europe in 2003."[57]

Current American agricultural practice also contributes to global warming through degradation of topsoil. Healthy topsoil contains vast quantities of soil bacteria, fungi, and other living and organic material that amounts to 44 tons of carbon per acre. Organic and sustainable agriculture uses this biomass to give crops the nutrients they need. Conventional commercial American agriculture, as we've seen, uses a lot of ammonium nitrate fertilizer instead. It also exposes the soil to the sterilizing effects of air, heat, and ultraviolet light. When tons of biomass in the soil die and decompose as a result of these conventional practices, carbon dioxide is released. So far, this source of CO_2 constitutes about seven percent of all the CO_2 in the earth's atmosphere.[58] In sum, if American agricultural techniques are adopted more widely to reduce the cost of food so that people around the world have more discretionary income for consumer items, agriculture's contribution to global warming will increase greatly.

Another aspect of American food consumption that people around the world tend to imitate as they become more affluent is, as we've seen, increased meat eating, which requires more grain and water. This tends to strain world food supplies. In addition, it contributes to global warming. The United Nation's Food and Agriculture Organization calculated that livestock is currently responsible for 18 percent of total greenhouse gas emissions (CO_2 equivalent), which is more than transportation.[59] Much of meat eating's large carbon footprint stems from the methane that livestock produce and emit. Worldwatch researchers Brian Halweil and Danielle Nierenberg write, "Belching, flatulent livestock emit 16 percent of the world's annual production of methane, a powerful greenhouse gas."[60] According to Pete Hodgson, New Zealand Minister for Energy, Science, and Fisheries, methane is 23 times more powerful than carbon dioxide as a greenhouse gas, and its contribution to global warming is increasing: "Atmospheric concentrations of methane increased by 150 percent over the past 250 years, while carbon dioxide concentrations increased by 30 percent."[61] Global methane emissions each year constitute a carbon dioxide equivalent of almost all the greenhouse gas emissions from the United Kingdom and Russia combined.[62]

Meat eating contributes to global warming also because it takes more fossil-fuel energy to produce protein from meat than from grain. Cornell University's David Pimentel writes, "It takes, on average, 28 calories of fossil-fuel energy to produce 1 calorie of meat protein for human consumption, [whereas] it takes only 3.3 calories of fossil-fuel energy to produce 1 calorie of protein from grain for human consumption."[63]

Meat eating exacerbates global warming also because it takes more grain and therefore more land devoted to agriculture to produce meat protein than vegetable protein, and the additional land devoted to agriculture to feed additional meat eaters often comes at the expense of rainforests. Forests are plowed and burned to create pasture for livestock or, more commonly, to grow soybeans that will be fed to livestock. Elisabeth Rosenthal reports in the *New York Times* that "deforestation creates carbon emissions through fires and machinery that are used to fell trees, and it also destroys the plant life that helps absorb carbon dioxide emissions from cars and factories around the globe."[64] In these ways, "deforestation . . . effectively accounts for 20 percent of the world's carbon dioxide emissions and 70 percent of the emissions in Brazil," where deforestation has been significant.[65] Soybeans produced on cleared land are sold to such agribusiness giants as Cargill and Archer Daniels Midland to feed cattle as far away as Europe and China.

✳   ✳   ✳

Besides greater consumption of meat, enormous increases in energy consumption accompany greater affluence when people imitate the American standard of living. China is a good example. I have already mentioned some figures supplied by Elizabeth Economy. "Some 14,000 new cars hit China's roads each day. By 2020, China is expected to have 130 million cars and by 2050—or perhaps as early as 2040—it is expected to have even more cars than the United States."[66] In addition, China plans "to relocate 400 million people—well over the entire population of the United States—to newly developed urban centers between 2000 and 2030. Furthermore, newly urbanized Chinese, who use air-conditioners, televisions, and refrigerators, consume about three and a half times more energy than do their rural counterparts."

Consider, for a moment, just air-conditioning. According to the US Department of Energy, two thirds of American homes have air-conditioners, and air-conditioning uses about five percent of all the electricity consumed each year in the United States.[67] In Brazil, by contrast, only eleven percent of households had air-conditioning in 2007, and in India the figure was two percent. Tens of millions of people in these countries, and ultimately some billions of people when we consider China and other heavily populated countries in the tropics, will want air-conditioning as they join the middle class and attempt to replicate the American lifestyle.

The need for air-conditioning is measured by cooling degree days, a metric of a climate's warmth. On any given day at any given location, when the day's average temperature is above sixty-five degrees Fahrenheit, cooling degree days accrue on that date for that location. The number of cooling degree days accrued equals the number of degrees that the day's average temperature is above sixty-five degrees Fahrenheit. For example, if the average temperature in Los Angeles on a certain day is eighty degrees Fahrenheit, Los Angeles has accrued fifteen cooling degree days on that date. The yearly cooling degree days for any location is just the sum of the cooling degree days accrued there in each of the days of the year. The average cooling degree days for the location is the average of this number over many years.

People living in warmer climates (with a higher yearly average of cooling degree days) generally need more air-conditioning than people living in areas where the climate is cooler (with fewer cooling degree days in the typical year). This is just common sense. The advantage of using cooling degree days as a metric is that it allows us to measure how much more electricity will have to be consumed worldwide if all other countries were to have the same benefit of air-conditioning that is part of the American way of life. The numbers are impressive. The average cooling degree days for Los Angeles is 837, whereas Chennai, India, typically has nearly 4,000 cooling degree days. New York City averages 639 cooling degrees days compared to 3,884 in Bangkok. Chicago's 460 cooling degree days is dwarfed by 3,438 in Manila and 3,386 in Mumbai. It's estimated, in fact, that the need for cooling in Mumbai alone equals about 25 percent of all cooling needs in the United States.[68]

The word "need" is used here without irony. People work more intelligently, effectively, and efficiently when temperatures are in the seventies Fahrenheit. Researchers in Japan found that for every degree of warmth greater than twenty-five degrees Celsius (seventy-seven degrees Fahrenheit), worker productivity dropped two percent. In Singapore the optimal office temperature seems to be about seventy-two degrees Fahrenheit. Thus, a Marshall Plan approach to world commerce requires that the billion or so people in the third world who are expected to become new consumers by 2025 have air-conditioning at their disposal.[69] Otherwise, they won't be able to compete. Nor can the use of air-conditioning be confined to workplaces. A major point of economic development is to allow people to have the consumer items that they want. Already, air-conditioner purchases are increasing by double digits annually in many third world countries.[70]

Because most electricity will still come from fossil fuels in 2025, the implications for global warming are enormous. In the relatively cool United States, air-conditioning in the average home releases about two tons of carbon dioxide into the atmosphere.[71] In third world cities with four or five or eight times the number of cooling degree days, releases will probably be much greater, even if the average home is smaller and the thermostat is set higher.

Travel is another climate-changing activity that is expected to increase with greater worldwide affluence. Salon.com aviation expert Patrick Smith noted in 2008 that "in countries like China, India and Brazil, emerging middle classes have spawned the birth of scores of new airlines. China alone intends to construct more than forty large airports over the next several years. In the United States, the number of annual airline passengers . . . is anticipated to double by 2025. Greenhouse gases from planes could rise to as much as five times current levels."[72] Flying uses on average 1.8 times the energy and generates 1.8 times the greenhouse gases per passenger mile as a single occupant of a relatively fuel-efficient (25 to 30 mpg) car.[73] As people fly more miles, where will all of the additional energy come from, and how will its production and use affect global warming and the availability of food?

Some people look to renewable fuels, biofuels such as ethanol, to replace such fossil fuels as oil, coal, and natural gas. In principle, biofuels are carbon neutral because they are made from plants that capture carbon from the atmosphere and just return that same carbon to the atmosphere when they are used. However, there are problems. In the United States about 95 percent of ethanol is made from corn, and growing corn uses a lot of conventional gasoline (to run tractors, etc.) and petroleum products (such as fertilizers). Additional conventional energy is used to transport the corn and process it into ethanol.

Douglas Tiffany, writing for the Federal Reserve Bank of St. Louis, finds that one BTU (British thermal unit) of fossil fuel energy is needed to produce between 1.25 and 1.36 BTUs of energy from ethanol.[74] In other words, 75 to 80 percent of the energy we get from ethanol we are actually getting indirectly from fossil fuels.

Another problem is that devoting a large part of the corn crop to ethanol raises the price of corn and competes with human consumption. Within six years of the US Congress mandating the use of ethanol in gasoline sold in the United States the price of corn tripled and nearly 40 percent of the American corn crop was used to make ethanol.[75] Corn is not the only crop at issue. China imports cassava chips, mostly from Thailand, to make biofuel, Elisabeth Rosenthal reports in the *New York Times*: "Driven by new demand, Thai exports of cassava chips have increased nearly fourfold since 2008, and the price of cassava has roughly doubled."[76] Between 2008 and 2010 the proportion of cassava production going to biofuels increased from 10 to 52 percent. The diversion of cropland from production of food to production for biofuels has already increased food prices enough to create instability in some third world countries: "Soaring food prices have caused riots or contributed to political turmoil in a host of poor countries . . . , including Algeria, Egypt, and Bangladesh, where palm oil, a common biofuel ingredient, provides crucial nutrition to a desperately poor populace." In all, biofuels consumed only one percent of world grain production in 2000, but six percent in 2010. In some cases food shortages and price increases result from farmers growing high-priced biofuel crops instead of producing a full range of food needed for human nutrition.

As we have seen, water shortages, desertification, global warming, increases in the human population, and the loss of farm land to factories, commercial complexes, residential housing, and roads combine to make feeding the human population difficult, and clearly impossible if everyone were to adopt a meat-rich American diet. In this situation it's obviously counterproductive, inefficient in the extreme, to use scarce water and cropland to make biofuels.

One reason why biofuels will not play a major role in mitigating global warming is the increasing availability of fossil fuels. Just as Julian Simon predicted, when something useful becomes scarce, its price rises and people devise new production methods that increase the supply. This development bodes ill, however, for global warming and its destructive impact on food availability in the future, because increased use of fossil fuels means increased emissions of carbon dioxide and other greenhouse gases. Jad Mouawad explains in the *New York Times*,

> Just a few years ago, the dominant theme in discussions about energy was of declining production and fear of running out of oil. . . . But . . . high energy prices led to a wave of successful oil and gas exploration in North America, including in fields that were deemed uneconomical only a few years ago. Using techniques like horizontal drilling and hydraulic fracturing, oil companies are tapping into deeply buried reserves in shale rocks and in the ocean's depths."[77]

Hydraulic fracturing, or "fracking" as it's commonly called, may pollute groundwater and thereby reduce food availability in the future. We still don't know. But even if natural gas can be obtained without environmental harm, it can't be used without harm. The result of more abundant, cheaper natural gas is that few new coal-fired power plants are being built, and some coal-fired plants are being converted to natural gas. By itself, this doesn't exacerbate global warming because using natural gas instead of coal to generate electricity reduces carbon dioxide emissions. However, natural gas is competing successfully also with renewable sources of energy such as wind and solar, thereby delaying conversion away from fossil fuels. We may now have enough natural gas to last seventy-five years. Global warming could get out of control if fossil fuels continue to dominate power generation for that length of time.

Continued or expanded use of coal to generate electricity is sometimes advocated on the grounds that in principle coal use can be carbon neutral. This is the promise of clean coal. The idea is to burn coal in such a way as to capture the carbon dioxide that is produced by combustion and sequester it underground. But there are a few problems with this approach. First, the technology to capture and sequester carbon dioxide is not yet in commercial use, so its cost is still uncertain.[78] With natural gas already cheaper than coal for the generation of electricity, it's not clear how on a business-as-usual commercial basis (that is, without the kind of government taxes and subsidies that would revolutionize energy markets) this new technology can gain market share.

Second, it can't be known for many years if sequestering will be successful—that is, if the CO_2 will really stay trapped underground or if it will, instead, leak into the atmosphere. Investing billions of dollars in this technology is therefore very risky as it may simply waste money and end up contributing massively to global warming. If governments are going to use their powers of taxation and subsidy to combat global warming, technologies that generate electricity from wind and sun are surer bets.

Finally, much of the growing energy use that threatens to exacerbate global warming is in vehicles powered by internal combustion engines—cars, trucks, and planes—which use oil-based fuels. Coal cannot replace oil for these purposes until electric engines dominate personal and commercial transportation, a prospect that may be enticing, but that is not on the immediate horizon. Another possibility is converting coal energy into a liquid or gaseous form. However, that is very expensive. In general, the prospects for greater use of coal are dimmed by the current increase in oil production.

Continued oil abundance is expected to delay all conversions from oil to sources of energy that don't contribute to global warming. Worse yet, the production of oil from unconventional sources uses much more fossil fuel energy than its production from traditional sources. The first of these new sources to come online in abundance is oil from tar sands. Canada is the major source of such oil in the United States. As you might imagine, it takes a lot of energy to separate tar from sand, and most of this energy comes from new supplies of natural gas made possible by fracking. Alex Farrell, a professor in the Energy and Resources Group at the University of California at Berkeley says, "All unconventional forms of oil are worse for greenhouse-gas emissions than petroleum."[79] The total greenhouse-gas emissions from tar sands, for example, including its production and use, are 15 to 40 percent higher than emissions from using conventional petroleum. Turning coal into liquid doubles the generation of greenhouse gases compared to conventional petroleum.

Taking all of these factors into account—the acceleration of economic growth in China, India, and elsewhere (more manufacturing, meat eating, cars, planes, air-conditioning, etc.) and the increased use of fossil fuels that require additional fossil fuels for their production, such as the production of oil from tar sands—we seem headed for a concentration of CO_2 in the atmosphere in the next fifty years that will eventually (there's a time lag) increase average world temperatures by three degrees instead of just two degrees Celsius. Such a change carries exaggerated versions of all the risks to agriculture discussed earlier. Irrigation will require much more water, and crop yields will be much lower in hotter weather. Significant global warming also threatens to make agriculture more difficult because the absence of freezing weather in winter will in many areas enable crop pests (as well as some human pathogens) to proliferate. Rising seas will reduce the availability of coastal cropland.

In sum, there is no way that everyone in the world can live the way Americans live today. Our way of life catalyzes global warming, which exacerbates all problems associated with the diminishing availability of food and water needed to feed a growing world population. As things are today, there isn't enough water to grow enough food of the type that Americans eat. Nor is there enough water and good land to grow enough cotton for everyone in the world to buy clothing the way Americans do. A globalized American lifestyle would put global warming on steroids, further impairing agriculture and aquaculture, as people use fossil fuels to power several times the current number of cars and airplanes, heat and cool larger homes and offices, mine more metal to make cars and other consumer items, produce more concrete for highways and airports, and generate more electricity to run many times the current number of consumer electronic devices. Thus, Americans can't gain employment in manufacture on the model of the Marshall Plan to create trading partners who will trade with us on a level playing field. We must look primarily to other approaches to lowering our unemployment.

We will find in later chapters that good jobs can be created for Americans in many areas, including in companies that mitigate global warming and in enterprises that help us adapt to climate change. Instead of the world coming to live in the unsustainable manner of contemporary Americans, the American way of life will likely change in ways that make it more sustainable. There is no doom and gloom, much less catastrophe in this, because the American standard of living as measured by human wellbeing and satisfaction need not be lowered in the least. First, however, we explore some of the more effective ways that are currently used to keep Americans working, including inefficient systems of transportation and health care.

CHAPTER 6
FUNCTIONAL INEFFICIENCY IN TRANSPORTATION

One way that our society fosters employment is to use fundamentally inefficient systems to meet some common needs, systems that use more human and natural resources than available alternate systems would require to attain the same level of wellbeing. The example in this chapter is transportation. Our society's inefficient transportation system relies predominantly on automobiles for transporting people and trucking for transporting goods. According to the United States Bureau of Transportation Statistics, travel in cars and light trucks accounted for 86 percent of passenger miles in 2005.[1] Cargo traveling by trucks in the United States accounted for 69 percent of cargo by weight and over 80 percent by value in 2006.[2] In addition to getting people and goods to their desired destinations, a major function of our predominant modes of transportation is to create jobs, more jobs than a more efficient system would create.

The importance of car manufacture to American employment was highlighted in 2009 when President Obama decided to bail out General Motors (GM) and Chrysler, $49.5 billion going to GM and $10.8 to Chrysler. Owing to the restructuring that the bailout financed, within a year GM was profitable and 55,000 of the 334,000 who had lost their jobs in the industry were already back at work. The President claimed, and independent analysts agreed,[3] that altogether the bailout had saved 1.1 million jobs.[4] Also in 2009, the Obama administration initiated the Car Allowance Rebate System, known as the Cash for Clunkers program. Three billion dollars were allocated to serve as incentives for people with old, gas-guzzling cars to trade in their cars for new, fuel-efficient models. According to the Center for Automotive Research (CAR), the program generated new vehicle sales of 998,000 in July and 1,262,000 in August of 2009, hundreds of thousands of cars beyond the norm for those months. These sales contributed significantly to the nation's

2.8 percent annual rate of growth in the third quarter of 2009.[5] These policies had major impacts on the American economy because the auto industry supports many American workers.

According to CAR's 2010 report, the manufacture and assembly of motor vehicles employs 313,000 people in the United States. But ten times that number of employees depend on motor vehicle manufacture when all intermediate jobs and spin-offs are considered. Intermediate manufacturing jobs include those in the manufacture of primary metals, fabricated metals, motor vehicle parts, plastics, and rubber goods.[6] For example, according to a federal study conducted at Cornell University's ILR School, "In 2008, 13% of the output of the U.S. steel industry was shipped to the motor vehicle industry, which is the steel industry's second-largest end market user."[7] Altogether, such intermediate manufacturing employs more than 192,000 people in addition to those employed directly in making cars.

Many more people are employed in intermediate nonmanufacturing jobs related to the auto industry. These include people in professional and technical services, administration, wholesale trade, retail trade, transportation and warehousing of vehicles, finance, insurance, and management. New-car dealerships alone, for example, directly employ almost 737,000 people, according to the CAR report, and the people who supply them with goods and services (other than cars) employ another 239,000.[8]

Yet more people are employed as a result of spin-offs from the employment numbers just cited. As the report from CAR puts it,

> There are 1,765,000 total spin-off jobs associated with U.S. automobile manufacturing operations. These are expenditure-induced jobs, created as a result of spending by the people employed in the direct and intermediate categories. As could be expected, a large portion of the spin-off jobs are in the non-manufacturing sector of retail trade, which employs 215,000 people [in automotive-related spin-off jobs]. When employees use their paychecks to purchase goods (including electronics equipment, clothing, food, and even new automobiles), employment is created to supply their demands.[9]

When direct, indirect, and spin-off employment are combined, car manufacture results in 3,145,000 jobs, parts suppliers employ another 3,286,000 people, and auto dealerships employ yet another 1,528,000, for a grand total of over 7,960,000 people. This amounts to 4.4 percent of employment and 3.5 percent of compensation in the private sector.[10] These jobs are widespread in the United States. According to Auto Alliance, there are at least ten thousand auto-related jobs in forty-seven states, and at least one hundred thousand such jobs in twenty states. The $500 billion dollars a year paid in compensation for auto-related work approaches the $525 billion spent on Medicare in 2010.[11]

Trucking employs a lot of people as well. According to the American Trucking Associations, 3.5 million people are employed as commercial truck drivers in the United States.[12] But this is less than half the story. Because most cars and trucks are powered by internal combustion engines that predominantly use petroleum products for fuel, our transportation system is responsible for many jobs in the oil industry as well. According to a 2009 study prepared by PriceWaterhouseCooper for the American Petroleum Institute (API), United States oil and natural gas companies have an even greater impact on American jobs and incomes than does the production and sale of cars and trucks. In 2007, the latest year for which figures were available at the time of the study, the oil and natural gas industries supported 9.2 million jobs, which was 5.2 percent of American employment. The associated labor income was $558 billion, representing 6.3 percent of all labor income in the country during that year.[13] According to the Bureau of Labor Statistics, more recent studies show that 75,000 jobs directly related to the oil and gas industry were created between 2009 and 2011, so the employment impact of the industry is increasing.[14] Not all oil and natural gas industry work is related to transportation. Petroleum is used to make plastics, fertilizers, and other products; oil is used to heat homes; and natural gas is used to generate electricity. Unfortunately, neither of the studies cited above separates the activities related to automotive transport from these other industrial activities. However, an association of American gas providers claims that their industry provided nearly three million jobs.[15] This accounting leaves more than six million jobs in the oil sector of the oil and natural gas industry, and most of the oil sector is devoted to automotive transportation.

It's safe to say that drilling for oil, refining petroleum, piping petroleum, transporting petroleum in tankers, transporting gasoline by truck to gas stations, and selling gas at those stations provide many jobs and a lot of income. And, of course, there are the indirect jobs at companies that make products needed for the oil and gas industry's automotive-related activities. These include jobs making oil tankers, making oil trucks, making pipes that transport oil, constructing gas stations, and so forth. Finally, there are all the jobs created when people in the above categories spend money at the mall, or enlarge their houses, or buy refrigerators.

We're still not done. For cars to be most useful, they need roads (and bridges and tunnels), which must be built and maintained. In March 2010, when President Obama signed a highway bill that extended the Highway Trust Fund, the Official Blog of Ray LaHood, then US Secretary of Transportation, described the measure in the first place as designed to "continue creating and sustaining transportation construction jobs." The blog continues, "One proven way to create good jobs in America is to build and maintain transportation infrastructure. By also authorizing the Highway Trust Fund through the end of 2010, this bill guarantees that states will be able to continue doing just that. The year-end extension means transportation projects employing thousands of workers can continue without the threat of disruption by furlough episodes like the one we experienced only two weeks ago."[16]

The Laborers' International Union of North America endorsed this reasoning. They noted in 2012 that according to the US Department of Labor, "more than 1.5 million construction workers are unable to find work. More than 2 million construction jobs have been lost since 2006, leaving the industry with 17.7 percent unemployment." A highway bill that funds transportation-related construction and maintenance not only provides needed jobs, the union contends, but also maintains a vital infrastructure that needs immediate attention. The union points out that "a fourth of bridges are structurally deficient or functionally obsolete and 169,000 miles of roadways are in poor or mediocre condition. About 3,580 bridges are closed because of safety hazards." This should come as no surprise because "the average U.S. bridge is 45 years old—dangerously close to the lifespan of 50 years." The union notes that safety is an issue as well. Due to the failure of upkeep, "poor road conditions have become a contributing factor in 53% of traffic fatalities, according to a Pacific Institute for Research and Evaluation study."[17]

Makers of construction equipment also endorse government investment in infrastructure. In his article for the Construction Equipment Guide, Dennis Slater writes,

> By funding the highway bill, Congress would actually be funding a jobs bill that would help keep one vital manufacturing sector operating in the United States. The companies my association represents in the construction equipment manufacturing industry are experiencing a depression, not a recession. Upwards of 40 percent of those working in this manufacturing sector have lost their jobs in this downturn, so this industry needs a fully-funded highway bill now.
>
> The simplest way to explain the importance of the federal highway bill to the construction equipment industry is this: a fully-funded highway bill will promote significant long-term funding and planning for serious construction projects, such as new bridges, new roads and other infrastructure improvements. Long-term planning means construction contractors have market certainty and can afford to buy new equipment. The more the bill is postponed, the harder it is for contractors to bid and plan for significant long-term construction projects, which leads to additional job losses.[18]

The promotion of automotive transport in order to create or maintain American jobs has a long history. After the Great Depression began in 1929, President Herbert Hoover allocated $175 million for road building to ease unemployment. The new Roosevelt administration did much more: "The celebrated first 100 days concentrated on jobs as the primary mission," writes Jane Holtz Kay, architecture and planning critic for *The Nation*.

> A bill to "employ the largest possible number" in "useful public works" was passed. In 1933 the Federal Emergency Relief Administration sent $500 million to state and local governments and $3 billion to Roosevelt's emergency Public Works Administration (PWA). . . . Almost half the 2 million workers paid would build street or highway projects. . . . The Civic Works Administration (CWA) boasted 500,000 miles of road building. . . . 80 percent of the New Deal's expenditures went to roads and construction. . . . From 1930 to 1940, surfaced road mileage would double to 1,367,000 miles.[19]

Again in 1941, as the war raging in Europe promoted full employment in the United States, Roosevelt was already concerned that the eventual peace and consequent reduction in armaments manufacture would increase unemployment. He therefore proposed a new look at a 1939 recommendation for a "limited system of national highways." This system eventually became the interstate highway system.

In sum, the association of jobs and automotive transport is close and long-standing. In 2012, Congress passed a bill that funded highway construction and maintenance over the following twenty-seven months. Highways were allocated $120 billion, of which $101 billion would come from fuel taxes and $19 billion from the general treasury. Representative Nick Rahall II, a West Virginia Democrat, said, "It means jobs." Barbara Boxer, a Democratic senator from California, claimed that the act would create a million jobs and save two million more.[20]

Today, when employment in support services, the provision of supplies, and economic spin-offs are added to direct employment in the manufacture of vehicles, the provision of petroleum products used by autos, and the construction and maintenance of roads and bridges, automotive transport provides many millions of jobs in the United States. In this sense it's highly functional. However, the system of transport that provides all of these jobs is fundamentally inefficient. Its use of human and natural resources doesn't produce the greatest human wellbeing. Yet, it's this very inefficiency that enables the system to promote so much employment.

*   *   *

Our inefficient transportation system is composed of *elements* that are for the most part produced efficiently. For the most part the steel used to make cars and trucks is mined and manufactured efficiently. Cars and trucks are manufactured efficiently. Roads are built and maintained efficiently. Oil drilling and petroleum refining are also usually efficient. In general, as in other sectors of an industrial economy, earth's resources are transformed through efficient uses of human labor time into products for human use. Competition requires such efficiency. Inefficient car makers and steel producers are driven out of business by competitors.

The transportation *system*, by contrast, is stunningly inefficient because the role that cars and trucks play is much larger than efficiency allows. In a truly efficient transportation system there would be a role for cars and trucks, but there would also be a much larger role for public transportation. Within metropolitan areas more people would travel by trolley, light rail, and bus, and between cities more people and freight would travel by train. Such a system would be more efficient, but would support fewer transportation-related jobs in the long term, and this, I suspect, is a major reason why we have so far retained so much inefficiency in the transportation sector.

There are two ways of demonstrating the inefficiency of our current level of reliance on automotive (and aeronautic) transportation. One way, which I'll do first, is to look at physical matters, such as fuel consumed per passenger mile and the space needed to accommodate a given number of travelers. The second way is to look at subsidies that, I hope to convince you, are often a sign of inefficiency.

Some of the physical facts are given by Marcia Lowe of the Worldwatch Institute. She points out that trains require less energy than cars or trucks to move a given number of people or amount of cargo because trains are more aerodynamic. In addition, less friction is generated when steel wheels meet steel rails than when inflated tires meet pavement.

> Measured by the energy required to move one passenger one kilometer under U.S. commuting conditions, an intercity train uses some 900 Btu [British thermal units] . . .—one-third the energy used by a commercial airplane, and one sixth the energy of an automobile with a sole occupant. Equivalent travel by urban rail uses roughly 1,100 Btu per passenger-kilometer; commuter rail consumes some 1,200.[21]

Greater energy efficiency translates into lower emissions of greenhouse gases.

Similar gains in fuel efficiency attend moving freight by train instead of truck. The fuel efficiency of moving freight is measured by ton miles per gallon, which measures how many miles a gallon of fuel can move one ton of freight. A fully loaded (80,000 pound) semitruck that averages 6.5 miles per gallon moves a ton of freight 130 miles for each gallon of fuel,[22] whereas freight trains move a ton of freight an average of 480 miles for each gallon of fuel.[23] In addition, "For every ton of goods moved one kilometer, freight rail emits one-third the nitrogen oxide and carbon monoxide, and one-tenth the volatile organic compounds and diesel particulates emitted by heavy trucks."[24] This suggests that hauling freight by rail instead of semitrucks reduces the negative impact of freight traffic on public health.

Mass transit also improves efficiency by reducing traffic congestion. Deborah Gordon, writing for the Union of Concerned Scientists, notes that "one fully occupied train can remove as many as 100 cars from the road during rush hour . . . [and] a bus can eliminate 40 cars."[25] Reducing traffic congestion saves time and fuel.

Passenger rail saves space as well. "Two railroad tracks can carry as many people as sixteen lanes of highway."[26] Saving space is particularly important in crowded cities, but it's also important in the countryside where more crops could be raised for human consumption if human traffic took up less space.

*   *   *

At this point you may wonder how we maintain a system that is physically so inefficient in a society that thinks of itself as rewarding efficiency and punishing inefficiency. The answer is subsidy. We subsidize automotive transportation much more than mass transportation alternatives. Hidden subsidies are often a sign of unrecognized inefficiency. Hidden subsidies make what is actually inefficient appear efficient because the subsidy allows prices that consumers pay to be low, and consumers assume that these low prices result from efficiency. Thus, the hidden nature of the subsidies makes what is actually inefficient appear efficient and therefore acceptable in our efficiency-oriented society.

Because most of the subsidies for automotive travel are hidden (usually in plain sight, as we'll see), travel by car is usually thought more efficient than public transportation. Critics of public transportation complain, in fact, that public transportation, whether by trolley, light rail, bus, or fast train, is almost everywhere subsidized, usually by the government. In general, critics maintain, people should pay for what they get in a free-market society. If a good or service has to be subsidized to attract more patrons, it seems that most people would rather do something else with their money than pay the full cost of that good or service. People would get the biggest bang for their buck (allocate their limited resources most efficiently) if they could have cash, which would allow them to buy what they really want most, rather than what subsidies have made artificially cheap (cheaper than the full price in a free market).

This is generally sound reasoning. Subsidies use limited resources; there's really no free lunch. When goods or services are subsidized, people who are not using them are paying part of their total cost, making it cheaper for those who do use them. But society, which includes both users and nonusers of the subsidized goods or services, is really paying the full cost anyway. The full cost is paid indirectly, in people's tax bills or in their bills for other goods or services. Eliminating the subsidy would promote fundamental efficiency. People who don't use the good or service would no longer be forced to pay for it. They could spend their money as they wish, thereby increasing the satisfaction that results from expenditures of human and natural resources.

Perhaps more surprisingly, eliminating subsidies can also improve the welfare of people who do want and do use subsidized goods and services. These people, too, are paying for subsidized items indirectly (through taxes or through higher prices on other goods and services that they buy). Elimination of the subsidy would allow these people to decide how much they really want to spend on the full array of items that the market offers. They might prefer to have back the money that they are using for the subsidy and spend that money on different things than what they are currently subsidizing. David Levinson, a public transportation critic at the University of Minnesota, applies this reasoning to public transportation: "Maybe you want transit. But maybe you would rather have the cash I am spending to provide you subsidized transit service so you can do something else with it. The only way to know what the best allocation of resources is, is to charge for things what they cost."[27]

Yonah Freemark summarizes Levinson's view by giving this example in *The Transport Politic*:

> You have two choices: Take a ride to your city's most beautiful park for a fare of $2 on your local bus (with the aid of a $2 subsidy chipped in by your local government), or walk to the nearest, less exciting park and buy an ice cream on the way for $3.00. Thinking about the relative merits of the two

possibilities, you might determine that the trip to the better park is actually the best deal (since it is cheaper for you), but for the society at large, it's more expensive. If you were charged the full $4 cost of providing the bus ride to the park, you might think twice and pick the ice cream option instead—which is cheaper for the society as a whole. But the mobility subsidy is providing an inappropriate incentive to do just the opposite and is causing people, Levinson writes, *"To behave inefficiently."*[28]

In sum, except where public goods are at issue, subsidies generally promote inefficiency because they deflect the use of limited resources from goods and services that provide people the greatest benefit, to those that happen to be subsidized. With subsidies, people are paying indirectly for things that might not otherwise be their highest priority purchases.

This is excellent reasoning, but not a good argument against public transportation and intercity rail in their competition with automobiles, trucks, and air travel. Travel by car, truck, and plane are actually much more highly subsidized than public transportation. So the above reasoning showing that subsidies tend to create inefficiency suggests the greater inefficiency of cars, trucks, and planes compared to urban mass transit and intercity rail.

A long history of subsidies tells the story. Jane Holtz Kay writes, "In the quarter century after World War II, Washington and the states allocated $226 billion for highways and for private cars and less than a quarter of that for public transportation."[29] Planes were subsidized also, mostly at the expense of railroads. According to former US Department of Transportation (USDOT) Secretary Coleman, as recounted on the website TrainWeb,

Between 1942 and 1962 a 10% rail ticket tax was levied on railroads as a war measure to discourage unnecessary travel. This tax generated revenues of over $5 billion, which went into the general revenue fund and, ironically, was used in some cases to build more airports and highways. In today's dollars, that probably would amount to about $100 billion and one wonders what would have happened if that money had been invested in rail service after the war. By the time the tax was lifted, the passenger train was already on the ropes.[30]

Trains Magazine gives more specific examples: "Washington's National Airport was built with federal funds and between 1941 and 1957 had cost the government $4 million to operate; the airport paid no taxes. At the same time, Washington Union Station [the city's rail terminal] was valued at $32 million and paid more than $6.9 million in taxes." Similarly, "the Pennsylvania Railroad modernized its Pittsburgh station in the 1950s only to see the taxes increased and the money spent to improve the Greater Pittsburgh International Airport."[31]

More generally, between 1971 and 2001, federal funding for air travel and highways was 63 times the funding for Amtrak, the government-run intercity passenger rail system—$1,890 billion to $30.1 billion.[32] And this bias has continued. In 2002, a typical year, USDOT allocated $32.3 billion for highways and $14 billion for aviation and airports, but only $5 billion for mass transit and just over half a billion dollars for Amtrak.[33]

These subsidies aren't hidden; they're in published budget reports. Still, most Americans don't think of them as subsidies. First, much of the funds come from taxes related to the transportation service being subsidized, and few people realize that these taxes don't cover the full budgetary outlay. The uncovered portion is the subsidy. Second, these allocations are called "investments," which suggests that they promote efficiency in the long run.

Still, these relatively visible allocations to promote automotive transportation and air travel are small potatoes compared to the hidden subsidies. These hidden subsidies are contained not in budget allocations but in goods, services, and facilities that we take for granted without realizing that we're not paying their full cost for the privilege of using them.

❋   ❋   ❋

Here's an enormous subsidy hiding in plain sight—"free" parking. The fact that it's free makes you realize once you think about it that you're not paying its full cost, since you're not paying any cost at all. But since you're not paying anything for it, you have no incentive to think about its cost. Thus, the subsidy for parking is hidden in plain sight.

Parking is actually one key to understanding the enormity of government bias in favor of automobiles in their competition with mass transportation. A survey in 1990 found that people park free 99 percent of the time when they use their cars.[34] But that's the clue: *"free" means subsidized.* In his magisterial study *The High Cost of Free Parking*, Donald Shoup cites a study done in 1990–1991 that gives low and high estimates for the total cost of providing off-street parking in the United States. Annualized capital and operating costs ranged from a low estimate of $79 billion to a high estimate of $229 billion, of which people paid only $3 billion to park their cars. So only between one and four percent of the total cost of parking was paid by people parking their cars. The rest was subsidy.

One way to appreciate the enormity of this subsidy is to compare it to the cost of Medicare in 2010, a year when Medicare costs occupied a lot of political attention because they were considered unacceptably high. In 2010 Medicare cost $525 billion.[35] The cost of parking, adjusting for inflation and for the increased number of parking spaces between 1991 and 2010, was between $154 billion and $453 billion *per year.*[36] So, creating and maintaining the parking infrastructure in the United States cost about half (somewhere between 30 percent and 70 percent) as much as Medicare, one of the three most costly government entitlement programs, and the co-pay for parking was only between one and four percent. Eliminating the subsidy through a gasoline tax would require a tax of between $1.62 and $4.78 a gallon.[37]

Failure to require motorists to pay at the pump or anywhere else for parking makes driving artificially cheap (that's the nature of a subsidy) and thereby influences people to drive more and take public transportation less. A study in thirty-three metropolitan areas by Bradley Lane of the University of Texas at El Paso concluded that a ten percent increase in the price of gas tends to increase the use of buses by four percent and the use of trains by eight percent.[38] This tendency was born out when a rise in gas prices to about $4 a gallon in 2011 was accompanied by a significant increase in the use of public transportation in both city and rural settings.[39] The percentage increase in the price of gas through a tax that covers the cost of parking, a tax of between $1.62 and $4.78 a gallon, would be somewhere between 36 percent and 120 percent (if gas costs $4 a gallon). So, failure to charge drivers for their parking results in an enormous underutilization of public transportation. This fact tends to be overlooked by critics of public transportation who complain that it shouldn't be subsidized because few people use it.

Since we don't charge drivers for most of the cost of parking, who pays for parking? Shoup answers,

> Everyone does, even if they don't drive. Initially the developer pays for the required parking, but soon the tenants do, and then their customers, and so on, until the cost of parking has diffused everywhere in the economy. When we shop in a store, eat in a restaurant, or see a movie, we pay for parking indirectly because its cost is included in the prices of merchandise, meals, and theater tickets. . . . Residents pay for parking through higher prices for housing. . . . We don't pay for parking in our role as motorists, but in all our other roles—as consumers, investors, workers, residents and taxpayers. . . . Even people who don't own a car have to pay for "free" parking.[40]

Parking continues to be available, most often at little or no cost to motorists, because most cities and municipalities require the provision of off-street parking when new buildings are constructed. The Urban Land Institute endorses this policy. "In an office park development, the provision of on-site parking for tenant and visitor cars is nearly as important as the building itself. . . . An allowance of four spaces per 1,000 square feet of net rentable space (or of one space per 250 net square feet) is an across the board ideal solution."[41]

Such parking requirements can add significantly to the cost of housing in crowded urban areas. Shoup gives this example from Los Angeles, which he considers typical. Zoning laws required that a nineteen-unit building have fifty-eight parking spaces (2.5 spaces per unit). Because the site was small, a two-level underground garage was needed to meet this requirement. At $80 a square foot, each parking space cost $41,600, adding $104,000 to the price of each unit.[42] That's "free parking."

Requiring such parking keeps the price for parking low (even as it increases the price of housing and many other items), thereby encouraging the use of cars instead of mass transit. Requirements that developers provide off-street parking encourage the use of cars also by increasing the distances people have to travel. Parking takes up space and thereby lowers population and commercial density. In urban settings where land is too valuable for ground-level parking, four off-street parking spaces in multilevel structures (called structured parking) occupy 1,200 square feet when access lanes and ramps are included in the calculation. Since this is typically required for every thousand feet of "net rentable space," parking takes up 20 percent more space than office space and stores combined.[43]

Where land is cheaper, parking is typically single level, usually outside. If the commercial establishment is multilevel, like most shopping malls and many office buildings, parking can occupy twice as much land as the stores, offices, and other forms of commercial activity that the parking is designed to serve. You can verify this for yourself. Just drive to the mall and look around. I say "drive to the mall" because the mall is for most people too far away to walk. But it's the parking that is largely responsible for the fact that most shopping is too far away for pedestrian access. There are myriad off-street surface parking lots between most people and the nearest mall, which is the main reason why the mall and other desirable shopping opportunities are so far away. A study of Albuquerque, New Mexico, shows, for example, that *even downtown* more land is devoted to parking than to all other uses combined. Similarly, half of downtown Buffalo, New York, is devoted to parking.[44] Shoup summarizes,

> Abundant parking makes it easier and cheaper to drive, but pandemic parking lots spread activities farther apart, making cars more necessary. Off-street parking requirements increase mobility by car, but they also reduce mobility by walking, cycling, and public transit. By reducing both propinquity and non-car mobility, the parking supply creates its own demand because a car is needed to get to most places.[45]

Jeffrey Zupan, co-author of *Public Transportation and Land Use Policy*, puts figures to the importance for public transportation of people and commerce being concentrated. He told a conference on transportation, "To get an hourly bus in the residential district, you have to have one house per quarter acre. To get one every half hour, it's seven an acre, and for every ten minutes, it's fifteen an acre." Needed commercial concentrations can be quantified as well. "To get an hourly bus you need to have 5 to 8 million square feet of retail space in the retail district; for one to come every half hour, it's 7 to 17½; and for every ten minutes in the CBD [Central Business District] downtown it's more than 20 million." Streetcars require more residential and commercial concentration and underground, unobstructed rail requires even greater concentration.[46] It should be noted, however, that Zupan's calculations are for the United States where, owing to free parking and other subsidies, driving is made artificially cheap. If people had to pay the full cost of their car travel, they would be more disposed to use public transportation, reducing the level of concentration needed for the practicality of public transportation.

The needed levels of concentration are not at all unusual in cities that restrict parking. Anyone who has visited London, Paris, or Manhattan has seen it. The relative lack of public parking encourages people to use public transportation, making it practical for the public transportation network to be more complete and helpful. With many riders, they can offer more frequent service, longer hours, more stops, and greater coverage. At the same time, with fewer parking lots and parking garages, commercial and residential use is more concentrated; everything is closer together. This propinquity makes it easier for people to bicycle or walk, or at least walk from the closest public transportation stop to their destination.

＊　　＊　　＊

Off-street parking requirements increase traffic congestion as well as distance. The more people use their cars (because low-cost parking makes driving cheap and because parking lots increase distances), the more cars there are on the roads and the greater the traffic congestion.

Free or low-cost on-street (curb) parking also increases congestion in city centers because drivers cruise streets near their intended destinations hoping to find on-street parking that is considerably cheaper than off-street parking. A study by the US Bureau of Public Roads in 1933 looked at car travel to the Department of Commerce Building. They found that on average driving time was twenty-five minutes, the search for curb parking took eight minutes, and walking from parking to the building took nine minutes.[47] A study in 1985 examined parking possibilities in Cambridge, Massachusetts, when curb parking cost fifty cents an hour and off-street parking cost three dollars an hour. Researcher Mary O'Malley found that it took her an average of

11.5 minutes to find curb parking in Harvard Square, during which time she cruised 1.27 miles.[48] Shoup concludes from these and other studies "that an average of 30 percent of the cars in congested traffic were cruising for parking. Cruising increases vehicle travel without adding either vehicles *or* real travel. The aggregate consequences of all this cruising—congested traffic, wasted time, squandered fuel, and polluted air—are staggering."[49]

This increased congestion hampers public transportation by bus. Buses generally use the same lanes of traffic as people cruising for parking spaces. Slowing down the bus increases the cost of bus travel because travel time contributes most to a bus's operating costs. Buses slowed by traffic congestion are also less attractive to travelers because it takes bus riders longer to get to their destinations and because congestion makes it more difficult for buses to maintain their schedules, thereby increasing the uncertainty of travel by bus.[50]

Traffic congestion is inefficient; it wastes time and money. A Texas Transportation Institute (TTI) report released in 2011 indicates nearly steady increases in the amount of time people spend stuck in traffic on American roads. In the country as a whole, commuters spent fourteen hours stuck in traffic in 1982 but thirty-four hours in 2010. The situation is much worse in some urban areas, such as Washington, DC (seventy-four hours), Chicago (seventy-one hours), and Los Angeles (sixty-four hours). Matters were even worse before the Great Recession of 2008–2009. TTI estimated that the monetary cost of traffic congestion in the Chicago metropolitan area alone was more than $9.4 billion in 2007. The average Chicago commuter consumed an extra fifty-two gallons of gasoline that year and experienced seventy hours of delay in commuter traffic, an amount of time equal to almost two weeks' work. In all, the cost in time and gasoline per Chicago commuter was $1,738, owing solely to traffic congestion.[51]

This figure doesn't include medical costs resulting from people breathing auto exhaust while sitting in traffic. A study of eighty-three cities by the Harvard Center for Risk Analysis concluded that traffic congestion-related emissions of three kinds of air pollution caused four thousand premature deaths in 2000, with a monetary cost of $30 billion (in 2007 dollars). This study did not consider the additional costs of medical care and lost income for people who were injured but not killed by this air pollution, nor did the study include the medical costs of people who ultimately died as a result of exposure to this air pollution but who, as is most often the case, had medical treatment before death. The study found also that in addition to costs related to air pollution, traffic congestion cost these eighty-three communities $60 billion merely as a result of wasted time and fuel.[52]

The situation would be worse today if the government hadn't invested in public transportation in the past. TTI (using constant 2010 dollars) estimates that public transportation saved the country $6.9 billion in 1982 and $12 billion in 2000 but $16.8 billion in 2010. Even so, merely as a result of wasted time and fuel, traffic delays in 2010 cost $101 billion, up from $21 billion in 1982 and $79 billion in 2000.[53]

In sum, "free" (and highly subsidized) parking adds greatly to the inefficiency of our transportation system. It adds to congestion, pollution, sprawl, and travel time as it harms human health and impairs development of more efficient public transportation. Shoup concludes, therefore, that a free market in parking is better than free parking. He advocates, for example, that cities cease requiring developers to provide a specific number of off-street parking spaces for commercial and residential properties. Instead, cities should allow developers to decide for themselves how much off-street parking to provide. This would allow developers to unbundle parking costs from other rental costs, thus reducing congestion and pollution as some renters of apartments sell one of their cars in order to avoid paying for a parking space. Some stores will want less parking so that they can lower their capital costs and thereby increase profit by attracting customers with lower prices on the items they sell. The result will be less traffic, less congestion, less wasted fuel, less wasted time, and improved public health.[54]

Shoup recommends that curb parking be charged a market price, which is a price just high enough that some parking is always available. This will not be intolerably burdensome to store owners and residents in areas of high cost for curb parking, Shoup contends, if the money collected is returned to the neighborhood for public works that improve the community, such as parks and street beautification.[55]

*   *   *

Many subsidies for cars are not related to parking or congestion. According to the US Census Bureau, in 2009 33,808 people were killed in car crashes. This amounted to 1.14 deaths for every hundred million vehicle miles traveled (VMT) by car.[56] According to the National Safety Council, the passenger death rate per hundred million VMT for travel by bus was only 7.5 percent of the death rate for travel by car, and the passenger death rate for travel by train was only half the rate for travel by bus.[57] So if everyone had traveled by bus instead of by car, only 2,535 passengers would have died in 2009, and if everyone had traveled by train, only 1,268 passengers would have died that year. This means that well over thirty thousand passengers died in crashes in 2009 because our transportation system is organized around cars instead of around such public transportation options as buses and trains.

The monetary value placed on a human life differs somewhat from one US government agency to another. In 2010 the Environmental Protection Agency valued a life at $9.1 million, whereas the Food and Drug Administration put the value at $7.9 million, and the USDOT used the value of about $6 million.[58] In the light of these facts, it seems reasonable to use the average of $7.6 million for the monetary value of a human life according to the US government.

Automobile insurance often provides benefits for people who die in car crashes, but even relatively high end auto insurance allows only $100,000 of liability coverage per accident victim. Assuming that people pay this much in liability insurance premiums related directly to their use of cars, most of the monetary loss associated with each death in an automobile accident is not paid for by any insurance, tax, or other expenditure directly related to driving. Subtracting the auto insurance cost of $100,000 per passenger death from the $7.6 million that each life is worth leaves us $7.5 million per death that is not paid for by any auto-related expenditure. This dollar figure represents a subsidy by society in general of our car-oriented culture. Multiply this $7.5 million by the additional thirty thousand people who die each year in accidents because they travel in cars instead of buses or trains, and the additional cost of travel by car instead of by safer public transportation amounts to $225 billion per year.

This reasoning yields results similar to those of the Harvard study cited earlier. That study put a figure of $30 billion for the cost of four thousand premature deaths each year that result from exposure to auto-generated air pollution when people are stuck traffic. Multiply four thousand by $7.6 million (auto insurance doesn't cover these deaths), and the result is $30.4 billion.

The cost of these deaths (both from accidents and air pollution) is reflected in life insurance rates, lower earnings by households who have lost a wage earner, lower productivity in society when a working adult is killed, public aid programs to support households whose wage earner has died prematurely, and loss of future productivity when young people are killed before their years of greatest productivity. Because these losses are not covered by the price of gas, vehicle registration fees, auto insurance, or any other automotive-related tax or expense, society is subsidizing travel by car to the tune of $255.4 ($225 + $30.4) billion a year (to cover auto-related deaths), in addition to all of the other subsidies noted earlier.

There's more. Consider national defense. In 1992, the Congressional Research Service found that independent studies estimated military spending needed for petroleum-related national defense at between $56 billion and $73 billion per year.[59] Adjusted for inflation between 1992 and 2010, this would be between $85.9 billion and $112 billion per year. Economist Jenny Wahl, making her own calculations and reviewing the work of several other researchers, calculated military spending for the same purpose at between 10 percent and 25 percent of the Defense Department's budget.[60] The 10 percent estimate corresponds to the lower of the preceding estimates, leading to the conclusion that the defense budget could be at least $86 billion less if we didn't have to defend our access to foreign sources of oil.[61] Because this additional defense expenditure isn't reflected in any driving-related tax, this $86 billion is another subsidy of our transportation system. Such military expenditures would not be necessary if our transportation system were dominated by forms of mass transportation powered by natural gas or electricity.

It remains to be seen, as the United States moves toward self-sufficiency in oil production, whether these expenditures will continue in the long run. They will almost certainly continue for at least the next several years because foreign policy agreements and commitments predicated on our previous need for petroleum, such as military commitments in the Middle East, cannot be abandoned quickly.

According to Mark Delucchi, who used Federal Highway Administration (FHWA) statistics to make his calculations, the cost of highway patrol and safety amounted to about $8 billion in 1990. The International Center for Technology Assessment adds,

> Other local police protection costs related to motor vehicles not covered in FHWA statistics add $5.4 billion in externalities. Fire protection costs attributable to motor vehicle use totaled between $1.4 and $3.2 billion in 1990 according to the Union of Concerned Scientists. Judicial and legal system costs imposed by motor-vehicle-related litigation adds an additional $4.8 to $6.2 billion. Jail, prison, probation, and parole costs run the taxpayer another $3.9 to $6.2 billion.[62]

Averaging these figures where a range is given, adding up the resulting averages, and translating the sum into 2010 dollars yields the figure of about $42.6 billion. People pay some of the litigation costs up front in their insurance premiums, but the total subsidy (the uncovered costs) of these services is at least $40 billion per year.

Another subsidy, whose payment is largely being deferred at this time, is for highway infrastructure. Our aging highway infrastructure needs enormous infusions of dollars each year, beyond revenues stemming from gasoline taxes that are put into state coffers and the Highway Trust Fund. As veteran federal highway administrator Frank Turner put it in 1986, "Highways grow old and wear out at fairly predictable ages and life spans, and therefore must be replaced or restored."[63] Ten years later he added, "The highway system has to be continually improved and replaced every minute of every day, and that is a large project in itself. There is a life to a mile of highway, about thirty to thirty-five years . . . , and the average age of the interstates' miles is getting to the point where overloads, cracks and other deteriorations are really showing."[64]

Unfortunately, public spending on roads hasn't kept up. The highway bill passed in 2012 included only $19 billion from the general treasury, to be spent over twenty-seven months, to augment money that comes from gasoline and other transportation-related taxes raised by federal, state, and local governments.[65] This is not nearly enough.[66] According to a report released in 2009 by the National Surface Transportation Infrastructure Financing Commission, maintaining and improving the current highway system between 2008 and 2035 requires additional funding each year (not every twenty-seven months) of about $90 billion.[67] Because delaying maintenance usually increases costs, this number is a low estimate of what we will pay if we wait until bridges become unsafe and roads start to crumble.

Let's summarize how much our transportation system costs each year in excess of what people pay for the privilege of driving.

$149 to $448 billion to construct and maintain parking infrastructure beyond what motorists pay for parking;

$101 billion owing to wasted time and fuel in congested traffic

$30 billion owing to deaths from exposure to air pollution in congested traffic

$225 billion for deaths in car accidents in excess of deaths in public transportation

$86 billion for national defense expenditures related to petroleum security

$40 billion for domestic security

$90 billion for road infrastructure

The total on the lowest estimate is $720 billion a year; on the high estimate it is over $1 trillion. Averaging these two figures, that is, using the figure of $860 billion a year, will not result in an overestimation because so many hidden subsidies are not yet included in the figures presented above. For example, I have not included: the cost of injuries from car accidents beyond the coverage of auto insurance; costs associated with death resulting from exposure to automotive-generated air pollution under conditions other than traffic congestion; healthcare costs of nonlethal air pollution; loss of income resulting from illness that stems from exposure to auto-generated air pollution; tax breaks for oil companies; and the loss of productivity and tax revenue that results from land being converted to highways in excess of the amount of land that would be need for a rail-oriented infrastructure.

Since Americans use about 138 billion gallons of gasoline each year,[68] paying at the gas pump for all $860 billion of annual subsidies would add $6.23 to a gallon of gas. People currently paying $2 a gallon would have to pay $8.23 a gallon just to pay for these annual subsidies. If gas prices go back up to between $3.50 and $4 a gallon, people would have to pay about $10 a gallon to cover all the true costs of using a gallon of gas.

Of course, we do pay for car-travel subsidies *as a society*; we just don't pay for it as drivers and riders. This is a classic case of subsidy-induced inefficiency. Because we are subsidizing cars whether we use cars or not, and that subsidy reduces the cost of using a car, free-market efficiencies are undermined because people aren't permitted to use their money in ways that they consider most conducive to their own advantage. They're locked into the car infrastructure. They're paying for parking whether they use it or not. Parking creates distances that make using a car necessary because public transportation alternatives are underdeveloped owing to a lack of public investment in them relative to public subsidies for cars.

This situation explains how a system that is physically inefficient, and therefore more monetarily expensive when all externalities are factored in, survives in our primarily free-market economy. The physically inefficient system is exempt from the most fundamental strictures of the free market. People don't have to pay the full cost of what they buy when they drive, and the government has reduced more efficient alternatives that would in a large segment of the market out-compete cars in a truly free market. But this government action makes sense. The inefficiency that it has created and maintains through subsidy is functional. As we saw early in this chapter, it functions to create and maintain millions of jobs.

*   *   *

The automotive approach to moving freight is integrated within our automotive-oriented transportation system. Large intercity trucks therefore benefit from the subsidies already noted. But, owing to the damage that large, heavy trucks do to the highway infrastructure, long-haul trucking deserves its own exhibit in the hall of infamous subsidies. Our highway infrastructure is deteriorating largely because heavy trucks are not paying their fair share of highway construction and maintenance costs.

A report of the General Accounting Office titled "Excessive Truck

Weight: An Expensive Burden We Can No Longer Support" maintains that an eighteen-wheel semi-trailer truck (with five axles and weighing the federal limit of eighty thousand pounds) causes ninety-six hundred times as much damage to a road surface when it rolls over that surface as a typical two thousand pound car with two axles.[69] What is more, the average truck travels many more miles per year than the ten thousand to fifteen thousand miles for the typical car. Although the semi is not fully loaded all the time, it is likely to travel many more miles per year fully loaded than the average car travels per year. So it's safe to say that the average eighteen-wheel semi (class 8 truck) damages our highways each year at least ten thousand times, and probably more than twenty thousand times as much as a relatively light passenger car.

I pay in Illinois a fee of $106 dollars to register my car, and this money is used largely, although not exclusively, for road construction and maintenance.[70] Also largely to fund road construction and maintenance, I pay 18.4 cents per gallon federal fuel tax and 19 cents per gallon state fuel tax. Because the national average state fuel tax is a little higher, the average American driver pays fuel taxes (federal and state) amounting to about forty cents per gallon.[71] If the average car is used to drive only ten thousand miles a year (a deliberately low estimate), and gets an actual (not an EPA estimated) twenty miles to the gallon in combined city and highway driving (an unfortunately realistic estimate when SUVs are counted as cars), the average car consumes five hundred gallons of gas per year and generates two hundred dollars in fuel taxes. (A Prius would generate only about half that amount in fuel taxes.) So the average car generates about three hundred dollars per year (one hundred dollars in registration fees and two hundred dollars in fuel taxes) in revenue for state and federal governments largely to defray the expenses of constructing and maintaining the nation's roadways.

If a large semitruck, such as a Kenworth, were to go one hundred thousand miles a year (the miles per year that the Kenworth Corporation uses to compare savings from increased fuel efficiency) and get five miles to the gallon (the low estimate on the Kenworth calculator), the truck would use twenty thousand gallons of diesel per year.[72] If combined state and federal fuel taxes were fifty cents per gallon (fuel taxes on diesel are generally greater than those on regular gas), the truck would pay ten thousand dollars in fuel taxes. (It would pay less if it were more fuel efficient and more if it were driven more than one hundred thousand miles in a year.) In Illinois, such trucks pay $8,545 ($550 of which is the Federal Heavy Vehicle Use Tax),[73] for registration each year. So the typical semitruck pays less than twenty thousand dollars in total road use taxes.

According to a 2009 report of the National Surface Transportation Infrastructure Financing Commission, merely maintaining our current system of roads (bridges and tunnels) requires average annual expenditures of $131 billion between 2008 and 2035. Recommended improvements require an additional $34 billion a year, for a total of $165 billion.[74] At the time of the report, there were a total of about 240 million vehicles on American roads,[75] of which 3 million were very heavy (class 8) trucks.[76] Assume that each truck causes only ten thousand (not twenty thousand or thirty thousand) times as much damage as the average vehicle, because many "average" vehicles are SUVs, light trucks, and cars heavier than the two thousand pound passenger car that was used in the original comparison of damages that different vehicles cause to the transportation infrastructure. Multiply three million heavy trucks by ten thousand and those trucks have the destructive impact of thirty *billion* average vehicles, which is more than 120 times the impact of all the other vehicles combined. (Thirty billion is more than 120 times the 240 million vehicles on US roads in 2009.) Assume, unrealistically, that heavy trucks cause only one thousand times as much damage as the average vehicle (if large SUVs are considered "average") and they still cause twelve times as much damage as all the other vehicles combined.

If heavy trucks should be paying only twelve times as much as all other vehicles combined for the construction and maintenance of the highway infrastructure, they should collectively be paying over $152 billion (of the $165 billion) annually, which is just over $50,000 annually for each of the three million heavy trucks. As we have seen, they are currently paying under $20,000 in fuel taxes and registration fees. Three million trucks paying $50,000 instead of $20,000 annually would raise an additional $90 billion dollars a year for surface transportation, which just about equals the annual shortfall of revenues needed to maintain and improve surface transportation in the United States.[77] So the failure of heavy trucks to pay their fair share through fuel taxes and vehicle registration fees is why we have a crumbling transportation infrastructure.

Earlier we saw that an additional gas tax of at least $6.23 a gallon would have to be paid by car drivers to make up for annual subsidies of automotive transportation. If trucks were paying their fair share to maintain and improve the nation's highways, $90 billion could be transferred from taxes on gas to taxes on heavy trucks. This would reduce the additional gas tax needed from other drivers to merely $5.58 per gallon, making a gallon of gas currently selling for $2 a gallon cost only a little over $7.50. Of course, if gas goes up to $3.50 a gallon, it would cost over $9 for a gallon of gas when all costs associated with using that gallon are included in its price. I'm afraid that's as good as it gets.

We saw earlier that long-haul trucking is physically inefficient compared to the rail alternative. A truck getting 6.5 miles per gallon hauls a ton of freight 130 miles per gallon of fuel, whereas a train hauls that ton of freight 480 miles per gallon.[78] Now we see that the system of hauling most intercity freight by truck is physically inefficient also, insofar as it requires enormous infrastructure maintenance. But such inefficiencies are functional in an economy that's fighting unemployment. Repairing roads creates many jobs. Driving trucks creates many jobs. And the current freight system, because it is so highly subsidized by the government, facilitates consumerism (another way that we keep people working) by making it easy and cheap (from the consumer's perspective) to have consumer items shipped. If trucking paid its full costs, items bought on the Internet, for example, would be more expensive to ship within the United States. Adding this expense to the cost of consumer items would dampen consumer demand, and such demand is the main driver of economic growth in our economy. A contraction of consumer demand usually slows economic growth and increases unemployment.

*   *   *

It's hard to justify the retention of inefficient systems because their very inefficiency suggests that more human wellbeing could be created using the same human and natural capital more efficiently. What is more, although inefficient systems create many jobs, so would their replacement by more efficient systems, at least in the short- and mid-term. For example, productive powers can be used to create a rail infrastructure—intercity freight and passenger rail as well as light rail within metropolitan areas—resulting not only in additional jobs during the construction of the system, but a more efficient and environmentally friendly transportation system. Such a system is also likely to be popular. Property prices tend to rise and commercial activity tends to increase near the stops of light rail networks in major metropolitan areas.[79] Motorists will be pleased with fewer large trucks competing with them for space on major intercity highways, and fast passenger trains can save consumers both time and money as compared to their paying the full costs of air or auto travel between cities. Repair costs on highways will go down as fewer heavy trucks use them. Family budgets would be improved because, according TTI, people who commute to work by public transportation currently save an average of eight thousand dollars per year in transportation costs.[80]

Poor people are likely to benefit most, which many people would consider a gain in social justice. Poor people benefit most because the current inefficient system relies on cars, and most poor people cannot afford reliable cars or cannot afford cars at all. The poorest fifth of Americans spends 42 percent of their annual household budget on the purchase, operation, and maintenance of their cars. That's more than twice the national average. Low-income people typically have older cars and more unexpected repair costs. More than 90 percent of former welfare recipients do not have access to a car, and yet three in every five jobs suitable for welfare-to-work program participants are not accessible by public transportation.[81]

None of this suggests that we shouldn't have cars or trucks. I don't foresee a time when a family wouldn't have a car; I just foresee a time when that car would seldom be used to commute to work. I don't foresee a time when trucks won't make local deliveries; I just foresee a time when freight arrives to the area by water or rail. I don't foresee a time when people won't drive or fly from city to city; I just foresee a time when it will be cheaper and more convenient to take fast passenger trains for most trips under five hundred miles.

The bad news is that when such a time arrives because a new infrastructure has been put in place, transportation will require less work because it is more efficient. The rail infrastructure is cheaper to maintain, which means that fewer construction workers will be needed. Fewer workers will be needed also at factories that make cement, at factories making large road-construction equipment, and so on. Families saving eight thousand dollars a year because someone takes public transportation to work instead of a car will need one less car in the family, and this will reduce the demand for new and used automobiles. It will also reduce the demand for workers at steel plants, and for sales people at automobile dealerships. So if we are serious about fighting unemployment, we need to consider how people will be employed if we eliminate much of our current functional inefficiency in the transportation sector. That is the topic of chapters 8, 9, and 11 through 13.

CHAPTER 7

FUNCTIONAL INEFFICIENCY IN HEALTHCARE

A betted by enormous fundamental inefficiency, healthcare employment remains strong in the United States and continues to grow, making this inefficiency nevertheless functional. According to a Bureau of Labor Statistics (BLS) survey "Occupational Employment and Wages—May 2012," nearly 7.65 million Americans are employed under the general category "healthcare practitioners and technical occupations," which represents an increase of about 135,000 workers in this category from the year before. This number includes chiropractors, dentists, anesthesiologists, family and general practitioners, obstetricians and gynecologists, physician assistants, podiatrists, respiratory therapists, medical and clinical laboratory technicians, registered nurses, and many others. Subtract the 55,000 veterinarians and there are still nearly 7.6 million people working to maintain or improve human health and vitality. But that's not all. The BLS lists nearly four million additional employees in "healthcare support occupations," such as home health aides, pharmacy aides, medical equipment preparers, physical-therapist aides, dental assistants, and others. Again, take away the veterinary assistants and there are still more than 3.9 million workers in this general category promoting human health.[1] Together, employees in these two general categories constitute about nine percent of American workers.[2]

But wait. There's more! The above figures don't include, for example, approximately 100,000 epidemiologists and other medical scientists, 114,000 rehabilitation counselors, 134,000 healthcare social workers, and over 200,000 postsecondary teachers of nurses and other healthcare professionals. Nor does it include 34,000 medical equipment repairers, more than a quarter million medical and health service managers, and over half a million medical secretaries.[3] In all, healthcare employs more than 11 percent of the American workforce.[4]

This should come as no surprise. CBS News reported in 2010 that health-care spending constituted 17.3 percent of our gross domestic product (GDP) and was rising fast. A report in 2012 by the Georgetown Public Policy Institute of Georgetown University put the figure at 18 percent.[5] If current trends continue, such spending would equal 19.3 percent of GDP by 2019[6] and 20 percent by 2020.[7]

This is good news for employment prospects in healthcare because, in general, when there's an increase in the percentage of GDP going to healthcare, employment prospects in healthcare improve. In 1960, for example, health-care spending constituted only 5.3 percent of GDP[8] and healthcare employed only three percent of American workers.[9] Since that time healthcare has consumed a larger chunk of our GDP and employed more Americans. Healthcare employment increased by an average of 3.8 percent annually between 1990 and 2011 and an additional cumulative increase of 29 percent is expected between 2011 and 2020.[10]

> Nursing will grow the fastest among healthcare occupations, by 26 percent, but that won't be enough to meet the demand. Barring some change, the shortfall will exceed 800,000 jobs, meaning the United States will have to continue to seek nurses outside its borders.
>
> After nursing, healthcare support occupations will grow the second fastest. . . . In particular, the demand for home health aides will grow at a rapid rate, by more than 700,000 positions. Mental health, substance abuse recovery support, and peer to peer support occupations are also expected to grow.[11]

Doctors will be in particularly high demand in the near future if current projections of a doctor shortage are accurate. "The Association of American Medical Colleges estimates that in 2015 the country will have 62,900 fewer doctors than needed. And that number will more than double by 2025," reports the *New York Times*.[12]

The Georgetown University report concludes that when all related jobs are counted—"hospital accountants, information specialists, medical equipment manufacturers, pharmaceutical sales representatives, doctor's office secretaries and the like"—healthcare industry employment will grow from 15.6 million in 2012 to 19.8 million in 2020.[13] Without a doubt, healthcare functions to create and maintain employment in the United States.

Increased healthcare employment and expenditure has also improved our health. Dr. David Brown points out in the *Washington Post*,

> In the 1960s, the chance of dying in the days immediately after a heart attack was 30 to 40 percent. In 1975, it was 27 percent, in 1984, it was 19 percent. In 1994, it was about 10 percent. Today it's about 6 percent. . . . In 1970, the death rate from coronary heart disease was 448 per 100,000 people. In 1980, it was 345. In 1990, it was 250. In 2000, it was 187. In 2006, it was 135. . . . About half the decline since 1980 is a consequence of better medical care.[14]

All in all, life expectancy in the United States improved by 8.3 years between 1960 and 2009, according to a 2011 report of the Organization for Economic Cooperation and Development (OECD).[15] But such improvements have come at a cost, Brown notes. "Over the same period, the charges for treating a heart attack marched steadily upward." Using constant 2007 dollars, treating a heart attack went from $19,500 in 1977 to $54,400 in 2007.[16]

Thus, as healthcare becomes more expensive and consumes an ever larger percentage of GDP, the healthcare industry functions, as intended, to improve human health as well as create jobs for an increasing percentage of the American workforce.

Even so, healthcare in the United States is extraordinarily inefficient. According to the Georgetown University report, in spite of its role in improving human health, "healthcare has experienced one of the lowest levels of productivity growth of all industrial sectors." In fact, the report contends, healthcare productivity actually declined by 0.9 percent per year between 1990 and 2011. This means that output declined in relation to inputs. The report claims that in the overall economy, by contrast, efficiency increased by an average annual rate of 2.2 percent between 1990 and 2011.[17] So healthcare has become less efficient as the overall economy has become more efficient. The report doesn't specify its methodology, but the charge of inefficiency is made also by the Commonwealth Fund in its review of the 2011 edition of the *National Scorecard on U.S. Health System Performance*. The review states, "Performance on indicators of health system efficiency remains especially low, with the U.S. scoring 53 out of 100 on measures that gauge the level of inappropriate, wasteful, or fragmented care; avoidable hospitalizations; variation in quality and costs; administrative costs; and use of information technology."[18]

The well-respected Institute of Medicine came to the same conclusion, claiming that the US healthcare system wastes thirty cents of every dollar spent, amounting to a total of $750 billion dollars in 2009. The report's breakdown includes $210 billion wasted on unnecessary services, such as repeated tests; $130 billion wasted on inappropriate delivery of services, such as services delivered in a hospital setting that could have been performed in a doctor's office; $55 billion wasted owing to insufficient preventive medicine; and $190 billion wasted on unnecessary paperwork and administrative costs.[19]

International comparisons also indicate the fundamental inefficiency of American healthcare. In 2009, for example, we spent $7,980 per capita on healthcare, which was more than twice the average among the forty countries included in an OECD survey, and almost 50 percent more than the second-highest spending country, Norway, which spent $5,352 per capita on healthcare.[20] What is more, in 2009 our healthcare spending was only 17.4 percent of GDP, whereas now, as noted above, it's 18 percent and seems headed toward 20 percent. By contrast, the average among the forty countries in the OECD survey is only 9.5 percent.[21]

Some may consider our high spending on healthcare worthwhile in light of our good results in some areas. In 2009, for example, only three out of thirty-four OECD countries surveyed had lower mortality rates for strokes,[22] and only eight had lower mortality from cancer.[23] However, on some other measures of health the United States fares poorly in international comparisons in spite of our extraordinarily high level of spending. In 2009, for example, twenty-four of the thirty-four OECD countries surveyed had lower mortality than the United States from ischemic heart disease.[24]

We have some of our poorest outcomes on the broadest and arguably most important measures of health. Of the forty countries surveyed by the OECD, thirty had lower rates of infant mortality than we do. Even worse, the decline in infant mortality among Americans between 1970 and 2009, a period of vast increase in healthcare spending in the United States, was less than the decline in thirty-six of the thirty-nine other countries that the OECD surveyed. Only the Russian Federation and India, which are not members of the OECD, had less improvement in infant mortality.

Life expectancy from birth was 78.2 years in the United States in 2009, but this was less than the OECD average of 79.5 years and much less than life expectancy in Israel, Australia, Spain, Italy, Switzerland, and Japan, which ranges from 81.6 years to 83 years.[25] In all, twenty-six of the other thirty-three OECD countries in the survey did better than us, and the only countries that did worse—the Czech Republic, Mexico, Hungary, Poland, the Slovak Republic, Estonia, and Turkey—are markedly poorer and spend on average less than one sixth of what we spend on healthcare.[26]

A different survey, this time of thirty OECD countries conducted in 2008, revealed that life expectancy increased in the United States by 3.1 years between 1986 and 2006. However, every other OECD country in the survey did better. The United States was dead last, suggesting that if trends continue Americans will be dead first.[27]

The United States does poorly also on measures of premature mortality, which is defined as the potential years of life lost (PYLL) when people die before the age of seventy. Potential years of life lost per one hundred thousand American women total 3,555 years. Only three of thirty-four countries surveyed by the OECD do worse—Hungary, Mexico, and the Russian Federation. Among one hundred thousand men, 6,133 years are lost, which is better than only six of the other thirty-three countries in the OECD survey.[28]

Life expectancy at age sixty-five is 17.3 years for American men and 20 years for American women, figures that are near the OECD averages of 17.2 for men and 20.5 for women. However, except for Denmark, the only countries in the OECD survey with lower life expectancy at age sixty-five are countries that are much poorer than the United States, such as Mexico, Hungary, Chile, Brazil, and Poland. And some relatively poor countries do better than we do, including Portugal, Greece, and Slovenia.[29]

In sum, healthcare has improved greatly in the United States over the past fifty years. In addition, it has provided an enormous and increasing number of job opportunities in recent decades and promises to provide even more jobs in the future. It is in both of these respects quite functional. At the same time, however, our healthcare system appears to be extraordinarily inefficient. We spend more than twice what most other developed countries spend on healthcare, both in absolute dollar amounts per capita and as a percentage of GDP, but our results on most measures are poorer than average. We have higher-than-average infant mortality, lower-than-average life expectancy at birth, lower-than-average improvement in life expectancy at birth, higher-than-average premature loss of life, and merely average life expectancy at age sixty-five. What accounts for such poor results from so much spending? What accounts for such inefficiency?

✻   ✻   ✻

My own experience with our healthcare system in 2006 illustrates several aspects of the problem. I'm basically a healthy person who hadn't had a physical exam for about twenty years before I met my wife. Grace thinks it's prudent to see a doctor once a year for a checkup, so I began doing so in 1997. In 2006 the family practice physician whom I'd been seeing for the preceding few years noticed some irregularity in my heartbeat. I couldn't feel it, so I wasn't aware of this irregularity, but she took it very seriously.

Some years earlier I had had irregular heartbeats that I could feel, and I wondered if this meant that I had a serious heart problem. I mentioned the irregularity to a good friend of mine who's a cardiologist. He suggested that I cut down on caffeine, which I did, and the problem was solved. This low-tech approach is characteristic of my friend, whose three rules for good health, stated only partly in jest, are these: (1) Don't go to the doctor; (2) If you do go to the doctor, don't let her put you in the hospital; and (3) If you do go to the hospital, don't let them operate. It was in the spirit of these rules that my earlier irregular heartbeat had been approached. No in-depth, costly, inconvenient, worrisome, and uncomfortable investigation was warranted, in my friend's opinion, because the kind of irregularity I described to him is not life threatening, which means that there was plenty of time to see if a simple life-style change would solve the problem.

This is an efficient approach. I lived and worked in Great Britain for a few semesters and had occasion to consult general practitioners who work for the National Health Service (NHS). Their approach to medical problem solving was similar to my friend's. But here in the United States the family practitioner who found my heartbeat to be irregular reacted entirely differently. She didn't want me to even leave her office before she had given me an electrocardiogram. My charges for the day, January 19, included $198 of lab charges for a blood panel, which I would have had as part of my normal physical, as well as $158 for the electrocardiogram and an additional $375 that I assume had something to do with the exploration of my heart anomaly.

The electrocardiogram and other investigation during my initial visit wasn't enough, however. I was told that I needed to see a specialist. At that point I could feel that I really did have an irregular heartbeat. I don't know for sure if I was just suddenly conscious of the irregularity that my family physician had detected with her stethoscope, or if the news that I had a heart concern that merited consultation with a cardiologist brought on an irregularity that had not existed previously. I suspect the latter, because I'm very suggestible.

In any case, the heart palpitations that I was now conscious of helped to convince me that I needed to see a cardiologist. After consulting with my friend the cardiologist, I went to see his cardiologist, who billed my insurance company $1,529 for work done on January 25. This included $411.00 for an echocardiogram of my heart, $252 for a Doppler echo exam of the heart, and $178 for Doppler color flow. I don't know what other work was done on January 25 to justify the remainder of the $1,529 bill reported to my insurance company.

I had an office visit with my new cardiologist on February 1, which cost $82. I then wore an ECG monitor for 24 hours, as reflected in the charge on February 13 of $855 for a report on its results. I was declared healthy in a letter from the cardiologist also dated February 13. "The results of your Stress Test have been received and reviewed. The results appear to be normal with no evidence of abnormalities." The price of this finding about my heart was already $2,144.

The finding announced in the letter dated February 13 wasn't considered definitive, however. My insurance company was billed $415 for a consultation with my cardiologist on that date. Then, on March 6, I had a battery of additional tests and charges to my insurance company: A stress test whose interpretation cost $435, a tomographic multiple test/read for $1,565, thallium/MCI for 213.60, Cardiolite for $152.70, a wall motion test for $320, and an ejection fraction test for $320. These additional charges add up to $3,421.30.

All but the first of these additional charges were billed by a physician other than my cardiologist, someone I never met.

I still looked perfectly healthy after all these tests and my heartbeat had become regular again, probably abetted by the news in the letter of February 13 that I have a healthy heart. The only anomaly found in all these tests was "mild to moderate aortic valve regurgitation," which was detected in the echocardiogram performed on January 25. This is what most of us call a heart murmur. Because it was mild to moderate, I was told by my cardiologist and by my friend the cardiologist, it should be detectable with a stethoscope. However, neither my family practice doctor nor the cardiologists could hear it. (Coming over for dinner one night, my friend the cardiologist brought his stethoscope to find out if he could hear what the other two physicians couldn't. He said he couldn't hear it either.) Because it couldn't be detected by a stethoscope, I was told, I may have had this condition all my life.

Thinking back, it would have been convenient to know about the heart murmur, if I actually had it when I was young, to avoid military service during the Vietnam War. On the other hand, if I had grown up knowing that I had a heart murmur I may have been discouraged from exercising. I've jogged a lot in my life and have run three marathons, exercise that has helped me to control my weight.

Even though everything looked good, my cardiologist told me that the tests taken might not reflect the true condition of my heart. I should be retested in six months. My insurance company was billed for tests on August 10: echocardiogram and interpretation ($650), Doppler echo test and interpretation ($365), and a Doppler Color flow test and interpretation ($450). I remember asking the echocardiogram technician in August if she could see a heart murmur, and she said that it was very clear, turning the screen toward me and pointing out something on the screen. I had no idea what I was supposed to be seeing and just took her word for it.

The total cost for tests and consultations related to my irregular heartbeat was $7,030.30. But that was the list price. Because my physicians and the associated laboratories were preferred providers for my insurance company, they actually charged the insurance company only about $4,000. They saved $3,000, quite a bargain. I was eventually required to pay out of pocket only $20.12, about one half of one percent of the actual charge.

Two years later a different family physician (my other one had moved away) found in the course of lab work related to my yearly physical exam that a liver enzyme was just outside the normal range. He suggested that I redo the test in three months. Upon hearing this news I had an irregular heart rhythm for three days. I knew enough not to tell the doctor.

✳   ✳   ✳

This story illustrates several sources of inefficiency in the American health-care system exposed by the research of Dr. John Wennberg over the last four decades. A major cause of inefficiency is that physicians make decisions for patients whose "informed consent" is most often ill-informed and automatic. American physicians tend to think that more healthcare is better than less, so no matter how great the supply of physicians, machines, and hospital beds, medical resources will seem inadequate to meet patients' medical needs as physicians perceive those needs. Physicians providing ever more services tend to drive up costs. But more medical care often harms rather than helps patients, which increases costs even more, and patients often don't even want so much medical care when they are fully informed and participate in shared decision making. Let's look at these elements one by one.

Dr. Wennberg shows first that physician belief is often the main deter-minant of healthcare decisions, notwithstanding the requirement of patient informed consent. In theory, when my family practice physician told me that I needed an EKG right there and then during my annual physical exam, I could have refused. No one would have tied me down to do it. But refusal never even occurred to me, and I have taught courses in medical ethics that cover the ethical importance of patients' autonomy and informed consent. Like most people, I assumed that the doctor knew what she was doing, so if she said an EKG was required, then it was required for my good health. I was in her office in the first place because I trusted her judgment about my health, so why would I question the need for an EKG when she told me it was necessary?

For the same reasons, I wouldn't have objected to a more conservative approach either. Upon noting my irregular heartbeat, a more conservative phy-sician would have asked questions designed to determine if I have other symptoms of heart disease. She would have asked, for example, if I run out of breath walking up stairs, if I ever have pain in my chest, and so forth. Upon hearing that I am aware of no symptoms associated with heart disease, the conservative physician would either have dropped the subject of my heart completely, or told me that I had what appears to be a completely benign irregular heartbeat. She would have told me that this is common and most often transient. She might have said that in view of this irregularity I should look out for the kinds of symptoms that she had just asked about and call her should I ever have any of them. In this case, too, I would have done what she recommended.

Dr. Wennberg first documented the overwhelming importance of physician belief for the use of medical resources when, as director of Vermont's Regional Medical Program (RMP), he compared the rates of elective hospitalization and surgery among thirteen different regions in Vermont in the early 1970s. His findings were published in the journal *Science* in 1973.[30] Different regions showed very different patterns of care: "In one region, tonsillectomies would be high, hysterectomies low, nursing home admissions low, and hospitalizations for pneumonia right in the middle. The next region would show a completely different pattern."[31] For example, Wennberg and his family lived in Waterbury Center, where by custom and proximity children received their care from physicians who practiced in the Morrisville hospital service area. Children in a neighboring community who lived within the Stowe school district, by contrast, were usually treated by a different group of physicians at a different hospital. "Among the children living in Waterbury Center, less than 20% received a tonsillectomy by age 15. Had our home been located 1,000 yards farther north, we would have been in the Stowe school district, where by age 15, more than 60% of children had lost their tonsils."[32]

There was no distinction between the populations of these two contiguous districts in race, ethnicity, or socioeconomic level, so Wennberg concluded that physician preference was the determining factor that accounted for a three-fold difference in tonsillectomies. He cites a study in Scotland that found similar differences among surgeons regarding tonsillectomies:

> Surgeons with a high proclivity to operate tended to stress the importance of the physical examination. For example, one surgeon thought that three

physical signs—infected material in the tonsil, reddening anterior pillars, and palpable cervical lymph nodes—were decisive and his rule of thumb was to operate on any child with two or more of these signs. . . . Among surgeons who were less quick to operate, the reverse was the case—much more stress was put on the history. A child who had suffered only the occasional bout of tonsillitis probably would not be a candidate for surgery, no matter how inflamed the tonsils might be on physical examination.[33]

Such differences in physicians' opinions about the need for tonsillectomies, which accounts for variations in per capita surgeries of this type, reflect the lack of medical consensus about this operation at the time of the Vermont study. Tonsillectomy was somewhat discretionary. Inguinal hernia repair, by contrast, wasn't considered optional. There was consensus, at least within the American medical community at the time, that surgery was normally required. Hence, there was little variation between different geographic areas in the per capita performance of this operation.[34]

Wennberg found lack of consensus among Vermont physicians about the need for many different kinds of medical interventions, resulting in very different performance patterns:

> Tonsillectomy rates per 1,000 population varied eleven-fold; hemorrhoidectomy five-fold; and removal of the uterus (hysterectomy) and surgery for an enlarged prostate (transurethral resection of the prostate, or TURP) varied three-fold from the highest to the lowest area. Hospital discharges per 1,000 in the highest area were 61% greater than in the lowest. Rates of hospitalization for broad classes of disease showed much more variation. Hospitalization rates for respiratory diseases, for example, varied 3.6-fold, while vascular diseases varied more than 2.1-fold.[35]

Wennberg is not the only doctor to stress the importance of professional opinion in the determination of treatment when there's a lack of medical consensus about what's appropriate. David Rieff, son of the writer Susan Sontag, writes about his mother's treatment for the cancer that ultimately caused her death. Ms. Sontag wanted to fight the cancer to the end, but most patients aren't so sure. Dr. Stephen Nimer, one of the oncologists who treated Sontag, told Rieff that doctors have almost complete power to influence such patients to accept or reject aggressive treatment when their cancer has progressed to the point that further medical intervention is probably futile. "There are ways to say things," Nimer told Rieff. "'This is your only hope.' Or you could say, 'Some doctors will say it's your only hope, but it has a 20 times better chance of harming you than helping you.' So I'm pretty confident I can persuade people."[36]

Physician opinion may also be the cause of significant differences among hospitals in the percentage of births done by caesarean section. A study released in 2013 found that in 2009 some American hospitals delivered only 7 percent of babies by C-section, whereas others used this method for 70 percent of deliveries. Even among healthy full-term pregnancies, which seldom call for a C-section, some hospitals performed the procedure 2 percent of the time while others did so 36 percent of the time.[37]

Wennberg and Rieff don't suggest that physician inclinations in matters where there is no medical consensus are guided by self-interest. They suggest that physicians tend to act on what they think is best for patients. But they act very differently, and Wennberg has isolated some factors that influence such differences of belief and behavior among physicians.

Supply of medical resources, Wennberg found in his Vermont study and again in his comparison of medical practice in Boston as compared to New Haven, is the main difference between high- and low-use areas:

> Having more hospital beds meant more hospitalizations. . . . Populations living in areas with more surgeons per capita had more surgery at all levels of complexity; areas with more general practitioners who performed surgery had higher rates of less complicated surgery; populations living in hospital service areas with more internists underwent more diagnostic tests, including laboratory tests, x-rays, and electrocardiograms.[38]

This pattern results, Wennberg claims, from the ingrained American belief that more medical intervention is generally better for patients than less. Consider a doctor's decision to hospitalize a patient. There's a dominant cultural bias in favor of hospitalization:

Both doctors and patients assume that the acute hospital setting, with all of its resources and concentrated medical skills, is a better place to deal with sick patients with guarded or uncertain prognoses than are other settings, like the patient's home or even the nursing home, where care is seemingly less organized, and there are fewer physicians and nurses available. Under such an assumption, the availability of beds becomes critical.[39]

Consider physician visits to chronically ill patients. Most people believe that patients benefit from more such visits, so doctors tend to spend the time when they are free from other duties visiting their patients. Where there are more physicians per capita, there are more physician visits per capita because each doctor has fewer patients to visit.[40]

Wennberg rejects the suggestion that physicians order unneeded hospitalizations and make unnecessary visits in order to increase their own incomes. Physicians can't be transgressing scientifically established professional norms in these matters, he claims, because "medical science provides no guidance on what the best practice interval between visits should be or when to hospitalize."[41] Lacking scientific evidence, most physicians assume that patients benefit from more medical services.

This assumption was probably why I was sent to a cardiologist for my irregular heartbeat. If there had been relatively few cardiologists in the area, family practitioners would have been accustomed to a different norm of referral. They wouldn't have referred a patient with a simple irregularity, because they would have assumed that the area's cardiologists could do more good with their very limited time if they worked on more serious cases of heart disease. I would have been spared the inconvenience and anxiety of additional medical tests and the healthcare system would have saved money.

In any case, the assumption that greater attention from the medical community is good for people—the assumption behind what Wennberg calls "supply-sensitive care" that drives up medical bills whenever medical services become increasingly available—is not shared by people in some other countries. Among forty countries surveyed by the OECD, the average number of practicing doctors per one hundred thousand population was 3.1 in 2009, whereas in the United States it was only 2.4.[42] Similarly, the United States had only 3.1 hospital beds per one thousand population, whereas the average among all forty countries was 4.9.[43] Simply having more doctors and hospital beds hasn't generated the level of supply-sensitive care in other countries that we have in the United States. Nevertheless, Wennberg's contention that supply creates use and cost in the *American* healthcare system is amply documented.

But the assumption behind this dynamic—that people are generally better off when they have more healthcare—is not supported by evidence. For example, Wennberg followed patients for up to three years who had been hospitalized in Boston and New Haven for heart attack, stroke, hip fracture, cancer, and intestinal bleeding. He found that in Boston, where there was a much larger supply of doctors and hospital beds per capita than in New Haven, patients with these conditions were readmitted to the hospital 60 percent more on a per capita basis than in New Haven. But the Boston patients did no better than those in New Haven. "The overall mortality for the cohorts during the entire period of follow-up was essentially the same in the two cities." Wennberg concludes, "The variation in supply-sensitive care appeared to be a case of overuse in Boston, not rationing in New Haven."[44]

Prostate surgery is another case in point. Many men over fifty have an enlarged prostate—benign prostatic hyperplasia or BPH. An enlarged prostate tends to restrict urine flow, which urologists assume impairs patients' quality of life by making it more difficult to pee. BPH can even obstruct urine flow completely, which is not only painful but dangerous and requires immediate medical intervention. In the 1970s many urologists believed that improving urine flow and heading off complete obstruction through removal of the prostate during an early stage of BPH was indicated for men whose rate of urine flow was below a certain threshold.

But prostatectomy carried a greater risk of death than many urologists recognized and was often accompanied by other outcomes that most patients wish to avoid. Postoperative mortality was estimated in 1975 to be less than 1 percent, whereas it actually turned out that "in Maine, 4.7% of Medicare patients 65 years of age and older were dead within three months of their prostatectomy. . . . Mortality reached 35% by six months for men who resided in nursing homes before their operation." These deaths may not have been caused by the prostatectomy, but they undermine the principal rationales for the operation, which were to improve patients' quality of life and head off the possibility of complete obstruction of urine flow at some later time. Wennberg notes, "In the months following the operation, quality of life is low because of the short-term effects of the surgery, so men who die so soon after surgery gain very little, if anything."[45] Among those who lived longer, a record of postoperative complications undermines claims of benefit to quality of life. Medicare data from Maine showed,

> Over a four-year period after surgery, 13% of surgery patients experienced a scarring (stricture) of the urethra that required treatment—sometimes additional surgery; 20% of men underwent further diagnostic workups, usually involving having a cystoscope inserted into the urethra; and 10% had a second prostatectomy. At the end of four years, only 52% of patients having a prostatectomy were still alive and free from one or more of the postoperative complications just listed.[46]

In the 1980s the Maine Urology Study Group found that prostatectomy, which had been justified in large part by its role in preventing death, actually reduces life expectancy: "*No matter what the age or illness level of the patient at the time of surgery, the chances of death from the surgery was not made up for by gains in life expectancy among those who survived the operation.*"[47]

The same results were found concerning treatments of many types near the end of life. Aggressive treatment does not tend to prolong life. Studies of Medicare expenditures during the last six months of life showed greater mortality among patients in high-spending regions, according to Wennberg's report on patients with hip fracture, colon cancer resection, and heart attack. "Compared to the lowest 20% of regions in per capita spending, survival in the regions ranking in the top 20% was worse: mortality for patients who had hip fractures was 1.9% higher; and for colon cancer and heart attack patients, it was 5.2% higher."[48]

What would account for these results? Why would more healthcare result in poorer outcomes? Sometimes unnecessary medical tests can increase the incidence of disease. Drs. Rita Redberg and Rebecca Smith-Bindman point out in the *New York Times* that "a single CT scan exposes a patient to the amount of radiation that epidemiological evidence shows can be cancer-causing. . . . A 2009 study from the National Cancer Institute estimates that CT scans conducted in 2007 will cause a projected 29,000 excess cancer cases and 14,500 excess deaths over the lifetime of those exposed." Yet, Drs. Redberg and Smith-Bindman note, "emergency room physicians routinely order multiple CT scans even before meeting a patient. Such practices, for which there is little or no evidence of benefit," they write, "should be eliminated."[49]

Dr. Sanjay Gupta, a neurosurgeon and correspondent for CNN, explains that a major factor is the incidence of mistakes in medical settings. "Each additional procedure or test, no matter how cautiously performed, injects a fresh possibility of error. CT and M.R.I. scans can lead to false positives and unnecessary operations, which carry the risk of complications like infections and bleeding."[50] Dr. Gilbert Welch notes that false positives in most cancer screenings vary from five to fifteen percent. A false positive for brain cancer, for example, which may happen easily owing to the appearance of a small mass on a brain scan, would typically lead to a biopsy. "The surgeon has to drill a hole through your skull and use a very fine needle to take a piece of the mass."[51] The potential for mishap is obvious. "Even routine operations like gallbladder removals," Gupta adds, "require anesthesia, which can increase the risk of heart attack and stroke."[52]

Common medications can injure people as well. Several times when I've had a cold, which my physician said was most likely a virus, I was offered an antibiotic even though antibiotics have no effect on such viral infections. The offer, which I declined, was made just in case the cold was actually caused by bacteria susceptible to antibiotics. But antibiotics can be dangerous, Gupta points out. "The more medications patients are prescribed, the more likely they are to accidentally overdose or suffer an allergic reaction."[53] He gives the example of a woman who had only a mild viral illness, but was prescribed an (ineffective) antibiotic to which she had a life-threatening reaction. "She developed joint pain and blisters on her chest and arms. . . . She ended up with sepsis, a bodywide infection, and spent two weeks in intensive care."

That patient survived, but many others have not. A 1999 report by the Institute of Medicine found that as many as ninety-eight thousand Americans die every year as a result of medical mistakes. Since that time, Gupta reports, "the percentage of doctor visits leading to at least five drugs being prescribed has nearly tripled, and the number of M.R.I. scans quadrupled." Partly as a result of this and other such increases, "a reasonable estimate is that medical mistakes kill around 200,000 Americans every year."[54]

In sum, beyond a certain point, which has long been passed by Americans with health insurance, increased medical attention is harmful to your health. Physicians are being encouraged for this reason to reduce healthcare interventions. One form of persuasion is to conduct clinical trials that show interventions to be useless or worse. For example, a study that was reported in July 2012 followed men with early-stage prostate cancer for fifteen years and found that those randomly assigned to no treatment (watchful waiting) did just as well as those whose prostates were removed. Anticipating the report of these results, in May 2012 the United States Preventive Services Task Force recommended that men no longer be tested for the prostate specific antigen (PSA) which signals the existence of early-stage prostate cancer, believing that the test puts men at risk of expensive, onerous, and dangerous interventions that tend to do more harm than good.[55] For the same reasons the task force also recommended against routine screening for ovarian cancer.[56] Already in April 2012 several panels of physicians made the same recommendation concerning forty-five medical tests and interventions, Roni Caryn Rabin writes in the *New York Times*:

> The list of tests and procedures they advise against includes EKGs done routinely during a physical, even when there is no sign of heart trouble, M.R.I.'s ordered whenever a patient complains of back pain, and antibiotics prescribed for mild sinusitis—all quite common.
>
> The American College of Cardiology is urging heart specialists not to perform routine stress cardiac imaging in asymptomatic patients, and the American College of Radiology is telling radiologists not to run imaging scans on patients suffering from simple headaches. . . .
>
> Even oncologists are being urged to cut back on scans for patients with early stage breast and prostate cancers that are not likely to spread.[57]

Peggy Orenstein reports in the *New York Times Magazine* that routine mammograms for women under fifty may do more harm than good and that for women over fifty the test should be performed every other year, not annually. For women in their forties, the screening reduces the risk of dying from breast cancer from .35 percent to .3 percent, a difference of one twentieth of one percent. On the other side, Orenstein writes, "for every 2,000 women screened annually over 10 years, one life is prolonged but 10 healthy women are given diagnoses of breast cancer and unnecessarily treated, often with therapies that themselves have life-threatening side effects."[58]

More recently, reports Jane Brody in the *New York Times*, some gynecologists are recommending against routine pelvic exams for apparently healthy women. The benefit "is not supported by medical evidence, increases the cost of medical care and discourages some women, especially adolescents, from seeing doctors. Moreover, the exam sometimes reveals benign conditions that lead to follow-up procedures, including surgery, that do not improve health but instead cause anxiety, lost time from work, potential complications and unnecessary costs."[59]

Not only the pelvic exam, but the entire annual physical for apparently healthy people seems to provide no medical benefit (and in my case as in many others leads to unnecessary anxiety, tests, and expense). Currently, about 44.4 million adults in the United States have such physical exams. If all adults did so, claims Dr. Ateev Mehrotra of the University of Pittsburgh School of Medicine, the result would be 145 million more such exams each year, consuming 41 percent of the time that primary care physicians have at their disposal to meet with patients. The annual physical would crowd out more productive doctor/patient interactions, like those that take place when people are actually sick.[60]

Guidelines such as these are designed to reduce inefficiency in the American healthcare system. Rabin reports, "Some experts estimate that up to one-third of the $2 trillion of annual health care costs in the United States each year is spent on unnecessary hospitalizations and tests, unproven treatments, ineffective new drugs and medical devices, and futile care at the end of life."[61] It's obviously inefficient to spend hundreds of billions of dollars on tests and procedures that do more harm than good, and by 2013 our nation's total healthcare bill was reported to be $2.7 trillion, not just $2 trillion.[62]

✳   ✳   ✳

In our society, however, efficiency is most often judged by consumer reactions to goods and services available in the marketplace. We tend to assume that if customers are getting what they want, their freely incurred expenditures are efficient, so long as they aren't subsidized, aren't hurting other people, and aren't degrading such public goods as clean air and water.

But healthcare is highly subsidized, which undermines the claim that healthcare in the United States must be efficient because it responds to consumer preferences. The vast majority of medical and surgical expenses in the United States are covered by some form of insurance. While customers at hardware stores pay for rakes as a condition of owning them, few patients in hospitals or clinics pay for medical services as a condition of receiving them. As already noted, of the approximately $4,000 that my insurance company was ultimately billed to determine that I have a healthy heart, I paid only $20.12. This is typical.

Amanda Bennett, executive editor at Bloomberg News, recounts in *The Cost of Hope* her husband Terence Foley's ultimately unsuccessful attempts to avoid death from cancer. Terence's initial surgery cost $25,000, but Terence and Amanda paid only $209.87. She writes, "The rest was covered by insurance—in reality by my employer, who footed the bill. Looking back, I find it astounding how little we knew both about the surgery itself, and about how much it cost."[63]

That surgery, and the accompanying treatments were successful insofar as Terence lived several more years, most of them in reasonably good health. But even watchful waiting during those years was quite expensive. Every three or four months Terrence and Amanda would go the Cleveland Clinic for Terence to have tests. "Three years, eight visits, from $4,500 to more than $5,300 each. That's more than $36,000 during a time when we were simply watching and waiting."[64] Because insurance covered almost all of this cost, Amanda was hardly aware of it.

When Terence had a relapse of cancer, he wanted everything done to try to save his life. So they tried Interleukin-2 (IL-2) even though his doctors realized, as Amanda put it later, "there most likely was zero chance that the painful and awful experience of taking IL-2 would have done him any good at all."[65] Such painful and futile efforts at the end of life are unfortunately common, in part because doctors tend to be overly optimistic about the possibility that treatments will benefit their cancer patients. According to a study published in 2000 in the British medical journal *BMJ*, two thirds of doctors overestimate the possibility of a cure. A subsequent study published the following year in the *Annals of Internal Medicine* found that doctors were honest with their patients about extremely poor prognoses only 37 percent of the time. Failure to communicate poor prognoses combines with subsidized healthcare to yield treatment that is painful, futile, and expensive.[66]

Amanda Bennett reflects at the end of her book,

> What if Terence and I were able to see more clearly some of the costs of the procedure? Would we have been able to make wiser choices? Less expensive choices? Even choices that might have made better sense for us?
>
> I believe we would have forgone the painful and ineffective IL-2 treatments because we would have had to think harder about it. As long as it was free—which it was, to us—Terence almost had to seize on even the tiniest possibility that it could help.
>
> And if there were a system in which we could see the prices for the scans—would Terence have had seventy-six of them? Was each and every one of them equally necessary to his care? Were some of them even harmful?[67]

In sum, Terence Foley's care illustrates what we all know. Healthcare costs are paid mostly by third parties, insurance companies and taxpayers, not directly by those receiving the services. This is the kind of subsidy that undermines claims that our healthcare system must be efficient because it is delivering care that people want. As we saw in the last chapter concerning transportation, giving people what they want is no sign of economic efficiency when people don't have to pay for what they're getting. Inadequate information reduces efficiency further.

But that's not all. Inefficiency in the American healthcare system is even worse than this. We saw earlier that the plethora of tests, medications, and procedures that Americans receive, contrary to expectation, tends to jeopardize rather than further their health. Equally surprising, Americans receive a lot of healthcare that they don't even want.

Consider, for example, hip replacement, an elective surgery studied in

Ontario, Canada, by Gillian Hawker and her colleagues. Hawker found that even in regions where per capita hip replacement surgeries were performed most frequently, more people were eligible for them than actually got them. This suggested that inadequate supply was depriving people of hip replacements that they needed. Hawker decided, however, to ask patients identified by clinical criteria as needing the operation if they actually wanted it. The overwhelming majority did not. Wennberg reports, "Only *14.9% of the patients in the high-rate region and only 8.5% in the low-rate region who were eligible for surgery, according to evidence-based clinical guidelines, actually wanted surgery.* This means that given the current stage in the evolution of their clinical problem, between 86% and 91% preferred medical management." Thus, "surgery rates in Canada were close to meeting need, *if only those who wanted surgery were the ones who actually got it.*"[68]

Studies of patient preferences regarding prostate surgery reached similar conclusions. Surgery is recommended for people with BPH who suffer from slow urination. The goal is to make it easier for them to pee, not to save their lives. And studies show that the operation does improve urine flow dramatically. However, men varied greatly in how disturbed they were by impaired urine flow in the first place. A study in Maine found, "There was virtually no correlation between objective clinical measures like urine flow and how greatly men were bothered by their symptoms."[69] So improved urine flow was not always perceived by patients as an important benefit. And one side effect, which most surgeons considered a normal outcome of surgery, bothered many patients a great deal. This is retrograde ejaculation, a condition in which ejaculation goes into the bladder instead of out of the penis. In sum, lack of interest in reducing their symptoms and distaste for a common side effect suggest that many patients for whom the operation was a success failed to have the improvement in quality of life that surgeons expected.

One way to determine if patients are getting what they really want is to educate them about their ailment, the procedure, and their role in medical decision making. For this purpose Wennberg and his colleagues developed what they call decision aids. Rather than rely on patients' informed consent after physicians make recommendations for elective surgery, the decision aid typically includes an informative video that explains the pros and cons of an elective procedure, including some relevant statistics. The video includes discussion of the issue by physicians who favor aggressive treatment and by those who oppose it. Awareness that there are differences of opinion in the medical community seems to empower patients to use information in the video to make independent decisions about their treatment that reflect their own values. For example, surgery for early-stage prostate cancer is not reliably associated with longer life because most prostate cancers grow so slowly that patients die of some other condition before the prostate cancer becomes lethal. Among patients who saw the video on this subject, 93 percent correctly answered a question on this matter and only 50 percent wanted to be screened for prostate cancer. Among a control group that had not seen the video, only 41 percent answered correctly and 97 percent wanted to be screened for prostate cancer.[70]

Wennberg writes, "A recent Cochrane review of randomized clinical trials comparing shared decision making . . . to obtaining informed consent through usual care showed an average 24% decline in demand for a wide range of elective surgeries and tests." These include treatment for chronic cholecystitis and silent gallstones, chronic stable angina (chest pain or other symptoms from coronary artery disease); hip and knee osteoarthritis; carotid stenosis (stroke risk from narrowing of the carotid artery); herniated disc or spinal stenosis (causing back pain or other symptoms); early-stage prostate cancer; early-stage breast cancer; and BPH.[71] Watchful waiting and other conservative forms of treatment that statistically produce equal or better clinical outcomes than elective surgery are often preferred by patients.

These results suggest that reliance on physicians' clinical judgment followed by patients' pro-forma informed consent is quite inefficient when compared to shared decision making with fully informed patients. Wennberg writes, "From a financial standpoint, an expected net reduction in utilization in the range of 25% would result in annual Medicare savings of $4 billion or more (in 2006 dollars) for the procedures listed" above.[72] It's inefficient to subject patients to operations and other procedures that, when fully informed, they reject.

Even more savings could be realized through shared decision making in end-of-life care. Studies show that most patients who express a wish to die at home die instead in the hospital, often in expensive intensive care units.[73] This occurs most often in regions with the greatest number of physicians (especially specialists) and hospital beds per capita. The use of aggressive forms of treatment as the standard of care in a region, abetted by a large supply of medical resources, carries over into aggressive end-of-life treatment regardless of patient wishes.

High spending doesn't improve patient satisfaction, either. "For example," Wennberg writes, "63% of respondents living in regions where Medicare spent the least gave their care a high rating (a score of 9 or 10), compared with 55% of those living where Medicare spent the most."[74] Nor does the per capita greater number of physicians in general and specialists in particular in high-spending regions reduce wait times to see a physician or ameliorate in any way the perception of a physician shortage.[75] Wennberg concludes that there is no physician shortage in the United States and that "we already have more than enough physicians to meet the needs of the aging Baby Boomer generation and any increase in need that may occur from insurance reforms that enfranchise the uninsured."[76] Our healthcare inefficiency stems largely from the erroneous belief that more medical treatment is preferred by and helpful to patients, which has led us to train more physicians, build more hospitals, and spend more money than actually promotes human health. Greater efficiency—better outcomes and enormous savings—would result from more conservative uses of medical resources.

But greater efficiency threatens incomes and jobs. Wennberg reports on the experience of the Intermountain Healthcare system in western Utah and southeastern Idaho. Using teams of medical professionals organized around the overall care of patients, Intermountain was able to lower the cost of managing chronic illness. "As their practice patterns became more efficient, fewer specialty services were needed; as care improved, hospitalization rates fell. . . . The net effect was a squeeze on revenue."[77] Fewer physicians and other hospital personnel are needed when healthcare is more efficient. Inefficiency functions to create and maintain jobs.

The economy-impairing effects of increased efficiency in healthcare were felt at the national level in 2014. In June of that year the Commerce Department revised downward its estimate of economic activity in the first quarter, determining that the economy contracted in that quarter by 2.9 percent. In addition to cold winter weather, the main culprit responsible for economic decline was reduced spending on healthcare resulting from improved efficiency as the Affordable Care Act was being implemented.[78] Again, inefficiency in healthcare has been responsible for some of our economic growth, so improved efficiency, other things being equal, results in economic decline.

Amanda Bennett was keenly aware of the jobs created at two of the hospitals where her husband was treated:

> Despite their sprawling size, neither hospital is huge, as hospitals go. Yet together they provide the livelihood for 7,648 people . . . , people who come to work here every day, park in the lots, eat lunch in the cafeterias, exchange small gifts at holiday sing-alongs. Each of the patients who sleeps here each night after gallbladders are removed, lumps excised, broken bones set, and new children ushered into the world helps 7.6 other people raise their families, pay their mortgages, and visit Walt Disney World. And they're just a microcosm of the millions of people around the country doing pretty much the same thing day in and day out. Checking blood pressure. Looking into eyes and ears. Taking blood.[79]

*   *   *

Another reason for the high cost of healthcare in the United States is the successful marketing of diseases by large drug companies holding patents on pharmaceuticals designed to combat those diseases. Inefficiency caused by such disease mongering will be explored in the next chapter in connection with the functional inefficiency of consumerism. Here we discuss drug-company-induced inefficiency only as it relates to the unusually high cost of drugs in the United States.

Drug companies keep their profits and our health bills high in part by marketing new drugs that enjoy patent protection when their older, equally effective drugs lose that protection. The older drugs can be manufactured by other makers at lower cost, eating into corporate profits, so the big pharmaceutical companies market the new drugs as superior even when they are not. Journalist Melody Petersen writes,

> The introduction of products like Clarinex, Lexapro, and Nexium followed a pattern. The government approved them, and the first boxes left the loading docks just months before the patent protecting the company's older product

expired. . . . Scientists who were independent from the makers of these drugs published reports saying they could find no evidence that the new products were better than the old. The independent scientists urged patients to save money by taking the generic, but their advice was drowned out by the din of the new advertising campaigns.[80]

Drug companies keep profits high also by increasing their prices much more rapidly than the general rate of inflation. For example, between 2008 and 2009, when there was no general inflation at all because we were in the midst of the Great Recession, drug companies increased the wholesale prices of prescription drugs an average of nine percent, raising to more than $2,000 the average cost of prescription medications that are taken daily.[81] Makers of generic drugs do the same thing when competition is lacking. For example, between 2008 and 2012, a prescription cream to relieve itching went from $18.17 a tube to $71.28 for the same tube. Another prescription cream, this one to kill scabies mites, went from $29.25 in 2008 to $71.08 in 2012. Profits soared at companies that make these drugs, one reporting an increased profit of 84 percent between 2011 and 2012, while another reported an increased profit of 76 percent during the same period. It's therefore no wonder that a pharmacy-benefits manager found that in the first five months of 2012 total spending on prescription dermatology medication increased 18.2 percent over the same period the previous year.[82]

When patents protect drug companies from competition and life is at stake, the cost of drugs can inflate enormously. Petersen reports,

In 2006 a drug called Avastin could cost cancer patients as much as $100,000 a year, depending on the dose and type of cancer. When doctors added a medicine called Erbitux to the standard chemotherapy regime for patients with advanced colon cancer, the cost of treatment rose to as much as $250,000. For patients with a rare disorder called Gaucher's disease, the needed drug, Cerezyme, could cost more than $600,000 a year.[83]

Worse yet, these very expensive drugs are often of little help. Studies showed that when Avastin was given to colon cancer patients at a dose that cost $50,000 a year, survival increased a total of only five months.[84] Yet nearly

70 percent of patients with colon cancer were taking Avastin within a year of its release in 2004.[85] Tarceva, a drug that costs $2,000 a month, extended the lives of patients with pancreatic cancer an average of only twelve days.[86] In all, Americans spent more than $23 billion in 2011 for drugs to treat cancer,[87] much of which provided little benefit.

Americans pay much more for these and other drugs than people pay in Canada and other countries, ABC News reported in 2011. For example, Celexa, prescribed for depression, costs $253 in the United States, but only $149 in Canada. Mirapex, prescribed for Parkinson's disease, costs $263 in the United States, but only $157 in Canada. Diovan, prescribed for high blood pressure, costs $253 in the United States but only $149 in Canada, and two prescription drugs for a range of mental health difficulties, oxazapam and Seroquel, cost only $13 and $33 respectively in Canada, whereas they cost $70 and $124 dollars here. The cancer drug Campath costs $2,400 in the United States, whereas the same drug sells for $720 in France, $660 in Sweden, $570 in Britain, and $500 in Italy. These differences reflect the fact that, unlike the United States, all of these other countries impose price controls on prescription drugs.[88]

The willingness within the United States to pay unusually high prices for drugs is a major element of inefficiency—high healthcare costs compared to benefits—in our healthcare system. This inefficiency results also in impressive pharmaceutical company profits. In 2011, Pfizer made more than $10 billion in profit, Johnson & Johnson $9.6 billion and Merck more than $6.2 billion. Such profits can't be justified as being needed to develop new drugs because in 1999 when the current class of drugs was being developed, Pfizer spent 17.1 percent of its income on R&D, while it spent 39.2 percent on marketing and administration. Johnson & Johnson spent 9.5 percent of its income on R&D and 38.2 percent on marketing and administration. Merck spent only 6.3 percent on R&D and 15.9 percent on marketing and administration.[89]

Drugs are not the only treatments for which Americans pay more than people in other countries. For example, an angiogram costs on average $914 in the United States, but only $35 in Canada; a colonoscopy averages $1,185 here, but only $655 in Switzerland; a hip replacement that goes for $40,364 in the United States costs only $7,731 in Spain and about $10,000 in Switzerland and France; C-sections cost three times as much in the United States as in

New Zealand and Great Britain; and an MRI scan for which Americans pay $1,121 cost people in the Netherlands only $319.[90]

Again, the high cost of American healthcare is a case of functional inefficiency. Just as unneeded tests, hospitalizations, and procedures keep people working, high prices allow more people to be employed in marketing, administration, customer relations, and a host of other jobs.

*   *   *

Health insurance is another area of functional inefficiency in our healthcare system. The United States relies much more than other advanced industrial countries on private for-profit health insurance to pay for medical care for the non-elderly. About 20 percent of what people pay to our health insurance companies goes for administrative costs and corporate profits; only 80 percent is spent on actual healthcare. The government-run Medicare system for the elderly, by contrast, spends only three percent on administrative costs; so 97 percent of its revenue pays for actual healthcare. Canada's single-payer healthcare system also spends about three percent on administrative costs, while the British National Health Service spends about five percent.[91] The Commonwealth Fund estimates that the United States could save $114 billion a year in healthcare costs merely by lowering its insurance administrative costs to the level common in countries such as Canada and Britain.[92]

Much of the private insurance coverage among Americans comes through their employers, which creates a lot of employment in business administration. According to the Bureau of Labor Statistics, there were in 2012 19,960 people employed as "compensation and benefits managers," the people in private companies whose tasks include managing health coverage for employees.[93] Some of the work of half a million medical secretaries in the United States is devoted to dealing with insurance issues, and much of the work of more than 218,000 insurance claims and policy processing clerks relates to medical insurance.

Because for-profit insurance companies avoid an expense whenever they can deny a claim, it's generally in the interest of these companies and their shareholders to spend money to deny claims so long as they save more money on the denials than they spend on administrative and legal costs defending them. This creates lots of work for lawyers, legal secretaries, and others in the fields of medical administration and adjudication.

One of the most inefficiency-inducing aspects of our private for-profit insurance system is the disincentive inherent in the system to fund preventive medicine. Advocates of the system claim that when people are free to choose their health insurers and the health insurers try to maximize profit, insurers will try to attract customers by improving their efficiency and their offerings to provide the best possible insurance coverage at the lowest possible price. The result will be low-cost health insurance that provides the necessary financial underpinning of medical and surgical care that keeps the American population as healthy as possible.

This reasoning is flawed. The private, for-profit insurance model encourages people to shop around for insurance to get the best deal. So people—more often the companies that employ them, as employers still provide most private health insurance—change insurers from time to time to get a better deal. As a result, on average, people change insurance companies once every six years.[94] Insurance companies therefore have little incentive to provide care designed to prevent chronic illnesses that won't appear for several years. By the time the illness arrives, the patient will probably be insured by a different company, or be old enough to qualify for Medicare.

This is one reason for the increase in type 2 diabetes in the United States, writes Ian Urbina in the *New York Times*. This disease, which comprises 90 to 95 percent of all diabetes, builds over time and is "linked to obesity and inactivity, as well as to heredity." Insurers often won't pay for preventive measures, because by the time significant medical intervention is required, the patient will probably be insured by someone else:

> Insurers, for example, will often refuse to pay $150 for a diabetic to see a podiatrist, who can help prevent foot ailments associated with the disease. Nearly all of them, though, cover amputations, which typically cost more than $30,000.
>
> Patients have trouble securing a reimbursement for a $75 visit to the nutritionist who councils them on controlling their diabetes. Insurers do not balk, however, at paying $315 for a single session of dialysis, which treats one of the disease's serious complications.[95]

Obesity is implicated in many forms of heart disease and cancer, so the failure of private insurance companies to cover measures designed to prevent or reduce obesity helps to explain why the American healthcare system is so inefficient. It helps to explain why we have poor health relative to the amount of money we spend on healthcare; why most other OECD countries spend much less and have better healthcare result.

Although private insurance companies promote inefficiency by failing to provide adequate coverage for preventive measures, even greater inefficiency results when people have no health insurance at all. Susan Sered and Rushika Fernandopulle write in *Uninsured in America*, "Americans without health insurance rarely go to the doctor for a checkup, rarely receive ongoing supervision of chronic problems, and rarely get treatment until pain becomes unbearable or intractable complications set in." As a result,

> small tumors may be left untreated until they become big and metastasize. Diabetes is not managed properly, leading to amputations, and end-stage renal failure, and expensive dialysis treatments. Asthma goes untreated until the individual ends up unable to breathe, turning blue in the emergency room. Hypertension progresses until it becomes a completely disabling disease, preventing the individual from working, bladder infections become kidney infections, and earaches become the source of hearing loss.[96]

When health problems get critical, however, we intervene. "In a bizarre economic and ethical twist," write Sered and Fernandopulle, "the chronically ill, if they are uninsured, are allowed to deteriorate to the point at which hospitals are legally required to take them in. They are covered if they have terminal cancer or renal failure, but not before."[97] Their end-of-life care, which begins in expensive emergency rooms and often ends in much more expensive intensive care units, does little for the quality or the length of their lives. It's futile inefficiency.

The Affordable Care Act (2010) is reducing significantly the number of people without health insurance in the United States, but many uninsured will remain. According to the Congressional Budget Office (CBO), there were about 53 million uninsured Americans in 2012, a number that would have increased to about 60 million by 2022 if the Supreme Court had overturned key provisions of the law. Because the court upheld those provisions, the CBO projects the uninsured to be 30 million in 2022.[98] That's still a large number given the enormous inefficiencies associated with lack of health insurance.

❋   ❋   ❋

In conclusion, the American healthcare system is extraordinarily inefficient, but that inefficiency functions to support many jobs and increase some corporate profits. We saw that employment in healthcare as a percentage of the American workforce increases as healthcare consumes a larger percentage of the American GDP. Imagine, then, the negative impact on employment if the current level of 18 percent of GDP were lowered to 12, which is still high by international standards. All other things being equal, about one-third of healthcare jobs would disappear. Since more than fifteen million people are currently employed in healthcare, this implies a loss of five million healthcare jobs if the US healthcare system were to become as efficient as systems that produce equal or better healthcare outcomes.

The actual net loss of jobs in the country would be less because the current level of public spending on healthcare reduces state spending on education and other public services.[99] Such reduced state spending costs jobs among teachers, police, and other public servants. Many of those jobs would be restored if states spent less on healthcare. Even so, the overall jobs picture would be much worse if healthcare were suddenly to become efficient in the United States.

Healthcare examined here and transportation examined in the preceding chapter are not the only areas of inefficiency that help to create employment in the United States. The ethanol program, for example, funds inefficient methods of energy production that function primarily to provide increased employment and profits in agriculture and grain processing.[100] Many defense programs are better designed to create jobs in the congressional districts of influential politicians than to defend the country. But details about these cases are unnecessary, as this chapter and chapter 6 illustrate and document the point well enough. Inefficient systems of providing necessary goods and services are one way that we fight unemployment in the United States.

Another way is to increase domestic consumption generally, which we turn to next.

CHAPTER 8
CONSUMERISM AND INDIVIDUAL DISCONTENT

"Why is unemployment so high?" asked David Leonhardt, the Economic Scene correspondent for the *New York Times*.[1] The answer he gave in 2011 was that consumers weren't spending enough money. The auto industry that year was on track to sell 28 percent fewer vehicles than in 2001, which was a year of recession. Oven and stove sales were expected to be lower than any year since 1992. The rate of discretionary service spending was also down. This is "a category that excludes housing, food and health care and includes restaurant meals, entertainment, education . . . and insurance." In past recessions the rate of discretionary service spending dipped only about three percent, but it was down seven percent in the wake of the Great Recession of 2008–2009. The result was continued unemployment. Leonhardt explains, "Business executives are only rational to hold back on hiring if they do not know when their customers will fully return."[2]

After previous recessions customers returned by borrowing money to spend on consumer items. The economic stimulus provided by such consumer spending furthered economic recovery and lowered unemployment. But the economic crisis of 2008 was based largely on overextension of debt. People bought houses by incurring mortgage payments that they couldn't afford and consumer items with credit cards that were now maxed out. With lending rules tightened and houses losing value, consumers could no longer increase their spending with new credit cards or home equity loans. Instead, they started to rebuild their credit ratings by paying down their debt and replenishing their depleted savings. This was prudent planning on their part, but impaired economic recovery and job growth.

The great twentieth-century economist John Maynard Keynes called this problem "the paradox of thrift." It's sensible for each individual and family to save when they have little money and the economic climate is uncertain. But what's rational and helpful for the individual is harmful for the economy as a whole, because the reduction in consumer demand that results from increased savings impairs economic growth and thereby perpetuates the dismal conditions that prompted saving in the first place. Because consumer spending constitutes about 70 percent of our gross domestic product (GDP),[3] its reduction impairs economic growth, job creation, and the reduction of unemployment.[4] This chapter and chapters 9 and 13 look at the possibility of increasing consumer spending so as to spur economic growth and reduce unemployment.

This is not a new idea. In the mid-1950s, marketing consultant Victor Lebow explained the importance of increased consumer spending in a modern economy:

> Our enormously productive economy demands that we make consumption our way of life, that we convert the buying and use of goods into rituals, that we seek our spiritual satisfactions, our ego satisfactions, in consumption. The measure of social status, of social acceptance, of prestige, is now to be found in our consumptive patterns. The very meaning and significance of our lives today express in consumptive terms. The greater the pressures upon the individual to conform to safe and accepted social standards, the more does he tend to express his aspirations and his individuality in terms of what he wears, drives, eats, his home, his car, his pattern of food serving, his hobbies.[5]

Lebow is here advocating not just consumption, or increased consumption, but *consumerism*, which is *the centering of life and its meaning around consumption*. Buying a new refrigerator is merely consumption if the old one broke down and the purchaser is just trying to keep food fresh with a new refrigerator of adequate size with convenient features that fits her kitchen decor. Buying a new refrigerator is an act of consumerism when discontent with the old refrigerator concerns not so much its functioning as its age and dated aspects of its design; when the purchaser's sense of self-worth is tied intimately to the social prestige associated with the model of refrigerator purchased; when gainful employment is considered primarily as a means of gaining money for an unending series of such purchases that are valued as much or more for their symbolic value as for their functions and esthetic features; and when it's common for people to strain their budgets or go into debt rather than forego such purchases.

The difference between consumption and consumerism can be seen in different reactions to money-making opportunities. CBS News correspondent Lara Logan reported that an ice-cream parlor in Paris closes for six weeks during the summer when the weather his hot, tourists are abundant, business would be brisk, and profits could be high. Yet the French owner, apparently without complaint from employees, closes the shop so everyone can take the kind of vacation that is now typical and expected in France. When Logan expressed surprise that the owner and workers would willingly forego so much income, a French editor at the journal *Le Figaro* whom Logan was interviewing replied, "The big difference is money, the place of money in your life."[6] The French enjoy many consumer items made available through industrialization, but they aren't as consumerist as Americans.

In the United States the owner and employees of such an ice-cream parlor would explain to their families that it's just the nature of their job to be working while others are on vacation, and that by doing so the family can purchase all kinds of goods and services that they otherwise wouldn't be able to afford. It would be taken for granted that buying more goods and services is more important in life than a vacation that coincides with other people's vacations. So, even though the French consume goods and services similar to those consumed in the United States, the place of consumption in their lives is different from its place in the lives of most Americans. The French are less likely to derive their sense of self-worth from their purchases, nor are they as likely to become discontented with items simply because they are no long new. Hence, they need less money and can prioritize a vacation over making a killing at the ice-cream parlor during hot weather. Consumerist Americans, by contrast, tend more to value what money can buy because buying things is considered the key to the good life. It's in this sense that we're a *consumer society*; a society with a *consumer culture*; a society where consumerism takes center stage. Only in such a society would anyone joke: "Who dies with the most toys wins."

Consumerism keeps Americans working in two ways. First, it gives workers a motive to work more rather than less because in their consumer role they want to buy more than they can currently afford. Second, consumerism provides an ever-expanding market for goods and services so that it remains profitable for businesses to retain productive employees. According to Victor Lebow, our economy needs not only what he calls "forced draft" consumption, "but 'expensive' consumption as well. We need things consumed, burned up, worn out, replaced, and discarded at an ever increasing pace. We need to have people eat, drink, dress, ride, live, with ever more complicated and, therefore, constantly more expensive consumption."[7]

In a sense, this consumerist strategy for reducing unemployment resembles the strategy of production for export examined in chapters 3, 4, and 5. The difference is that domestic consumer demand can spur job creation in construction and services as well manufacturing, and the jobs created in these areas will for the most part be within the country. Manufactured goods can be shipped around the world, so creating jobs through manufacturing, whether for export or for domestic consumption, puts American workers in competition with workers around the world, most of whom have the competitive advantage of receiving much lower wages. However, American consumer demand for construction and most services creates jobs primarily within the United States, not elsewhere.

Except for prefabricated components and structures, which convert some construction work into manufacturing jobs, people have to be in the United States to build a school, courthouse, home, highway, or electricity-generating facility. Similarly, except for services that can be mediated by electronic communication, such as computer programming, telemarketing, and medical consultation, service workers have to be in the country to do their work. A surgeon may use telecommunication to consult with other medical professionals who may be anywhere in the world, but she has to be right there in the operating theater to actually perform the operation. Telemarketers who could be anywhere in the world may generate consumer interest in a new restaurant, but the cooks and waiters have to be right there in the restaurant to serve customers. The same is true of most teachers, rehabilitation specialists, counselors, busboys, lawyers, fire fighters, nurses, police officers, prison guards, dentists, sanitation workers, retail sales professionals, school principals and most other managers, and many more.

As with the other approaches to lowering unemployment, consumerism is evaluated here according to four criteria. First, does it actually reduce unemployment? We will see that for the most part it does. Second, is it a viable option given the American character, the American way of life, and the American political system? Most certainly it is. Third, can consumerism lower unemployment without unacceptable levels of environmental harm? We'll see in chapters 12 and 13 that many, but certainly not all fields within the service sector can, within environmental constraints, increase indefinitely, allowing the economy to grow and create jobs without limit. Finally, is the increase in employment created by consumerism fundamentally efficient? Are the devotion of human time, effort, and training, and the exploitation of natural resources needed for consumerism to lower unemployment the best ways to use these human and natural assets to promote human wellbeing? Unfortunately, we'll see, consumerism is about as inefficient as the American healthcare system examined in the last chapter.

This chapter relates consumerism to individual wellbeing; chapter 9 relates it to social wellbeing; and chapter 13 discusses the consumption of services which, because they have low environmental impact, can proliferate indefinitely to create ever more economic growth and jobs.

❋   ❋   ❋

Because consumerism is the main driver of economic growth in the United States, the case for increasing consumerism is strengthened by the case for economic growth in general. In other words, if economic growth is good and consumerism is the main way to achieve it, we have a reason to value consumerism. As noted in chapter 1, Harvard University economist Benjamin Friedman claims that economic growth is, indeed, generally beneficial. The benefits start with attractive products, increased employment opportunities, and improved working conditions:

> New products and new ways of organizing productive activity are usually
> the essence of what creates economic growth: within the last century, for
> example, first automobiles and airplanes, then television, and then consumer

electronics appeared, while at the same time work on farms and in dirty factories increasingly gave way to cleaner, less physically demanding jobs in modern manufacturing facilities and in the rapidly expanding service sector.[8]

Other benefits of economic growth include the ability to fund better public sanitation and health care that make life safer and longer. We can also afford more travel that makes life more interesting. We can afford more entertainment that makes life more fun. Friedman writes, "Having at least some financial resources is even helpful in maintaining marriages, perhaps because it allows young couples to live on their own instead of with their parents."[9]

Friedman stresses improvements in psychological wellbeing that attend economic growth. He notes that people tend to feel good when they compare themselves favorably with either other people or with their own previous condition. The comparison with other people can never improve the psychological wellbeing of the population at large because half the population will always be below average, and research consistently shows that poorer people *within* any given country are less happy than richer people within that country. But when the economy is growing and the vast majority of people are becoming richer, comparison with one's former condition can make people happy and optimistic across the income spectrum. "In particular," Friedman claims, "when people know that they are moving ahead compared to their own past experience, they feel less need to get ahead of other people too."[10]

My life history is typical for people of my generation. I didn't have a television, now I can afford one; I didn't have color TV, now I do; I didn't have a computer; now I can afford one; I didn't have Internet access, now I do; I had slow Internet access, now my access is faster; I didn't have a high definition flat-screen TV, now I do. I had to share a bedroom (much of the time) with my brother while growing up, whereas my daughters (often) had rooms of their own. Amidst such improvement of personal circumstances it's easy to feel good about one's place in the world. But when such improvements stop, people quickly and easily become morose. Having gotten used to a certain set of conveniences and toys, they become bored unless and until they can acquire a new set. Having become used to improvement, they are disgruntled by stagnation. Although their car is better than the one they had years ago, they want one that is better still. (Seat warmers for winter and air-conditioning for summer that can be activated remotely from inside a house or other building several minutes before intended car use *without turning on the car's motor* would be welcome progress from my point of view.)

The observation that progress improves spirits is not new. Adam Smith wrote in *The Wealth of Nations*,

> It deserves to be remarked, perhaps, that it is in the progressive state, while the society is advancing to the further acquisition, rather than when it has acquired its full complement of riches, that the condition of the laboring poor, of the great body of the people, seems to be the happiest and the most comfortable. It is hard in the stationary, and miserable in the declining state. The progressive state is in reality the cheerful and the hearty state to all the different orders of society. The stationary is dull; the declining melancholy.[11]

In addition, when spirits are thus high, people tend to act better toward others, including those less fortunate than themselves. Adam Smith writes in *The Theory of Moral Sentiments*, "Before we can feel much for others, we must in some measure be at ease ourselves. If our own misery pinches us very severely, we have no leisure to attend to that of our neighbour."[12] In better personal circumstances, we can afford to be more charitable. John Miller, a contemporary of Smith's, is clearer. When people "find less difficulty in the attainment of bare necessaries . . . [they] are more at liberty to cultivate the feelings of humanity . . . ; and the various rights of mankind, arising from their multiplied connections, are recognized and protected."[13] Friedman gives the example of efforts to reduce discrimination:

> Experience suggests that most people are more willing to support anti-discrimination policies and to accept the risk that their advantage over others might erode if they are confident that, even if this should happen, their own living standard will rise over time nonetheless. Economic growth creates that confidence, and thereby makes the personal risks that come from eliminating unfair discrimination more readily acceptable.[14]

Similarly, Americans generally support equal educational opportunity. But attempts to equalize opportunities between society's haves and have-nots require programs, such as Head Start, which provide free prekindergarten education for children in poor families. Middle-class families are more willing to pay for such benefits directed at the poor when their own incomes are rising, as they generally are in a growing economy, than when their own incomes are stagnant or declining, as they generally are when the economy stalls or goes into recession. Equal-opportunity policies are thus more politically viable in a growing economy.[15] Again, according to Friedman, when the economy is growing and people have more than they need for urgent individual and family needs, they are more likely to support public initiatives that provide parks, schools, and other public meeting places that enrich opportunities for people to socialize with fellow citizens. Such venues and the publicly sponsored events that take place in them tend to bring together citizens of different classes, religions, professions, and ethnicities. The resulting contact among citizens helps to create and maintain one of the prerequisites of democracy, tolerance for and acceptance of fellow citizens as worthy partners in the direction of the country. Also, when the economy grows and people have more money to spend they tend to give more to charitable organizations, thereby in most cases helping poorer people, a value that is esteemed in most moral codes. Helping poor people reduces inequality, which is generally considered an advance in fairness and an effective method of forestalling social unrest.

Reviewing US history, Friedman shows that for the most part eras of moral improvement—"movements *toward* openness, tolerance, mobility, fairness, democracy"[16]—correspond with periods of economic growth and prosperity, whereas movements away from the realization of these ideals correspond to periods of economic stagnation or decline. The Populist Free Silver Movement, for example, received its impetus between 1880 and 1895 when farm families, who still constituted a majority of households, were in desperate economic circumstances because the price of food was declining relative to the cost of living (owing mostly to increased agricultural output in the United States and abroad). Populists whose political inclinations reflected views formed during this period of decline opposed immigration long after recovery had begun. Beginning in the 1880s they supported increasing restrictions on immigration, with the successful exclusion of Chinese immigration in 1882 and a ban on the immigration of contract labor in 1885. Reconstruction in the South ended during the Populist era, racist Jim Crow laws were instituted, and the Ku Klux Klan thrived. Populists inveighed against Catholics and Jews. William Jennings Bryan, the last of America's major Populist politicians, campaigned to bar non-Christians from teaching at American universities.[17]

People whose political views were formed under the more favorable circumstances of the mid-1890s, by contrast, formed the backbone of the Progressive era (1895–1919). This was the era of Horatio Alger stories of people going from rags to riches on the basis of hard work and good fortune. Women were given the vote. Immigration continued to be a concern, but Progressives favored assimilating rather than excluding immigrants. The Progressive era saw the influence of the Social Gospel in mainstream Protestant churches, which made serving the poor a major goal of Christian activism. The National Association for the Advancement of Colored People was established. The Seventeenth Amendment to the Constitution provided for the direct election of US senators. The rich sharing with the rest of society was institutionalized by the new income tax. Corporate greed was opposed also by antitrust activism at the federal level.[18]

The succeeding decade, by contrast, the decade of the 1920s, was economically impoverishing for most Americans. The Ku Klux Klan was revived. Immigration was severely restricted. Antitrust activism was abandoned by the Harding and Coolidge administrations. Taxes on the rich were lowered.[19]

The post-World War II economic boom (1945–1973) saw the racial integration of baseball and of the military, the Civil Rights Movement, the GI Bill, the expansion of state universities to offer higher education to an increasing percentage of the American population, the provision of medical insurance to senior citizens through Medicare, the building of the Interstate Highway System, the creation of the Environmental Protection Agency, steeply progressive income taxes, and the beginning of the Women's Movement for greater gender equality.

Friedman traces the same tendency in Britain,[20] France,[21] and Germany[22] for economic growth to engender progressive policies and economic decline to promote movement away from openness, tolerance, mobility, fairness, and democracy. The only exception to this rule in the United States, Friedman claims, was the Great Depression (1929–1939). New Deal legislation was designed to help the poor in society. Friedman accounts for this exception in part by crediting the charisma of President Roosevelt and his commitment to social justice. He points out also that many people saw the New Deal as the only alternative to the extremes of fascism, which was taking over in Germany, and communism, which had taken over in Russia. Finally, the scope of the economic problems was so widespread in the 1930s that almost everyone felt touched by it. Friedman sums up, "Most people understandably exhibit generosity when they are doing well and defensiveness when they are doing badly. But they nonetheless pull together when they see their very lives threatened and the entire social and political structure in which they live thrown into imminent danger."[23]

In general, not only does economic growth foster tolerance, equality, equal opportunity, and democracy, these positive social conditions, in turn, foster additional economic growth. A society characterized by great inequalities between rich and poor tends to be unstable, and such instability inhibits the kind of investment needed for economic growth. A society in which subgroups are mutually hostile instead of tolerant and respectful is also unstable. On the other hand, a society where all children have reasonable educational opportunities is more likely to have a productive workforce that fosters economic growth. A society that is democratic is more likely to have public funds spent for productive public services, such as schools and healthcare, rather than have those funds illegally siphoned off and squandered by corrupt public officials who in undemocratic societies are unaccountable to fellow citizens. Thus, the moral benefits of economic growth—greater tolerance, equality and democracy—improve prospects for further economic growth in a virtuous circle of moral, social, and economic improvement.

Finally, economic growth also has fiscal benefits. Unemployment concerns are tied to concerns about public debt because one way of increasing employment is for the government to employ people, as it did under the New Deal in the 1930s and as it did even more during World War II. The problem with this solution to unemployment is that unless the government is running a budget surplus, which it seldom is, the government must borrow money if it is to lower unemployment by simply giving people jobs. However, economic growth can improve the situation in two ways. First, as the economy grows, public revenues generally increase, making it possible for the government to employ more people without incurring additional debt. Second, the most important measure of public debt is not the amount of money that the government owes, but the amount of debt as a percentage of GDP, because the size of the economy (GDP) measures the resources the government can draw upon to pay its debts. The larger the GDP, the easier it is for the government to make needed payments from its tax revenues. Few economists worry, therefore, if federal debt is 40 or 50 percent of GDP, because this leaves the government plenty of tax revenue to make payments when they are due. But when federal debt goes past 80 percent most economists become concerned. They worry that interest on the debt will take so much public money that the government will not be able to pay for its vital programs.

Faster economic growth is the answer to these worries. At the end of World War II, federal government debt was about 120 percent of GDP. Budgets for the next twenty-five years were more often in slight deficit than in slight surplus. Nevertheless, as a result of economic growth the federal deficit in 1970 was under 40 percent of GDP.[24] So economic growth can help reduce unemployment not only by creating job opportunities for workers in the private sector, it can also increase opportunities in the public sector by allowing the government to borrow money to employ people without increasing the country's debt burden as a percentage of GDP.

* * *

Given these multiple benefits of economic growth—reinforcing improvements in job opportunities, equality, democracy, and tolerance—it's worth looking at the means of promoting economic growth. One of the principal means is consumerism. As already noted, consumer spending constitutes 70 percent of American GDP,[25] so one of the most reliable paths to economic growth and general social improvement is growth in the consumer sector of the economy. In addition, consumerism appears to be good because many consumer items are desired by most people simply because, given the choice of living with them or without them, they would choose to live with them. People think that these *consumer items improve the quality of human life*.

Like American healthcare, consumerism is to a large extent effective even though it's highly inefficient. Just as our healthcare system has improved American health in spite of its inefficiencies, many consumer items are desirable notwithstanding inefficiencies inherent in consumerism.

Here are some of my favorite things—consumer items that I enjoy—items which I think improve the quality of my life: One is my refrigerator. I don't think I'm alone in finding that it's convenient to have an electric refrigerator rather than an ice box that requires a regular infusion of ice from outside the house. It's helpful if the refrigerator is big enough to contain all the food that you want to eat for a week so that you don't have to go shopping more often. If the refrigerator has a freezer, that helps even more. If the freezer has an automatic ice maker, that's an added convenience. And if the ice maker is attached to a lever outside the refrigerator door so you can get ice (either cubes or crushed) delivered into a glass or pitcher without even having to open the refrigerator door—well, what's not to like?

When my children lived at home, I also enjoyed having a house large enough for each child to have her own room. It gave each of my daughters a sense of independence. Central heating in the house is another plus. The year that we lived in university housing in Aberdeen, Scotland, without central heating renewed my appreciation of it. Central air-conditioning is almost as helpful where I live now, in central Illinois, because the summers can be really hot. I realize that humanity survived in prehistory without large houses, central heating, and central air-conditioning, so I'm not claiming that these items are essential for human survival. I just claim that their possession improves the quality of life. Wanting these consumer items doesn't strike me as evidence that I've been infected by noxious consumerism. I want central heating and air-conditioning because they increase my comfort and that of my family and guests.

Computers and word processors are also attractive to me. I wrote two books longhand with a pencil on legal pads and can attest to the life-improving nature of word processing for authors. High-speed Internet connection is great, too, for non-fiction authors like me who like to spice up their work with a few actual facts. In many cases the facts are just a Google away. Although I'm not one to carry a cell phone, much less a smart phone, my wife finds these items convenient and fun. What's more, her phone and iPad give her access almost everywhere to the Internet and to pesky pieces of information whenever we disagree.

I enjoy radio and television. I think my life is improved by being able to hear news or music while driving down the highway or resting my eyes at home. (I'm not asleep!) And although most prehistoric people would probably have been more than satisfied with a 27-inch color TV, watching movies and sports on a 52-inch flat screen high definition TV is better, in my opinion. Again, I don't think that my enjoyment indicates that I've made a religion of consumption. Nor do I think excessive materialism is indicated by my enjoyment of our clothes washer and drier, our vacuum cleaner, and a host of other goods.

There are professional services, too, that I believe improve the quality of my life. I don't think that I'm particularly vain, but I still appreciate the quality of haircut that I get from a professional barber in contrast with what I could do myself or what a friend with scissors might do for (or to) me. Because I appreciate my computer, I appreciate the services of people who fix computers when they malfunction. The same goes for all of the other technologically complex goods that I have and enjoy, whether refrigerator, water heater, central heating, central air-conditioning, indoor plumbing, or television. Other services that I appreciate include garbage collection, as well as the news gathering and reporting services of periodicals and of radio and television stations that enable me to become a more informed and engaged citizen. I have also had occasion to appreciate the services of lawyers, real estate agents, and insurance agents.

Medical and dental services shouldn't be ignored. One of my daughters needed emergency surgery for internal bleeding that could have been life threatening. I appreciate ambulances, as well as other medical services, in such situations. Another of my daughters was treated successfully for a difficulty during one of her pregnancies. All three daughters benefited from removal of their wisdom teeth. As with the goods that I appreciate, these services and many more improve my quality of life and the quality of life of others whom I care about.

On this accounting, it seems that increased consumption is a win-win-win

202 **FUNCTIONAL INEFFICIENCY**

situation. It promotes economic growth that has many positive results—moral and political as well as economic. It seems to promote tolerance, openness, mobility, fairness, and democracy, while at the same time lowering unemployment. In addition, many of the items that consumers purchase improve the quality of their lives. What's not to like? Why is consumerism criticized?

❊   ❊   ❊

One critique of consumerism concentrates on the disconnection between increased consumption and associated economic growth, on the one hand, and human happiness (or, more generally, human wellbeing or flourishing) on the other. According to the social and psychological studies reported by economist Richard Layard in his book *Happiness*, above a per capita income of $20,000 in 2005, increased income and associated consumption do not increase happiness. There has been no increase in the general level of happiness in the United States since 1950 even though living standards have more than doubled. Statistics in most other advanced counties go back only to 1975, but there again, happiness has not increased in Britain or Japan in spite of significant increases in material standards of living since that time. Similarly, studies of individuals show that they have on average become no happier as their incomes have increased. In continental Europe the picture is mixed, with some happiness increase in Italy and significant decrease in Belgium, but the overall picture shows no general increase in happiness in western European countries comparable to increases in their material standards of living since 1975.[26]

Among countries that are or were poor, such as India, Mexico, the Philippines, Brazil, and South Korea, economic growth coincided with (and presumably caused) increases in happiness. People were on average so poor in these countries that additional material comforts made a difference to their happiness. They had yet to reach the $20,000 per capita per year threshold.[27]

Economist Robert Frank believes that we should take seriously the results of happiness research that relies primarily on responses to questionnaires because people tend to be consistent in their responses. Asked eight months after the initial survey, most people respond as they did earlier. Also, friends tend to rate people's happiness the same as they rate it themselves.

In addition, Frank writes, people whose "brain-wave patterns emanate disproportionately from the left prefrontal region . . . are much more likely to call [themselves] happy. . . . [Such] brain-wave data are also remarkably consistent."[28] (A Tibetan monk who was enrolled in a study of such brain-wave activity had brain-waves indicative of happiness much higher than the norm.) What is more, "people who are classified as happy by the various measures are more likely to initiate social contact with friends, a step that mental health professionals regard as indicative of psychological wellbeing."[29]

Finally, people classified as happy are "less likely to suffer from psychosomatic illnesses, such as digestive disorders, headaches, and rapid heartbeat. Happy persons are also less likely to be absent from work and less likely to be involved in disputes at work. . . . And happy people are much less likely than unhappy people to attempt suicide, the ultimate behavioral measure of unhappiness." In short, *the happiness discussed in this literature refers really to human wellbeing in general. If questionnaire research shows that increased riches don't make people in rich societies happier, there's reason to think that increased riches don't improve psychological wellbeing in general.* There is a genuine disconnect between riches and human wellbeing.

Further evidence of this disconnect comes from statistics about depression. Depression indicates unhappiness, and it has increased in the United States and other countries as living standards have risen. Currently in the United States about fifteen percent of the population experiences clinical depression before the age of thirty-five and six percent experience clinical depression in any given year. But if we can trust people's memories, only two percent of those who had reached the age of thirty-five by 1960 recalled years later that they had ever experienced clinical depression before age thirty-five.[30] Public policy professor Robert Putnam reports additional research in *Bowling Alone*:

> Depression has struck earlier and much more pervasively in each successive generation, beginning with the cohorts born after 1940. For example, one study reported that "of those Americans born before 1955, only 1 percent had suffered a major depression by age 75; of those born after 1955, 6 percent had become depressed by *age 24*. Psychologist Martin Seligman concludes that "the rate of depression over the last two generations has increased roughly tenfold."[31]

As already noted, suicide suggests poor quality of life. "Between 1950 and 1995 the suicide rate among adolescents aged fifteen to nineteen more than quadrupled, while the rate among young adults aged twenty to twenty-four, beginning at a higher level, nearly tripled."[32] Between 1999 and 2010, the suicide rate among adults between the ages of thirty-five and sixty-four increased by almost 30 percent.[33]

More common indications of psychic distress are headaches, indigestion, and sleeplessness, which Putnam terms "malaise." In the mid-1970s, the incidence of malaise among older and younger people was essentially the same. But since that time older people's afflictions have diminished while those of middle-aged and especially of younger people have increased. "Even among the financially comfortable the generation gap in malaise widened steadily," Putnam writes.[34]

Alcoholism is another indication of unhappiness (or, more generally, lack of wellbeing). Early in the twentieth century alcoholism decreased as people's incomes went up, but in the second half of the century alcoholism increased along with income. In recent surveys more than a quarter of young white men report having problems with alcohol, whereas only 15 percent of men aged sixty-five and older remembered having had such problems. Death statistics that don't rely on anyone's memory tell the same story. Death from cirrhosis of the liver has increased since 1950 in every rich country except France.[35]

Crime statistics also suggest that increased wealth does not improve happiness or overall human wellbeing. In the nineteenth century crime increased in the squalor of industrial cities, but then declined until World War I as people became more prosperous. It was assumed that decreasing crime naturally accompanied increasing wealth. However, in most rich countries crime soared during the postwar economic boom between 1950 and 1980. Although crime has declined significantly in the last two decades, it still isn't as low as it was when society was much poorer two generations ago.[36]

Why is there such a disconnection between increased wealth and consumption, on the one hand, and increased happiness or wellbeing, on the other? Why don't people perceive their lives to be better as they become richer and better able to afford lots of consumer items, many of which I find quite helpful and enjoyable?

✻ ✻ ✻

Part of the reason is what psychologists call adaptation, which leads easily to two levels of addiction that rob consumption of its advantages. People tend to adapt to what they consider desirable as well as to what they would like to avoid. The new condition, whether initially good or bad, becomes their new normal; they typically settle down before long to the same level of satisfaction as before the welcome or unwelcome change. Psychologist Daniel Gilbert writes,

> Able-bodied people are willing to pay far more to avoid becoming disabled than disabled people are willing to pay to become able-bodied again because able-bodied people underestimate how happy disabled people are. As one group of researchers noted, "Chronically ill and disabled patients generally rate the value of their lives in a given health state more highly than do hypothetical patients [who are] imagining themselves to be in such states." Indeed, healthy people imagine that eighty-three states of illness would be "worse than death," and yet, people who are actually in those states rarely take their own lives.[37]

Adaptation to positive changes occurs when the initial happiness of getting the newer, better car, computer, television, kitchen counter top, or whatever wears off, and what gave us such initial pleasure becomes part of our new normal that we take for granted.

Adaptation can lead to the first level of addiction, because adaptation to positive elements in our lives makes continuation of the benefit necessary for continued happiness, at least in the short run. Layard writes, "When I get a new home or a new car, I am excited at first. But then I get used to it, and my mood tends to revert to where it was before. Now I feel that I *need* the bigger house and the better car. If I went back to the old house and car, I would be much less happy than I was before I had experienced something better."[38] Gilbert adds, "Not knowing what we're missing can mean that we are truly happy under circumstances that would not allow us to be happy once we have experienced the missing thing. It does *not* mean that those who don't know what they're missing are *less* happy than those who have it."[39]

The television series *Little House on the Prairie*, which ran from 1974 to 1983, depicted a family living under conditions typical of late nineteenth-century rural western America. There was no family car, no radio, no television, no dirt bikes, no Xbox, no computer games, yet everyone in the family is depicted as reasonably happy. Was this realistic? Why didn't the kids commit suicide on a cold night somewhere between the house and the outhouse? Family members were not depicted as bothered by failure to have items and conveniences that we take for granted because they had never had them. Such items were not part of normal life for them. Does this mean that most of us could be equally happy without these items? Certainly not; we are addicted to these items as part of normal life. Most of us would miss them sorely. Should they be taken away, our symptoms of withdrawal would be quite serious, and we would never entirely escape a sense of loss so long as we could remember life with them.

This is the first level of addiction; we need to retain new, better things in order to avoid unhappiness upon their loss. This level of addiction is abetted by the fact that on average a loss makes people twice as unhappy as an equivalent gain. This is called "loss aversion." For example, when psychologist Daniel Kahneman asked students how much they would pay for a certain coffee mug, the average price was $3.50. But when he gave these mugs to a different set of students and asked for what price they would be willing to sell the mugs that they now owned, the average price was $7. In another experiment, subjects were told of a gambling opportunity. On the toss of a coin the subjects would either lose one hundred pounds (very British), or they would gain a certain amount of money. How much gain would the subjects require to induce them to take the bet? It turned out to be two hundred pounds. Again, a loss is felt twice as much as a gain.[40] This suggests that when people are addicted to consumer items that they enjoy, the sacrifice they experience in giving them up is much greater than the sacrifice they would make to acquire them in the first place. So once we have our fancy cars, computers, etc., we are addicted to them in the sense that we don't want to give them up and are willing to spend money to maintain and replace them as needed. This is good news for workers who make and repair cars, computers, and all of the other consumer items that we currently own and enjoy.

❋   ❋   ❋

But our productive economy requires that most people be afflicted with a second, higher level of addiction to consumer items. Because productive efficiency constantly increases so that fewer workers are needed to produce a given volume of product, consumption must continually *increase* in order to keep unemployment at bay. It's not enough that people be addicted to the products that they own so that they have them fixed when they are broken and replace them when they wear out. They need to be addicted also to additional acquisitions, to replacement of what's (perceived as) good by what's (perceived as) better; and such replacement must proceed at an ever accelerating rate. In other words, consumers in our society must be in a nearly constant state of discontent with what they already have if their purchases are to be sufficient to keep the economy growing fast enough to keep people working.

This is not a new or radical observation. Charles Kettering, head of research at General Motors from 1920 to 1947, made this observation in 1929 in an article entitled "Keep the Customer Dissatisfied." He recounts a conversation with one of the country's great bankers about the purchase of a new automobile. The banker had just bought a new car and thought it "a rotten shame" that he had to accept so much depreciation on the one he traded in. He told Kettering, "You are the fellow who is to blame. You, with all your changes and refinements, made me dissatisfied with the old model" which, he acknowledged with regret, still "ran like new." The banker observed, "The only reason for research is to keep your customers reasonably dissatisfied with what they already have." Kettering agreed:

> There are no places where anyone can sit and rest in an industrial situation. It is a question of change, change, change, all the time—and it is always going to be that way. It must always be that way for the world only goes along one road, the road to progress. Nations and industries that have become satisfied with themselves and their ways of doing things, don't last. While they are sitting back and admiring themselves other nations and other concerns have . . . been moving ahead. . . .
>
> If everyone were satisfied, no one would buy the new thing because no one would want it. The ore wouldn't be mined; the timber wouldn't be cut. Almost immediately hard times would be upon us.
>
> You must accept reasonable dissatisfaction with what you have and buy the new thing, or accept hard times.[41]

Victor Lebow recognized in the 1950s that the new medium of television was the most powerful conduit of the needed message. "Television actually sells the generalized idea of consumption. It promotes the goal of higher living standards." Regardless of the individual product being advertised, the regime of advertising ensures that "the consumer's highest loyalty is actually towards his standard of living, toward the goals, aspirations, and wants which comprise the reason for his existence."[42] When watching television, "the family thinks only partly in terms of the individual items that satisfy its aspirations. The real goals are to *look* better, *dress* better, *travel* better."[43] These goals are linked inextricably with present dissatisfaction. People want to look, dress, and travel better when they are discontented with their current appearance, dress, and travel.

Even apart from TV ads, watching television engenders discontent because characters on television are much richer than average Americans, so "the more television people watch, the more they overestimate the affluence of other people."[44] When people's sense of self-worth is tied to what they own, as it is in a consumer society, raising the perceived norm of material possessions increases the number of people who are discontented with what they own as it increases the number who believe that their own possessions are poor compared to the social norm. Like commercials, programming content thus promotes the discontent that is essential to consumerism.

TV watching tends to engender discontent even with one's own body and with that of one's intimate partner. In one experiment women's moods became worse after they were shown pictures of beautiful models. As part of the same series of experiments, men who were shown pictures of beautiful models expressed more discontent with their wives after viewing the pictures. TV commercials and shows are replete with images of beautiful women, so watching TV tends to lower self-esteem in women and reduce marital contentment among men, thereby impairing wellbeing.[45]

According to Lebow, "Nobody has better understood this [the importance of discontent to increased consumption] nor more conscientiously sought this than the automotive industry." They have successfully inculcated the idea that "owning a more expensive car signifies the consumer's rise on the economic ladder." This may seem to contradict the producer's goal of brand loyalty. If the consumer's next car is more expensive than the last, how can it be the same brand? The major car companies have reconciled the desire for ever-greater luxury with brand loyalty to the major companies, General Motors, Ford, and Chrysler, by maintaining "a hierarchy of automobiles, corresponding to promotions in the consumer's social rank."[46] One can go from a Ford to a Mercury to a Lincoln, all produced by the Ford Motor Company. One can go from a Chevy to a Buick to a Cadillac, all made by GM.

This is the form of consumerism that Lebow endorsed when he said that massive unemployment can be avoided in the American economy only if people center their lives around new products and make a religion of consumption. To quote him again, "We need things consumed, burned up, worn out, replaced, and discarded at an ever increasing pace. We need to have people eat, drink, dress, ride, live, with ever more complicated and, therefore, constantly more expensive consumption."[47] We must be habituated not just to living with the new, but to experience pain when we can't get a steady supply of what's newer. This second level of addiction is not like being addicted to central heating at the first level; its loss would hurt, but its failure to improve or expand causes no pain associated with first-level addiction. People afflicted with second-level addiction, by contrast, can avoid pain only when their consumer items continually increase or improve. Just as drug addicts feel pain in the absence of increasing doses of drugs, or "better" drugs, people afflicted with second-level addiction to consumer items need the supply available to them constantly to increase and improve.

This is why historian Christopher Lasch considers consumerism to be a form of addiction. Like drug addicts, second-level consumer addicts constantly need more in order to avoid the pain of dissatisfaction. In a consumer society "the need for novelty and fresh stimulation becomes more and more intense, intervening interludes of boredom increasingly intolerable."[48] Layard agrees:

> One reason why happiness has not risen, despite our higher standard of living, is that we get used to the higher living standard. At first, extra comfort gives extra pleasure, then we adapt to it, and our pleasure returns towards its former level. Indeed, the pleasure is largely associated with the change in income rather than its level. To some extent it is like the classic forms of addiction, such as alcohol or drugs, where you have to increase the dosage all the time to get the same enjoyment.[49]

The consumer is like a spoiled child who is less interested in her toys than in the novelty of getting new toys, which is exactly what is needed if consumption is continually to increase. According to Lasch, "Advertising serves not so much to advertise products as to promote consumption as a way of life. It 'educates' the masses into an unappeasable appetite not only for goods but for new experiences and personal fulfillment."[50]

This second-level addiction is by its nature almost always associated with frustration and therefore unhappiness. The addict experiences satisfaction only temporarily before increased doses of the addictive substance or experience are required for another transient episode of happiness. Because larger doses (of whatever it may be) are increasingly difficult to obtain, the addict is subject to periods of frustration that are longer and more bothersome, which may explain why few self-help books recommend addiction. In the case of consumerism, second-level addiction typically runs up against limited financial resources. Lacking enough money to buy all the products that they find attractive, consumer addicts experience continual frustration. To the extent that such addiction is foundational to our growing economy, it's no wonder that increasing riches that allow people to buy more of what they want has generally not increased happiness or wellbeing among consumers.

*   *   *

A related reason for increasing individual discontent in our consumer-oriented economy is that consumption is fostered in large part by advertising that induces irrational fears and raises false hopes of personal improvement.

According to Christopher Lasch, the advertising industry

> upholds consumption as the answer to the age-old discontents of loneliness, sickness, weariness, lack of sexual satisfaction; at the same time it creates new forms of discontent peculiar to the modern age. . . . Is your job boring and meaningless? Does it leave you with feelings of futility and fatigue? Is your life empty? Consumption promises to fill the aching void; hence the attempt to surround commodities with an aura of romance; with allusions to exotic places and vivid experiences; and with images of female breasts from which all blessings flow.[51]

Purchases made under the inducement of such advertisements are almost certain to disappoint because the benefits that ads associate with products are almost never realized. The mouth-freshening toothpaste almost never engenders sex with a beautiful person, as the ad suggests. Drinking the right beer almost never brings forth a fun party or picnic with fifty friends who think you're wonderful. The expensive underwear almost never looks the same on the purchaser's body as on the model's. Buying the rugged 4x4 vehicle almost never transforms ordinary men into rugged he-men who go over the mountain instead of around it (especially where I live in central Illinois). To the extent that people are influenced by the associations in the ad to buy what's advertised, they are almost certain to be disappointed. This helps to explain why increasing wealth has not improved happiness.

The consumer way of life is so pervasive that many ordinary people engage in what is popularly called "retail therapy." Regardless of the reason for their sadness, they go out and buy something, anything, to make themselves feel better, as if a purchase could actually alleviate what's bothering them. Again, most people are bound to be disappointed, as they're looking for happiness in all the wrong places.

Advertisers also promote increased purchases that don't increase happiness by inculcating irrational fears in the consuming public. Advertising suggests that your child will not succeed in school without the special tutoring or the special educational computer program or the new educational video game being advertised. If your child has trouble learning to read (a fairly common occurrence), parent-consumers are told that the child may have dyslexia, a (much rarer) condition that can be treated for a price.

Many irrational fears that promote consumption are related to healthcare and account for some of its inefficiency and its increasing cost as a percentage of our GDP. Does your child fail to pay attention to you and seems to crave activity all the time? She may suffer from attention deficit and hyperactive disorder (ADHD). There are drug treatments you can buy after you've bought the services of a physician who can prescribe them. Fear induces purchase. Who would risk condemning his child to academic failure? Worse yet, your semiliterate pogo-stick of a child may lack friends as a result of suffering from "social anxiety disorder," which is distinguished from shyness merely by its inclusion in the *Diagnostic and Statistical Manual of Mental Disorders*, a listing that suggests the need for professional treatment by real doctors.[52]

Alternatively, your illiterate offspring may be a social pariah because she's depressed. Depression, like all of the problems mentioned here, does exist, and it seems to be increasing in the United States in spite of our increasing affluence. But like dyslexia and ADHD, the chances that your child suffers from depression and needs medication or some other form of special intervention are slim compared with the probability that your child is (perish the thought) normal. In 2006, Americans, who make up at most six percent of the world's population, took 66 percent of the antidepressants consumed.[53] Is it more likely that people around the world are massively depressed and don't do anything about it, or that drug company ads have aroused irrational fears among American consumers of untreated mental disorders? Your answer to this question indicates more about your common sense than about your mental health.

Here's another kind of health-related purchase motivated by fear. Children are in danger of extremely rare physical ailments that may be treatable in the future with stem cells from their own umbilical cords. Accordingly, parents are urged to spend more than $2,000 to have their child's umbilical cord preserved indefinitely for possible use. More than a quarter of a million families have bought this service from a company called Cord Blood Registry even though medical science suggests that "cord-blood treatment will never be a widespread procedure." The cord contains only enough blood to treat a small child, and cord blood cannot help with genetic disorders because the stem cells in the cord blood have the same genes as the child.[54]

In case you think I'm being cynical, consider the title of a talk given by pharmaceutical executive Neil Wolf explaining the success of his company's drug Detrol. The title was "Positioning Detrol (Creating a Disease)."[55] The disease is "overactive bladder." The drug was designed originally to treat incontinence, which is a real medical problem, but one that afflicts many times fewer people than can be convinced by clever advertising that nature is calling them too often to the bathroom. This is not a unique case of getting people to worry about their physical or mental health when they are normal. Journalist Melody Petersen reports, "In 2003 Vince Parry, pharmaceutical branding expert, wrote in the industry magazine *Medical Marketing & Media* that marketers were taking their ability to create new disorders 'to new levels of sophistication.' He called this process 'the art of branding a condition.'"[56] It's all the better if the condition is a normal part of the human condition because then, if the condition can be made to seem like a disease for which treatment is desirable or required, large swaths of the human population may be convinced to buy a company's new drug.

The general routine is this: A pharmaceutical company comes up with a drug that may ameliorate to some small extent a problem that is for the vast majority of people simply among the many normal inconveniences or difficulties of life. Anxiety, depression, and other mental disorders are particularly handy in this context because there are few physical symptoms or indications, making them "open to conceptual definition." After getting the drug approved by the FDA the drug company starts marketing as a disease the (heretofore normal, often mental) problem that the drug is supposed to alleviate. Petersen gives these examples:

> Few Americans had heard of an illness called panic disorder . . . before Upjohn began marketing a drug called Xanax to treat it in the 1970s. Likewise, few people knew they could be suffering from something called generalized anxiety disorder if they worried too much until GlaxoSmithKline told them that a pill called Paxil could ease its symptoms. And in 2000, millions of women learned they might suffer from something called premenstrual dysphoric disorder, or simply PMDD. News reports of the disorder began just as marketers at Eli Lilly repackaged Prozac in a lavender and pink capsule, renamed it the sweeter-sounding Sarafem, and began selling it to treat this new disease. Lilly's television ads promoting the "new" drug showed a frustrated woman trying to untangle a shopping cart from a messy lineup of carts in front of a store. "Think it's PMS?" the announcer asked. "It could be PMDD."[57]

Ads like these promote consumerism in the United States in a way that's illegal in almost every other industrialized country. Except for New Zealand, the United States is the only country to allow direct-to-consumer advertising of prescription drugs.[58] To the extent that sales are generated and consumerism promoted by marketers engendering and then playing on people's (mostly unrealistic) fears, the economy grows through increased consumer demand without anyone getting any happier. For example, people who used to think that their rhythm of bathroom use was just a little annoying now can fear that they suffer from a disease. Worse yet, the fear continues because the new pills provide only partial, if any relief. And who's to say what counts as adequate relief? Who defines the proper rhythm for the use of bathrooms? There's a large range of normal. In sum, marketing through fear is one way that people can get richer through economic growth that doesn't make anyone any happier or improve anyone's wellbeing.

*   *   *

The consumer culture seems to inhibit happiness and individual wellbeing also because it tends to substitute less satisfying for more satisfying activities and aspirations. For one thing, people in a consumer culture are oriented to what they can buy, which invites them to look at their work activities primarily from the perspective of monetary gain, rather than from the perspective of any joy or fulfillment they might find in the work itself or in its connection to nonmonetary goals. Studies by psychologists Tim Kasser and Richard Ryan suggest that greater orientation toward monetary goals rather than toward affiliation with others, community goals, and self-acceptance is correlated with poor psychological wellbeing. They write,

> Highly central financial success aspirations in the first two [of their three] studies were associated with less self-actualization, less vitality, more depression, and more anxiety. . . . Comparable results were obtained in a third heterogeneous adolescent sample when interview ratings of global functioning, social productivity, and symptoms of behavior disorders [oppositional and conduct disorders] were assessed.[59]

The bottom line here is that primary orientation toward the external, monetary rewards for work is bad for psychological wellbeing. But why would that be?

One reason is expressed in the so-called hedonic paradox. The paradox is this: People who take personal happiness as their goal tend to be less happy than people who care less about their own happiness than about other projects, tasks, or goals that they consider important. It's when people throw themselves into a project or cause—climb that rock face, learn that foreign language, protect the rights of animals, defeat candidates from the opposing party, create a community organization that will build a new public park— that they are happiest. Concentration on one's own happiness weakens commitment to any such project or goal because the project or goal is valued only contingently insofar as it is perceived to augment happiness. But such contingent commitment is a lesser commitment and therefore produces less happiness. Think of the happiest people you know. It's most likely that they have commitments to projects, causes, and people beyond any commitment that they have to attaining happiness for themselves.

Juliet Schor reports on the baleful effects on children of consumerism and of the associated orientation toward external instead of internal rewards. Toy sales in the United States increased 20 percent between 1995 and 2000. The United States, with less than 6 percent of the world's population and about 25 percent of the world's GDP,[60] consumes 45 percent of the world's toys.[61] These figures reflect "an upsurge in materialist values," greater interest in having than in doing, among children, Schor writes.

> Children's top aspiration now is to be rich, a more appealing prospect to them than being a great athlete, or a celebrity, or being really smart, the goals of earlier eras. Forty-four percent of kids in fourth through eighth grades now report that they dream "a lot" about being rich. And nearly two-thirds of parents report that "my child defines his or her self-worth in terms of the things they own and wear more than I did when I was that age."[62]

This increase in materialism coincides with increasing distress among American children. "Diagnosis of attention deficit disorder and attention deficit hyperactivity disorder have risen dramatically, and record numbers of kids are taking drugs to help them achieve self-control and focus. . . . Teasing and bullying is rampant in schools, and includes a new protagonist, the 'alpha girl,' a mean-spirited social enforcer."[63] Schor's studies and those of other scholars indicate a causal relationship; increased materialism is largely responsible for the decline in the mental health of American children. "Involvement in consumer culture leads to problems."[64] By the same token, "Children with emotional problems will be helped if they disengage from the worlds that corporations are constructing for them. The effects operate in both directions and are symmetric. That is, less involvement in consumer culture leads to healthier kids, and more involvement leads kids' psychological well-being to deteriorate."[65]

As with adults, TV watching by children contributes significantly to their immersion in the consumer culture, as TV is the main vehicle of advertisement. "Television induces discontent with what one has, it creates an orientation to possessions and money, and it causes children to care more about brands, products, and consumer values."[66] Such

> higher levels of consumer involvement result in worse relationships with parents (as measured by both the parental attitude scale and the likelihood of fighting or disagreeing with parents). That's the first causal link. The second is that as children's relations with their parents deteriorate, there is an additional negative effect on well-being. Relating poorly to parents leads to more depression, anxiety, lower self-esteem, and more psychosomatic complaints.[67]

Studies concentrating on teens have found that increased materialism corresponds with increases in such risky behaviors as smoking, drinking, and using illegal drugs, as well as such anti-social behavior as carrying weapons, skipping school, and vandalism.[68]

In sum, Schor finds,

> Materialism is correlated with lower self-esteem. It is correlated with higher rates of depression and anxiety. Materialism is related to psychological distress and difficulty adapting to life. People who value money and conventional success are less likely to experience positive emotions, such as happiness and joy, and they are more likely to experience negative ones, such as anger and unhappiness. Materialism is also related to elevated levels of physical symptoms, such as headaches, stomachaches, backaches, sore muscles, and sore throats. These results have been found in samples of men and women, teens and adults, across income groups, and for students and nonstudents. And they hold up across countries. . . . The more strongly a person subscribes to materialist values, the poorer is his or her quality of life.[69]

✳   ✳   ✳

Considerations of personal addiction, irrational fears, physical distress, family discord, and disappointed promises suggest that consumerism reduces happiness and wellbeing. Increases in divorce, clinical depression, suicide, alcoholism, drug abuse, and crime also suggest decreased happiness and wellbeing. All of this implies that consumerism is inefficient as a method of promoting human wellbeing. Enormous quantities of human and natural resources are expended without producing improvements in the human condition, except insofar as consumerism tends to keep unemployment at bay. Thus, consumerism seems to be a form of functional inefficiency.

But how inefficient is it? According to the World Happiness Report issued in 2012 by Columbia University's Earth Institute, the happiness index of the United States was about 174 on a scale of 200, whereas the happiness index of France was close to 172, making Americans less than two percent happier than the French.[70] Two years earlier, researchers at Stanford University reported that welfare in France is three percent lower than welfare in the United States, all things considered.[71] Yet, figures from the United Nations Statistical Yearbook indicate that private household consumption in France constitutes only about 61.5 percent of GDP, compared to 70.5 percent in the United States,[72] making the proportion of GDP devoted to household consumption in France only 87 percent of the proportion of GDP devoted to household consumption in the United States. Because France's GDP is only 70 percent as large per capita as GDP in the United States, consumers in France spend only sixty-one cents for every dollar spent by Americans on consumer items, even as they get 97 or 98 percent as much benefit as Americans.[73] The French are clearly getting a lot more bang for the buck, as it requires only 63 percent as much household expenditures on consumer items in France as in the United States to yield equivalent levels of human satisfaction. Stated otherwise, it takes about 59 percent more input of consumption in the United States than in France to get an equivalent output in human satisfaction. This suggests significant inefficiency in the promotion of human welfare through consumption in the United States as compared to France.

Compare this with the inefficiency of American healthcare exposed in chapter 7. On most measures of health, France has somewhat better health outcomes than the United States while the French spend less than half of what we do on healthcare. According to the OECD, Americans spent $8,233 per capita on healthcare in 2010 while the French spent only $3,974.[74] When it comes to healthcare spending, therefore, the French get in excess of 105 percent more bang for the buck than Americans. As we have seen, household consumption in France yields about 59 percent more bang for the buck. Comparing America's 59 percent greater inefficiency in consumption with its 105 percent greater inefficiency in healthcare yields this conclusion: In comparison with France, consumer spending in the United States is about 56 percent as inefficient in promoting happiness or wellbeing as US healthcare spending is in promoting health. A review of outrageous inefficiencies in American healthcare suggests that 56 percent of such inefficiency is still an impressive amount of inefficiency.

What is more, consumption is 70 percent of US GDP, whereas healthcare spending, which is largely but not entirely a subcategory of consumption, is only about 18 percent of GDP. Because expenditures on consumption (including healthcare consumption) are more than 3.5 times expenditures on healthcare alone, total inefficient spending on consumption (56 percent of more than 3.5) is twice as great as the total of inefficient spending on healthcare. If you take out the healthcare component of consumer spending (treating all healthcare expenditures as consumer spending) the result is that about an equal amount of inefficiency exists in non-healthcare consumer spending as in healthcare spending. Thus, *consumerism as a method of creating enough demand to lower unemployment is, equal to healthcare, a prime example of functional inefficiency.*

However, not all of this inefficiency stems from the problems of individual discontent discussed in this chapter. Some of it stems from the relationship of consumerism to social disaffection discussed in the next chapter.

We can conclude at this point that consumerism passes the tests of creating jobs in the United States while being politically acceptable. Its compatibility with environmental sustainability will be discussed in chapter 13, where we'll see that consumption of certain kinds of services can increase indefinitely without significant environmental harm. But there is no way for consumerism to be actually efficient as a method of promoting human flourishing. It's fundamentally inefficient even though it is functional in the sense of reducing unemployment.

CHAPTER 9

CONSUMERISM, COMPETITION, AND SOCIAL DISAFFECTION

We examined in the last chapter evidence that consumerism and the increased wealth that it represents and helps to promote don't improve human happiness or wellbeing. Explanations for this phenomenon centered on factors of individual psychology. In this chapter we examine the effect of consumerism and increased wealth on human welfare in light of the inherently social nature of human beings. Our social nature helps to explain further why consumerism doesn't augment happiness or wellbeing and is therefore fundamentally inefficient.

✳   ✳   ✳

First, because we are social by nature, we tend to compare our condition with that of others; we tend to want to keep up with the Joneses. In fact, many of us derive our greatest satisfaction from getting ahead of the Joneses, from doing better than other people. Thus, many consumer items are what economists call *positional goods. Any good is a positional good to the extent that its enjoyment is conditional upon competitive comparisons with the consumption patterns of others in society.* When consumer items are primarily positional goods, increased wealth and greater GDP can't augment happiness in society as a whole because as many people as before remain *relatively* poor.

Adam Smith noted in *The Wealth of Nations* the importance of what we now call positional goods. He pointed out that the desire for gold and other precious metals rests largely on the fact that they are rare. He writes,

> With the greater part of rich people, the chief enjoyment of riches consists
> in the parade of riches, which in their eye is never so complete as when they
> appear to possess those decisive marks of opulence which nobody can possess
> but themselves. In their eyes the merit of an object which is in any degree
> either useful or beautiful, is greatly enhanced by its scarcity, or by the great
> labour which it requires to collect any considerable quantity of it, a labour
> which nobody can afford to pay but themselves.[1]

Human evolution may help to explain why people in societies characterized by significant inequality are delighted by invidious contrasts with others.
As Darwin showed, species change and new species emerge as traits of successful individuals are passed down biologically from generation to generation. In evolutionary terms, successful individuals are those who manage to
pass down more traits than others. Success depends on mating and in the
human case having the material and emotional wherewithal to provide for the
next generation for at least the first several years of life. Males of higher rank
in primate groups tend to have better than average access to mates, and both
males and females of higher rank tend to have better than average access to the
material requirements of nurturing their young. Thus, social position may be
emotionally important to human beings as a legacy of our evolutionary past.

This doesn't mean that all humans are emotionally impelled to fight their
way to the top of the social ladder. The impetus for such competition depends
in large part on social context, the context of significant inequality. Foragers,
for example, people who live by hunting and gathering in relatively egalitarian
social groups, emphasize sharing and reciprocity rather than competition and
individual distinction in their social relationships. Individual distinctions can
lead to jealousy and social disruption that foragers can't handle because they
have no police or jails. In addition, a successful hunt is liable to yield more
meat than the individual or nuclear family can consume without waste, so it
makes sense to share with others. Those others, in turn, will share meat when
they are successful in the hunt. No one, even poor hunters, can be allowed to
starve or to be socially isolated because there are few social means of restraining
disruptive individuals. Hence, the foraging way of life tends toward egalitari-
anism. Social relationships are as important among such people as among any
people, but distinguishing oneself as an individual isn't the best way to be

successful socially and biologically. The most successful people in Darwinian terms are those known to cooperate well with others.[2]

As people in society become more specialized and society becomes materially richer, it's possible to sequester disruptive individuals, so it's no longer necessary to avoid invidious distinctions between haves and have-nots. As social hierarchy becomes steeper, therefore, it becomes more useful to compete for individual distinction because people at the low end of the hierarchy may lack what they need to live and reproduce successfully. Thus, people are emotionally predisposed through their evolution to compete more fiercely for social distinction in social contexts of greater inequality. Medical researchers Richard Wilkinson and Kate Pickett put it this way,

> If inequalities are bigger, so that some people seem to count for almost everything and others for practically nothing, where each one of us is placed becomes more important. Greater inequality is likely to be accompanied by increased status competition and increased status anxiety. It is not simply that where the stakes are higher each of us worries more about where he or she comes. It is also that we are likely to pay more attention to social status in how we assess each other. Surveys have found that when choosing prospective marriage partners, people in more unequal countries put less emphasis on romantic considerations and more on criteria such as financial prospects, status and ambition, than do people in less unequal societies.[3]

Modern societies are less egalitarian than forager societies, so individual social distinction is more important. As Thorsten Veblen noted in *The Theory of the Leisure Class*, because consumption is the principal means of competing for social distinction in modern societies, people view themselves and are viewed by others in large part by what they are able to buy and display.[4]

It should come as no surprise, therefore, that among people in rich countries where there are significant differences in buying power between the rich and poor, the relatively rich are happier than the relatively poor. Economist Richard Layard found, for example, that among the top quarter of the population in the United States (as measured by income), 45 percent reported that they were "very happy," but among the bottom quarter only 33 percent considered themselves "very happy." Only 4 percent of the top quarter considered themselves "not very happy," whereas 14 percent of the bottom quarter said they were "not very happy." Similar differences were reported for the top and bottom quarters of the population in Britain.[5] Another study compared the top 10 percent by income with the bottom 10 percent. Among the top 10 percent, 55 percent reported themselves to be "very happy," 1.8 percent said they were "not very happy," and none reported being "not at all happy." Among the bottom 10 percent, by contrast, only 43.9 percent reported themselves to be "very happy," 7.1 percent said they were "not very happy," and 5 percent reported being "not happy at all."[6] Combined with the finding that overall happiness in society doesn't increase with increased per capita income above $20,000 a year, these results suggest that relative income remains a source of happiness or unhappiness for many people even when the society as a whole gains no increase in happiness from increased income.

This finding agrees with common sense. Who wants to be stuck with a black and white television (except the odd philosopher) when everyone else has color? Who wants to be able to afford only a vacation in a neighboring state when most others can afford to vacation overseas? (Not even the odd philosopher.) Thus, income in general is a positional good in wealthy societies like ours, which makes it easy to understand why society as a whole doesn't exhibit increased wellbeing as it becomes wealthier. To the extent that people seek increased consumption in an inegalitarian society in order to avoid envy and to gain joy or self-esteem by keeping up with or ahead of the Joneses, increased consumption can't increase overall happiness or wellbeing in society at large. No matter how much individuals strive for distinction, only 10 percent of people can be in society's top 10 percent. Similar calculations apply to other percents. Thus, increased consumption to avoid envy and attain self-esteem can't increase total wellbeing in society.

Support for this conclusion comes from studies showing that people are so concerned with their social position that they are willing to have lower income, which requires that they consume less, if the income of others in society is lowered even more. In an experiment at Harvard University students were asked to choose which of two imaginary societies they would like to inhabit. In one, the average earnings were $25,000 a year, but they would earn $50,000 a year. In the other, the average earnings were $200,000 a year, but the students in question would earn $100,000. The students understood that they could have more of what money can buy (bigger houses, more powerful cars, etc.) with $100,000 than with $50,000. Nevertheless, the majority of students preferred to earn only $50,000 a year rather than $100,000 a year, presumably because they didn't want to be relatively poor even if their income and consumer purchases were doubled. Happiness thus depends not so much on absolute as on relative income and consumption in rich, inegalitarian societies.[7] The reason is presumably that especially in such societies, as Adam Smith noted, riches are to a large extent positional goods. They are valued because they enable people to keep ahead of the Joneses. They give people pleasure largely because others don't have them. Such pleasure would be destroyed completely if one's own increased riches were acquired in the context of other people gaining even more.

Further support for this view comes from studies that compare desires for individual consumption in societies with different degrees of inequality. If increased inequality motivates greater interest in individual distinction through consumer purchases, we should expect that people in more unequal societies would be more interested than those in more equal societies in individual (or family) consumption. And this is exactly what we find when we compare the United States with western Europe.

One of the most important measures of income inequality in a society is called the Gini Index. According to this index, a score of zero means that everyone in society has the same income, whereas a score of one means that one person in society has all the income. The lower the score, the more equal the society. Our Gini coefficient in 2003, for example, was 0.47, while the Gini coefficient for France was 0.33 and for Germany 0.38, showing that our society is considerably more unequal than French and German society. The median for the world's industrial economies was just 0.31, which indicates even greater equality.[8] Sweden is the most equal society, with a Gini coefficient of 0.23 in 2005.[9] Accordingly, Americans resist high taxes so that they can spend as much of their income as possible on purchases that they make as individuals (and families), which is to say, on consumer purchases. Citizens in more egalitarian France and Sweden, by contrast, are more willing to forego some individual consumption (which could be used to distinguish themselves as individuals) in favor of public projects funded by taxes. In the United States, people pay taxes—at municipal, state, and federal levels—amounting to about 26 percent of GDP, whereas in France the tax burden is about 46 percent of GDP and in Sweden it's 52 percent.[10]

In general, people in more egalitarian wealthy societies, having less evolutionary imperative to distinguish themselves as individuals, work fewer hours, produce less for individual consumption, and consume less as individuals. So inequality is one factor that spurs consumerism in the United States as people seek to improve their social position through what Veblen called "conspicuous consumption." This increases our wealth, our per-capita GDP. But it doesn't increase overall wellbeing because for every winner in the competition for relative distinction there is a loser. To this extent, expenditures of human and natural resources to increase riches are wasted and therefore fundamentally inefficient.

✳   ✳   ✳

But if addressing unemployment with increased consumption fails to promote maximum human flourishing, why do we do it? Is it all just keeping up with the Joneses in a relatively unequal society? I don't think so. Much of our activity is individually rational. It results from what I call *compulsory consumption*, which is distinct from trying to keep up with or ahead of the Joneses.

Consumption is compulsory to the extent that purchases reflect not just the product's attraction in itself, the way I like my refrigerator, or the desire to keep up with or ahead of the Joneses, but additionally (or instead) *the desire of the consumer to avoid some kind of social sanction.* Such consumption is not compelled in any absolute sense, the way people are compelled to fall when they step off a diving board. Very little compulsion in social life is so absolute, as the comedian Jack Benny once illustrated. His public persona included extreme stinginess. He got a big laugh when he failed to reply immediately to a thief's demand, "Your money or your life." After ten seconds of Benny's hesitation, the thief repeated the demand, as the audience laughed, and Benny replied, "I'm thinking it over."[11] The compulsory consumption considered here seldom involves loss of life, but it still puts significant weight on the decision-making scale in favor of consumption. Although purchases made under these conditions are often rational, they generally yield less personal gratification than purchases made simply because the consumer likes the product. The fact that much of our consumption is compulsory in this sense is among the reasons that increased consumption doesn't increase overall happiness in society.

Even though I'm not trying to keep up with the Joneses, I'm a better consumer than I would otherwise be because I'm not immune to *social pressure*, which is the **first** and lowest level of compulsion toward consumption. I live in a suburban area where people have lawns. An environmentally conscious colleague of mine, who's braver than me, planted a wildflower garden in his front yard to avoid the work, expense, and environmental damage associated with creating and maintaining a green lawn in central Illinois. One of his neighbors called the police, claiming that his house was an eyesore. Fortunately, the public official who investigated the complaint could recognize a wildflower garden when he saw it, so my colleague avoided a hefty fine. But he couldn't avoid the visible displeasure of most of his neighbors. Apart from my colleague's example, it would never even occur to me to risk displeasing my neighbors in this way. Instead, I cut my lawn regularly and every year I have a company aerate the soil and spread the appropriate deadly chemicals at prescribed intervals. Because people invented ways of producing green lawns in central Illinois, I find it necessary to pay for the creation and maintenance of such a lawn. Invention is the mother of necessity. I tell my environmentalist friends that I'm hoping to get the Greenpeace award for the greenest lawn.

As this example illustrates, compulsory consumption differs from the social competition of attempting to keep up with or ahead of the Joneses insofar as social competition can take place without punishment. I may feel bad about the age of my refrigerator or the size of my TV, but no one else need know or care. Consumption is compulsory whenever others do care and impose some form of socially sponsored punishment for failure to buy what's for sale.

*   *   *

A **second**, more stringent, level of compulsion exists when failure to purchase products results not only in social disapproval, but a *socially imposed disability*.

Sometimes the physical landscape is structured to make consumption compulsory. Where I live in Springfield, Illinois, having a car for local transportation isn't optional for most people, but required by the distances between the places most people need to go and the inadequacy of reliable and convenient public transportation to get there. People without cars are thus disabled. In general, the inefficiency of the American transportation system examined in chapter 6 is functional, that is, it create jobs, largely because it makes cars and other forms of automotive-related consumption compulsory.

Social disapproval can also debilitate the under-consumer. Imagine submitting a job application produced on a typewriter. This was the norm forty years ago, but today such an application would be so odd as to be futile because it would suggest that the applicant is a countercultural weirdo. Here the punishment for failure to adopt contemporary technology is material, not just social. Refusal to buy and use the new technology reduces employment possibilities, not just invitations to the summer block party, even if the typed application contains all the information in as easily legible form as an application printed out in various colors and several different cleverly designed fonts on a laser printer.

Economist Robert Frank and public policy expert Philip Cook point out that where competition is fierce, as in job applications and sales, relative position among contestants is very important, and consumer purchases can improve one's relative position. Looking like a successful person gives other people the impression that you are competent and therefore that you can be trusted with their business. Hence, it makes sense for a salesman to borrow money to buy a more expensive suit than he can really afford to impress customers. Frank and Cook write, "The more important the job, the more important—and the more expensive—it is to look the part. An aspiring Hollywood agent is ill advised to show up for lunch driving an eight-year-old Ford Escort. In one sense, he cannot afford to buy the new Porsche Carrera; but in another sense, he cannot afford not to."[12]

Frank and Cook note also the need for increasing cosmetic surgery to avoid a personal appearance that is below current standards. The popularity of cosmetic surgery, they point out, has altered our standards for normal appearance. A nose that would once have seemed only slightly larger than average may now seem jarringly big; the same person who once would have looked like an average fifty-five-year old may now look nearly seventy; and someone who once would have been described as having slightly thinning hair or an average amount of cellulite, may now feel compelled to undergo hair transplantation or liposuction.[13]

The same considerations apply to the whiteness of one's teeth. Toothpaste companies advertised for decades that using their product would whiten your teeth, but mostly what they did was at best reduce the rate at which your teeth became yellow. In the last couple of decades, however, teeth whitening products and services have so improved that it is now possible actually to brighten one's teeth to a noticeable extent. This raises the bar of whiteness for socially acceptable teeth. Young people especially are now subject to social punishment if their teeth are as yellow as they tend to become without use of these products. Such people are handicapped in the dating game. Again, invention is the mother of necessity.

Sociologist Juliet Schor gives other examples from the intimate sphere:

Nicole Brown Simpson [the murdered, former wife of O.J. Simpson] and her three sisters, members of a well-off Orange County family, all had breast implants. One suspects the purpose was to get and hold desirable (rich?) men in the "marriage market." Some [women] I interviewed were quite explicit on this point. "Single women . . . well, we tend to spend more money on making ourselves look attractive, be it staying in shape or getting your hair done, waxing, all that kind of stuff. It's just the cost of doing business."[14]

The logic of benefit here is the same as with other positional goods. As more women have their breasts enlarged to gain competitive advantage in certain segments of our mammocentric society, the standard for appropriate breast size increases. The net effect is that whatever competitive advantage women were seeking by having larger breasts will be canceled out overall, as one woman's gain will be another's loss. But this competition does not itself make having breast implants a case of compulsory consumption. It's compulsory consumption because the improved position that results does more than increase the sense of self-worth that comes from having larger than Jones-size breasts. Consuming the services of cosmetic surgeons is compulsory consumption because there are social sanctions for failing to do so. Larger breasts than nature provides have become increasingly prerequisite to a successful social, professional, and personal life in some areas and social groups. A woman with natural-size breasts runs a greater risk of losing Mr. Right in these groups. Thus, like much compulsory consumption, the net effects are not neutral, but negative. There's no net gain in society, but women in general lose because they must increasingly subject themselves to expensive surgery, which can't be pleasant or perfectly safe. However, as with consumerism generally, money changes hands, the economy grows, and jobs are created.

Human height is another example. It's generally believed to be an asset, especially for men in our society, to be tall relative to median height, just as it's generally an asset for women to have larger-than-average breasts. This makes short stature a mild social disability; it correlates with reduced opportunities and success. It is now possible to increase a person's height two to four inches through abdominal injections twelve to fourteen times a week over a period of three to seven years before age twenty with synthetic human growth hormone (hGH).[15] Intended originally for children with particular physiological or genetic disorders that result in notably short stature, in 2003 the Food and Drug Administration approved its use in children whose only problem was that they were projected to be in the bottom one percentile in height, as if being short was a disease.

It's understandable that parents want to protect their children from the negative consequences of particularly short stature, but even if the treatment is perfectly safe, the net effect is no gain for society at all. No matter what medical science produces, *some children*, one percent of them if my calculations are correct, are going to be shorter than the other 99 percent. All that hGH can do is change the individual identities of the children in that category. The overall level of pain in society increases as more and more children are subjected to years of injections by parents and doctors trying to keep them out of the shortest one percent, with no possible gain at the societal level. Even the children treated successfully may not be helped psychologically in the long run, because getting two abdominal shots a day for half a decade might remind them that height is desirable in our society and that their parents consider them deficient in this respect, as the few inches of height that they gain will still leave most of them shorter than average.

What is more, the shots come at a considerable price, $10,000 to $20,000 per year, which is not usually covered by insurance.[16] Poor parents can't afford the shots, so very short poor kids are put at an additional competitive disadvantage in a society where poverty and short stature are already problems. Many people would consider this unfair. In sum, because there's always a shortest one percent, society as a whole is no better off for the cost, pain, and inconvenience of treatments that reallocate the stigma of short stature except, as with consumerism generally, that the practice supports economic growth and creates jobs.

*　*　*

The typed job application is a sign of oddity and the cheap suit a hint of incompetence, but like unenhanced breasts and thinning hair, they need not actually inconvenience anyone other than the person put at a competitive disadvantage. A **third** level of compulsory consumption exists when failure to purchase and use something actually *inconveniences others*. This consideration often applies to the purchase and use of newer communication technologies. Writing in 1998, Juliet Schor calls this "the social dimension of technological change."

> When the telephone was introduced, life without one posed no problems. But as phones became widely disseminated throughout the population, practical difficulties arose. Alternative forms of interpersonal communication declined. . . . Paying a social visit without an advance phone call became less acceptable among the middle classes. Today [1998] rotary phones, already inadequate for accessing certain services, have become nearly obsolete. Callers get annoyed if you don't have an answering machine. In business, voice mail, faxes, and mobile phones are standard, and they are becoming so in private life. As more and more people buy these items, substitutes disappear and life without them becomes more vexing.[17]

Yet again, invention is the mother of necessity. When new models and systems are created and widely disseminated, one is often compelled to buy them. This is different from the planned obsolescence in the automobile industry after World War II, because older cars often worked well even if they were out of style. You needed the new model primarily to feel good about yourself (keeping up with the Joneses), and possibly to avoid some social disapproval (level one compulsory consumerism) or competitive disadvantage (level two compulsory consumption). At worst, you were disadvantaged by the *attitudes* of others, not by their *needs*. The purchase of new communication technologies, by contrast, is for many people more compulsory because of the way business is done today—many employers really *need* to stay in touch with their employees through recently developed means of communication. Failure to purchase and use the new technology may thus be reasonable grounds for losing one's job because of the inconvenience it causes.

✳   ✳   ✳

A **fourth** level of compulsion exists when the *life chances of one's family* are jeopardized by failure to increase consumption. Perhaps the most expensive example of increased consumerism tied to extravagance made rational by society's increasing inequality concerns home purchases and public schools. In the United States, public school education is central to most children's chances of success in life, making it rational for parents to seek good public schools for their children. In most places, property taxes constitute a major part of public school funding, and property taxes reflect in large part the market prices of homes in the school district. In a competitive society such as ours, rational parents want schools for their children that are better than average. They therefore spend increasingly on their houses. One result is that home sizes have increased, going from a median size of 1,600 square feet in 1980 to a median size of 2,400 square feet by 2004.[18] Being larger, these newer homes are more expensive to buy and maintain. But living in an area where such houses are common means living in an area where more money is spent per capita on schools. Thus, in order simply to retain a quality of education for their children that keeps the kids in their relative position with peers, households have to spend more money on housing.

Financial support for schools is not the only factor. Research shows that children benefit educationally from the higher socioeconomic status of class-mates independent of how much is spent per pupil on education in the school district.[19] Thus, another reason for parents to spend more money on housing than they can perhaps afford is to allow their children to attend school with children from families of higher socioeconomic status.

The effect of better public schools on house prices is well documented. Elizabeth Warren (now United States senator from Massachusetts) and Amelia Warren Tyagi, wrote in 2005,

> A 2000 study conducted in Fresno, California, (population 400,000) found that, for similar homes, school quality was *the single most important determinant of neighborhood prices*, more important than racial composition, commute distance, crime rate, or proximity to hazardous-waste site. A 1999 study conducted in suburban Boston showed that two homes less than half a mile apart and similar in nearly every aspect would command significantly different prices if they were in different elementary-school districts. Schools that scored just five percent higher than other local schools on fourth-grade math and reading tests added a premium of nearly $4,000 to nearby homes.[20]

In the five years after the University of Pennsylvania invested in the public schools of its west Philadelphia neighborhood, median home values went from $60,000 to $200,000. More generally, they write, "looking at the period from 1984 to 2001 we find that housing prices for families with at least one minor child at home grew at a rate three times that of other families."[21] Robert Frank cites a study based on the 2000 census showing that median house prices increase most in areas of greatest income inequality. Again, inequality increases consumer spending by making it rational to purchase what one really can't afford because a social sanction accompanies failure to purchase. Many families had their houses foreclosed in the wake of the Great Recession because they had spent more for their houses than they could afford.

*　　*　　*

The gravest form of compulsory consumption, the **fifth** and final level, concerns *physical safety*. Here we approach the Jack Benny level of compulsion. It's rational for people to consume beyond their financial safety zone when rich people in a highly unequal society purchase large, expensive vehicles, such as heavy SUVs. Frank gave this example in 2007,

> Today's entry-level Honda Civic . . . at 2,500 pounds is about the same size as 1985's Honda Accord, whose current model weighs 3,200 pounds. For about the same real price, an Accord buyer in 1985 could buy today's Civic and in the process do better on virtually every performance dimension. . . .
>
> But people who buy a 2,500 pound Civic today will incur a significant risk that they wouldn't have incurred in their 1985 Accords, because they must now share the road with 6,000-pound Lincoln Navigators and 7,500-pound Ford Excursions. The odds of being killed in a collision rise roughly fivefold if your car is struck by one of these large vehicles.[22]

The fact that many other people spend a lot of money to buy extremely large vehicles makes it rational for people of more moderate income to do the same. Thus, again, the inequality in society that enables some people to spend more money on vehicles rationally motivates additional consumption by others.

The fact that so much consumption is in some sense compulsory helps to explain why increased riches don't improve overall happiness in society. It's not that people don't enjoy their consumption, including consumption that's compulsory. Many people like me who find it necessary to use the Internet enjoy it. Many people who buy large SUVs in part to improve their safety on roads that contain many heavy vehicles also enjoy the extra room that SUVs afford. Many people who are forced by competition at work to dress for success enjoy fine clothes. Nevertheless, the aspect of compulsion in such purchases means that in society overall, the pleasure taken in these products may not be as great as could be obtained through alternative uses of time or money absent such compulsion. People are not as happy, all things considered, as they could be.

*   *   *

Consumerism also detracts from human wellbeing by eroding social connections, which public policy professor Robert Putnam calls "social capital" in his landmark work *Bowling Alone*. Because we are social animals, we thrive when social capital is high and suffer when it is low. In the most general terms, "social capital refers to the connections among individuals—social networks and norms of reciprocity and trustworthiness that arise from them."[23] Putnam quotes L. J. Hanifan, state supervisor of rural schools in West Virginia, who wrote in 1916 that social capital refers to

> good will, fellowship, sympathy, and social intercourse among the individuals and families who make up a social unit. . . . The individual is helpless socially, if left to himself. . . . If he comes into contact with his neighbor, and they with other neighbors, there will be an accumulation of social capital, which may immediately satisfy his social needs and which may bear a social potentiality sufficient to the substantial improvement of living conditions in the whole community.[24]

Reciprocity is central to the existence and benefits of social capital because it means that individuals who help others are eventually helped in return. Yogi Berra famously illustrated reciprocity this way: "If you don't go to somebody's funeral, they won't come to yours."[25]

Social capital has declined in the United States since World War II, as evidenced in the increase in divorce and the decrease in almost all forms of volunteering and social engagement in churches, bowling leagues, political parties, and the like.[26] Declining social capital continues in the new century in the form of increased loneliness, defined as a want of intimacy. During the first decade of this century, according to a study by AARP, the percentage of adults forty-five and over who reported themselves to be chronically lonely (meaning "lonely for a long time") increased from 20 percent to about 34 percent.[27]

Decreased social capital has physical consequence. Putnam reports, "The more integrated we are with our community, the less likely we are to experience colds, heart attacks, strokes, cancer, depression, and premature death of all sorts. Such protective effects have been confirmed for close family ties, for friendship networks, for participation in social events, and even for simple affiliation with religious and other civic associations."[28] In fact, "Statistically speaking the evidence for the health consequences of social connectedness is as strong today as was the evidence for the health consequences of smoking at the time of the first surgeon general's report on smoking."

Putnam presents some theories to explain this phenomenon:

First, social networks furnish tangible assistance, such as money, convalescent care, and transportation, which reduces psychic and physical stress and provides a safety net. If you go to a church regularly, and then you slip in the bathtub and miss a Sunday, someone is more likely to notice. Social networks also may reinforce healthy norms—socially isolated people are more likely to smoke, drink, overeat, and engage in other health-damaging behaviors. . . . Finally . . . , [socializing] might actually serve as a physiological triggering mechanism, stimulating people's immune systems to fight disease and buffer stress.[29]

Marriage is a form of social interaction that results in happiness as well as health. "Married people," Putnam maintains, "are consistently happier than people who are unattached, all else being equal. . . . In study after study people themselves report that good relationships with family members, friends, or romantic partners—far more than money or fame—are prerequisites for their happiness. . . . Not only in the United States but around the world . . . , happiness is best predicted by the breadth and depth of one's social connections."[30]

Consumerism impairs personal ties in several ways. One of these is its tendency to increase financial anxiety. People whose main goal is to buy things are encouraged by the commercial culture to spend as much money as they can, which typically results in significant credit card and mortgage debt, and these debts often lead to anxiety about repayment. Putnam reports that "financial anxiety is associated with . . . less frequent attendance at church, less volunteering, and less interest in politics. Even social activities with little or no financial cost are inhibited by financial distress. In fact, the only leisure activity positively correlated with financial anxiety is watching TV."[31]

Increased consumption tends to harm children by eroding family ties and inhibiting development of social skills by dividing family members physically. When I was growing up, we had only one TV set, so my sister and I had to compromise on what to watch when our parents weren't around. This helped us develop social ties (we still speak) and social skills. When our parents were present, we watched whatever they watched. We learned forbearance. The family was together and engaged in the same experience, which encouraged interaction.

Since that time, social wealth has allowed and consumer orientation has promoted increased house size. New single-family houses have gone from an average of under 1,000 square feet in 1950 to 1,600 square feet in 1980 to 2,400 square feet by 2004. Family size, by contrast, has decreased.[32] Thus, the possibility increases of each child having her or his own bedroom and of there being a playroom to boot. TVs are now cheaper so it's increasingly possible for each child to have her or his own TV in her or his own room. In 1970 only 6 percent of sixth graders had a TV in their bedroom, but by 1999 77 percent had one.[33] The bedroom is likely to include a host of other devices—computers, DVD players, electronic games, and so forth—that children can use to entertain themselves without interacting with family members or peers.

*　　*　　*

TV watching is implicated in both increased consumerism and the weakening of personal ties needed for human flourishing. As Victor Lebow realized as long ago as 1955, "Television actually sells the generalized idea of consumption. It promotes the goal of higher living standards." Increasingly since that time, television has fostered consumerism and is now associated with high emphasis on consumption. At the same time, Putnam claims,

> dependence on television for entertainment is not merely *a* significant predictor of civic disengagement. It is *the single most consistent* predictor that I have discovered.
>
> People who say that TV is their "primary form of entertainment" volunteer and work on community projects less often, attend fewer dinner parties and fewer club meetings, spend less time visiting friends, entertain at home less, picnic less, are less interested in politics, give blood less often, write friends less regularly, make fewer long-distance calls, send fewer greeting cards and less e-mail, and express more road rage than demographically matched people who differ only in saying that TV is *not* their primary form of entertainment.[34]

Consumerism leads to financial anxiety and to more TV watching among those who are more socially disengaged because of their anxiety. Increased TV watching, in turn, leads to more consumption, additional anxiety, less civic engagement, poorer health, and less happiness. Worse yet, TV watching seems itself to be addictive and lead to unhappiness independent of its relationship to financial anxiety. People who report their own dependence on TV watching report also higher-than-average levels of headaches, indigestion, and sleeplessness. In addition, "Like other addictive or compulsive behaviors, television seems to be a surprisingly unsatisfying experience. Both time diaries and the 'beeper' studies find that for the average viewer television is about as enjoyable as housework and cooking, ranking well below all other leisure activities and indeed below work itself."[35] But the consumer culture thrives on and therefore encourages TV watching because the TV is such an important means of advertising.

*   *   *

We saw in chapter 8 that consumerism is a fundamentally inefficient way of promoting human flourishing because its use of human and natural resources exacerbates such problems as drug addiction, irrational fears, family discord, physical distress, clinical depression, alcoholism, divorce, and suicide. This chapter suggests that it also erodes the social capital on which flourishing depends. In light of these facts, can a case still be made for increased consumerism?

An advocate of consumerism might respond by citing the work of Harvard economist Benjamin Friedman discussed in chapters 1 and 8. Friedman contends that economic growth correlates well with many healthy *social* values, such as social mobility, openness, tolerance, fairness, and democracy.[36] To the extent that consumerism is needed for economic growth (and increased job opportunities), perhaps, contrary to the contentions of Putnam and Schor that we've just considered, consumerism has beneficial effects at the social if not at the individual level. Perhaps these beneficial social effects are sufficient to justify continued consumerism to fight unemployment.

Unfortunately for this defense of consumerism, Putnam's work shows that when consumerism reduces social capital it also impairs attainment of the very same goals that Friedman claims are advanced by economic growth. Consider, for example, democracy. Putnam reports, "From the 1950s to the

1960s growing numbers of Americans worked for a political party during election campaigns, ringing doorbells, stuffing envelopes, and the like. Since 1968, however, that form of political engagement has plunged."[37] By 1996 the number of people who said that they had been contacted by a party was up, but the number who said that they worked for a party was down. "While membership in a political club was cut in half between 1967 and 1987, the fraction of the public that contributed financially to a political campaign nearly doubled."[38] Political parties had become more professionalized. They took in more money and spent increasingly on the services of paid professionals.

This is consumerism in the political arena. It erodes democracy because democracy, rule by the people, is by definition an interpersonal activity. As Putnam puts it,

> You tell me what you've heard and what you think, and what your friends have heard and what they think, and I accommodate that new information into my mental database as I ponder and revise my position on an issue. In a world of civic networks, both formal and informal, our views are formed through interchange with friends and neighbors. Social capital allows political information to spread.[39]

But as we've seen, as people enmeshed in the consumer culture try to earn as much money as possible to buy all that they want, social capital, including the civic networks essential to democracy, diminishes. An indication that buying the services of political professionals degrades democracy is decreasing knowledge among the public about such basic matters as which party controls the House of Representatives.[40] An indication that buying the services of professionals has increased since Putman wrote in the late 1990s is the continually increasing costs of political campaigns.[41]

Consumerism also threatens tolerance, another of the values prized by Friedman which Friedman thinks, perhaps correctly, is promoted by economic growth. The problem is that the decline of social capital, an effect of the consumerism used to promote economic growth, jeopardizes tolerance. Writing in the late 1990s, Putnam sounds prescient when it comes to the erosion of social capital jeopardizing the willingness to tolerate and accommodate opposing views and individuals:

> If participation in political deliberation declines—if fewer and fewer voices engage in democratic debate—our politics will become more shrill and less balanced. When most people skip the meeting, those who are left tend to be more extreme, because they care most about the outcome. . . . Controlling for all the standard demographic characteristics—income, education, size of city, region, age, sex, race, and job, marital and parental status—Americans who describe themselves as "very" liberal or "very" conservative are more likely to attend public meetings [and] write Congress . . . than their fellow citizens of more moderate views.[42]

To those who might say that more extreme individuals, because they feel strongly about issues, have always been disproportionately represented in public deliberations, Putnam replies that this tendency has been exacerbated in recent decades by the decline of political participation among people with more moderate views. "In the 1990s self-described middle-of-the-roaders were about *one half* as likely to participate in public meetings, local civic organizations, and political parties as in the mid-1970s."[43] The twenty-first century has seen increased political polarization that impairs democratic decision making.

The consumerist erosion of social capital threatens to increase extremism, too, because consumerism leaves more people socially isolated, and socially isolated individuals are more likely to fall prey to extremist political views and organizations.[44] Sociologist William Kornhauser wrote in the 1950s, "People divorced from community, occupation, and association are first and foremost among the supporters of extremism."[45]

In general, Putnam finds, the younger generation in the United States tends to be more tolerant than previous generations on matters of gender and race equality. But within each generation, those who are more socially engaged (with the exception of those whose major social engagement is within fundamentalist churches) are more tolerant than those with fewer social ties. The same is true regarding toleration of dissenting and unpopular political views. During the McCarthy era of the 1950s, for example, people involved in citizen-participation initiatives were found to be more tolerant of controversial speakers than those not involved.[46] It has been shown more recently that "citizens of high-social-capital states are far more tolerant of civil liberties and far more committed to racial and gender equality than citizens of low-social-capital states."[47]

Friedman mentions increasing fairness as one of the advantages of economic growth. Increasing social capital also correlates with increasing fairness, as can be seen by comparing the 1950s and 1960s with more recent decades. Social capital was high in the 1950s and 1960s and the gap between rich and poor was relatively small. Starting around 1970, however, social capital began to decline as the gap between rich and poor increased.[48]

This correlation is no coincidence. Unions are a form of social capital; they are associations where people typically gather to discuss and decide matters of mutual interest. Fighting for higher wages, unions helped to reduce the gap between the rich and poor from the 1930s to the 1960s. Between 1935 and 1945, for example, union membership increased from 12 percent to 35 percent of the workforce, and wages increased dramatically.[49] Between 1947 and 1973, while the social capital represented by union membership was still high, workers' (inflation adjusted) wages rose along with their increased productivity, both doubling during that time. This was fair. As union membership has declined, however—by 2012 unions represented only 11.3 percent of workers, a 97-year low[50]—so has the fair distribution of extra wealth stemming from increased worker productivity. Between 1980 and 2005, worker productivity increased 71 percent, but (inflation adjusted) wages increased only 19 percent, while the top one percent of earners increased their share of GDP from 8.2 percent to 17.4 percent.[51]

Nonunion forms of social capital also promote fairness. Hazardous waste sites are typically located near poor neighborhoods and towns. Economist James Hamilton found, however, that companies deciding where to discard hazardous waste tend to avoid communities where they are likely to encounter organized opposition.[52] Here, social capital in the form of community organization increases fairness.

Social mobility, another value that Friedman claims is advanced by economic growth, is also advanced by social capital. Education and other elements of child welfare are key elements in such mobility, and child welfare improves with social capital. For example, Putnam writes,

"Community psychologists have long noted that child abuse rates are higher where neighborhood cohesion is lower."[53] In a group of at-risk children whom researchers followed for several years, "the best predictor of which children successfully avoided {behavioral and emotional} problems was the degree to which they and their mothers were enmeshed in a supportive social network, lived in a socially supportive neighborhood, and attended church regularly."[54] Another study shows a correlation among African-American children of high social capital with lower rates of depression. Finally, social capital improves student performance beyond what can be done by more education-specific measures, such as reducing class size, as illustrated in a comparison of student performance on standardized tests given in both North Carolina and Connecticut. North Carolina ranks number forty-one among the fifty states on such measures of student performance as SAT scores, achievement tests, and dropout rates, whereas Connecticut ranks number nine. The main statistical difference between the states is social capital: the informal social capital of people visiting with friends and playing cards and the formal social capital of people participating in clubs, attending church, etc.

In sum, Friedman points out that economic growth promotes openness, tolerance, mobility, fairness, and democracy. However, social capital also promotes these values. If economic growth requires ever-increasing consumer demand, we have a dilemma, because consumerism erodes social capital, thereby impairing attainment of these values. Unless a different, non-consumerist means of generating economic growth can be deployed, we will have to choose between two incompatible ways of promoting openness, tolerance, mobility, fairness, and democracy—economic growth and increased social capital. In light of the toll that we have seen consumerism to exact on individual psychological wellbeing, advocates of economic growth may have a hard time showing that continued economic growth promotes human welfare, all things considered, even though it seems essential to the reduction of unemployment.

*   *   *

Again, it seems that a great deal of the consumerism needed to underpin economic growth is functional but inefficient. Consumerism is functional insofar as the economic growth that it enables provides jobs and reduces unemployment. It's inefficient insofar as a great deal of human and natural capital is expended without net improvement in human wellbeing.

Another concern about consumer-driven economic growth is that it seems to run up against environmental limits. Chapters 12 and 13 consider this issue and conclude that many types of service-sector growth can continue indefinitely without significant environmental harm. When the economy grows through increasing provision of such services there are no environmental limits to economic growth. We'll find, however, that much of this service-sector growth results from consumerism and therefore suffers from the limitations of consumerism; it's fundamentally inefficient even though it's functional (it reduces unemployment).

CHAPTER 10

IDLING WORKERS II

MORE VACATIONS AND PAID LEAVES,
FEWER HOURS, AND EARLIER RETIREMENT

As we saw in chapter 2, unemployment is a morally devastating and even physically burdensome way of idling workers, which is why politicians of all stripes consider it important to keep unemployment numbers low. Idling workers through society-wide decreases in the number of hours worked per week, increases in days of paid vacation, increases in paid family leaves, and earlier retirements often have less negative effects. Consequently, these are among the methods that have been used for over a century to idle workers and curtail overproduction.

Idling workers can be environmentally benign. When people in industrial societies work fewer hours and therefore (other things being equal) have less money to spend during their time off than they would have if they worked more, their activities are usually less burdensome on the environmental than when they work and spend more. Relaxing on the beach, reading a book, playing tennis, and watching TV do not tax the environment as much as buying and using cars and other such material goods. With less money to spend there is less pursuit of leisure activities with greater environmental impact, because such activities—racing cars, flying private planes, yachting, and even taking commercial flights to distant vacation spots—are relatively expensive. There is less environmental impact, for example, when a family saves money by using its car to reach its vacation destination than when it spends more money to fly to a more distant vacation spot, possibly overseas. In general, then, idling workers meets one of the conditions of promoting employment. It can be relatively environmentally sustainable.

In the long run, it meets the goal of reducing unemployment as well. The great economist John Maynard Keynes, writing in 1930, attributed some of the high levels of unemployment experienced at that time to what he called *"technological unemployment.* This means unemployment due to our discovery of means of economizing the use of labour outrunning the pace at which we can find new uses for labour."[1] Keynes is here stating one of the presuppositions of this book. Unemployment stems at least in part from the fact that technological progress improves labor (meaning industrial or manufacturing) efficiency, so we need fewer workers to produce what people want and need. For this reason, some people are thrown out of work.

Keynes recognized that economists tend to think that people have insatiable needs. Thus, according to these economists, our economy will provide enough work for people no matter how efficient our production. In the long run, people's insatiable demand for goods and services will make it profitable for employers to continue paying workers to be productive because consumer demand is a bottomless pit that can absorb production no matter how much our improved efficiencies increase abundance.

Keynes disagreed with this view. He writes that human needs

> fall into two classes—those which are absolute in the sense that we feel them whatever the situation of our fellow human beings may be, and those which are relative in the sense that we feel them only if their satisfaction lifts us above, makes us feel superior to, our fellows. Needs of the second class, those which satisfy the desire for superiority, may indeed be insatiable; for the higher the general level, the higher still are they. But this is not so true of the absolute needs—a point may soon be reached, much sooner perhaps than we are all of us aware of, when these needs are satisfied in the sense that we prefer to devote our further energies to non-economic purposes.[2]

Keynes apparently didn't think that the demand for products stemming from the desire for superiority was truly insatiable. Instead, he claimed that limitations on consumer demand stemming from limits on people's needs, both absolute and relative, would divert people from economically related tasks. Consumption would fall well below what was needed to keep everyone working full time. In order to keep most people working at all, he thought, "we shall endeavor to spread the bread thin on the butter—to make what work that is still to be done to be as widely shared as possible. Three-hour shifts or a fifteen-hour week may put off the problem for a great while."[3]

Keynes clearly underestimated the potential for consumer demand to increase. Our productive capacities have increased about four-fold since 1930, but the fifteen-hour week is nowhere considered full-time. Yet, he was not entirely wrong either; the number of hours worked by average employees has fallen significantly as our productive powers have increased. Thus, idling workers has proven helpful in forestalling unemployment.

Industrialized countries have reduced the average length of the workday and work week and increased the number of vacation days and holidays, with consequent reduction in the number of hours most people work per year. For example, in France the average worker spent 66.1 hours per week on the job in 1870, 65.9 in 1900, 48.0 in 1929, 45.9 in 1960, and 38.5 in 2000. This decline in the number of hours worked per week is typical. In the same time periods, Sweden's workers went from working 69.6 hours per week in 1870, to 56.0 hours, 48.0 hours, 43.4, and finally 37.7 hours in 2000. Belgians between 1870 and 2000 went from working over 72 hour per week to working about 37 hours per week, while Americans went from working 62 hours per week to working about 40 hours per week. In general, Americans and others in the New World, such as Canadians and Australians, tend in recent decades to work more hours than western Europeans in the Old World. On average, people in the New World work about 40 hours per week, whereas those in the Old World average only 37.5 hours.[4]

Declines in hours worked per week are reflected in declines in hours worked per year. In 1870 workers in most Old World (European) econo-mies spent more time on the job than workers in such New World econo-mies as the United States, Canada, and Australia. In 1870, French workers spent 3,168 hours on the job each year and workers in Belgium 3,483 hours, whereas people in the United States worked only 3,096 hours. This pattern was reversed, however, in the 1970s. For the last four decades Americans have worked more hours than their European counterparts. In 2000 Americans worked 1,878 hours per year, while Belgians worked 1,547 hours, and the French only 1,443 hours. Since work is typically forty hours per week in the

United States, the four hundred hours per year that Americans work more than the French represents ten weeks of additional work.[5]

This disparity reflects and is partly caused by differences between the New and Old Worlds regarding the idling of workers through vacations and holidays. In both the Old and New Worlds vacations and holidays increased between 1870 and 2000. France, for example, had eighteen days of vacation and holidays in 1870 but thirty-six in 2000. Sweden went from eleven to thirty-eight days, and Belgium from eighteen to thirty-three. The United States, by contrast, although increasing vacations and holidays between 1870 and 2000 from four days to twenty days, lagged significantly behind European countries throughout the period.[6]

There is little doubt that the increase in idling workers between 1870 and 2000 reflects and responds to the increased productivity of workers over the decades. We can have more material abundance than our ancestors while working fewer hours largely because each hour that we do work we produce more than our ancestors did. And decreased hours worked has helped to contain unemployment by reducing overproduction. Imagine what our unemployment problems would be today if full-time employment was sixty hours per week. It's hard to imagine how we would absorb the fruits of all that productive activity. Thus, it appears that idling workers can be environmentally sustainable and that over the long run it reduces unemployment. But is it efficient? And would increased worker idling be politically acceptable in the United States? The present chapter concentrates on these two questions.

* * *

Much debate about worker idling in recent years has centered on what many people consider the next step in reducing work hours to contain unemployment—France's legally mandated thirty-five-hour workweek. Has it improved employment prospects in France? Is it efficient in the sense of resulting in as much dollar productivity per hour of work as the alternative forty-hour week? Is it monetarily efficient enough to allow French products to compete globally with products made where the workweek is longer? Is it efficient in the fundamental sense of using human and natural resources to produce maximum human flourishing?

The law requiring firms employing twenty or more people to maintain a thirty-five-hour workweek took effect in February 2000. It mandated a reduction of four hours of work per week from the previous norm of thirty-nine hours. Smaller firms were given an additional two years to establish a thirty-five-hour work week. The law still allows people to work more than thirty-five hours in a week, but non-managerial workers, and even some managers, must receive overtime pay if they average more than thirty-five hours per week in any given year.[7]

Has it worked as intended to curtail French unemployment? Opinions differ and I can't tell who's right. The Socialist Party claimed during the 2011 presidential campaign in France that the law had created around 350,000 jobs.[8] The following year, however, an expert panel headed by business executive Louis Gallois claimed that France had lost 750,000 industrial jobs during the preceding decade and that France's trade balance was deteriorating. The new Socialist government seemed to accept these findings,[9] and economists Marcello Estevao and Filipa Sa conclude their study with the claim that "the 35-hour workweek in France failed to create more jobs."[10] On the other hand, French unemployment declined with the advent of the thirty-five-hour week. The French unemployment rate was over 10.5 percent in 1998 and 1999, shortly before implementation of the thirty-five-hour workweek and then dropped to a low of 8 percent two years after implementation. It has been up and down since that time and averaged over 10 percent in 2012[11] after three straight quarters of zero economic growth.[12] The significance of these figures is uncertain, however, because the entire euro zone was stagnant in 2012. Perhaps unemployment would have been worse (or not as bad) without the thirty-five-hour week. I really don't know.

Worker pay was reduced very little, if at all, as the work week diminished, thereby increasing the per-hour cost of labor. The government compensated firms for the extra cost of labor by giving them rebates on their social security contributions. Economists Estevao and Sa write, "The official argument was that productivity increases together with cuts in social security contributions might even lead to a reduction in labour costs, so that firms would not need to cut monthly wages for the policy to be sustainable."[13]

Journalist John Carney and financial analyst Vincent Fernando argued in

Business Insider in 2009 that the French are, indeed, among the most productive workers in the world, and that they are certainly more productive than Americans. They write,

> France has $36,500 GDP/Capita and works 1,453 hours per year. This equates to a GDP/Capita/Hour of $25.10. Americans, on the other hand, have $44,150 GDP/Capita but work 1,792 hours per year. Thus Americans only achieve $24.60 of GDP/Capita/Hour.
>
> This puts the French . . . at about $0.50 GDP/Capita/Hour over the US. It may sound small at first, but add that up across millions of people, and a few decades. Now you've built a lesson for the rest of the world to learn.
>
> Winning is not about working hard. It's about working smart . . . and less.[14]

Even if $.50 per hour isn't statistically significant, it seems that thirty-five-hours-a-week French workers are reasonably efficient as measured by monetary productivity per hour of work.

Is the thirty-five-hour workweek efficient also in the sense of allowing French products to compete successfully with products made in countries where people work more hours per week? Opinions differ. The international news provider France 24 reported in 2012 that "Many [French] employers claimed that it [the 35-hour workweek] bloated labour costs and blunted their ability to compete in world markets."[15] The same year, France's Socialist government also expressed concern that French labor costs were too high for French products to remain competitive in international markets.[16] But Prime Minister Jean-Marc Ayrault told French radio, "There will be no rolling back on the 35-hour week because it is not the cause of our difficulties."[17] The government's response was to lower labor costs not by increasing the number of hours worked per week, but by cutting the payroll tax that companies must pay.

Not everyone agrees, however, that French labor costs are too high. Claude Mailly, secretary general of the relatively militant labor union Force Ouvrière, disputes that claim. More telling because it comes from a more neutral source, foreign exchange figures supplied by Trading Economics, which provides economic indicators for 196 countries, show that France is not losing ground in international competition. Countries that are uncompetitive internationally generally import more than they export, because consumer goods are generally produced more efficiently elsewhere than in those countries. But beginning in 1999 France's trade balance with the rest of the world, although up and down on a yearly basis, has been slightly positive, with 2011 being a relatively good year.[18] It would seem that France continues to be competitive internationally in spite of (if not because of) its thirty-five-hour workweek. The United States, by contrast, runs considerable trade deficits year after year even though we have a forty-hours-per-week standard. Also, the French competitiveness problem couldn't be too bad because three thousand American companies have established a presence in France and employ more than half-a-million thirty-five-hours-per-week French workers.[19] In sum, on the efficiency measure of international competitiveness, French workers seem to be competitive enough.

✳   ✳   ✳

What about efficiency in the most fundamental sense? Does the thirty-five-hour week maximize the human welfare that results from expenditures of human and natural resources? If popularity is any measure, it does, as demonstrated by the political difficulty of significantly altering the law. Nicolas Sarkozy ran for president of France in 2007 as head of a conservative party (UMP) which opposed the thirty-five-hour week as promoting inefficiency and economic decline. But after winning the election Sarkozy and the UMP made only minor alterations to the law. Then in 2011, when Sarkozy was up for reelection, Jean-François Copé, the leader of UMP, again expressed opposition to the law, saying in a press interview that ending the thirty-five-hour law is "inescapable" and telling a party meeting, "We invite workers to work more and better. . . . The 35 hours must no longer be taboo." Yet even he declined to endorse outright repeal of the law, calling only for its fundamental revision.[20] After the Socialists defeated Sarkozy and the UMP in 2012, the new Socialist Party Prime Minister, Jean-Marc Ayrault, raised a storm in October of that year when he suggested possibly changing the law to allow thirty-nine instead of just thirty-five hours in a full week of work. He soon "clarified" his comments to rule out any such possibility.[21] It seems at the very least that, regardless of its wisdom, the thirty-five-hour law is as popular in France as

Social Security and Medicare are in the United States, making its abolition a third rail in French politics.

It's easy to see why. In 2009, CBS News reporter Lara Logan investigated reasons for the law's popularity, and found evidence that the thirty-five-hour workweek and associated long annual vacations and numerous public holidays make efficient use of human and natural resources to further human welfare. She interviewed Stephane Marchand, a senior economics editor at the conservative French newspaper *Le Figaro*. In the United States such editors are thought of as workaholics on constant call because their job security and advancement depend on successful competition with other papers. Even in France, as a manager Marchand often works more than thirty-five hours a week. However, in compensation for long hours, the thirty-five-hour-week law provides him with extra vacation time. So instead of the five weeks of paid vacation, which is standard in France, Marchand told Logan that he and others in his position take eight weeks of paid vacation. In addition, France has twelve public holidays each year which give managers like Marchand and most other French workers even more days off.[22]

You don't have to be French to find the French approach attractive. Logan interviewed Katherine Melchior Ray who left a senior management position at Nike in the United States to work in the French fashion industry. Although her French job is just as high-powered as her former American job, she now takes weekends off and enjoys her five weeks of vacation each year. She told Logan, "I don't check in, I don't check my e-mail. I don't call on the phone and no one expects me to. You really go on vacation." In sum, she says of her five weeks of vacation, "It feels just great."[23] Ray claims in addition that such vacations may be economically beneficial. She noticed that "People came back [from vacation] and it was like everyone had had 10 shots of espresso; they were just ready to go. They were like Eveready bunnies;[24] everyone was going together and there was a team work that was inspiring."

No one doubts, however, that French GDP is lower than it would be if French workers spent more time on the job. For their free time, French workers give up some money, some services that money can buy, and some individually owned material possessions. The popularity of the thirty-five-hour workweek suggests that the French consider the trade-off to be beneficial overall.

*   *   *

Some other worker-idling strategies besides reducing the standard workweek seem also to improve human welfare. Consider maternity leaves. The International Labour Organization (ILO) of the United Nations established minimal standards of maternity leaves at fourteen weeks, during which pay should be at least two-thirds of full-time pay. Except for Norway, all western European countries exceed the ILO standard's length of maternity leave, and all except Britain and Ireland exceed the standard for the percent of full-time pay. Austria, France, Luxembourg, the Netherlands, and Spain provide sixteen weeks at full pay. The western European average is nineteen weeks at 86.5 percent of pay.[25] United States law, by contrast, requires twelve weeks of leave, which applies only to employers with fifty or more workers, and requires no pay at all. Monetary loss may influence many American women to return to work in advance of twelve weeks.[26]

Paid leave following the birth or adoption of a child seems to improve wellbeing. A 2011 report by Human Rights Watch (HRW) documented the baleful effects on American workers who were given little paid leave when a new child entered their family. HRW interviewed sixty-four people from around the country. "Parents said that having scarce or no paid leave contributed to delaying babies' immunizations, postpartum depression and other health problems, and caused mothers to give up breastfeeding early."[27] This HRW report supports the findings of a study in 2005 that documented a reduction of six or seven percent in symptoms of postpartum depression for every additional week of maternity leave. Infant as well as maternal health is improved by paid maternity leaves. A study in 2010 found that if the percentage of infants being breastfed for at least six months was increased from the current 43 percent in the United States to 90 percent, nine hundred infant deaths would be prevented and $13 billion would be saved each year. Extended paid maternity leave encourages such healthful breastfeeding. It was found in Canada that by increasing the length of paid maternity leave from six months to one year the number of infants breastfed for at least six months increased 40 percent. Median time of breastfeeding doubled in California after introduction of their mandatory family leave policy. Congruent with this evidence, a sixteen-nation European study from 1969 to 1994 documented a 20 percent decline in postneonatal deaths and a 15 percent increase in childhood survival to age five when the entitlement to paid parental leave was extended to fifty weeks.[28] In addition, HRW found, "Many who took unpaid leave went into debt and some were forced to seek public assistance,"[29] so payment during leave is crucial. In sum, at least one form of idling workers, mandated extended paid family leaves upon the birth or adoption of a child, is fundamentally efficient insofar as the time off work not only reduces over-productivity, but promotes human wellbeing by increasing beneficial activities and reducing negative outcomes.

Extended higher education is another way of idling workers, as it places people who would seek full-time employment in a context where studying without pay is the norm, and most individuals work only part-time if at all. Better-educated individuals help our industries remain competitive because they are more competent workers. They can also provide more competent services in such vital areas as teaching, healthcare, scientific research, and communication technologies. In addition, such people earn higher salaries and are generally happier than those with less education.[30]

However, there is irony here. More highly educated individuals generally command higher salaries because they are more productive than their less-educated counterparts. Ironically, their greater productivity may exacerbate the original problem of over-productivity that results in endemic unemployment. If the unemployment problem results from too much labor efficiency in highly developed industrial societies, idling workers in higher educational programs that subsequently improve labor efficiency is not a permanent solution. It alleviates the problem of unemployment temporarily while laying the groundwork for its exacerbation at a later time. In other respects, on the other hand, higher education appears to improve human wellbeing insofar as it promotes happiness.

The same cannot be said of idling workers through incarceration. People don't seem to enjoy it and, unlike higher education, it diminishes rather than increases employment prospects upon completion. Also, a higher proportion of ex-convicts than of the general population are antisocial, often engaging in illegal activities. Incarceration is therefore best kept to the minimum necessary to contain socially disruptive individuals.

In sum, on the measure of fundamental efficiency, it seems that giving people longer paid family leaves and more higher education tends to promote human welfare even though it tends to lower GDP (at least in the short run). In the French context, shorter workweeks also seem to improve human well-being as measured by popular preference. In addition, because idled people tend to have less disposable income, their lifestyle is more likely to be environmentally sustainable. So idling workers in these ways, but not through more incarceration, seems an efficient use of human and natural resources.

*   *   *

But can these methods of idling workers and the benefits of their use be transferred to the American context? There may be cultural differences between Americans and Europeans that place greater political limits in the United States than in Europe on the practice of idling workers to combat unemployment.

About half the difference in annual hours of work between Americans and Europeans stems from differences in the number of days of paid vacation. Americans typically have about two weeks of paid vacation each year whereas western Europeans typically have about five.[31] What is more, when European Union workers become sick during their vacation time (so sick that they wouldn't be able to work if they weren't on vacation), they have the right to more vacation time because the time when they are ill is covered by sick leave. So if an EU worker is on a three-week vacation and ill during two of those three weeks, she has the right to two weeks of additional vacation to make up for the two weeks she was sick.[32]

I don't see comparable vacation times or rules in America's future any time soon. The prospects for extending American vacations seem particularly dim in light of the fact that many Americans don't even take the full two weeks that they are given. In 1992, for example, a study found that Americans took, on average, only twelve of the fourteen days of their allotted vacation.[33]

It's hard to imagine, too, that American employers will any time soon agree to pay family or maternity leaves of six months or more at 65 or 75 percent of salary as is common in Europe. The United States has negative balances of payments with the rest of the world, so it seems unlikely that our government would promote, or that our businesses would accept, a worker-idling strategy that tends to reduce international competitiveness by increasing labor costs.

In addition to differences in the number of paid vacation days and in family leave policies, Americans work more hours per year than western Europeans because Europeans enjoy more generous social programs than Americans, and Americans may be less willing than Europeans to spend taxpayer money on such programs. For example, in Europe everyone has health insurance regardless of their income or job status, so no one has to continue working to remain insured or work additional hours to afford insurance. Staying with France as our main example, the government helps families with children additionally by defraying some household expenses that most Americans pay primarily out of pocket. France gives all families with two or more children a child allowance meant to defray some of the expenses of raising a child. In 2012 families with two children under twenty years of age received a monthly benefit of almost 128 Euros, or about $165. For each additional child, the family received (approximately) an additional $210 each month.[34] Single parents received more.

Childcare is also subsidized. Poor families with a child under three years-of-age received about $560 per month toward paying for the childcare of their choosing in 2012. Every family with such a child, rich or poor, received at least $220 per month for this purpose. But if the childcare is from an approved association or company, every family received at least $580 dollars a month, with the poorest families getting almost half again as much. Poor and lower-middle-class families also received a "Back-to-school allowance (ARS)" for children between the ages of six and eighteen. This was worth about an additional $400 per year, depending on family income and the number of children in the family. But wait! There's more! Poor families also received a family income supplement worth about $215 a month, and poor families with three children could get an additional one-time payment of $1,250 to defray the expenses of moving.[35]

In the light of all these benefits, people in France and others in Europe who enjoy similar benefits can work fewer hours per week, fewer weeks per year, and earn less money without becoming truly impoverished. This may help to explain why Europeans are more willing than Americans to forgo income in order to have more time off of work. When Americans, Germans, and Swedes were asked whether, given their current rate of pay, they would like to work more hours, fewer hours, or their current number of hours, Americans were more likely than the Europeans to prefer working more hours in spite of the fact that, as we've seen, Americans already work more hours than Europeans.[36]

An alternative to the elaborate European system of social support for families is proposed for the United States by political economist Robert Skidelsky and philosopher Edward Skidelsky. However, it would still require more taxpayer support than Americans may be willing to provide to foster the idling of workers. The Skidelskys propose providing everyone with a basic income. Unlike a minimal income, which is means-tested and goes only to the relatively poor, the basic income that they envision "is an unconditional payment to all citizens, ideally at a level high enough to give them a genuine choice of how much to work."[37] Many people, they think, would work less if they were endowed with such a basic income, thereby solving or reducing problems of unemployment that stem from overproduction.

One concern about the Skidelskys' plan is the cost. The Skidelskys meet this concern by pointing out that the problem of unemployment exists precisely because people have become too productive, so there must be the wherewithal to pay for such a basic income. The other main objection is that a basic income will discourage many people from working, as they will be able to get by with little or no work. The Skidelskys reply that this is true, but it's exactly the desired result—reduce unemployment by idling workers without unemployment. The voluntary idling that the basic income promotes doesn't detract from human wellbeing as does unemployment.

Another method of idling workers without unemployment is through retirement, but retirement ages differ among advanced industrialized countries. The retirement age in the United States is currently sixty-six for those wishing to get full benefits from Social Security.[38] The age is scheduled to increase to sixty-seven in the next several years, and there are Social Security incentives to delay retirement to age seventy.[39] Among other OECD countries, only Norway places retirement at sixty-seven, and 60 percent of Norwegian workers are eligible for full retirement as young as age sixty. In other OECD countries, retirement ages range from sixty to sixty-five, although there is a trend toward increasing the age of retirement. In France it is currently sixty-two.[40] In general, Americans are idled less by retirement than are western Europeans, just as workweeks, paid vacations, paid holidays, and paid family leaves idle Americans less than they idle western Europeans.[41]

*   *   *

Whether it's a robust western European-style social safety net, earlier retirement with full benefits, or a basic income, it remains to be seen if idling workers through social provision of necessities and some comfort can be politically acceptable in the United States. According to sociologist James Russell, the strong European social safety net stems at least in part from conservative acceptance of Catholic teaching going back to St. Augustine. Augustine taught that rulers are superior to those who are ruled, making equality and democracy inappropriate. The ruled have a duty of obedience to their superiors. But rulers owe mercy and care to the ruled. In a world beset by original sin, rulers have the responsibility to promote the good of the community conceived as an organic whole. After the Middle Ages, Russell writes, "Order based on hierarchy and obedience, but with obligations of the higher to the lower classes, would culturally mutate into contemporary European conservative acceptance of the welfare state. Conservatives would be able to see in the welfare state a way to socialize their obligations to the less privileged."[42]

In the New World, by contrast, greater individualism prevailed. This results in part from the greater influence of the Calvinist doctrine of predestination. The Puritans considered worldly success an outer sign of inner virtue, which implies that poor people are poor because they lack inner virtue and therefore deserve their unenviable condition. Therefore, no one has an obligation to help them; they should help themselves. Frontier conditions also favored this individualist view. On the frontier people start relatively equal (compared to social starting places in the Old World), so success and failure can be attributed largely to an individual's hard work and intelligence, making the fruits of success and failure individually deserved. Again, no one has an obligation to alter economic results that reflect just rewards. Americans thus favor equality of opportunity but are less willing than western Europeans to pay for a social safety net that ameliorates inequalities of outcome.[43]

An additional consideration is the stronger role of labor unions in western Europe than in the United States. Longer vacations and shorter work weeks have been major demands of European labor unions.[44] The greater strength of labor unions in Europe compared to the United States may reflect the greater harshness of working conditions during the Industrial Revolution in Europe. The American frontier, besides encouraging the kind of individualism at odds with unionization, afforded an avenue of escape from some of the harshest nineteenth-century conditions, thereby weakening the appeal of labor unions for many American workers.

People tend to think collectively also when they are under attack. Most countries in western Europe experienced military conflict on their soil between 1936 and 1945. Under such conditions it's obvious to people that they cannot extricate themselves from horrific conditions and provide good lives for themselves through individual action. Writing of experiences in Great Britain during World War II, for example, political scientist Malcolm Pearce and historian Geoffrey Stewart point out that many people of all classes shared the experience of evacuating their children to the countryside. Regardless of class, they also shared rationing food; they shared time in bomb shelters; they shared the risk of death from German bombs; and they shared entertainment. This had a leveling effect that paved the way for Labour Party electoral victories at the end of the war and socialist legislation in the years that followed.[45] Presumably, similar experiences produced similar results in other western European countries, leading to stronger unions, a greater sense of social solidarity, and less reliance on the kind of individualism that inhibits unionization and the construction of a more robust social safety net in the United States.

Extensive maternity leave with little loss of pay, one of the ways that Europeans idle workers more than Americans, may be largely a response to low birthrates in Europe. Italy, Spain, and Greece, for example, have birthrates near 1.3 children per woman,[46] whereas 2.1 children per woman is the replacement rate, the rate at which a population remains steady. At 1.3 a country could lose half its population in less than fifty years.[47] No European country has a birthrate as high as the replacement rate, so extensive maternity leave with little loss of pay and a social safety net that includes payments to families simply for having children and generous support for early childcare

are designed at least in part to boost birthrates. The United States enjoys a higher birthrate without these employer- and government-provided benefits.

If these are the reasons for a stronger safety net and acceptance of reduced hours of work in Europe as compared to the United States, the prospects for increasing idling in America to combat unemployment seem dim. We can't change or reproduce centuries-old religious influences, nineteenth-century experiences of the Industrial Revolution, or twentieth-century social bonding during World War II, nor does the American birthrate warrant the kind of pronatalist policies that are common in Europe. If these are the major bases for European acceptance of idling, Americans may seem doomed to remain relative workaholics and either suffer consequent unemployment or use some other methods of reducing unemployment, such as more inefficient systems of transportation and healthcare.

✳   ✳   ✳

A different understanding of the reasons for Americans working so many more hours than western Europeans provides a more promising basis for altering American practices in a way that reduces unemployment. It seems that there must be a different explanation for differences between Europe and the United States, because if the different work habits of Europeans and Americans really reflected the deep-seated different world views of St. Augustine and Calvin, or the influences of the Industrial Revolution and World War II, it would be difficult to explain why Americans worked the same or fewer hours than many Europeans until the 1970s. As noted earlier, in 1870 Americans worked on average fewer hours per year than most western Europeans. Americans worked 3,096 hours per year, while the French worked 3,168 hours and the Germans 3,284 hours. In 1900 the figures are 2,938 for the United States versus 3,115 and 3,056 for the French and Germans. In 1950 the French and Germans were still working more hours than Americans. But by 1973 positions were reversed, with Americans working more on average than people in what are now Europe's two largest economies. What happened?

Increased inequality happened. People tend to work more hours as inequality increases. In the last four decades income and wealth distributions in the United States have become increasingly unequal. The Gini Index score of the United States went down dramatically (reflecting increased equality) from the late 1930s to the mid-1950s (from 0.44 to 0.36), but by the late 1970s it was up again (reflecting increased inequality) to just over 0.40.[48] It has continued to increase since that time, reaching 0.47 by 2003.[49] Nobel Prize-winning economist Joseph Stiglitz writes,

> By 2007, the year *before* the crisis [the Great Recession], the top 0.1 percent of America's households had an income that was 220 times larger than the *average* of the bottom 20 percent. Wealth was even more unequally distributed than income, with the wealthiest 1 percent owning more than a third of the nation's wealth. . . . In the first post-recession years of the new millennium (2002 to 2007), the top 1 percent seized more than 65 percent of the gain in total national income. While the top 1 percent was doing fantastically, most Americans were actually growing worse-off.[50]

Gains after the next economic crisis, the Great Recession of 2008–2009, were even more concentrated among the richest Americans, according to Stiglitz: "The top 1 percent of Americans gained 93 percent of the additional income created in the country in 2010, as compared with 2009."[51]

As we saw in chapter 9, inequality is much lower in other industrial countries. In 2003 the Gini Index score for Germany was 0.38 and for France it was 0.33. It was only 0.23 for Sweden in 2005. The average for all members of the OECD, the world's industrial economies, was just 0.31, compared to 0.47 for the United States.[52]

This difference in levels of inequality helps to explain why Americans work longer hours than western Europeans. We saw in chapter 9 that there may be biologically based reasons for people to concern themselves increasingly with their social position as social inequality increases. Writing during the Gilded Age in 1899, Thorsten Veblen contended in his landmark work *The Theory of the Leisure Class* that much of people's demand for consumer goods stems from the desire for self-esteem, which requires attaining material riches comparable to that of society's elite. He wrote, "The motive is emulation—the stimulus of an invidious comparison. . . . All canons of reputability and decency and all standards of consumption are traced back . . . to the usages and thoughts of the highest social and pecuniary class, the wealthy leisure class."[53] Accordingly, the higher the top end of the income spectrum compared to average workers, that is, the greater the inequality in society, the higher the standard of consumption that average workers use for self-comparison. This higher standard of consumption increases the level of consumption needed by average people for an acceptable level of self-esteem.

Recent research shows that average people are willing to work longer hours to earn more money to afford the higher standard of consumption needed for self-esteem as that standard is raised by the increasing affluence of the rich compared to the rest. As we've seen, people in the United States worked fewer hours on average than those in western Europe when the Gini Index in the United States was falling, that is, when equality was increasing. But when the Gini Index of European countries continued to fall while that in the United States began to rise, Americans started working more than western Europeans. As the disparity between inequality in the United States and Europe has increased, so has the disparity in hours worked.[54]

The same effect can be seen in studies on a smaller scale than the national level. Richard Wilkinson and Kate Pickett report in *The Spirit Level* on two studies of women's propensity to work. In one study it was found that "women who were married to employed men . . . were more likely to take a job themselves if they lived in an area in which men's incomes were more unequal." On an even more personal level, a study "using data within the USA found that married women were more likely to go out to work if their sister's husband earned more than their own husband."[55]

Sociologist Juliet Schor found an additional reason why increases in inequality correlate with increases in hours worked. Increases in inequality in the United States have been created in part by lowering the real income of most workers. By the time Shor's book was published in 1992 it had become a common belief that American families can no longer "make it" on a single income, hence the increased work participation of married women, including those with small children. She writes, "In one sense, workers are choosing these extra hours. . . . But the pressure to work the hours *has* come from companies. In return for a 1970s standard of living, employers are now demanding far more hours. . . . *Just to reach their 1973 standard of living, they must work 245 more hours, or 6-plus weeks a year.*"[56] This trend continued into the current century. Production and nonsupervisory workers, who make up 81 percent of the nonagricultural workforce, saw their real hourly earnings decline by 8 percent between 1973 and 2005 even as their productivity rose 55 percent.[57] Their extra productivity went to richer people. Inequality increased and the majority of workers needed to work more hours to make ends meet.

Another factor that encourages more work hours from each employee is the fringe benefit system in the United States. Fringe benefits constitute an increasing percentage of the total compensation of American workers, largely because of increases in the cost of healthcare and therefore of medical insurance. These benefits compensate for part of workers' reduced earnings. But employers want to minimize the number of employees who qualify for medical and other employee benefits, so they tend to hire fewer workers and require each employee to work longer hours to meet company goals. This can have a direct effect not only on the average number of hours worked by employees, but also on the number of unemployed. After the recession of the early 1980s, which caused widespread unemployment in the steel industry, the industry prolonged unemployment by requiring workers to work overtime, Schor claims.

> In 1983, USX issued a directive to plant managers (which was subsequently leaked) ordering them to use overtime, specifically so that they could avoid calling back laid-off workers. This decision was based on the desire of the company to avoid re-entitling workers to benefits. The situation in the mining industry at the time was similar; the coal companies demanded overtime in the midst of severe unemployment. And in the auto industry, the United Autoworkers' Union has calculated that in 1988 overtime resulted in the loss of eighty-eight thousand jobs.[58]

Here we see the opposite of idling workers through a shorter work week to create employment opportunities and lower unemployment. In the United States there is a history of requiring or encouraging workers to work more hours, which reduces employment opportunities and increases unemployment. Europeans don't share this history, as most fringe benefits are provided universally by the state, regardless of employment status. The provision of benefits therefore does not encourage European employers to hire fewer workers and require that each worker spend more hours on the job.[59]

Also relevant to idling workers is the greater role of unions in Europe. Unions in both the United States and Europe fight to increase pay and vacation days, which would idle workers, increase equality, and reduce the incentive to work more hours to afford a decent standard of living. When private sector union representation increased in the United States between 1935 and 1945 from 12 percent to 35 percent,[60] equality increased as well. As we have seen, the Gini coefficient went from 0.44 to 0.36 between the late 1930s and the mid-1950s.[61] By 2012, however, according to the Bureau of Labor Statistics of the US Department of Labor, unions represented only 11.3 percent of workers[62] and, as we've seen, the Gini coefficient indicated greater inequality.[63] In Europe, by contrast, union agreements cover a much larger percentage of workers[64] and the Gini coefficient is much lower, reflecting more equal societies.[65]

In sum, the difference between the United States and western Europe does not depend primarily on entrenched and ineradicable beliefs and practices concerning religion, the Industrial Revolution, and World War II. It depends primarily on factors that can be changed—the level of unionization in the workforce, the provision of benefits by the state instead of by employers, and the general level of inequality in society. Because union membership increased from the 1930s through the 1950s, there is reason to think that it can increase again. In fact, were it passed, a bill called The Employee Free Choice Act would probably go a long way toward increasing union representation in the American workforce. The act would authorize union representation upon the signature on a card of half an employer's nonmanagement workers. This is sometimes called "card check." No union representation election, which gives employers opportunities illegally to influence employees to reject union representation, would be required. With greater union representation, greater equality in society is probable; our Gini coefficient would go down. Thus, the pressures of inequality to work more hours than are worked in Europe would decrease.

There is reason to think also that in the future American employers will assume less responsibility and the state will assume more responsibility for healthcare, retirement income, and other fringe benefits of employment that currently discourage many employers from hiring more workers. The state has already assumed increasing responsibility for employee benefits, such as those regarding retirement benefits and healthcare for the poor and aged.

What is more, employer costs of providing fringe benefits puts American companies at a disadvantage in the global marketplace because it saddles the Americans with costly labor-related obligations that are greater than those of their European competitors. If history is any guide, American businesses don't like government involvement unless it's clearly to their advantage, at which point they lobby for it vigorously. Hence, it's likely that the government will continue to increase its role in the provision of fringe benefits.

The Affordable Care Act is a case in point, as it provides government support to make health insurance more affordable for people who don't have jobs. The Congressional Budget Office (CBO) projected in February 2014 that about 2 million people will choose to drop out of the labor force in order to spend their time on other pursuits. In other words, they'll choose voluntary idling over gainful employment.[66] Thus, as American conditions become more like those in western Europe—more government support, greater equality, and stronger union representation—there is reason to believe that American workers will, like their European counterparts, prefer more leisure to more pay.

Even under current conditions most American full-time workers favor working fewer hours. Although American full-time workers are not as interested as Europeans in shorter working hours, more American full-time workers would like shorter hours than would like longer hours.[67] What is more, a study published in 2004 compared the contribution to happiness of eighteen specific activities and found that working ranked seventeenth. Only commuting to work was worse, suggesting again that Americans would be happy to work less. As Derek Bok notes, "The most striking result . . . is that almost all of the most pleasurable activities of the day take place outside of work—having sex, being with family, seeing friends, and so forth."[68]

Sociologist Juliet Schor reports that "millions of working parents see their children or spouses far less than they should or would like to. 'Working' mothers complain they have no time for themselves."[69] Additionally, Schor reports, "In a 1978 Department of Labor Study, 84 percent of respondents said that they would like to trade off some or all of future income for additional free time. Nearly half (47 percent) said they would trade *all* of a 10-percent pay raise for free time."[70] Similarly, a study reported in 1996 showed that the overwhelming majority of workers at some large law firms would prefer a 10 percent cut in both pay and work hours to their current situation.[71] More recently, a survey by the Families and Work Institute found that whereas one half of women with children under eighteen currently work full time, only a quarter of these women would do so if their financial situation enabled them to work less.[72] Thus, idling or partial idling is quite attractive to many Americans, which may improve the prospects for idling to become increasingly acceptable in the United States.

✻   ✻   ✻

But if it were politically acceptable, would it be an example of functional inefficiency—inefficiency that functions to lower unemployment—or would idling workers be efficient as well as functional? In most respects the American situation is the same as what we've discovered in discussions of France and several other European countries. If the input is the nation's work potential and the output is GDP, idling workers (without unemployment) is certainly inefficient; with less idling the country could have a higher GDP per capita, as the United States does, for example, in comparison with France. If the input is the nation's work potential and the outputs are products for export and a positive balance of trade with other nations, it would seem again that idling workers is inefficient because it adds to the cost of products and thereby inhibits foreign sales. However, if the input is an hour of work and the output is the productivity of that hour, idling workers (without unemployment) may actually increase efficiency.

Regarding nonmonetary values, some forms of idling, as we've seen, are fundamentally efficient because they promote human welfare with little expenditure of human and natural resources. These include idling workers through more generous family leave policies and higher education that is not so costly that it leads to enormous student debt. I know of no reason why positive outcomes wouldn't be as great in the United States as in Europe. Idling by such means seems to be fundamentally efficient. But when it comes to simply having fewer hours in the standard workweek, more days of paid vacation, and earlier retirements with adequate income, results in the United States may differ from those in Europe because of differences in the way that leisure time is used.

Consider the possibilities of reducing the number of hours in the standard workweek and increasing the number of paid vacation days. On the one hand, it seems that Americans who desire less time at work would benefit from the resulting increase in leisure time because, besides being desired, leisure is not a positional good. It appears to be exempt from the general rule that most people feel deprived if others get more than they get. We saw earlier that a survey of Harvard University students showed that they would prefer less income if most others had even less than them to more income if others had even more than them. But the same result didn't apply to leisure time. The same researchers at Harvard asked their students if they would prefer a world in which they had two weeks' vacation and everyone else had only one week to a world in which they had four weeks of vacation when everyone else had eight. Only 20 percent of students chose the first option, showing that although they envy other people's income, they don't envy them their leisure.[73] Similar results were obtained by researchers in Sweden when they compared the positional nature of income versus leisure.[74] For the most part leisure, unlike income, is not a positional good. Some people can enjoy increased leisure without this benefit reducing the happiness of others.

These results suggest that overall happiness could be increased in society, at least among people who are not so poor that they are materially deprived, if people got their wish to work less and earn less. Because income is primarily a positional good, if the normal income in society went down as people worked less, average happiness would not diminish, because happiness with one's income in rich societies depends on one's income relative to the incomes of others. If income in general went down, relative positions would remain the same at a lower level of income, so total happiness would remain the same. Because leisure isn't a positional good (or is one to a much lesser extent than income), and people generally desire more leisure than they currently have, increased leisure in society would increase total happiness. Even if one's amount of leisure remained the same relative to that of others in society, one would experience the benefit of enjoying more leisure because that enjoyment doesn't depend on invidious contrasts with the leisure available to others.

According to this reasoning, life has improved in the United States in recent decades because leisure has increased. A study published in 2007 shows that leisure, defined as time spent away from both market (paid) and non-market (unpaid) work, increased about 14 percent between 1965 and 2003. "Men and women decreased their total work hours by 8.3 and 7.8 per week, respectively,"[75] even though women's paid work increased by 3.8 hours per week during this period.[76] Home production (unpaid work) declined among women by more than 10 hours per week, and this offset their increased participation in the market. But has this increase in leisure improved wellbeing?

In Europe it seems that idling workers without greater unemployment improves human flourishing because people use much of their free time to cultivate personal relationships and participate in political and civic life, which most psychologists believe contribute to human wellbeing more than the extra goods and services that people could afford if they worked more hours.[77] In other words, Europeans use their increased free time to strengthen the kinds of social capital that we saw in chapter 9 to be so important for human flourishing.

But the United States, according to sociologist Monica Prasad, has been much more consumer oriented than western Europe since World War II.[78] This orientation affects the fundamental efficiency of giving Americans shorter work weeks and more vacation days. As work hours among Americans decreased by about eight hours per week between 1965 and 2003, time devoted to childcare ultimately increased by two hours per week, which would seem to promote social capital and flourishing.[79] However, the overwhelming majority of extra leisure time was devoted to watching TV. "More than 100 percent of the increase in leisure can be accounted for by the increase in time spent watching television. . . . This increase in television is offset by a 3.9-hour-per-week decline in socializing (going to parties, bars, etc.) and a 3.1-hour-per-week decline in reading (books, magazines, letters, etc.)." In addition, "civic activities fell by thirty minutes per week [and] education (omitting students) fell by eighteen minutes per week."[80] Thus, rather than strengthen social capital as in Europe, increased leisure seems to weaken it in the American context, making it difficult to determine the fundamental efficiency of giving workers more vacation days and shorter work weeks. Increased TV watching promotes consumerism which, as we've seen, tends to harm people individually and socially.[81] Declines in social engagement that accompany increased leisure threaten social capital. These negative outcomes may more than offset the benefits of giving workers their desired reductions in work.

A similar uncertainty attends idling workers through early retirement. On the one hand, according to a report by the Center for Retirement Research at Boston College, most retired people think that retirement has improved their lives. When retired respondents were asked if they would characterize their retirement as "very satisfying, moderately satisfying, or not at all satisfying," over 60 percent rated it as very satisfying and more than 32 percent as moderately satisfying, leaving only 7.5 percent who found it not at all satisfying. When asked to compare life in retirement with life during the latter years of their employment, more than half of respondents found retired life to be better than working life. Almost one third found the two "about the same." Only 16.9 percent found retired life worse.[82]

A significant circumstance inclining retirees toward dissatisfaction was poor health. However, more significant was the involuntariness of retirement. Some people retire involuntarily because of diminished health, and many of these people may not be ready psychologically or financially for retirement. Others retire involuntarily because they have lost their jobs and can't find another. They are actually unemployed people who became "'discouraged workers,' that is, people willing to work but who decide to drop out of the labor force."[83] We know that unemployment reduces life satisfaction, so it's no surprise that retirees who are really unemployed are among the least satisfied retirees.

Researchers found, as one might expect, that "defined benefit pension wealth [traditional employer-provided retirement income], defined contribution pension wealth [such as 401(k) retirement accounts, and] Social Security . . . all increase retirement satisfaction." Perhaps because of the additional security it provides, defined benefit plans lead to more satisfaction than defined contribution plans. However, and this is perhaps surprising, the effect of increased income and wealth is in any case very small,[84] probably because retirees generally need less money to maintain their lifestyle than working people. Retirees usually have diminished responsibilities for children, no need to pay for work-related clothing or travel, and more time to shop carefully so they get more of what they want from their limited income, making 75 percent of preretirement income enough for most retirees.[85]

However, like most Americans, retirees tend to spend much of their increased leisure time watching television. According to the Bureau of Labor Statistics, in 2012 Americans over the age of fifteen who were not employed watched on average eleven more hours of TV per week than those who worked full time.[86] An earlier study revealed that this kind of difference applies to older as well as younger people. In 2003 and 2004, men aged fifty-five to fifty-nine who were out of the labor force spent 10.5 more hours watching TV than those in this age group who worked full time, and men aged sixty to sixty-four who were out of the labor force watched on average fourteen hours more TV than their contemporaries who worked full time. Women in both age groups increased their TV watching by more than eleven hours when they were out of the labor force.[87]

It is people in these age groups who would increasingly be leaving the labor force through early retirement if such retirement were used more than at present to idle workers so as to decrease unemployment. Human welfare may be impaired rather than enhanced because Americans use their free time to watch TV, which increases the type of consumerism that was shown in chapters 8 and 9 to harm individuals psychologically and erode the kind of social capital that is essential for human flourishing. Thus, the benefits of more people taking early retirement may be less than the harm it causes, making early retirement with adequate income a fundamentally inefficient way of combating unemployment.

✻   ✻   ✻

In sum, idling workers through longer paid family leave and increased, affordable opportunities in higher education are functionally and fundamentally efficient. They improve prospects for lowering unemployment, at least in the short run, while promoting human welfare, all things considered. Idling workers through increased incarceration, by contrast, is clearly fundamentally inefficient, although it's functional insofar as it reduces unemployment. It's a case of functional inefficiency. But idling American workers through shorter workweeks, more paid vacations, and earlier retirements with adequate income, although functional regarding the reduction of unemployment, may or may not be fundamentally efficient.

CHAPTER 11
PHYSICAL INFRASTRUCTURE AND PUBLIC GOODS

P utting people to work in manufacturing for export, we've seen, is limited by environmental constraints as well as by the decreasing need for workers in manufacturing. Inefficient systems of transportation and healthcare continue to create and maintain millions of jobs, but this is an undesirable way of combating unemployment because the fact of their inefficiency means that alternative uses of human and natural resources would result in greater human satisfaction (wellbeing, flourishing). Consumerism currently promotes more employment than any other category, but its inextricable link to individual discontent and social disintegration makes consumerism less than ideal, which motivates a search for alternatives. One alternative, idling workers, combats unemployment in ways that are mostly environmentally sustainable. Its association with individual discontent and social disintegration is neither intrinsic nor universal. But people can't live by idling alone, certainly not if we want to have a growing economy.

Building and improving our physical and human infrastructure promises to promote economic growth and combat unemployment within environmental limits. *Installing new physical infrastructure related to energy and transportation*, the topic of this chapter, *does more. It creates jobs while actually reducing our impositions on the environment, thereby paving the way for the indefinite continuation of economic growth that's environmentally sustainable.*

Infrastructure is the set of background conditions that a society needs in order to be relatively productive. According to the American Society of Civil Engineers, it includes "the physical framework [for] transporting goods, powering factories, heating and cooling office buildings, and enjoying a clean glass of clean water."[1] For example, transportation facilities are required in a relatively productive industrial society because industrial processes use raw materials and manufactured components from around the world. Modern agriculture, too, uses inputs that may come from afar. In addition, most workers don't live within walking distance of their places of employment, so transportation facilities are needed for people to go to and from work, whether they work in mining, manufacture, construction, agriculture, or service. Once produced, manufactured and agricultural goods must be transported to the point of sale. Thus, poor transportation facilities hamper productivity, making goods and services more expensive as a result of additional costs and delays in getting materials, components, and people to the sites where they are needed for production, and add costs again when finished products are shipped to points of sale or use. Poor transportation facilities may even preclude the commercial viability of some products; perishable agricultural foods, for example, require quick transport to points of sale. Our infrastructure therefore includes such aids to transportation as roads, bridges, railways, light rail, airports, seaports, and inland waterways, including locks and dams.

Nonhuman energy is similarly fundamental to productivity. Mining, agriculture, and manufacturing use such energy to produce goods, and transportation uses energy to move products and people. So the means of acquiring and transporting nonhuman energy are part of society's infrastructure. This includes electric generating facilities, the mines and wells used to procure fuel for electricity generation, oil refineries, natural gas pipelines, and the electricity grid. Clean water is similarly needed for agriculture, manufacture, and human consumption, so the means of gathering, cleaning, transporting, and recycling water are part of the nation's infrastructure.

Although the American Society of Civil Engineers fails to note it, some services are also part of our infrastructure. Protection of lives and property are among these services. People don't work productively when their lives are constantly in danger, so a state that protects human life from unjustified attack is part of society's infrastructure. Because a major motivation for productive employment is the acquisition of private property, laws, police, and courts that protect private property are necessary as well.

Modern mining, manufacture, construction, agriculture, and service require investment to maintain and improve productivity. Consumers, who promote economic growth through purchases of goods and services, also need financial institutions to facilitate some of their purchases, especially big ticket items such as houses and cars. So a financial sector capable of providing funds for business investments and private purchases also forms part of our country's infrastructure. This includes banks and the stock market.

Educational institutions are part of the country's infrastructure, too. Private firms need an educated workforce as a background condition for efficient production just as much as they need energy, transportation, law enforcement, and financial services. It isn't realistic to expect private companies to teach their workers how to read, write, tell time, do math, and follow a schedule, because such education would cost companies too much money. So employers locate where there is an education system capable of endowing people with these abilities before they enter the workforce.

Many items of infrastructure are **public goods**. Goods are called public when their benefits can't be confined to a single individual or small group. National defense is the classic example. If anyone in the country is protected from attack or invasion by a foreign power, everyone else in the country is protected as well. For this reason it's not in the self-interest of any individual or small group to provide national defense privately, as their private resources would benefit others who pay nothing. Each person reasons that it's in her self-interest to let other people provide national defense so that she can benefit from national defense without paying for it. This would allow her to use her money for other goods or services that she might enjoy privately, like a new car or a bigger house. Because everyone tends to reason this way, national defense and other public goods won't be created or maintained unless the state takes on this role, paying for these public goods with forced contributions (taxes).

Endorsement of taxes to pay for public goods isn't a recent or particularly left-wing position. Adam Smith endorses this view in *The Wealth of Nations*, writing that the state

> has the duty of erecting and maintaining certain public works and certain public institutions, which it can never be for the interest of any individual, or small number of individuals, to erect and maintain; because the profit could never repay the expense to any individual or small number of individuals, though it may frequently do much more than repay it to a great society.[2]

Free-market conservative economist Friedrich Hayek expresses the same view in *The Road to Serfdom*, a 1940s-era antisocialist tract beloved of conservatives to this day,

> Where . . . it is impracticable to make the enjoyment of certain services dependent on the payment of a price, competition [the free market] will not produce the services; and the price system becomes similarly ineffective when the damage caused to others by certain uses of property cannot be effectively charged to the owner of that property. In all these instances there is a divergence between the items which enter into private calculation and those which affect social welfare; and, competition may have to be found to supply the services in question. Thus, neither the provision of signposts on the road nor, in most circumstances, that of the roads themselves can be paid for by every individual user. Nor can certain harmful effects of deforestation, of some methods of farming, or of the smoke and noise of factories be confined to the owner of the property in question or to those who are willing to submit to the damage for an agreed compensation.[3]

Thus, many infrastructural items, such as roads, secure banking, and the enforcement of property rights are public goods. They can't be provided to anyone in a form needed to underpin economic prosperity without becoming available to many others as well. Their maintenance therefore requires public action, which is why, for the most part, governments build roads with tax dollars, governments fund police and courts to enforce property rights, and governments regulate the banking industry.

Some public goods, those that are not made by human beings, are not usually counted as part of the nation's infrastructure. Clean air and potable water, for example, are public goods—no one can benefit from them unless many others benefit as well—but they are not typically considered part of the country's infrastructure. This is because they are not products of human invention and creation. Instead, human-made methods of preserving these public goods are part of the nation's infrastructure, such as scrubbers on the smokestacks of coal-burning electric power plants (to protect air quality) and water purification systems at factories that use ambient water that is released back into the environment. Because these infrastructural items are needed to protect environmental amenities that are public goods, state regulation is required to insure their creation, use, and maintenance.

Many infrastructural items that are public goods are also private goods because they are privately owned. For example, our country's freight railroad infrastructure, airlines for both freight and passengers, much of the country's electric generating facilities, and most financial institutions are owned by private corporations. As a result of private ownership, some of the benefits of these infrastructural items are not shared by others; corporate profits go exclusively to owners of these corporations. However, these privately owned items of infrastructure are still public goods because, as infrastructure, they underpin commercial activity, thereby supporting economic growth and job creation from which most Americans benefit. Thus, they are public goods, but not only public goods. Many other items of infrastructure, by contrast, such as police, courts, and most roads and bridges are publicly owned and are therefore more exclusively public.

Just as many public goods are also private goods, many goods that are primarily private are also to some extent public. Consider the good of an attractive front lawn and house exterior. These are generally considered private goods. People take pride in the appearance of their houses and curb appeal adds resale value to them. But neighbors benefit as well because the good appearance of your house helps to maintain or improve property values in the area, and passersby benefit as they enjoy the view of your landscaping. The essence of a public good is that its enjoyment can't be restricted to people of the purchaser's choosing. Thus, we have here private goods with a public good aspect. This is why there are covenants in some neighborhoods specifying many details of outside maintenance of home and garden.

There are many other examples. Your education helps you to gain employment and additional education helps you to increase your pay. Education is thus a private good. But because an educated workforce is essential to the success of an industrial society, it's part of the country's human infrastructure and as such helps to maintain and augment commercial activity needed for economic growth and job creation. Because society in general benefits from your education, it's a public good as well as a private good.

Saving money by installing an energy-saving geothermal heating-cooling system in your home is another private good insofar as it reduces your utility bills and increases the sale price of your house. But it's a public good insofar as it saves energy, thereby reducing the need for energy production and so reducing the generation of associated air and water pollution. Your private good thus helps to maintain the public goods of clean air and potable water. Similar public good aspects attend use of fuel-efficient cars. You save money at the gas pump, but the public benefits from cleaner air. An additional public benefit of fuel-efficient vehicles has been (but may no longer be if we attain oil independence) reduction of the nation's dependence on foreign sources of oil. Such reduced dependence increases the nation's security without increased spending on the military. It also helps the economy by improving the country's balance of payments. We don't have to sell as much overseas to maintain economic health when we buy less from overseas. More money is left in our country for investments or consumer purchases that can result in job creation when we are sending less money overseas for petroleum.

This chapter and the one that follows look at the prospect of addressing unemployment problems by investing in infrastructure and public goods. The present chapter focuses on items of physical infrastructure, and the one that follows concerns our human infrastructure. I use the same four tests as before: efficiency/inefficiency, job-creating potential, environmental sustainability, and political acceptability, but these two chapters differ from most of the other chapters in this book insofar as they uncover functional *efficiencies*, rather than inefficiencies. Uncovering efficiencies that function to promote employment aligns these chapters with a great deal of mainstream economic thought. This is good news. Pessimists will be pleased by findings in chapters 13 and 14 that the economic-growth potential of infrastructural development can be realized only if the fundamental inefficiencies associated with consumerism increase.

❋   ❋   ❋

The job-creating potential of investments in infrastructure and public goods has two aspects. Jobs are created while infrastructural items are being produced, and, because we are talking about infrastructure that underpins and augments economic growth and job creation, jobs are created by having a better infrastructure after it has been produced. We begin with the latter issue, comparing economic growth and employment with and without an adequate infrastructure related to surface transportation, water and wastewater, electricity, airports, inland waterways, and marine ports.

According to the American Society of Civil Engineers, the United States currently invests too little in these infrastructural items and is on a path to invest too little in the future. The engineers write, "Our projections included both the cost of building new infrastructure to service increasing populations and expanded economic activity; and for maintaining or rebuilding existing infrastructure that needs repair or replacement. The total documented cumulative gap between projected needs and likely investment in these critical systems will be $1.1 trillion by 2020."[4] By 2040 the cumulative gap between what the United States will spend if current patterns of funding continue and what is needed to maintain and improve infrastructure in these areas will be $4.7 trillion.[5] This figure includes $3,664 billion (above current expenditure trends) needed to fund surface transportation infrastructure, $144 billion for water/wastewater infrastructure, $732 billion for electricity infrastructure, $95 billion for airports, and $46 billion for inland waterways and marine ports.[6]

Without the increased investment in these areas of infrastructure to close the gap between current funding trends and future needs, the engineers explain, inadequate infrastructure

> will result in higher costs to business and households as a consequence of less efficient and more costly infrastructure services. For example, travel times will lengthen with inefficient roadways and congested air service, and out-of-pocket expenditures to households and business costs will rise if the electricity grid or water delivery systems fail to keep up with demand. Goods will be more expensive to produce and more expensive to transport to retail shelves for households or to business customers. Business related travel, as well as commuting and personal travel, will also become more expensive. As a consequence, U.S. businesses will become less efficient. As costs rise, business productivity falls, causing GDP to drop, cutting employment and ultimately reducing personal income. Higher costs will also render U.S. goods and services less competitive internationally, reducing exports and decreasing dollars earned and brought into the U.S. from sales to international customers.[7]

In short, inefficiencies caused by inadequate infrastructure impair the growth of GDP, thereby reducing business profits and employment opportunities in most areas. The cumulative costs to businesses of failure to maintain and improve infrastructure, according to the civil engineers, will be $1,219 billion by 2020 and $5,811 billion by 2040 (using constant 2010 dollars). Households will experience a loss of $611 billion by 2020 and $2,850 billion by 2040,[8] which translates into an annual loss of disposable income per household of $3,000 through 2020 and $6,000 between 2021 and 2040.

When households lose income they usually spend less money, resulting in less employment among those who would provide them with goods and services. The civil engineers claim that by 2020 3.5 million jobs will be lost as a result of underinvestment in infrastructure and that by 2040 inferior infrastructure will reduce employment opportunities by 7 million jobs.[9] Hardest hit will be

> large, labor-intensive industries such as retail, medical services, and restaurants. . . . This is the long-term result of households . . . reducing purchases (restaurant meals, home improvements, consumer electronics, new furniture, for examples), deferring services (medical care), and the long-term reduction in business sales that will particularly affect construction spending.[10]

However, inefficiencies resulting from infrastructure decline will increase employment in some areas, such as "automobile repair services, truck driving, and highway passenger services."[11] Owing to congested air space and degraded inland waterways, more people will travel by car, leading to an increased need for highway passenger services. For the same reasons, more goods will be shipped by truck, leading to an increased need for truck drivers. More truck drivers will be needed also because road maintenance will be so poor that travel times are increased, which means that more trucks and drivers will be needed to move the same amount of freight each year. Opportunities for jobs in automobile repair services will increase because the poor state of roads as well as their increased congestion will cause more damage to cars from wear and tear as well as from accidents. Such job creation is an example of functional inefficiency which, we saw in chapter 6, abounds in the transportation sector. But the cost of this inefficiency is great, according to the civil engineers:

In 2010, it was estimated that deficiencies in America's surface transportation systems cost households and businesses nearly $130 billion. This included approximately $97 billion in vehicle operating costs, $32 billion in travel time delays, $1.2 billion in safety costs, and $590 million in environmental costs. If present trends continue, by 2020 the annual costs imposed on the U.S. economy from deteriorating surface transportation infrastructure will increase to $210 billion, and by 2040 to $520 billion.[12]

These losses impair the growth of GDP and inhibit job growth. Cumulatively, the economy will lose $900 billion by 2020 as a result of poor surface transportation, causing the loss of nine hundred thousand jobs. By 2040, the cumulative economic loss is expected to be $2.7 trillion, but the job loss is only four hundred thousand as a result of (what I call) functional inefficiencies. "As productivity deteriorates along with infrastructure degradation," the engineers write, "more resources will be wasted in each sector. In other words, it may take two jobs to complete the tasks that one job could handle without delays due to worsening surface transportation."[13] But the jobs created or preserved will be at relatively low levels of pay in auto repair, retail sales, and truck driving compared to the higher-paying jobs in the knowledge-based, high-tech sector that could be created in a more efficient economy. When the economy loses $2.7 trillion, $2.7 trillion less is available for salaries, and overall employment will still be down by four hundred thousand jobs merely as a result of failure to invest in this one sector of physical infrastructure—surface transportation.

Because similar degradation is expected in several sectors, inefficiencies in one sector will not be ameliorated by increased efficiencies elsewhere. This increases the overall negative impact of failure to maintain and improve infrastructure. For example, inefficiencies due to inadequate air transportation infrastructure can't be compensated for by the efficient use of highways if highways are in such disrepair that their use doesn't increase efficiency. In addition, inefficiency in one sector causes inefficiencies elsewhere because the sectors are interdependent. Deterioration in our water infrastructure, for example, will reduce efficiencies related to energy as well as water because many electric generating facilities boil water (to create steam) and use water in cooling. Electricity and water are needed, in turn, for manufacturing of many types, including the manufacture of auto parts needed in the transportation sector. And "transportation of all modes is required to deliver parts and equipment to all types of infrastructure systems, including transportation facilities."[14]

Such negative synergies account for the enormous cumulative impact of our failure to maintain and develop infrastructure, the loss amounting to $1.83 trillion by 2020 and $8.66 trillion by 2040.[15] According to the engineers, these cumulative losses could be avoided through infrastructure investments of $1.1 trillion by 2020 and $4.7 trillion by 2040 above current trends of spending on such infrastructure. Because the needed investments are considerably lower, especially in the 2040 timeframe, than the losses consequent upon failure to invest, investing in infrastructure is generally very good for economic growth and for job retention and creation.

This explains why, over nearly a sixty-year period, investment in infrastructure and economic growth have gone hand in hand in the United States. Between 1950 and 1979, investment in such core areas of infrastructure as transportation, water management, and electricity transmission averaged 4.0 percent per year, as overall growth in the GDP averaged 4.1 percent per year. Between 1980 and 2007, by contrast, public investment in these areas fell to an average of 2.3 percent per year and GDP grew at an annual rate of 2.9 percent.[16]

❋   ❋   ❋

The calculations above concern growth in the economy and in job opportunities that result from *having* an adequate infrastructure in the areas of surface transportation, water and wastewater, electricity, airports, inland waterways, and marine ports. But this is only part of the story. Jobs are created also, almost immediately, in *the process of maintaining and improving infrastructure* in these and other areas. This is the focus of research conducted by the Political Economy Research Institute at the University of Massachusetts for the American Alliance for Manufacturing.

The Institute considered jobs created under the three categories discussed in chapter 6: First, jobs created directly by investments in infrastructure, such as jobs in road construction. Second, jobs created indirectly by investments in infrastructure, such as increased job opportunities in the production of steel, cement, and other materials used in infrastructure development. Finally, employment created when people with direct and indirect jobs spend the money they earn. These "induced" employment effects of infrastructure development include many jobs in services, such as retail sales.[17]

Government will catalyze employment in all three categories whenever it spends money. However, some types of expenditures generate more jobs than others. According to the Institute, for each billion dollars of government spending in the energy sector, for example, more than 16,700 jobs are created. In transportation the figure is nearly 19,000 jobs, and in water infrastructure it's more than 19,700 jobs. By contrast, tax cuts that would enable people to buy more of whatever they want as consumers would create fewer jobs. Even if taxpayers spent all of the money made available to them through a tax cut, a billion dollars would provide only about 15,000 new jobs. One reason is that much of the money spent by consumers goes to overseas manufacturers of goods and services, whereas a higher percentage of money spent on infrastructure stays in the United States. Most of the jobs from infrastructure spending are for construction, which can't be outsourced.[18] In addition, the figure of 15,000 new jobs is unrealistically high because people don't spend all of the money that they receive from tax cuts.[19] They pay down debts and save some of the money that is newly available to them. And the more that tax cuts go to relatively affluent households, the greater the percentage of the tax cut that is saved, further lowering the number of jobs created.

Returning money to taxpayers who save it is important because savings promote economic health and growth as they fund private-sector investments that help to increase productivity. Some economists worry, therefore, that increased government spending on infrastructure will "crowd out" investments in the private sector, thereby hurting the economy in the long run. The Institute agrees that this is an issue, but notes that the crowding out argument is valid only under certain highly specific conditions:

> These circumstances would be when: 1) all the economy's real resources are being fully utilized, i.e. workers are fully employed, and the existing productive apparatus is being run full-tilt; 2) the economy's financial resources are similarly already being fully used up in financing productive invest-

ment projects; and 3) new public investment spending makes no contribution toward expanding the economy's productive capacity—i.e. it is not succeeding in its purpose of increasing the overall size of the economic pie.[20]

We have seen that these conditions do not apply to the United States at this time. Unemployment is one of our major difficulties, so public investment will not be competing with private investors for available workers. Perhaps more important, increased investments in infrastructure, whether funded publicly or privately, according to the civil engineers, are necessary conditions for maximum economic growth. Finally, taxpayers aren't shortchanged by infrastructure investments that preclude tax cuts, because taxpayers are helped little by tax cuts that put them out of work owing to inadequate infrastructure; tax cuts that they must spend on increased car repairs resulting from poorly maintained roads; or tax cuts that are eaten up by increased electricity rates stemming from deteriorating electric power plants or an inefficient electricity transmission grid.

Other studies have come to similar conclusions by comparing the employment effects of spending money on nonmilitary infrastructure instead of giving people tax breaks or spending tax money on the military. The federal government spends more on the military for national defense than on any other category of public goods. Those expenditures increased from 3 percent of GDP to 4.3 percent during the Bush presidency. In 2009 this represented an *increased* outlay of $175 billion per year on the military.[21] Dialing back military spending to 3 percent of GDP and using that money for other public goods, argue economists Robert Pollin and Heidi Garrett-Peltier, would provide many more jobs and greater economic stimulus than either continued high levels of military spending or the return of the money to American taxpayers for personal consumption. They estimate that $1 billion in defense spending generates only 8,555 jobs, whereas the same amount of money devoted to personal consumption generates 10,779 jobs. Better than both of these alternatives, however, is spending on such public goods as construction for weatherization/infrastructure (12,804 jobs), education (17,687 jobs), and mass transit (19,795 jobs).[22] These economists conclude that shifting $175 billion a year from defense spending to spending on a combination of education, mass transit, and construction for weatherization/infrastructure would increase employment by more than 1.2 million jobs *without a single extra dollar being collected in taxes or spent by the government.*

* * *

Many infrastructure investments, besides promoting economic growth and job creation better than tax cuts, can reduce the tension between economic growth and environmental sustainability. Consider the energy sector. Thomas Casten, co-founder and CEO of Trigen Energy Corporation, argues that we waste enormous amounts of energy in the form of excess heat from coal- and natural-gas-fired electricity plants because we fail to connect the plants to other buildings that could use this excess heat for heating and cooling.

> The standard way of removing this heat is to draw in water from a river or lake and cool the spent steam so it condenses to water. This transfers much of the energy to the water. This is why so many power plants were built beside rivers and lakes. An alternative approach, also widely practiced, is to reject the leftover heat into a cooling tower, which evaporates water to remove the heat, and then sends the heated vapor into the air.[23]

As a result of wasting this heat, the typical electricity generating facility converts only 33 percent of the energy in the original fossil fuel into electricity. Efficiency could be improved to about 85 percent if smaller plants were built near factories, universities, medical centers, and city centers where the energy that is currently wasted could be used for both heating and cooling.[24]

In addition, because trigeneration uses excess heat for heating and cooling buildings, it avoids using water for this purpose and thereby saves water as well as fuel resources. This is not a trivial consideration. Michael Webber writes in the *New York Times*, "Our energy system depends on water. About half of the nation's water withdrawals every day are just for cooling power plants. . . . All told, we withdraw more water for the energy sector than for agriculture."[25] So investments in the infrastructure of electricity generation that gradually replace current facilities with trigeneration facilities would not only improve energy efficiency and security, but also conserve an irreplaceable and scarce resource, water, thereby improving our food security.

But there's more. Natural gas, although a fossil fuel, emits only about half the carbon dioxide per unit of energy as coal. Owing to increasing supplies of natural gas stemming from hydraulic fracturing (fracking), natural gas is now cheaper than coal for electricity generation. This makes the current time ideal for the replacement of coal-fired facilities with natural gas facilities. In fact, the process has begun already. As a result of its price going down, natural-gas-generated electricity increased by 25 percent in the United States between 2008 and 2012 and now equals, or more than equals, the amount of electricity produced by burning coal.[26] And the transition isn't confined to the United States. In 2013 the coal industry had to scale back its plans to export coal because overseas demand is lacking. Even China, a major coal importer, is taking steps to reduce its reliance on coal by requiring greater efficiency from its coal-fired electricity plants and by developing nuclear and renewable power.[27]

Greater energy efficiency and less emission of CO_2 would result if, in the process of Americans switching from coal to natural gas, a switch was made also from conventional stand-alone electricity plants to trigeneration facilities. Such a transition is facilitated by the fact that natural gas is better suited than coal to the generation of electricity in smaller plants, just the kinds of plants that can be located near universities, shopping centers, factories, hospitals, and other major consumers of electricity, heating, and cooling.

However, the natural gas story is not completely positive. Fracking involves the injection of chemicals into the ground, and this creates four concerns. First, oil and gas companies have been reluctant to reveal all details about these chemicals, making it difficult to monitor possible leakage to groundwater or to lakes and streams to ensure the safety of drinking water. The companies are now required to reveal the chemicals they use on private land in some states. On federal land the government requires identification of chemicals used in fracking, but only *after* they have been used.[28] Second, and worse, the oil and gas industry lobbied successfully to have fracking exempt from some key provisions the Clean Air Act, the Clean Water Act, the Safe Drinking Water Act, the National Environmental Policy Act, and the Superfund Act, suggesting industry resistance to getting its environmental act together.[29] Third, fracking requires a lot of water, millions of gallons a day, according to Webber. It's not clear that there will be enough water available for fracking to continue indefinitely.[30] Fourth, both adding and subtracting water from the earth's crust may provoke earthquakes, leading to the suspicion that some quakes in Oklahoma in 2013 resulted from fracking.[31] These are among the reasons why natural gas is mentioned most often merely as a transitional fuel.

Finally, it's not certain that the use of natural gas obtained through fracking reduces greenhouse gas emissions below the emission rates of coal-fired plants. Methane, a greenhouse gas with heat-trapping properties twenty-five times greater than carbon dioxide, leaks from gas wells. Eduardo Porter reports in the *New York Times* that "replacing coal with gas would reduce greenhouse gas emissions only as long as the leakage of methane into the air from gas production did not exceed 3.6 percent."[32] The National Center for Atmospheric Research found that leakage over 2 percent negates the CO_2-reduction effect of substituting natural gas for coal in electricity generation. In 2011 the National Oceanic and Atmospheric Administration reported that the rate of leakage in gas and oil fields in California, Colorado, and Utah ranged from 2.3 percent to 17 percent.[33] Other estimates of leakage range from 2 percent to 9 percent.[34] In addition to these leaks, which take place in the production process, oil and gas wells leak methane increasingly as they age and lose their integrity.[35] Some energy experts say that leaks can be minimized in cost-effective ways, but this is yet to be demonstrated in practice, and "cost-effective" is not the same as "costless."[36] In 2014 a study by researchers at Stanford University, MIT, and the Department of Energy's National Renewable Energy Laboratory concluded that because of such leaks, switching vehicles from oil to natural gas doesn't ameliorate global warming through reduced emissions of greenhouse gases.[37]

For all of these reasons, investments in new energy infrastructure should concentrate on renewable and inexhaustible sources of energy—especially wind and solar energy. The US Energy Information Administration (EIA) publishes an "Annual Energy Outlook" that compares the price of electricity generated by various means in power facilities which, begun now, would start producing electricity five years in the future. According to the projections made in 2013 for facilities that would become operational in 2018, the national average levelized cost of electricity from wind turbines will be less than that of the cheapest (national average) electricity produced in new facilities using coal, nuclear fission, geothermal, and biomass.[38]

In this report, the average levelized cost of land-based wind generation is cheaper even than natural gas produced in facilities with advanced carbon capture and storage (CCS), a system that's needed to minimize emissions of CO_2 when natural gas is burned. Using constant 2011 dollars, the cost of electricity from plants entering service in 2018 are $93.4 per megawatt-hour for natural gas, but only 86.6 for land-based wind energy.[39] This is a disparity of $6.8 per megawatt-hour of energy. And the disparity continues to widen. The EIA Annual Energy Outlook published in 2014 concerning energy that would become available in 2019 expects natural gas energy to cost on average $91.3 per megawatt-hour, whereas wind will cost only $80.3, a disparity of $11 per megawatt-hour,[40] an increased disparity of nearly 40 percent in one year. Nor is the EIA the only organization that considers land-based wind energy to be cheaper than electricity produced by natural gas. The global investment bank Lazard found in 2013 that the cost of energy from wind ranges from $48 to $95 per megawatt-hour (depending on the windiness of the region) while the next cheapest source of electricity, natural gas, ranges from $61 to $89 per megawatt-hour.[41]

The prospects for coal are particularly grim. New coal plants perform worse than wind energy even when externalities (the harmful side effects of its mining, transportation, and use) are excluded from the calculation. However, according to economist and climate expert William Nordhaus, generating electricity from coal causes 21,000 premature deaths in the United States each year, primarily as a result of emissions of sulfur dioxide.[42] The most efficient approach to electricity generation therefore includes phasing out dependence on coal, not retrofitting coal-fired power plants to reduce sulfur emissions, because retrofitted plants would perpetuate high levels of CO_2 emissions in the generation of electricity. The attempt to reduce drastically the emission of CO_2 from coal-fired plants through systems of carbon capture and storage (CCS) in new or retrofitted plants is not helpful either. First, this so-called "clean coal" is an unproven technology. Second, even if it works, it would increase the direct cost of electricity from coal by at least 40 percent,[43] making electricity from coal much more expensive than wind energy, and would do nothing to reduce the negative environmental and health effects (not yet included in the calculations above) of coal *mining*.[44]

In sum, it makes no sense to build new plants to produce more expensive electricity from coal or nuclear fission when wind energy is already cheaper. However, geothermal, solar, and biomass development makes sense in regions where these sources of energy are abundant, making costs less than the national average, and research in these areas is called for because, unlike coal and nuclear energy, costs are coming down.[45] Recent reductions in the cost of photovoltaic solar energy (solar PV) are particularly impressive. In the EIA Annual Energy Outlook published in 2011, electricity produced by solar PV is projected to cost on average $210.7 per megawatt-hour when projects begun that year produce electricity in 2016.[46] The report two years later put the average cost of PV solar at $144.3 per megawatt-hour in 2018,[47] and the following year's projection for 2019 was an average cost of $130 per megawatt-hour.[48]

Off-shore wind farms are especially promising. The United States currently has not one wind turbine in its coastal waters, writes Marissa Newhall of the Clean Energy Group, whereas "the U.S. Department of Energy estimates that more than 4,000 gigawatts of electricity—more than four times what the U.S. power system can currently produce—could be generated from winds blowing above coastal waters."[49] The water of the Atlantic Coast's continental shelf is relatively shallow for over 200 miles, making wind development there less costly than it would be elsewhere (in deeper water). Electricity demand is great along the East Coast and transmission costs would be relatively low from off-shore wind farms because the wind farms would be relatively close to the end users of the electricity.[50]

The job-creating potential of offshore wind development is impressive. These include jobs in manufacturing, construction, engineering, operations, and maintenance. According to the National Wildlife Federation, "Over 40,000 people are currently employed in the offshore wind industry in Europe, with over 300,000 jobs expected by 2020. . . . America's wind industry currently employs over 75,000 people, and research shows that approximately 300,000 jobs and over $200 billion in new economic activity could result from a robust American offshore wind industry."[51]

In keeping with this information about wind and solar, a Stanford

University study found that New York State could all but eliminate its dependence on fossil fuels by 2030 and save money in the process. Forty percent of the state's power would come from wind turbines, most of them offshore, 38 percent would come from several solar energy technologies, and the rest from a variety of geothermal, tidal, and hydroelectric sources.[52]

Major investment in solar energy makes sense in New York State, according to the Sierra Club's Paul Rauber, because the price of solar energy is going down so fast that within two or three years solar energy will become as cheap as the relatively expensive residential electricity available in California and New York.[53] The energy conversion of New York State would pay for itself in seventeen, or possibly as few as ten years, the Stanford researchers maintain, because although initial capital costs would be high, the state would have no costs for fuel and would save annually $33 billion on health costs and $3.2 billion a year on avoided climate-change-induced coastal erosion and extreme weather events. The plan "would also create a net gain in manufacturing, installation and technology jobs because nearly all the state's energy would be produced within the state."[54]

There is a long list of helpful energy-related infrastructural investments that save money in the long run, create more jobs than would be created through tax cuts or alternative investments, and make the economy more sustainable by reducing its burden on the environment. Many investments concern energy efficiency, which refers to the efficiency of energy consumption, rather than the efficiency of its production. Researchers from Georgia Tech and Duke University reported in 2010 on the effects of nine strategies to reduce energy consumption in the District of Columbia and sixteen southeastern states in residential and commercial buildings and in industry (RCI). These strategies include new building codes with third-party verification and expanded weatherization assistance programs for the residential sector; tighter commercial appliance standards and commercial retrofit incentives in the commercial sector; and industrial plant utility upgrades and industrial improvement policies in the industrial sector. The estimated benefit of implementing these nine policies is nearly three times the estimated cost. Using constant dollars and a seven percent discount rate, total costs during the 20-year period 2010 to 2030 are $31.5 billion and total benefits are $126 billion.[55]

"Consumers in the south could save $41 billion in reduced energy bills in the year 2020 [and] $71 billion in 2030," which translates into savings by the typical household of $26 per month in 2020 and $50 per month in 2030, by which time residential electricity rates would be 17 percent lower than they would be without these programs.[56]

As we have seen, electricity generation typically requires a lot of water. Because the nine energy efficiency programs would save electricity they also would conserve water, an estimated 8.9 billion gallons in 2020 and 20.1 billion gallons in 2030.[57]

The nine policies would also generate a great deal of employment—380,000 jobs in 2020 and 520,000 in 2030. This compares favorably with the job-creating potential of investments in other energy-related sectors in the south. For every $1 million dollars of infrastructure spending in the south, spending in the electric utility sector adds only 5.6 jobs and in the natural gas sector 8.4 jobs. But the nine efficiency measures which reduce the need for energy is projected to add 16.5 jobs per $1 million of spending, more than double the average of the other two.

*   *   *

There are many other areas where money spent on infrastructure improves our economy more than money spent on other projects or that reverts to consumers through tax cuts. Consider, for example, money spent on our water resources. Protecting and improving beaches promotes recreational tourism. Restoring wetlands improves hunting and promotes ecotourism. And preserving aquatic habitat promotes continuation of lucrative fishing and dining industries.[58]

Transportation spending is particularly helpful because it could reduce much of the inefficiency that, we saw in chapter 6, afflicts the American transportation system. Light rail systems, for example, improve efficiency in several ways. Energy is saved when a person travels by rail instead of driving a car. The form of energy used constitutes another saving. Cars use gasoline, which contributes to global warming and aggravates our country's balance of payment problems when much of our petroleum comes from overseas. Light rail, by contrast, uses electricity that is cheaper, employs domestic energy sources, and those domestic sources can increasingly come from renewables, such as wind power, which don't contribute to global warming. Light rail also reduces traffic congestion in metropolitan areas, thereby improving efficiency by saving people time when they shop or commute to work. Light rail reduces the need for parking, which frees up land for more productive pursuits. And when this land is used more productively, it generates tax revenue that relieves the tax burden of most people. Mass transit also reduces air pollution, which improves human wellbeing directly through better health and indirectly through reduced monetary costs related to healthcare and absence from work.

Poor people are helped most because they tend to live in some of the most polluted areas, and they are least able to afford reliable cars to get to work. Helping the poorest among us improves social justice, according to most accounts, and in any case relieves the tax burden on people of means who would otherwise be called upon through private charity or tax contributions to help the poor. People of means benefit from mass transit also, even if they never use it themselves, because travel by car becomes faster when fewer cars are on the road.

All of these benefits attend the *existence* of improved mass transit. In addition, the *creation* of mass transit provides a host of jobs. As we've seen, nearly twenty thousand jobs are created per $1 billion dollars spent, more than twice the job-creation benefit of military spending.

Generating an intercity rail infrastructure also creates a lot of jobs, improves efficiency, and reduces environmental damage. Federal Railroad Administrator Joseph Szabo said in 2012,

> Local officials know that every dollar you spend on rail infrastructure generates three times more in economic output and job creation. And while these projects aren't finished overnight, the economic benefits often arrive before initial rail construction takes place. That includes a rise in land values and wages. It includes new growth, new jobs, and a huge windfall for local economies.[59]

Ray LaHood, former US Secretary of Transportation, gives two examples. In Brunswick, Maine, "an extension to Amtrak's Downeaster service is expected to bring more than $7 billion in new development, 10,000 new jobs, and $75 million in annual state revenue." In Normal, Illinois, "improved rail service to St. Louis and Chicago has already generated $200 million in private investment in the city's central business district where the occupancy rate is now 100 percent."[60] Other Illinois cities are benefitting as well. In nearby Rochelle, a railcar manufacturer won a contract in 2012 worth $352 million to supply railcars to California and to three Midwestern states. Taxpayers are creating American jobs, LaHood claims, "Our Buy American requirement ensures that rail projects, from trains and tracks to new stations, are built with American hands and with American-made parts and supplies. And right now, railway suppliers have locations in 49 states and D.C., creating good-paying jobs across the country."[61]

In addition, according to former Secretary LaHood, "passenger rail is three-times more energy-efficient than car travel and six times more efficient than air travel." Intercity passenger rail is more energy efficient than air travel because it takes much less force to roll a train along its tracks than to lift tons of metal, luggage, and passengers into the air.[62] For this reason, the *Ecologist* reports, a round-trip flight from London to Paris creates between 110 and 172 kilograms of CO_2 per passenger, whereas a round trip by fast train (Eurostar) generates only 17 kilograms per passenger.[63] Intercity rail is more energy-efficient than car travel because there is less friction when metal rolls on metal than when the rubber meets the road. Also, more weight per passenger is moved in car travel (on average just over 1.5 passengers per three thousand-pound vehicle), and because electric motors waste less energy than internal combustion engines. Passenger rail saves space as well because "a single dedicated high-speed passenger rail line can carry more capacity than six lanes of freeway."[64] And high-speed passenger rail saves travel time, as it can average over 100 miles per hour without having to stop for people to get snacks or go to the bathroom. Passenger rail even saves time compared to air travel for most trips under five hundred miles and for almost all trips under three hundred miles because people don't have to arrive so early for security checks, and trains most often take people closer to their final destination (except, of course, for those whose final destination is an airport).

We saw in chapter 6 how inefficient it is to move freight intercity by semitruck. The trucks use much more fuel per ton of freight than freight trains, do costly damage to our roads, contribute to road congestion that wastes a lot of time and money for travelers in cars, and jeopardize the safety of people in smaller vehicles. Our economy would run more efficiently with a freight rail network that replaces most intercity trucking.

* * *

Our economy would run more efficiently also with a new electricity grid, a so-called "smart grid," to transmit electricity. Our current electricity distribution system sends electricity to homes, factories, and businesses using meters to monitor how much electricity is sent to each customer. A smart grid system does this and more. It allows customers to install smart meters that allow them to reduce their electricity bills by adding electricity to the grid. Households with photovoltaic displays (PV), for example, may use some of the energy they generate on a sunny day to add electricity to the grid. This is most welcome on hot summer days when air-conditioning strains the supply of electricity and threatens brown-outs. The money that customers can save on their electricity bills encourages the installation of PV without additional government subsidies, and utilities gain because the cost of electricity to the utilities is at its highest at times of greatest use, especially hot sunny days. Smart meters can similarly encourage factories to install environmentally sustainable wind turbines because they know that they can recover some of the wind turbines' cost by selling their excess electricity.

A smart grid also allows the price of electricity to vary from times of least demand to times of greatest demand. This will encourage car owners to use more battery-operated vehicles because they can program battery charging for the middle of the night when electricity is overabundant and therefore cheap. It will discourage overuse of air-conditioning on hot days when electricity is in short supply and therefore much more expensive. Many people who currently set their thermostats at 70 degrees Fahrenheit may thus be influenced to set their thermostats at 75 degrees to save money. Ron Pernick and Clint Wilder wrote in *Clean Tech Nation*, "Residential customers with smart thermostats were shown [in a study in Oklahoma] to have reduced demand by up to 57 percent during peak times, compared with customers without them. And for customers participating in variable peak pricing, average energy consumption dropped as much as one third during the highest-priced periods."[65]

Many more examples could be given of infrastructural repair and development related to energy and transportation that would improve efficiency, help our economy to grow, and provide employment. Many bridges need repair, as does our natural gas distribution network.[66] Rather than consider these and other projects in detail, let's now consider how such infrastructure projects rate according to the four criteria used in this book: job creation, efficiency/inefficiency, environmental sustainability, and political acceptability.

Much of the argument given so far in support of infrastructure development has been that creating, maintaining, and repairing infrastructure creates more jobs than alternative uses of the money needed for these tasks, and that having a well-developed infrastructure is necessary for the kind of economic growth that keeps people working. Infrastructure development clearly passes the test of job creation.

The economy grows faster with an improved infrastructure precisely because such an infrastructure improves the efficiency of activities basic to industrial civilization, such as energy generation and transmission and the transportation of people and products. Infrastructure development isn't a case of functional inefficiency; it's actually functional and efficient.

Much of the efficiency of infrastructure development comes from harnessing the forces of nature in more sustainable ways, such as by substituting natural gas, wind, and solar energy for coal in the generation of electricity, and by using less energy-intensive systems of transportation, such as rail and light rail, in place of the more energy-intensive systems of transportation by cars, trucks, and planes. Infrastructure investment and development passes the test of environmental sustainability. For this reason, it also paves the way for indefinite economic growth in service sectors, discussed in the next two chapters, which don't draw heavily on environmental resources. *Although most of these services have some negative environmental impacts, so long as those impacts are more than compensated for by an improved infrastructure that reduces overall environmental damage, our economy can grow sustainably into the indefinite future. This fact is central to the positive message of this book.*

Only the fourth issue remains to be addressed: the political acceptability of such investments in infrastructure. Our current deficits in all of the areas of infrastructure discussed in this chapter suggest that forces opposed to this approach to job creation are formidable. Opposition stems largely from reluctance to pay taxes for this (or almost any other) purpose. Many items of physical infrastructure are publicly owned public goods, such as interstate highways. As publicly owned, their creation and maintenance depend on tax-supported government expenditures. Many other items of physical infrastructure are privately owned but are also in large part public goods, such as privately owned power plants and railways. Privately owned pubic goods benefit private owners more than others, but they are public goods since private owners don't capture all of the benefits. Because the public benefits as well, private owners are reluctant to pay for the entire expense of creating and maintaining these goods. They count on the public to pay for that part of the benefits that accrues to the public. Again, taxes must be raised for this purpose. Most people resist taxes because they prefer to spend their money at their own discretion. Thus, tax receipts tend to be insufficient to pay for needed infrastructure whether it's owned publicly or privately.

However, if history is any guide, the physical infrastructure of the United States can be developed in ways needed to improve efficiency and promote economic growth. Such developments will not happen automatically or without a fight, but they are definitely politically possible. We can have greater reliance on light rail, intercity passenger trains, and intercity freight trains, and less reliance on cars and trucks as a percentage of transportation miles for both people and freight. We can have cars and trucks that use less petroleum. We can have greater reliance on renewable sources of energy, such as wind (or something different and better), and less reliance on coal and oil. We can have a smart electricity grid. We can build commercial and residential buildings that use energy more efficiently. And we can employ millions of people in the generation-long process of making these improvements in infrastructure.

One reason to believe that such change can take place is that since the beginning of the Industrial Revolution monumental change in transportation and energy infrastructure over a fifty-year period is the universal norm. Think back over fifty-year intervals starting in 1800. Picture a well-settled country such as England in 1800, and then picture it in 1850. By 1850 transportation had been revolutionized by steam locomotives and steam ships, and the nature and location of manufacturing had been altered by steam engines in factories. The scene looks quite different in 1900 because the rail network is much more extensive and trains move faster, although they are still powered by steam. Dynamos appear on the landscape. Electricity is beginning to light homes and factories and people move not only by horse and train but also by trolley, in North America as in Europe. Cities expand as light rail allows longer commutes to work. By 1950 cars are everywhere and horses have all but disappeared from metropolitan areas. Transportation powered by electricity, much of it underground, is the norm in the largest cities. Paved roads are common where they were rare fifty years earlier. But these are mostly two-lane roads that make intercity travel by car much slower than the interstate highways that will replace them by 2000. In France, Japan, England, Spain, and other countries, fast trains powered by electricity instead of steam or diesel were common in 2000. Nuclear power, nonexistent in 1950, provided 20 percent of electricity in the United States and 75 percent in France by 2000. Since 2000, natural gas has been replacing coal for electricity generation in the United States, followed closely in percentage of growth by wind power. In sum, change of the sort called for in this chapter is the norm, not the exception.

Our current failure to maintain infrastructure can't be caused by endemic reluctance to pay for it, because if Americans were always averse to paying for infrastructure we wouldn't have the infrastructure that we're currently failing to maintain. I regularly discuss political and economic issues by email with some very conservative Tea-Party-sympathizing individuals. They are suspicious of government programs, but I haven't found one who objects to the government having funded the interstate highway system. They just don't yet recognize that fast trains, wind turbines, and light rail are for the twenty-first century what the interstate highway system was for the twentieth. And those individuals may never come around. But they're old, like me. The next generation and the one to follow, people who need jobs, will probably recognize what's needed in the current century just as the older generation recognized what was needed previously.

Young people are already turning away from cars and driving, our dominant modes of transportation. "For six decades," writes John Schwartz in the *New York Times*, "Americans have tended to drive more every year. But in the middle of the last decade, the number of miles driven—both overall and per capita—began to drop."[67] The change began before the Great Recession of 2008–2009. Michael Sivak, a researcher at the University of Michigan's Transportation Research Institute reports that "rates of car ownership per household and per person started to come down two to three years before the downturn."[68] Aging baby boomers are retiring and therefore drive fewer miles because they don't have to commute to work. But the greatest changes are among young people who now seek driving licenses in smaller numbers than in previous generations. Between 2001 and 2009 driving by young people declined 23 percent. Part of the explanation may be that they use social media to connect with friends. In addition, many workers now telecommute to work, and many others increasingly use public transportation.[69] Public transportation is increasingly popular also to reach some destinations to which access by car is often arduous. Hence, the revival of train service to Cape Cod.[70]

Global competition and global warming are additional reasons to believe that succeeding generations, if not the older generation, will fund needed infrastructural maintenance and development. Efficiency is a key to international competition, and this includes efficiency in the generation and transmission of power as well as in the transportation of people and goods. By 2013 even Texas Republicans were starting to advocate new fees and taxes to pay for transportation infrastructure needed to reduce congestion and increase efficiency.[71] Nationally, Alberto Cardenas, former chairman of the Florida Republican Party and now head of the American Conservative Union, chastises fellow Republicans who prefer lowering taxes to increasing federal spending on transportation infrastructure. Like national defense, Cardenas argues, transportation infrastructure is a public good that our tax dollars should support.[72]

Global warming is a factor as well as international competition. It was widely reported after Superstorm Sandy hit New Jersey, New York, and Connecticut that skepticism among people in the area about global warming was washed away overnight. Reluctance to pay for ways of ameliorating the extent and impact of climate change disappeared as well. Infrastructural projects to protect the coastline suddenly gained political traction and journalistic attention. One idea, for example, is to protect New York City with a giant swing gate like the one that currently protects Rotterdam, Europe's most important port. The gate could be placed across New York's Narrows, the sea lane between Brooklyn and Staten Island, at a cost of at least $6.5 billion. In June 2013 New York's Mayor Bloomberg proposed a $20 billion plan to protect the city from the effects of climate change.[73] New infrastructure projects like these can be expected to generate untold numbers of jobs in the next fifty years because, as journalist McKenzie Funk puts it, "By deciding to adapt to climate change—a decision that has already been partly made, because significant warming is already baked into the system—we have decided to embrace a world of walls."[74] Building walls creates jobs. In addition, renewable sources of energy become more price-competitive when the cost of coping with climate-change disasters is factored into the price of energy from fossil fuels.

Right-wing Republicans and powerful business interests are starting to line up on the side of changes in infrastructure that will mitigate the effects of climate change. The insurance industry, hit by $35 billion of insured property losses in 2012 compared to a decade average of only $24 billion, is not at all skeptical of climate change, which it expects to create more severe storms and greater losses of insured property in the future. Some conservative Republicans endorse a carbon tax to reduce greenhouse gas emissions. Eli Lehrer, a former vice president of the conservative Heartland Institute, considers a carbon tax consistent with conservative orthodoxy, writes Eduardo Porter in the *New York Times*. "It is a broad and flat tax whose revenue can be used to do away with the corporate income tax—a favorite target of the right. It provides a market-friendly signal, forcing polluters to bear the cost imposed on the rest of us and encouraging them to pollute less. And it is much preferable to a parade of new regulations from the Environmental Protection Agency." Former Republican congressman Bob Inglis of South Carolina supports a carbon tax for these reasons and claims a dozen Republicans in the House and eight in the Senate are of the same opinion. Even ExxonMobil supports a carbon tax to mitigate global warming.[75]

Four Environmental Protection Agency (EPA) administrators appointed by four Republican presidents—Nixon, Reagan, and both Bushes—endorse President Obama's decision in 2013 to combat CO_2 emissions through new

EPA regulations and through increased support for investments in clean energy technology. They note that under Republican presidents, "The United States led the world when nations came together to phase out ozone-depleting chemicals. Acid rain diminishes each year, thanks to a pioneering, market-based emissions-trading system adopted under the first President Bush in 1990. And despite critics' warnings, our economy has continued to grow." They urge such can-do activism immediately to address global warming.[76] Perhaps of greater importance, reports Coral Davenport in the *New York Times*,

> at least 29 companies with close ties to Republicans, including ExxonMobil, Walmart and American Electric Power, are incorporating a price on carbon into their long-term financial plans. . . . The development is significant because businesses that chart a financial course to make money in a carbon-constrained future could be more inclined to support policies that address climate change.[77]

One motivation for corporations to take this course seems to be concern about production and profitability in a warmer world. Coca-Cola, for example, sees climate change as disrupting the supply of needed inputs for their products—potable water, sugar cane, sugar beets, and citrus fruits. Many other companies worry that global warming will increase financial risk and lower GDP.[78] Hence, there are increasingly strong voices within the Republican as well as the Democratic establishment in favor of energy policies designed to combat global warming.

In sum, although Winston Churchill may not have actually said this, the quote commonly attributed to him may be correct: "You can always count on Americans to do the right thing—after they've tried everything else."[79] With regard to physical infrastructure we have to a large extent been trying everything else since about 1980, such as by failing to maintain our roads, bridges, and electricity grid. Now, bipartisan considerations of jobs, economic growth, and competitiveness, the kinds of considerations that produced our present infrastructure, are beginning to have their customary influence, and it is politically feasible that employment possibilities will abound in the next few decades as we produce this infrastructure. Fewer jobs will be needed to maintain the new physical infrastructure once it has been created than are needed to create it in the first place, but an economy with an improved physical infrastructure will grow more quickly and thereby continue to create jobs of many kinds. Its growth will also be environmentally sustainable into the indefinite future because the kinds of infrastructural developments discussed here tend to reduce dramatically the impact that economic growth has on the environment. Thus, infrastructure development is functionally efficient as well as politically possible.

Such development will not take place without a fight. Negative reaction from the coal industry was swift in June 2014 when the Obama administration unveiled plans to regulate carbon dioxide. The plan is to reduce by 2030 CO_2 emissions from power plants to 30 percent below their level of emissions in 2005.[80] But, as Paul Krugman pointed out at the time, even the research in opposition to limits on CO_2 emissions, sponsored by the US Chamber of Commerce, claimed that such regulations would have negative financial effects amounting to no more than a small fraction of one percent of income. And these slightly negative numbers are under attack as being unduly pessimistic.[81] What is more, the coal industry currently employs only one sixteenth of one percent of American workers,[82] which limits its political clout.

In sum, just as railroads and coal power won in the nineteenth century, and automobiles and electricity won in the twentieth century, Americans can make light rail and renewable energy win in the twenty-first century. Americans usually adapt to technological change when it improves profitability and economic competitiveness. And a more environment-friendly infrastructure can lay the groundwork for indefinite economic growth and unlimited job opportunities in service sectors discussed in the next two chapters.

CHAPTER 12
HUMAN INFRASTRUCTURE

Improving our country's human infrastructure, like updating our physical infrastructure, will create many jobs, improve our international competitiveness, and contribute to indefinite economic growth. Here we concentrate on education as a major contributor to the creation and maintenance of the kind of human infrastructure needed in today's high-tech economy.

Education is primarily a service with relatively low environmental impact, so its continued growth is environmentally sustainable. However, the difficulty of gaining political acceptance for investments in physical infrastructure, discussed in the preceding chapter, is mirrored by controversies surrounding investments in education, from preschool through grad school, even though there's consensus that an educated workforce is an essential public good. According to a study for the Brookings Institution,

> Economists have long believed that investments in education, or "human capital," are an important source of economic growth. Over the last 40 years output has risen about 3.5 percent a year. Growth in the productivity of labor, the major driver of increases in wages and standards of living, has measured about 2.4 percent per year. The contribution of education to labor productivity growth is estimated in different studies to be between 13 and 30 percent of the total increase.[1]

The reason is that more educated workers are "more . . . adaptable, can learn new tasks and new skills more easily, can use a wider range of technologies and sophisticated equipment (including newly emerging ones), and [are] more creative in thinking about how to improve the management of work."[2]

The proliferation of such skills helps the economy in general because it improves the prospects for American firms to compete successfully in the global marketplace and because it lowers unemployment and increases personal income, which reduces crime and improves the functioning of civil institutions. Although international competiveness in the production of manufactured goods will not provide a great deal of employment, it's nevertheless necessary. If we weren't competitive in these areas, Americans would increasingly import manufactured items as its manufacturing infrastructure declined. Increased imports would jeopardize the economy through a worsening balance of trade (we would become an even greater international debtor than at present) and decline of our manufacturing infrastructure would make us ever more dependent on the willingness of other countries to lend us money so we could buy the manufactured goods that are central to our material affluence.

Improving our educational infrastructure is important also because educated workers suffer less unemployment and earn higher salaries than their less-educated peers. The US Bureau of Labor Statistics reports that in 2012 unemployment among workers with doctorates or professional degrees was between 2.1 and 2.5 percent, whereas it was 8.3 percent among those whose highest academic attainment was a high school diploma and 12.4 percent among those who had failed to complete high school. Those with master's degrees had lower unemployment than those with bachelor's degrees; those with bachelor's degrees had lower unemployment than those with associate's degrees, etc. Weekly median earnings followed the same pattern, highest for those with professional degrees and doctorates and lowest for those who failed to complete high school, with others falling in between in accordance with educational attainment.[3]

Because education is so important to the economy, and our economy is now integrated within a global economy, much concern is expressed whenever American students fare poorly on international tests comparing their educational proficiency with that of students in other developed countries. For example, in 2009 the Program for International Student Assessment (PISA) ranked American fifteen-year-olds fourteenth in reading and twenty-fifth in math among the thirty-four members of the Organization for Economic Cooperation and Development (OECD).[4] Arne Duncan, US Secretary of Education said that the tests "show that American students are poorly prepared to compete in today's knowledge economy. . . . Americans need to wake up to this educational reality—instead of napping at the wheel while emerging competitors prepare their students for economic leadership."[5]

All of this suggests an American willingness to invest in education, a key pillar of the nation's human infrastructure. But this is not always the case. In general, current American discussions of education focus on two kinds of approaches to educational improvement, whether at the preschool, primary, secondary, or tertiary level. One approach is cheap and the other is more expensive. I will show that the cheap approaches are generally ineffective and that some relatively expensive approaches more than pay for themselves through the economic impact of their superior results. In addition, the expensive approaches provide more jobs than the cheaper alternatives, and promise to promote human flourishing through their noncommercial as well as their commercial effects.

*   *   *

The most popular cheap approach to the improvement of K–12 education is generally called "school reform" and embraces the 2002 No Child Left Behind (NCLB) legislation. The basic NCLB approach assumes that resources for schools are sufficient and would produce needed results (as measured by electronically graded student test scores) if only teachers were better at educating students. Reformers seem to think that most public school teachers aren't sufficiently talented, motivated, or hard-working. So, as originally conceived, the law uses the sticks of reduced funding and unemployment to motivate teachers and principals to work harder to help their students. Many school reformers also want to motivate teachers with the carrot of increased pay for particularly successful performance. Accordingly, reformers tend to demonize teachers' unions because the unions support tenure for teachers (eliminating the stick of job loss) and pay scales according to seniority (eliminating the carrot of increased pay).

In order to reduce the baleful influence of unions and to create competition in education that resembles the competition in free markets that generally improves efficiency, reformers favor nonunionized alternatives to traditional public schools: publicly financed charter schools and publicly financed school vouchers that parents can use to send their children to private schools. Reformers believe that such schools will outperform most traditional public schools. Ultimately, reformers think, many traditional public schools will close, their teachers and principals losing their jobs, when their students fail to perform at or above grade level in math and English, while the charter and voucher schools will thrive through more efficient use of the same resources. Thus, the country gets better results without increased spending on education.

That anyone interested in education still believes this is testimony to the strength of resistance to spending more money on education as infrastructure and public good. In the first place, although teachers are the most important influence *within the school* on educational outcomes, reform critic Diane Ravitch reports, high-quality analyses have formed a consensus: "teachers account for around 10–20 percent of achievement outcomes."[6] Blaming teachers alone for poor results in international comparisons is therefore wrong. As one might guess, parents are important as well. A study for the Center for Public Education of the National School Boards Association looked again at the result of the 2009 PISA tests and found that regardless of socioeconomic status, fifteen-year-olds did markedly better on the tests "whose parents often read books with them during their first year of primary school." In addition, the study found, "monitoring homework; making sure children get to school; rewarding their efforts and talking up the idea of going to college," all correlated with significantly higher test scores.[7]

Statistically, the most significant influence on educational outcomes is neither parents nor teachers but poverty. A larger percentage of children are in poverty in the United States than in other OECD countries. Adjusting for this factor (that is, comparing American students only with foreign students of similar socioeconomic status) improves the ranking of American students among those in the thirty-four OECD countries from fourteenth to sixth in reading and from twenty-fifth to thirteenth in math.[8] In fact, on the 2009 PISA tests, Ravitch writes, "American schools in which fewer than 10 percent of the students were poor outperformed the schools of Finland, Japan, and Korea," three of the countries with the best overall results. "As the proportion of poor students rises, the scores of US schools drop."[9]

Interstate comparisons also suggest the importance of poverty rather than unions for student performance. While the reform movement blames teachers' unions for low test scores, Ravitch notes that students in highly unionized states such as Connecticut, New Jersey, and Massachusetts have higher scores than students in states with few teachers' unions, such as those in the South,[10] where there is more poverty. Additional evidence that poverty is important comes from findings that as the income gap between rich and poor American families increases, the gap in educational attainment between children in rich and poor families increases as well.[11]

Poverty and inequality are therefore major impediments to overall American achievement on international tests. Yet the school reform movement alternates between ignoring the problem of poverty[12] and claiming that it isn't really important.[13] Why? Because reformers are looking for cheap solutions to the woes of American education and reducing the effects of poverty on educational achievement requires a lot of additional money spent on the education of children before they reach the age of five, as we shall see.

Besides failing to recognize that current research does not favor blaming teachers alone for poor student performance, reformers seldom notice that charter and voucher schools, their preferred alternatives to traditional public schools, fare no better without extra infusions of money. Although some charter schools seem to work wonders, as do some traditional public schools, educational outcomes in most charter schools are either no better or are worse than results in comparable traditional public schools, according to a study by Stanford University's Center for Research on Educational Outcomes (CREDO). The study, which included

> more than 70 percent of the nation's students attending charter schools, . . . found that there is a wide variance in the quality of the nation's several thousand charter schools with, in the aggregate, students in charter schools not faring as well as students in traditional public schools. . . . Seventeen percent of charter schools reported academic gains that were significantly better than traditional public schools, while 37 percent of charter schools showed gains that were worse than their traditional public school counterparts, with 46 percent of charter schools demonstrating no significant difference.[14]

What is more, some charter schools celebrated for their amazingly good outcomes benefit from extraordinary levels of financial support, much of it from private donors and foundations. For example, the Harlem Children's Zone, whose two charter schools in New York City are justly praised in the 2010 documentary film *Waiting for Superman* for its excellent results working with impoverished students and their families, has assets of over $200 million. Its founding director earns $400,000 a year. Another school justly praised in the documentary for excellence is the SEED boarding school in Washington, DC. But it spends $35,000 per pupil per year, about three times as much as DC spends on students who attend public schools.[15] The academically successful KIPP network of charter schools also spends considerably more money per pupil than is spent at most traditional public schools.[16] Contrary to the belief of most reformers, it seems that additional funds may be needed for better results than currently obtain in most public schools.

So far, school vouchers, which help families send their children to private schools with public money, do not improve academic outcomes either. Milwaukee has had a voucher system for over twenty years, and "on average the students in voucher schools achieve the same test scores as those in regular public schools."[17] Overall, according to federal assessments, Milwaukee still has one of the nation's worst performing school districts.

In sum, experience in the United States suggests that charters, vouchers, and computerized tests designed to weed out underperforming teachers and schools are no substitutes for spending additional money on education. Experience to date suggests also that unionization isn't a major obstacle to improved education in the United States.

Nevertheless, reformers are correct that teaching is important to the educational process (even if it can't compensate completely for failures due to poverty and lack of parental involvement). However, few reformers have considered what, besides punishing unsuccessful teachers, it takes to improve teaching. Here is where international comparisons provide insight. A study conducted by McKinsey & Company found that teachers in countries with the most successful students—Singapore, Finland, and South Korea—"recruit 100% of their teacher corps from the top third of the academic cohort, and then screen for other important qualities as well. In the U.S., by contrast, 23% of new teachers come from the top third, and just 14% in high poverty schools."[18]

How could we become more like these other countries? The authors of the study write, "Our market research suggests that raising the share of top-third+ new hires in high-needs schools from 14% to 68% would mean paying new teachers around $65,000 with a maximum career compensation of $150,000 a year."[19] This is far more than most teachers currently make in the United States, where teacher salaries have declined for more than a generation. In 2011 the average starting salary for teachers was $39,000 a year, and the average after twenty-five years of teaching was $67,000 a year. These salaries are 14 percent lower than those of professionals in other fields that require similar levels of education and price teachers out of home ownership in thirty-two metropolitan areas.[20]

Yet, recent studies suggest that society at large benefits so much economically from excellent teaching that salaries for really good teachers would increase enormously if teacher pay reflected all their contributions to social wellbeing. A study led by Harvard University economist Raj Chetty concluded that an excellent kindergarten teacher—not necessarily the hero of a heartwarming movie, just someone in the top 14 or 25 percent instead of the bottom 14 or 25 percent by teaching quality—has a lasting positive impact on students. The students of the better teachers have greater levels of college attendance, college graduation, home ownership, retirement savings, and lifetime earnings. If such kindergarten teachers were to receive the full monetary worth of the lifetime benefits they provide for twenty students in a year, their salaries would be $320,000 a year.[21] In sum, rather than follow the reform model of trying to improve education without additional funds, several strands of research suggest that spending more on teacher salaries is justified and necessary to improve student performance.

Teacher training and support are important as well, according Jal Mehta, an education researcher at Harvard Graduate School of Education:

> Teaching requires a professional model, like we have in medicine, law, engineering, accounting, architecture and many other fields. In these professions, consistency of quality is created less by holding individual practitioners accountable and more by building a body of knowledge, carefully training people in that knowledge, requiring them to show expertise before they become licensed, and then using their professions' standards to guide their work.

We also need to develop a career arc for teaching and a differentiated salary structure to match it. Like medical residents in teaching hospitals, rookie teachers should be carefully overseen by experts as they move from apprenticeship to proficiency, and then mastery. Early- to mid-career teachers need time to collaborate and explore new directions [so] they can refine their skills.[22]

Such approaches yield good results in other countries. "High school teachers provide 1,080 hours per year of instruction in America compared with fewer than 600 in South Korea and Japan [countries with better test results on international exams], where the balance of teachers' time is spent collaboratively on developing and refining lesson plans."[23]

All of this, raising teachers' salaries, evaluating teachers through peer and administrative attention rather than by student test scores, and allowing teachers to spend more time preparing lessons in collaboration with colleagues, takes money. Yet, if current research is correct, the money spent is less than gains to society, assuming that we don't pay good kindergarten teachers the full $320,000 a year that they're worth to society. Thus, this approach improves efficiency.

At the same time, this kind of program to improve student performance provides excellent employment opportunities. Consider how many more teachers will be needed if teachers spend more time than at present mentoring, collaborating with, and assessing their colleagues. All other things being equal, if our high school teachers were to spend on average only 600 instead of 1,080 hours per year in direct instruction, we'd need 80 percent more high school teachers than we currently employ. Additional professionals would be needed to evaluate teachers through peer reviews rather than through student test scores because the peer-review process is more labor intensive.

Another educational approach that provides jobs and helps students is tutoring. Troubled teenagers who disrupt classes and then fail to complete high school tend to pay attention to their work and instructor when they are tutored either individually or in groups of just two or three. Intensive tutoring combined with group behavioral counseling resulted in students who are poor, previously disruptive, and deficient in grade-level math skills gaining the equivalent of three years improvement in those skills after just one year of tutoring. The cost was about $4,000 per student, mostly to pay counselors and tutors.[24]

The money spent to employ additional professionals in education would for the most part be drawn from tax receipts, and raising taxes to meet increased expenses in education would reduce the money available for household consumption. But this, too, is a gain for employment, according to economists Robert Pollin and Heidi Garrett-Peltier. They estimate that for every $1 billion spent on education 29,100 jobs are created, but when the same $1 billion is spent on household consumption only 14,800 jobs are created.[25]

In addition, consider how many jobs would be created if more students were given the opportunity to be educated in boarding schools as are students in Washington, DC's SEED program, which "has remarkable rates of graduation and college acceptance" but costs $35,000 per student per year.[26] Even without the proliferation of such boarding schools, the Political Economy Research Institute estimated in 2009 that $4.7 billion of investment is needed annually above current levels of investment in constructing, renovating, and adding to school buildings.[27] Many more construction-related jobs would be created by a national program of providing boarding school education for all underprivileged high school students. Widespread imitation of the Harlem Children's Zone would create many service jobs in education, social work, and healthcare, because one of the keys to the success of those schools is provision to children and their families of a broad array of social and medical services.

Thus, the job-creating potential of spending money on K–12 education is almost limitless. And the money is well spent in two senses. It creates more jobs than any other use of the money except spending on public transportation and, like public transportation, it increases social wealth. Because the increase in wealth results from more students completing postsecondary school programs, let's look now at the current state of higher education in the United States.

✻   ✻   ✻

Considerations of cost impair postsecondary as well K–12 education, even though, as with K–12, increased public support would create millions of well-paying jobs and improve our economy. Like all education, higher education is a public as well as a private good. It's a private good insofar as people's earnings increase as they attain associate's, bachelor's, and master's degrees. But it's also a public good, writes journalist Catherine Rampell. "Economists have found that higher education benefits communities even more than it benefits the individual receiving the degree. Studies show that an educated populace leads to faster economic growth and a more stable democracy. . . . The post-World War II economic boom, for example, has been attributed to increased college enrollment thanks to the G.I. Bill."[28] In recent years, however, "There has been a shift from the belief that we as a nation benefit from higher education, to a belief that it's the people receiving the education who primarily benefit and so they should foot the bill."[29]

One way to recognize the public benefits of higher education is to see how closely they are tied to the private benefits that accrue primarily to successful students. According the US Bureau of Labor Statistics, median weekly earnings for someone with a master's degree is $1,300 whereas for a bachelor's degree it's $1,066. If the master's degree represents two years of full-time study after the bachelor's degree, the percentage wage increase per year of study is over 10 percent.[30] Similarly, even if it takes on average three years of full-time study (a rather generous allotment of time) to go from an associate's degree to a bachelor's degree, the income increase (from $785 to $1,066 per week) is over 10 percent per year of study. The same is true if it takes on average three years of full-time study for those without a high school diploma to obtain one, because median weekly earnings go from $471 to $652.[31] These are private benefits of higher education.

Currently, the median income per year for full-time work is about $40,000. If each year of additional schooling increases the income of the average worker by at least 10 percent, the median worker gains $4,000 of additional income with each year of additional schooling. Assuming that people work about forty years in their lifetimes, lifetime earnings increase by $160,000 for each year of additional schooling. Again, these are private benefits.

If median earnings increase with inflation and therefore remain $40,000 per year in real dollar terms, 10 percent increased lifetime earnings will bring in money that remains the equivalent of today's $160,000. Yet an extra year of K–12 schooling today costs only about $12,000, making the return more than thirteen times the cost. Impressive returns apply even when education is considerably more expensive. Full time study at colleges and universities, for example, can easily (although they don't necessarily) cost $40,000 a year. Similarly, high school study at a boarding school like the one in the SEED program costs $35,000 a year. Yet, even at these higher rates the benefit is still at least four times the cost. Thus, it is cost effective to publicly fund not only K–12 education, but college and university education at least through the master's degree even at high cost per year because the private monetary benefits to our citizens average at least several times the cost.

But why should the public pay for such private benefits? They should pay because it's a good investment that spurs so much economic growth that taxpayers will gain in the long run. Suppose that, in real dollar (inflation adjusted) terms, the average cost of an additional year of education in high school were to go from the current $12,000 to $20,000, so that we could incorporate many of the improvements that would make our system more like that of countries whose students are more successful on international tests. Suppose that community-college education costs the same, and that college and university education costs $40,000 a year. The average (inflation adjusted) cost to taxpayers of an additional year of education would be what is now equivalent to about $30,000. Because the government would collect about 20 percent of the additional earning in tax receipts (assuming that historical patterns of tax collection continue), and the additional earnings for a lifetime are the inflation-adjusted equivalent of $160,000 today, the government would eventually collect the equivalent of $32,000 (20 percent of $160,000) for each year of education provided at completely public expense.

Taxpayers who don't benefit directly as participants in these educational programs would gain owing to accelerated economic growth and reduced need for taxpayer support of workers who are paid so little that they require food and housing assistance from the government. Because people with more education and better-paying jobs engage less in criminal activity, taxpayers save also through reduced expenses for security and corrections. These gains would more than compensate taxpayers who aren't direct beneficiaries. Even if the government borrows to fund these educational programs, thereby adding to the interest that must be paid on the national debt, the benefits to the US Treasury are greater than such additional interest. Only the direct beneficiaries whose incomes increase as a result of additional education would pay any more than extra interest on the public debt. But the additional taxes that they pay would merely be taxes on the *extra income* that they make as a result of their improved education.

The OECD gives an even rosier picture. They find that "over the course of his working life, a tertiary-educated man in the U.S. can expect to earn almost $675,000 more than a man with no more than an upper secondary or postsecondary non-tertiary education." For a woman the figure is $390,000. It is in the financial interest of US taxpayers to fund additional years of higher education, according to the OECD, because

> U.S. taxpayers . . . on average . . . bear a cost (direct and indirect) of $45,554 to support a man in higher education and $45,618 to support a woman in higher education. . . . In the long run, however, taxpayers will recoup this investment many times over through the increased income taxes that tertiary-educated workers typically pay, as well as savings from the lower amount of social welfare benefits these individuals typically receive. Overall, the net public return in the U.S. amounts to $232,779 for each tertiary-educated man, and $84,313 for each tertiary-educated woman.[32]

* * *

In spite of the economic advantages of spending more public money on higher education, the current trend in the United States is in the opposite direction. Higher education is starved of funds, as politicians try to provide this public good on the cheap. In constant dollars, public support for higher education went down from $8,670 per full-time student in 2001 to $5,896 per full-time student in 2012, a reduction of over 30 percent.[33] Between 2011 and 2012 alone state funding for higher education dropped 7.5 percent. Between 2008 and 2012, writes Eric Kelderman in the *Chronicle of Higher Education*, "more than a dozen states . . . slashed tax dollars for colleges by more than 20 percent." Arizona cut 37 percent and New Hampshire 36 percent.[34]

One result of reduced public support for higher education is higher tuition.

Between 1985 and 2012 the percentage that students and parents have to pay for education at public universities has risen from 23 percent of the total cost to 40 percent of total cost.[35] As government pays less, students and their parents pay more for tuition. In 2012 CNN Money reported, "Over the past decade, average annual tuition for a year of community college has risen 40 percent to $3,122. ... At 4-year public universities, the cost has risen 68 percent to $7,692."[36] Virginia illustrates this trend. Between 2006 and 2011 in-state tuition rose 50 percent at the University of Virginia, as the state cut back its contribution to only 8 percent of the total budget of its flagship campus.[37]

The increasing cost of higher education has resulted in mounting debt among those who go to college. As recently as 2002, total student debt was $200 billion;[38] by 2014 it was $1.1 trillion. Almost 39 million Americans now have student loan debts, and the average debt is nearly $30,000.[39] According to the Federal Reserve Bank of New York, "Student loan debt is the only form of consumer debt that has grown since the peak of the consumer debt in 2008. Balances of student loans have eclipsed both auto loans and credit cards, making student loan debt the largest form of consumer debt outside of mortgages."[40] Student loan debt is growing fastest in percentage terms among people sixty and older, more than tripling between 2005 and 2013 from $700 million to $2.2 billion. Increased student loan debt among this group is assumed to stem primarily from borrowing so that children or grandchildren can attend college.[41]

An indication that the level of student loan debt is too high is an accelerating rate of default. During 2012 the percentage of student loan debt that was ninety or more days delinquent increased among those aged sixty and older from 9.6 to 12.9 percent, subjecting many seniors to automatic deductions from their social security checks. People between forty and forty-nine years of age fared worse, as delinquency in this group went from 11.9 to 16.1 percent during 2012.

In addition to problems of default, high levels of debt discourage home purchases and entrepreneurial activity, thereby impairing economic recovery and growth. Lauren Asher of the Institute for Student Access and Success notes, "Things like buying a home, starting a family, [and] starting a business ... may not be options for people who are paying off a lot of student debt."[42]

Brent Ambrose, a professor of risk management at Penn State, is especially concerned about small businesses because they create 60 percent of new jobs. Unemployment may be exacerbated by student loan debt because such debt may impair the ability of entrepreneurs to get the capital that they need to start new businesses.[43] Also, when people in great debt get a job and earn some money, they have to use much of their income to pay debts. Less goes to new purchases that stimulate the economy and provide jobs for others.

Another result of declining public support for higher education is that fewer students attend colleges and universities. In California, for example, where funding for the University of California (UC), California State University (CSU), and the California Community Colleges has been falling for a generation, the Public Policy Institute of California notes declining interest among high school graduates in attending any four-year college. "Enrollment rates at UC and CSU have fallen by one-fifth over the past five years," the Institute reports, "from about 22 percent of all high school graduates to below 18 percent. Among the state's most highly prepared high school graduates, the enrollment rate has declined even more—from around 67 percent to 55 percent."[44]

Declines like this exacerbate the long-standing problem of stagnating percentages of American students going to college and earning bachelor's degrees. In 2006 the Advisory Committee on Student Financial Assistance of the US Department of Education reported that owing to the high cost of college and inadequate financial assistance, many American students from low- and moderate-income families who are qualified to go to college either don't enroll in the first place or drop out before completing a bachelor's degree. The Advisory Committee "projected that as many as 2.4 million bachelor's degrees would likely be lost this decade [the first decade of the twenty-first century], as the number of high school graduates increases and their academic preparation for college-level work improves. An update released in May 2008, noting a significant enrollment shift from four-year to two-year public colleges between 1992 and 2004, revised the estimate upward to 3.2 million."[45]

One approach to increasing the number of graduates in the United States without increasing tax support for higher education (that is, one proposal to improve higher education on the cheap) is to have more classes taught online in "the hope that college courses taught online can drive down the cost of a degree, and make it easier for working students to complete their college education."[46] In such courses, instructors communicate with students only electronically. One version of this approach is for universities to offer what are called Massive Open Online Courses (MOOCs), in which an online lecture can potentially reach millions of people all around the world, either simultaneously or "asynchronously" on the students' preferred schedule. Many people think that personnel costs are reduced when one lecturer is doing the work that requires many lecturers in face-to-face teaching. Economist Tyler Cowen writes, "Online education will be extremely cheap. Once an online course is created, additional students can be handled at relatively low cost, often close to zero cost."[47]

Before pointing out some negatives, let me note that online offerings can certainly promote learning. Like a good book or movie, a series of online lectures from world-renown authorities who are also excellent lecturers can stimulate and inform the general public as well as students enrolled in higher education. As a result, human flourishing can be advanced through the joy of learning and through an improved ability, distributed widely in the population, to understand and solve both individual and social problems.

However, as the basis for courses in higher education aimed at generating university credits that lead to university degrees, such courses have major drawbacks. *Esquire* magazine's editor at large, A. J. Jacobs, found that in such courses, "The professor is, in most cases, out of students' reach, only slightly more accessible than the pope. . . . For MOOCs to fulfill their potential [their providers] will have to figure out how to make teachers and teaching assistants more reachable, more like local pastors, less like deities on high."[48]

A common approach to online education addresses this problem with more modest online courses produced by locally available instructors. Again, there is a positive side to this. *Combining* online elements with traditional class meetings in credit-generating courses can improve educational experiences at universities. The student who is shy can more easily participate in class discussions online. So can the student who thinks of a good point after class. Students who miss class occasionally can often gain online access to lectures they've missed, and students who were in the class can use online resources to review class material before an exam. So there is no problem with online education when used in the context of traditional classes. The problem is *substitu-*

tion of online content for traditional classes—online credit-generating classes where students' *only* access to class is through electronic media.

Two problems prevent such classes from improving higher education at low cost. First, such classes are unlikely to save money if they meet the need that students have for access to and regular feedback from their teachers. In fact, answering a question or clarifying a point online—through email, Blackboard (an Internet platform for online courses), or some other electronic medium—is more labor intensive than answering a question or clarifying a point during a face-to-face class. For this reason, when my university, the University of Illinois at Springfield, introduced online classes, class size was capped at twenty students compared to thirty-five in most other courses. The cap in online courses was raised to twenty-five for budgetary reasons a few years later.

The second problem is that fewer students complete online than face-to-face courses. The Community College Research Center at the Teachers College at Columbia University studied the enrollment history of fifty-one thousand community-college students in the State of Washington between 2004 and 2009. "Thirty-three percent of the students . . . enrolled in at least one course online during the five-year period. Students in an online course had an 82-percent chance of completing the course, compared with a 90-percent chance in face-to-face courses. Among students in remedial courses, the gap was even wider," 74 percent compared to 85 percent. A similar study of students in the Virginia community college system, which followed forty thousand students over four years, came to the same conclusion—that online students are less likely to complete courses. "A combination of technical difficulties, a lack of structure, and isolation" seems to account for less persistence in online than in traditional courses.[49] Thus, on average, when online classes are done properly, they don't save money and they depress instead of increase rates of completion. The move toward more online education is thus likely to exacerbate the dropout problem in US higher education without saving money.

A perennial suggestion in the United States when budgets are tight is to encourage and support increasing private sector contributions to the provision of public goods because, being subject to competition, private-sector organizations are thought (by some people) to be more efficient than public institutions. Thus, we can get the result we want more cheaply. Just as this reasoning leads to support for school vouchers in K–12 education, it favors for-profit colleges in higher education.

Unfortunately, the combination of public support and profit motive has created perverse incentives. Large for-profit institutions such as the University of Phoenix, which has more than 450,000 students, and others with more than 100,000 each, such as Education Management Corporation, Career Education Corporation, DeVry, and Kaplan, get most of their revenue from the federal government because their students get federal Pell grants, Stafford loans, veterans benefits, and the like. In 2009, for example, Kaplan got 91.5 percent of its revenue from the federal government. Enrolling students who qualify financially for government help is therefore in the interest of these for-profit institutions whether or not the students qualify academically for their chosen courses of study. Tamar Lewin reports in the *New York Times* that undercover videos made for the Government Accountability Office showed "deception or fraud at 15 for-profit colleges, including two Kaplan campuses." Kaplan recruiters in Florida and California made "false or questionable statements to prospective students—suggesting for example, that massage therapists earn $100 an hour, and that student loans need not be paid back. . . . Dozens of current and former Kaplan employees said the videos painted a representative picture."[50] Education Management Corporation, the second largest of the for-profits, received $2.2 billion from taxpayers in 2010, which constituted 89.3 percent of corporate revenues that year. It was sued by the federal government, for having recruiters who

> were instructed to use high-pressure sales techniques and inflated claims
> about career placement to increase student enrollment, regardless of appli-
> cants' qualifications. Recruiters were encouraged to enroll even applicants
> who were unable to write coherently, who appeared to be under the influence
> of drugs or who did not own a computer—despite the fact that the students
> were seeking to start online programs.[51]

It's not surprising that completion rates at for-profit colleges are dismal. Not only are many of the students ill-prepared, but teaching is largely online, which has poorer outcomes than face-to-face education, even in the relatively intimate setting of community colleges. Online teaching is featured at these for-profit institutions because they spend about 30 percent of their revenue on advertising and marketing,[52] much more than public institutions such as community colleges and state universities. So if the overall education is to be cheaper at for-profits than at state colleges there must be significant savings elsewhere—in the method of teaching.

Finally, as a result of insufficient qualifications, unrealistic expectations, and impersonal instruction, students at for-profits default on their loans much more than others. Students at for-profits constitute only 12 percent of those in higher education, but about half of those defaulting on their student loans. Deanne Loonin, a lawyer at the National Consumer Law Center who works with low-income borrowers, told Lewin, "About two-thirds of the people I see attended for-profits; most did not complete their program; and no one I have worked with has ever gotten a job in the field they were supposedly trained for."[53] So, for-profit institutions of higher education are part of the problem, including the budgetary problem related to Americans failing to earn degrees and obtain other professional credentials after the completion of high school.

* * *

The failure of Americans to earn degrees in higher education bodes ill for US competitiveness worldwide. A 2006 report from of the Advisory Committee, "Managing Our Future: How Financial Barriers to College Undercut America's Global Competitiveness," asserts "America's global competitiveness depends not only on investment in research, science, and technology, but also on investment in human capital—higher education." Increasingly, the jobs of the future require at least a bachelor's degree. If we don't have workers to fill these jobs, the work will go elsewhere, to countries with a better-prepared workforce. Thus, America will have slower economic growth, lower average salaries, and reduced tax receipts compared with a scenario of increased investment in higher education. And recent studies indicate that the United States is falling behind global competitors: "Statistics that highlight differences in educational attainment show that our competitors are equaling or surpassing us in educational achievement."[54]

The OECD reports that in 1995 the US higher education graduation rate was 33 percent, second only to New Zealand among nineteen OECD countries with comparable data. However, by 2010, although the United States had increased its graduation rate to 38 percent, it ranked thirteenth among twenty-five OECD countries with comparable data, as the OECD average nearly doubled from 20 percent to 39 percent. Another indication of relative stagnation in higher educational attainment among Americans is that the United States is the only OECD country whose workers nearing retirement (fifty-five to sixty-four year-olds) have just as much postsecondary attainment as workers near the beginning of their careers (twenty-five to thirty-four year-olds.)[55]

The employment effects of our failure to invest well in higher education are already being felt. Steven Greenhouse reported in the *New York Times* in 2012, "Even though nearly 13 million Americans are still out of work, many employers complain that they cannot find the right people to fill myriad job openings—for example, specialists in medical information technology or operators of computer-controlled manufacturing machinery. All told, the nation's employers have 3.4 million job openings, according to the Bureau of Labor Statistics," that employers can't fill. Preparing students for these jobs could lower the country's unemployment rate 2.3 percent.[56] These factors justify spending much more than at present on continuing education and certificate programs similar to those that currently exist at Northern Virginia Community College, UCLA, Miami Dade College, New Jersey's Rutgers University, and Sinclair Community College in Dayton, Ohio, leading to certificates in such fields as digital marketing, green marketing, renewable energy, cyber security, and geospatial information systems.

Such continuing education and training is not an alternative to traditional higher education at community and four-year colleges because in the vast majority of cases students require postsecondary education to qualify for these programs. Few students can go directly from high school to specialized certificate programs in cyber security and geospatial information systems without college-level mathematics. Marketing specialists need college-level economics and verbal skills. So increased support for higher education in general, leading to increased higher educational attainment in the country at large, is needed as a precondition for accelerating growth in employment and in the economy through specialized training in many areas.

Other programs in postsecondary education, by contrast, such as programs in nursing, are available to those who have only completed high school, but many of these programs languish for lack of funds. The nursing program at Wake Technical Community College in Raleigh, North Carolina, for example, has a waiting list of 1,000 for 275 student slots. The college can't expand its program in spite of a current shortage of nurses that is expected to increase to 260,000 by 2025,[57] because its state funding fell 21 percent between 2009 and 2012, a loss of revenue only partly offset by increased tuition.[58]

Business reporter Robert Kuttner notes that through additional training in such areas as nursing and early-childhood education, the service sector can improve the economy by generating better paying jobs. Kuttner argues that as service jobs dominate the economy, there is danger that employment prospects will be dominated by jobs for salespeople, health aids, personal care aides, and office clerks, which have salaries near the poverty line for a family of four.[59] In order to create more well-paying middle-class jobs in the service sector, Kuttner proposes increased expenditures on higher education to professionalize and improve the quality of jobs and service in such areas as "education and care for the young, the old, and the sick."[60] For example, with one extra year of post-secondary education, a person can move from being a certified nursing assistant (CNA) to being a licensed practical nurse (LPN), thereby earning $20 an hour instead of just $8, the pay differential being justified by improved healthcare.[61]

Currently, we don't have enough workers qualified to take these and myriad other jobs because our budgetary commitment to higher education is inadequate. Community college is the most affordable option, but less than one-third of students who begin a two-year associate's degree finish it within seven years, largely because students have to take care of families by earning money while they're going to school. Fully funding students' tuition at community colleges and at state universities and granting a living allowance besides would be an excellent investment in America's human infrastructure.[62]

Such investment in higher education is justified on noncommercial grounds as well. Even when expenditures on higher education don't result in degrees that allow former students to earn greater income, they often stimulate life-long learning that people enjoy and also promote human flourishing by improving the general level of problem-solving capability in society.

*   *   *

Additional social gain and employment possibilities stem from spending more money on preprimary education as well, mainly to counteract the baleful effects of poverty on educational achievement. Education begins at birth. The US Chamber of Commerce's Institute for a Competitive Workforce has recognized that

> The first five years are the most critical in the development of a child's brain. During these early years, children begin to develop their cognitive, social, emotional, and language skills and start to relate to and interact with the world around them. In fact, from birth to age three, children grow and learn at the most intense rate; these are the years when children are learning how to learn.[63]

We've seen that American schools do very well on international comparisons of achievement when the proportion of students from impoverished families is less than 10 percent. Much of the reason is that more affluent families tend to speak to their children more than families that are struggling financially. Ginia Bellafante reports in the *New York Times*, "Reflexively, the affluent, ambitious parent is always talking, pointing out, explaining: Mommy is looking for her laptop; let's put on your rain boots; that's a pigeon, a sand dune, skyscraper, a pomegranate. The child, in essence, exists in continuous receipt of dictation." Discussing the work of psychologists Betty Hart and Todd R. Risley, Bellafante writes, "What they found was not only a disparity in the complexity of words used, but also astonishing differences in sheer number. Children of professionals were, on average, exposed to approximately 1,500 more words hourly than children growing up in poverty. This resulted in a gap of more than 32 million words by the time the children reached the age of 4."[64] This is one reason why children of rich families score much better than children of poor families on school readiness exams before entering kindergarten.[65]

Another reason is the greater access of rich families to high-quality preprimary childcare. Women today comprise about half the workforce, compared to only about one third in 1969. Today, in nearly half of the households with children, both parents work outside the home, and in another quarter of households a single parent works outside the home, leaving only a quarter of children with a stay-at-home parent, most often the mother.[66] In light of the importance of language development and other forms of intellectual stimulation in the early years of life, improved educational attainment depends in large part on preprimary childcare and education. Children need a lot of one-on-one interaction in their first three years with intelligent, well-educated, conscientious caregivers who stay with them during the day while their parents are at work, giving them the stimulation they need to realize their potential. Minimum-wage, poorly educated babysitters who change jobs often in search of better employment won't do.

More needs to be invested in preschool for three- and four-year-olds as well. Studies beginning in the 1960s of the high-quality Perry Preschool Program in Ypsilanti, Michigan, support the claim of enormous benefits from such preschool education. According to a study by the Brookings Institution, the children in Ypsilanti spent two-and-a-half hours per day for thirty weeks each year "supplemented on a weekly basis with one-and-a-half hour home visits by the child's instructor," with the result that "at the age of twenty-seven, participants in the program were found to have levels of educational attainment 0.9 years greater than non-participants." If, as we've seen, one year of increased education increases lifetime earnings by $160,000, 0.9 years of increased education increases lifetime earnings on average by $146,000. But that's not all, according to the Brookings' researchers. The

> difference in educational attainment likely understates the productivity improvements of program children, who also experienced gains in non-cognitive characteristics, including persistence and diligence. Also these narrow economic benefits were supplemented by numerous other benefits, including reduced rates of teenage pregnancy and dramatically lower rates of criminal activity relative to [impoverished] children who did not receive the program.[67]

Research by the Committee for Economic Development (CED) offers monetary figures for these additional benefits, writing, "The Perry Preschool program is estimated to generate nearly $230,000 in benefits per student, much of which is attributable to avoiding the tangible and intangible costs of crime. The long-term follow-ups of these targeted model programs suggest that every dollar invested will return [to society] about $4 to $16 dollars."[68] By 2080 the economy will be $2 trillion larger as a result of these programs, which equals about $7,700 of increased income per capita.[69] This has a clear implication for job growth, as people spending this additional money will create jobs. It also means that the average taxpayer will have more than enough extra earnings to pay higher taxes for the additional interest on the debt incurred in order to institute such programs.

State budgets will be helped in the process, according to the CED: "For every dollar spent on preschool, states are projected to recoup 50 to 85 cents in reduced crime costs and 36 to 77 cents in school savings"[70] (during the K–12 years, because states will have lower costs for remedial education and behavior control).

Americans would also do better on the PISA, the international test that measures student achievement. As we have seen, critics of current educational policies in the United States point to our children's lackluster performance on this test. High-quality preschool could change this. The test is scored so that the median score internationally on each component is always five hundred points, with a standard deviation of one hundred points. This means that two-thirds of test takers score between four hundred and six hundred points.[71] Research under the auspices of the OECD shows that for every dollar spent on a child's preprimary education, the average child gains 1.6 points on the test. For every reduction by one student in the pre-k class, the average child gains 1.5 points on the test. A country's average test score goes up by 4.3 points for every additional 1 percent of its children who attend preprimary education, and the country's average goes up ten points for every one year of increased duration in preprimary education.[72]

The downside is that quality preschool programs are expensive because they

employ teachers with bachelor's degrees and training in early childhood education or development. Well-qualified teachers expose children to extensive vocabularies and knowledge that stimulate curiosity while preparing them to read, write, and count. Educated teachers also demonstrate positive communication skills that boost children's self-confidence and self-control. Attracting and retaining well-qualified preschool teachers requires compensation that is equal to that of elementary school teachers.

Small class sizes and low child/teacher ratios are also important to maintain classroom order and provide individual student attention.[73]

These considerations apply equally to early-childhood education before the age of three as to preschool for three- and four-year-olds, Robert Kuttner writes.

High-quality early childhood education cannot be delivered by a workforce of high-turnover, untrained, minimum wage workers. In France, where there is a national policy of universal, child-development-oriented early education, pre-kindergarten teachers are required to be more highly trained than public school teachers. They must get additional course credits in public health and early child development, and they are compensated accordingly.[74]

For about $50 billion a year, Kuttner calculates, we could gain all of the social and economic benefits of high-quality early-childhood education and permanently employ two million people in well-paying jobs, jobs that can't be outsourced overseas. And, as we've seen, the $50 billion would be returned to taxpayers several times over in the form of less criminality, reduced need of government benefits for the poor, better workers, more productivity, faster economic growth, and higher salaries that result in increased tax revenues from the beneficiaries of high-quality early-childhood education when they grow up and enter the workforce.

The Committee for Economic Development suggests evaluating expenditures on pre-k childcare and education the way that we evaluate other investments. "Annual rates of return on preschool investments are estimated at 10 percent or higher each year over the students' lifetimes, exceeding the 6 to 7 percent average rate of return typically expected of government programs and the stock market."[75] Secure investments don't get much better than that.

In sum, if we want better results from our educational efforts—students who compete better on international exams, and a more highly educated workforce to compete globally in a high-tech world—we'll need to spend a lot more money than at present on high-quality day care for children from birth to three years of age and on high-quality preschool for three- and four-year olds. Yet, as we've seen, it's worth it. If we think of it as an investment, the rate of return compares favorably with other investments.

* * *

Increased investment in education at all levels is clearly justified on the first three of the four criteria used in this work. Such investment would create millions of well-paying jobs. Economic efficiency would be improved. And although education requires a physical plant, like most services, education causes much less disturbance of the earth per employee than is caused by employment in such fields as mining, manufacturing, and construction. Relatively speaking then, expanding opportunities in education is environmentally sustainable.

But is such long-term investment in our human infrastructure politically feasible in the United States? Certainly our current deficits in all of the areas discussed in this chapter suggest that forces opposed to this approach to job creation are formidable. The most popular proposals to solve problems in K–12 education are attempts to get better results without increased funding, including blaming teachers and principals when students perform badly on computerized tests, substituting charter and voucher schools for traditional public schools, and reducing the influence of teachers unions. Similarly, states have reduced their spending on postsecondary education with a consequent increase in for-profit colleges and online classes.

The trend is equally discouraging in early-childhood education. In 2006, for example, Illinois became the first state in the nation to authorize state subsidies for all three- and four-year-olds to attend preschool. However, owing to budget constraints, this "Preschool for All" legislation only provided preschool for some. In its first year it provided preschool for only ten thousand of the fifty thousand children from disadvantaged backgrounds that it was designed to serve.[76] Since then, Illinois budgets have only gotten worse, reflecting a national trend. The National Institute for Early Education Research at Rutgers University reports that state funding for pre-k education was more than half a billion dollars less in the 2011–2012 school year than in the previous year. This represents a drop of more than $400 per child in just one year. Over the previous decade the drop had been more than $1,100 per child per year in constant dollars.[77] We are clearly moving in the wrong direction, against all economic information about how to improve our human infrastructure, accelerate economic growth, and provide more well-paying jobs to more people.

The problem, according to researchers at the Brookings Institution, is that like most investments, the costs of improving our human infrastructure are up front and the benefits come later. Unfortunately, they write, "the political system tends to be biased against making such investments. However," they add, "any business that operated this way would likely fail to succeed. A similarly dim prospect may be in store for a country that fails to take advantage of such solid investment opportunities."[78]

That is the key—get Americans to think of government investments in human as well as in physical infrastructure the way that they think of business and personal investments. To those who claim that current budget deficits and public debt preclude such investments at this time, it can be answered that we made similar investments when the federal government's financial situation was considerably worse. In 1944 and 1945 the annual federal government deficit was over 20 percent of GDP,[79] yet the GI Bill that funded higher education for returning World War II veterans was passed in 1944. The federal deficit's annual rate in the first quarter of 2013, by contrast, was under 6 percent of GDP and falling rapidly.[80] I've never found a Tea Party enthusiast, skeptical of government involvement in the economy, who thinks the GI Bill was a bad idea. Everyone seems to recognize that, like the interstate highway system in our physical infrastructure, the GI Bill was a productive investment in our human infrastructure, without which America's postwar economic boom would not have been possible.

Current opposition to government programs is actually out of character for Americans because it's driven by ideology, whereas historically Americans have been influence more by pragmatism, by whatever works. That's how we came to be such a successful country. Historically, before the "Reagan Revolution" of 1980, the Republican Party wasn't antigovernment; it was pro-business. Its major financial backers are still pro-business, which is why, as we saw in the last chapter, Republicans are starting to call for more government spending on transportation infrastructure and climate-friendly energy generation.

The same is true of human infrastructure. The US Chamber of Commerce is, according to its self-description, "the world's largest business federation representing the interests of more than 3 million businesses of all sizes, sectors, and regions." It funds the Institute for a Competitive Workforce, which "promotes the rigorous educational standards and effective job training systems needed to preserve the strength of America's greatest economic resource, its workforce. . . . ICW connects the best minds in American business with the most innovative thinkers in American education, helping them work together to ensure the nation's continued prosperity." ICW doesn't support ineffective cheap solutions to insufficiencies in our human infrastructure. Instead, in 2010 it put out the policy document, "Why Business Should Support Early Childhood Education."[81] This document doesn't represent the views of utopian visionaries, but the calculations of business-oriented people who operate according to principles of enlightened self-interest. They have crunched the numbers and figured out how to maximize the bottom line.

Republican economist Glenn Hubbard, who helped President George W. Bush devise tax cuts, shares this opinion. Discussing inequality in America, he told Adam Davidson of the *New York Times Magazine*, "The real question is 'What can we do to improve the earnings of lower- and middle-income Americans?'" His answer: "That's about increased education and skills training, and that may require higher government spending."[82] Hubbard continues to be concerned about our country's debts, but he recognizes increased spending on education to be an investment, not just an expenditure.

This kind of thinking seems to be catching on among Republicans as well as Democrats. In July 2013 a telephone poll sponsored by the First Five Years Fund found that 60 percent of registered Republicans and 84 percent of registered Democrats favor increased expenditures on public preschools financed by increased taxes on tobacco products. Ron Haskins, a former political adviser to President George W. Bush, maintains that "there's a sincere and growing concern on the part of a lot of Republicans about how to increase economic opportunity."[83]

Many business leaders see short-term as well as long-term benefits of early-childhood education. It provides jobs, improves the ability of low-income parents to work outside the home, reduces the need to provide expensive special education programs for ill-prepared students, and lowers the rate of repeating grades at great expense. Thus some red states, such as Oklahoma,

Georgia, and West Virginia, are among the nation's leaders in offering free, public preschool. The ideological battle against such programs is still strong in the US Congress, but people outside Congress from both the left and right and from both business and labor are increasingly recognizing and supporting preprimary education as a solid investment.[84]

To suppose that such thinking cannot hold sway in the United States is to suppose that our national character has changed from pragmatic and business-oriented to ideological and self-destructive. This could happen, but there's no reason to believe that it has happened already.

Resurgent enlightened self-interest is affecting higher education as well. After an 11 percent reduction of state funding nationwide between 2008 and 2012, thirty states increased their funding for higher education in fiscal 2013. Overall funding was down just 0.4 percent, and that was because some large states continued reductions, including a 6 percent funding decline in California.[85] But California now projects its own turnaround. In fall 2012 it approved Proposition 30, which raises taxes largely in order to increase funding for higher education.[86] State funding for higher education increased by 5 percent in fiscal year 2014.[87] The governor's proposal for the following year included allocations that would increase state funding for higher education by 20 percent over four years, during which time tuition would not increase.[88]

Besides enlightened self-interest, continued failure to maintain and improve our human infrastructure conflicts with our long-standing support, at least in theory, of equal opportunity. Derek Bok, former President of Harvard University, writes, "Among the core values of our society is the goal of giving all Americans an equal chance to succeed according to their abilities and aspirations. Huge majorities of the public accept this principle and consider it fundamental to the American Dream."[89] To the extent that there is an ideological and not just a pragmatic impulse regarding education in the United States, it's the ideology of equal opportunity that, like enlightened self-interest in the business community, inclines policy makers to invest in high-quality education at all levels for all Americans.

In sum, needed increases in public support for education at all levels is not a given; it will take a lot of persistent effort and success isn't assured. However, there's no reason to think that such investments in our human infrastructure are beyond realistic possibility in the contemporary American context. These investments, like those in our physical infrastructure, are functional (they increase job opportunities), economically sound, in keeping with our aspiration to provide all Americans with equal opportunity, and fundamentally efficient.

CHAPTER 13

THE SERVICE SECTOR AND INDEFINITE ECONOMIC GROWTH

We saw in chapter 11 that investments in physical infrastructure can create many jobs, reduce our economy's burden on the environment, and create the conditions for indefinite economic growth. We saw in chapter 12 that investments in education to improve our human infrastructure similarly create many jobs and facilitate indefinite economic growth. But where, other than in these two broad sectors, is this growth supposed to occur? What are we to do with the ever-growing economic potential that investments in physical and human infrastructure foster?

We are primarily a consumer society, with consumption constituting 70 percent of our GDP, so our economic growth is most plausibly associated with indefinite growth in consumption. Such economic growth is concentrated in three different, although somewhat overlapping areas of consumer goods: manufactured goods, constructed goods, and services. We saw in chapters 3, 4, and 5 that production of manufactured goods for export is not a promising avenue for reducing unemployment. First, owing to technological advances in manufacturing, fewer and fewer workers are needed to manufacture goods, especially in advanced industrial countries, including the United States. Second, there are environmental limits to the production of manufactured goods. These considerations apply equally to manufacturing goods in the United States to meet domestic consumer demand as to manufacturing goods for export. A third consideration limiting the potential of employing more Americans in the manufacture of goods in the United States to meet domestic demand is that increased American demand for manufactured goods is often met by foreign manufacture of goods that Americans import. In such cases, increased consumer demand for manufactured goods may create more jobs overseas than at home.

For the most part, construction undertaken to meet domestic consumer demand does not suffer from the liability of creating more jobs overseas than at home. With the exception of prefabricated houses, most jobs created by home construction in the United States are performed by people residing in the United States. Imports may increase as well, because many components of a traditionally constructed house may still come from overseas: faucets, milled lumber, aluminum or vinyl siding, etc. Still, most of the jobs are American jobs. Better yet, most construction work has not been eliminated by technological improvement. Although the copper and plastic pipes used in modern houses are manufactured with fewer labor hours than were the galvanized steel pipes of generations past, the labor hours of plumbers installing that pipe are not nearly so greatly reduced. Although wood is milled with fewer workers now than in the past, carpenters using the wood have become only marginally more efficient. Substituting drywall for plaster increased construction efficiency greatly after World War II, but drywalling today is almost as labor intensive as it was sixty years ago. In sum, construction can create a lot of jobs.

However, construction for personal consumption (as opposed to construction of some public goods, discussed chapter 11) meets some of the same environmental limits as manufacture for personal consumption. A larger house that affords each child her own room, each parent his and her own office, and includes three full bathrooms, a playroom, a den, and lots of storage space takes more material to construct than a house half its size. It also takes more energy to heat and cool. The same applies generally to the construction of more retail floor space, such as additional shopping malls, more office space, more factories, more commercial warehouses, and more private storage. All of this suggests that if consumerism is to keep the American economy growing at a rate that reduces unemployment, services will have to play the largest role, because manufacturing and construction run afoul of environmental limits.

Concentration on services doesn't mean that our economy is postindustrial, as if it has left industry behind. The signal achievement of the Industrial Revolution was increased output for each input of human labor. The United States at the end of the first decade of the twenty-first century still manufactured about as much as China. As we have seen, however, increasingly efficient industrial methods of manufacture require the employment of relatively few

Americans, which is why the economy needs to emphasize services in order to keep people working. Thus, far from being postindustrial, as if the efficiencies of industrialization were in the past or unimportant, the American economy needs to emphasize services because it's hyperindustrial. It's more industrially efficient than ever, and such hyperindustry is at the root of both the opportunity and economic necessity of concentrating on services to promote economic growth.

Environmental limits play some part in most services, but the provision of many services is much more environmentally friendly per increment of GDP than manufacture and construction. Typically, the greatest environmental impacts of service work and its associated GDP come from using materials and nonhuman energy as a precondition for the service or in the process of providing the service. Services differ considerably in these respects and therefore in the extent to which they require the use of materials and nonhuman energy, so some services are much more environmentally friendly than others. For example, the service of training people to fly their own one- or two-engine prop planes is not environmentally friendly. For that service to grow, more such planes must be constructed and a lot of fossil-fuel energy expended in their use. Weight-loss coaching, by contrast, has very little environmental impact and can therefore be expanded even more than people's waistlines without environmental limit. This allows an economy focused on environmentally benign services to grow indefinitely, especially because continuing improvements in our physical infrastructure reduce the impact of our economy on the environment. This chapter looks at the potential for services, especially those that meet consumer demand with little environmental impact, to spur unlimited economic growth and reduce unemployment. Our final assessment will concern the fundamental efficiency of the resulting economy dominated by a consumerist orientation toward (relatively) environmentally benign services.

✳   ✳   ✳

Many services that people provide are not part of the formal economy because they are performed free of charge. When a fifteen-year-old babysits his five-year-old sister, a woman rakes the leaves in her yard, a man vacuums the house, a parent prepares an evening meal, or friends discuss the pros and cons of one of them accepting a new job, valuable services are performed, but typically no money changes hands. Such services are crucial to a healthy society, but they are not the focus of the current discussion because they don't provide gainful (monetary) employment; they therefore don't add to GDP or reduce unemployment. The focus here is on gainful employment that can add to GDP or reduce unemployment.

In 2011 American employment was highly concentrated in the service sector. The top eight, and nine of the top ten occupations were in that sector: Retail salespersons, (approximately) 4.5 million employees; Cashiers, 3.3 million; Office clerks, 2.85 million; Combined food preparation and serving workers, including fast food, 2.8 million; Registered nurses, 2.7 million; Waiters and waitresses, 2.3 million; Customer service representatives, 2.2 million; Janitors and cleaners, except maids and housekeeping cleaners, 2.1 million; and Secretaries and administrative assistants, except legal, medical and executive, 1.95 million.[1] There are many other service providers as well. There are many nurses, for example, such as licensed practical nurses, who are not counted in the nurse category because they aren't registered nurses. There are many secretaries and administrative assistants who are not included above because they serve executives or serve in the legal or medical professions. Maids and housekeeping cleaners aren't included above. Thus, even more than the figures above indicate, service work dominates current employment in the United States.

According to the Bureau of Labor Statistics, the dominance of service work will be greater in 2020 than at present. Between 2000 and 2010, employment in "Goods producing, excluding agriculture," a category that includes mining, construction, and manufacture, declined from more than 24.5 million to only 17.7 million.[2] Although the civilian labor force is expected to grow by 10.5 million between 2010 and 2020,[3] this sector is expected to create only 1.8 million additional jobs, leaving it more than 5 million short of where it was in 2000. The service sector, by contrast, created nearly 5 million more jobs in 2010 than in 2000, growing from 107.8 million to 112.7 million, and is projected to create almost 18 million new jobs between 2010 and 2020.[4] Thus, the future of employment in the United States is tied much more closely to service work than to manufacture and construction. From an environmental perspective, this is good, because much service work is environmentally benign.

*   *   *

There are six major interrelated and overlapping reasons for the increase in the provision of services for pay in our economy: increased institutional complexity; technological change; time constraints; declining social capital; increased insecurity; and greater affluence. Ultimately, these six catalyze growth in the service sector. They all respond to consumer demand, even though some services meet consumer demand only indirectly.

Many services are required in our economy because of increased **institutional complexity**. As the tax code becomes more complex, for example, it is in the interest of individuals and businesses to hire tax professionals. When laws of contract become more complex our need for attorneys and their staffs increases. The more we trade internationally in an increasingly global economy, the greater the need for experts on foreign laws and languages. The more our property is intellectual rather than material, the greater the need for attorneys specializing in intellectual property rights. The more our laws are geared to preventing financial fraud, the greater our need for accountants and auditors. The more government rules affect business interests, the greater the demand for lobbyists to educate and persuade legislators and government administrators. These are net gains for employment in the service sector and they are relatively environmentally friendly. These services do not require for their provision significant use of physical material or nonhuman energy and therefore can in principle increase indefinitely.

Because they are part of production rather than consumption, there is sometimes debate about possible inefficiencies associated with the proliferation of these services. The services add to the efficient promotion of human wellbeing only if, all things considered, the context that requires them adds to human wellbeing that, economists assume, is advanced by the economy's increasing ability to meet consumer demand. For example, more experts on international law are needed in an increasingly global economy. The work of experts in this area is consistent with the economy efficiently serving consumers (and presumably human wellbeing) only if, as most economists believe, globalization results in such greater productivity that consumers are better off paying indirectly for the services of experts on international law than they would be in a world of nation-based economies that could forego such services. Similarly, the work of lawyers specializing in intellectual property rights is justified from the perspective of overall efficiency only if the existence of such rights improves economic output, as again most economists believe, more than the cost of the service work of lawyers and others who are needed to run our regime of intellectual property rights. The goal is still to improve prospects for consumer satisfaction, which is assumed to advance human wellbeing.

Some services are attacked as lowering overall efficiency, reducing economic output, frustrating consumer demand, and impairing human wellbeing. The ultimate value of some lobbying and of some government regulations that encourage lobbying is called into question on this basis. Still, efficient or not, these services provide relatively environmentally friendly service jobs. At worst they are cases of functional inefficiency.

✻   ✻   ✻

Some services that help productive businesses exploit **technological change**, by contrast, may detract from job creation, all things considered, precisely because they improve efficiency. Teaching people in an office how to use new computer programs, for example, is *relatively* environmentally friendly, even though it presupposes a context of computer manufacture and the subsequent expenditure of energy in computer use. But it is productive only insofar as it enables the company to operate more efficiently than it would without the use of increasingly sophisticated computer applications. The company is getting more output per unit of input, and the input spared is most often labor hours. It's mostly a case of substituting the use of capital, computers and other electronic technologies, for people, such as secretaries, clerks, and messengers. Thus, on the whole, computer services to businesses tend to reduce rather than increase overall employment. This doesn't mean that they're bad, only that, like many efficiency improvements, they're bad for the reduction of unemployment.

In general, however, technological change increases overall employment. It does so not by improving business efficiency but by increasing consumer demand. Technological change creates new possibilities for human survival, enjoyment, and fulfillment. In large part, the technologies in question meet consumer demand directly, not through services to business, sometimes by giving people new and better ways of meeting persistent human needs and desires.

Consider healthcare. The enormous growth in the healthcare sector of the economy, discussed in chapter 7, largely reflects the increasing ability of healthcare professionals to address age-old problems of disease and infirmity. Most of the millions of jobs created are service jobs. I talked to a woman who spent a night in an emergency room and she told me she had been visited by at least twelve different hospital employees, each with a specialized service task—delivering something to keep her comfortable, checking measurements on some complex piece of equipment, and so forth. In general, the hospital environment was very consumer oriented from the perspective of the process (as pleasant as possible) as well as the result.

Some of these new jobs serving consumers of healthcare are very environmentally friendly. Fifty years ago, for example, there were no clinical ethicists—people who work, usually in hospitals, to help medical professionals and their patients determine the best course of treatment for disease, disability, and degeneration. When doctors had very limited ability to address physical maladies, there were fewer choices to be made among treatments, and there was relatively little risk that patients would be kept alive for long periods of time against their will. Now that we have the ability to keep some people alive indefinitely, issues arise as to patients' desires and who will speak for patients who cannot speak for themselves. Clinical ethicists (or people playing that role) are needed to help patients sort through their options in accordance with their own deepest values. Many patients also need help deciding who should speak for them when they are no longer able to do so themselves.

Among the largest opportunities for increased employment related to technological changes in healthcare are technologies that enable people to live longer. Combined with slower immigration and lower birthrates, increased longevity means that the average American will be older in coming decades. The United Nations projects that the number of Americans over sixty-five will increase 8.1 percent between 2010 and 2050.[5] A more recent projection by the US Census Bureau, the first to incorporate information from the 2010 census, estimates that in 2056, for the first time in US history, the number of Americans over sixty-five will be greater than the number under eighteen.

Perhaps more important, the share of the population that is aged eighteen to sixty-four (working age) is projected to decline from 62.7 percent to 56.9 percent between 2010 and 2060.[6]

Many economists worry that this demographic change will impair growth in per capita GDP (as well it may) and strain retirement programs, because each worker will have to support a larger number of retirees. A typical worry is expressed in "Buttonwood's Notebook" in the *Economist*: "With more dependents to care for, it is very hard to imagine how we will pay down our debts. And it is also very hard to imagine how one can possibly expect government spending to shrink significantly."[7]

The potential for reducing unemployment is less often mentioned. Yet in healthcare one person's tragedy often underpins another person's living. More old people will need more services from healthcare professionals as well as from personal aids. Consider just the expected increase in the incidence of Alzheimer's disease. Because people become more susceptible as they age (only one in seventy-seven has the disease among people sixty-five through seventy-four, whereas one in three has the disease among people over the age of eighty-five), it's expected that the current population of Alzheimer's patients, 4.7 million, will balloon to 13.8 million by 2050.[8] Little wonder, then, that three of the four occupations expected to grow most between 2010 and 2020, according to the Bureau of Labor Statistics, will increasingly serve older Americans. They are registered nurses, expected to increase by 712,000 jobs; home health aides, expected to increase by 706,000 jobs; and personal care aides, expected to increase by 607,000 jobs. In light of projected demographic changes, imagine how many more will be needed between 2020 and 2050.[9]

Nursing is critical. Research done in 2002 showed that for each extra patient that a nurse had to care for above a nurse-patient ratio appropriate for a given patient population, an additional seven percent of patients died. The study concluded that, given the current nursing shortage and consequent inadequate staffing of hospitals by nurses, 20,000 patients die each year in the United States who would not have died but for the shortage of nurses. In addition, nurses are critical for reducing suffering among the ill.[10] It's hard to overestimate how many nurses will be needed by 2050.

A lesser but still considerable number of healthcare-related jobs are tied to technological change related to reproduction. For example, many couples who can't conceive a child turn to in vitro fertilization. The woman is injected with hormones so that more than one ovum is ripe for harvesting in a single cycle; some ova are then harvested; some or all of the harvested ova are combined with the man's sperm in vitro (in glass), and one or more resulting embryos are placed in the woman's uterus. All of this creates service jobs in healthcare to meet consumer demand.

If the woman doesn't have viable eggs, the eggs of a donor may be used instead of hers. There is now a thriving industry in egg donation, sociologist Arlie Hochschild reports:

> In a 2006 study of more than one hundred advertisements seeking egg donors published in sixty-three college papers . . . , a quarter offered potential compensation exceeding $10,000. Guidelines issued by the American Society for Reproductive Medicine, the nonprofit arm of an industry group, take no issue with the commercial purchase of eggs, but urge limits on their price. A client should pay no more than $10,000 for an egg, they suggest. But ads in newspapers at Harvard, Princeton, and Yale on average promise donors $35,000. . . . [In general,] for every extra one hundred points in a university student's SAT score, the advertised fee rose by two thousand dollars.[11]

If the woman can't carry a pregnancy, then the service of a surrogate may be employed. Immunosuppressive drugs now make it possible for a woman to carry safely to term a fetus that is not related to her biologically. The technologies of freezing and transporting ova and sperm (or embryos if in vitro fertilization takes place close to home) make it possible for the unrelated surrogate to be anywhere in the world. Accordingly, although many service jobs are created in the United States by surrogacy, many of the surrogates themselves reside overseas, particularly in India. Many healthy Indian women need money, will perform the service of carrying a fetus for less money than would an American, and tolerate pregnancy-related restrictions on their behavior, including dormitory housing away from their families during pregnancy.[12]

Technological change creates a host of jobs in other sectors of the economy as well. Computer technicians serve consumers indirectly when they design and maintain websites and create apps for smart phones. They serve consumers directly when they fix computers and teach people how to use new computer programs. Whether in healthcare or other domains, it seems that service employment created by technological change can increase indefinitely.

*　　*　　*

In general, consumerism promotes service sector employment by imposing increasing **time constraints** on many people, and it seems that this employment, too, can increase indefinitely. As we've seen, more people (at least try to) work more hours to afford all the consumer goods and services that they want in an increasingly consumer-oriented society. Consumerism is largely responsible, therefore, for the increase in women's work participation in the United States. Hochschild writes,

> Steadily from 1900 on—and dramatically after the 1970s—homemakers of yesteryear became the working women of today. Women made up 18 percent of the American workforce in 1900, 28 percent in 1970, and a stunning near-50 percent by 2010. Today, 70 percent of all American children live in households where all the adults work. So who now would care for the children, the sick, the elderly?[13]

The answer is an increasing number of service providers in the formal economy. Many household services performed for pay, such as child minding, house cleaning, meal preparation, and party planning, were traditionally performed free of charge by stay-at-home moms. Insofar as household members enjoy having someone else perform these tasks, the services are part of consumption by the household and production by the service workers. Insofar as this service work releases a household member to join the paid workforce outside the home, these services contribute to additional production as well.

According to labor economist Richard Freeman, American women work outside the home in the formal economy more than do their European counterparts roughly to the same extent as American families now pay for services that women traditionally performed at home without pay. "In 2005," Freeman writes,

> 59.3 percent [of American women] were in the workforce. . . . American
> women worked more hours than women in Europe and Japan while also
> having more children. . . . American women averaged 28.7 hours per week
> in the market, whereas European women averaged 20.7 hours per week. . . .
> What American households have done is to *marketize* household activity.
> They use cleaning services to clean their homes. They buy meals in restau-
> rants or as takeout. They send their children to day care.
>
> The evidence on eating is illustrative. Americans spend twice as much
> on restaurant meals per capita as do Europeans, and as a result, the United
> States employs approximately twice as many persons per capita in the restau-
> rant and hotel business . . . as European countries such as France.[14]

Because American women get all of this paid help, they don't work longer
hours than their European counterparts; they just do more work for pay and
less domestic work for no pay. Because other people get paid for this domestic
work, the economy is larger than it would be if there were fewer hours of
paid employment, and this helps to explain why the US GDP is larger than
that in France and other European countries. Even if women worked outside
the home merely because they enjoyed such work more than housework and
were willing (contrary to what normally occurs) to reduce net family income
to avoid housework, per capita GDP would increase. Replacing a situation
where a woman stays home and takes care of her family with one where she
earns $18,000 a year and pays $20,000 a year for services that compensate for
her absence from the home increases per capita GDP, all other things being
equal. In the more common situation, where the woman working outside the
home earns considerably more than the family pays in compensating services,
per capita GDP increases even more.

However, women entering the paid workforce instead of staying home
may not directly lower unemployment. Such women move from idling to
employment, which tends to exacerbate unemployment problems. Of course,
as we've seen, these women also require additional services as a result of
working outside the home, and this creates jobs for others. The jobs thus
created may merely equal the additional work-force participation of the formerly idle women. Indirectly, however, this system tends to reduce unemployment because it represents a net increase in employment that stimulates

economic growth. We'll see in the next chapter that such growth facilitates infrastructural developments that create additional employment possibilities, thereby further reducing unemployment.

The best services from the employment perspective are those that serve consumers without increasing productive efficiency and with relatively little adverse environmental impact. These are services in the don't-do-it-yourself sector of the economy. Dog walking offers among the most environmentally friendly service employments (assuming that the walker picks up the poop). No extra buildings are constructed, and very little extra fossil-fuel-using transportation need be involved. The same is true of a host of other services that respond to the increasing inability of Americans to find the time to do for themselves what people did for themselves in previous generations. Consider wedding planning. Hochschild quotes a woman, Laura Wilson, who had hired a wedding planner for her impending marriage to Trevor in Los Angeles because their schedules were so full:

> Trevor was getting up at 3:30 a.m. every morning, heading for the office (a law firm) by 5:00 a.m., and not getting home till around 7:00 p.m. I was working full time, too. We'd only left ourselves six months to plan the wedding. My mother lives in Missouri. My maid of honor works in New York. We were all scattered and low on time.[15]

Laura's mother thought at first that she could help plan the wedding. When she and Laura's father had married decades earlier in Missouri she had never heard of a wedding planner and just had a little reception in the church basement. But standards have risen in our more affluent society. In 2010, with or without a planner, the average wedding cost $28,000.[16] Increasingly, people want to experience a wedding fantasy, which is why one in ten weddings is now planned professionally. Laura's mother realized that she couldn't be much help creating the fantasy wedding, telling Hochschild, "We live so far away and my husband and I both work full time." Time constraints and distance (in our mobile society) argue for professional help. This adds to GDP without increasing burdens on the environment, assuming the professionally planned wedding is no more materially elaborate than one people plan on their own.

Time constraints are an element in many other service sector jobs that have little environmental impact. There are many simple tasks that people know how to do for themselves but hire other people to do because they don't want to take the time to do it themselves. Increasingly, electronic media allow people inexpensively to advertise services and contact potential customers. TaskRabbit, for example, established in 2008 by IBM software engineer Leah Busque, was among the first to use electronic media to bring together service providers and needy patrons in the same vicinity. It enables service providers to advertise services such as mailing items, delivering items, shopping, doing laundry, copyediting, putting together gift baskets, assembling Ikea furniture, and much more. Borrowing some of its features from dating websites, TaskRabbit gives potential customers information about service providers along with ratings given the services by previous customers. The providers respond to customer requests with price bids as well as their credentials, and customers can choose among those making bids. According to Patricia Marx, writing in the *New Yorker*,

> Today, according to TaskRabbit, there are more than four thousand "Rabbits" (errand runners), in nine cities. According to the company, twelve per cent are young female professionals, ten per cent are college students, twenty-five per cent are retirees, and fifteen per cent are stay-at-home mothers. Over the past four years, there have been twelve thousand, five hundreds loads of laundry washed and folded . . . ; twenty thousand, four hundred cupcakes delivered; and eighty iPad2s purchased on launch day for eager technophiles. The average price for a task is $45. . . .
>
> Dan Buck, a twenty-seven-year-old actor and screenwriter, told me [Marx] over the phone from L.A. that he makes $450 to $600 a week on TaskRabbit by serving, as he puts it, as a rented husband or boyfriend. "I deal with women mostly, because the men in their lives don't clean, don't know how to set up an entertainment center, or have never learned about cars," he said.[17]

Presence on the Web is not always necessary for services like this to thrive in the time-constrained environment of contemporary America. Hochschild writes, "Even in small towns like Auburn and Lewiston, Maine, shop bulletin boards and local papers might display a notice for Rent-a-Husband, a handyman service that cleans out your garage and hangs your pictures. If in 2011 you called 1.877.99.HUBBY, you would be contacting a nationwide chain with five offices in Maine."[18] Elsewhere, Kids in Motion will escort the children of busy parents to and from soccer games and music lessons. Rent-a-Mom will have someone wait at your house for the kids to come home from school and bake cookies with them.[19] It's not obvious to me why there would be any particular environmental or economic limit to economic growth based on the proliferation of such services.

✳   ✳   ✳

Services that respond to **declining social capital** can also increase without limit. These are jobs that result from people no longer having as many close personal contacts as people had in previous generations when social capital was greater. Because consumerism tends to erode social capital, these jobs are indirectly dependent on the rise of consumerism.

Perhaps the most obvious example of a service that responds to declining social capital is Rent-a-Friend. According to one survey one-in-four Americans claims to have no "close friends." This invites a service that provides consumers with someone who will act like a friend when you need it, so long as you are willing to pay. Here's an advertisement by a woman named Holly, who offers entanglement-free support:

> Ever have a day when you just needed to vent to a good friend and get their feedback to give you another perspective, or to validate your thoughts, or to tell you that you really are fine? What happens if you don't have the energy to do the other side of the friendship, where you support them in their struggles? And suppose you were starting to feel like their solutions fit them but not you? That's when you need me to be your *rent-a-friend*.[20]

Holly charges $50 for problems that are "Short and Sweet," $75 for "Average" problems, and $100 for "Complex" problems. Other Rent-a-Friend services include providing company while going out to dinner, seeing a movie, working out, sorting photos, and taking trips.[21] Hourly rates for "friends" found on Rentafriend.com, which gets one hundred thousand unique views a month, range from $10 to $160, none of it for sex.[22]

Another service that wouldn't exist if social capital were better is Rent-a-Grandma. To help people get the feel of a traditional family dinner, an elderly woman of your chosen ethnicity—including Italian, African-American, and Mexican—will accompany you while you shop, cook, and eat dinner, all the while teaching you about traditional cuisine.[23] There would be no call for such a service in a traditional society with a lot of social capital because in such societies traditions are handed down from one generation to the next on a daily basis in the course of living together.

Many of the child-minding and child-transport jobs in our economy are created as much by our loss of community (our loss of social capital) as by parental time constraints. A man who had lived with his wife and children for several years in the 1990s in a small town in Switzerland contrasts life there with life in the United States:

> People had lived in that place since the thirteenth century. They thought of the town as theirs, and looked after it because it was. Our kids could go anywhere because there were always people watching out. For them it was a big shock to come back to the States. Here each family is on its own. Couples move from place to place, like we do. No one feels part of anything larger. It's like we're a collection of bits and pieces floating in a vast sea.[24]

✳   ✳   ✳

The decline in social capital creates jobs in part because it promotes **increased insecurity**. As we just saw, when people move regularly and don't know their neighbors, they feel insecure about their children's safety because they can't count on neighbors to watch their children at play, hence the proliferation of child-minding services. Generalized fear of the larger society promotes employment also in security products and services of all kinds. Protective service occupations employed 3.3 million people in 2010 and are projected to employ 3.67 million in 2020.[25] By 2009, according to journalist Rich Benjamin, "roughly 10 percent of the occupied homes in this country [were] in gated communities. . . . Between 2001 and 2009, the United States saw a 53 percent growth in occupied housing units nestled in [such] communities."[26] They offer increased private-sector jobs in protective services as private security personnel keep watch on individual houses and check people into and out of the community.

Both public and private sector service jobs are created by insecurity when society increases the percentage of its population that is incarcerated. We saw in chapter 2 that the United States incarcerates more than 750 people per 100,000 of population, whereas England and Wales incarcerate only 153 per 100,000, Canada incarcerates only 116, France 96, and Germany 90 per 100,000.[27] The chapter pointed out that idling most inmates by disallowing their participation in meaningful work contributes to lowering unemployment. The point here is that high levels of incarceration, justified by security considerations, lower unemployment further by offering long-term employment in services to inmates. Nearly half a million people are employed in the United States as correctional officers and jailers.[28] Others are employed providing nutritional, medical, and other services to the prison population.

For-profit organizations specializing in the provision of incarceration facilities and services are keenly aware of the employment and profit implications of maintaining America's unusually large prison population. The 2005 annual report of the largest of these organizations, the Corrections Corporation of America, states what's obvious, but still chilling:

> Our growth is generally dependent upon our ability to obtain new contracts to develop and manage new correctional and detention facilities. . . . The demand for our facilities and services could be adversely affected by the relaxation of enforcement efforts, leniency in conviction and sentencing practices or through the decriminalization of certain activities that are currently proscribed by our criminal laws. For instance, any changes with respect to drugs and controlled substances or illegal immigration could affect the number of persons arrested, convicted, and sentenced, thereby potentially reducing demand for correctional facilities to house them.[29]

In short, if ordinary Americans stop feeling insecure about the effect on their lives of illegal drug use, illegal immigration, or other illegal activities, prison service work will decline. If they stop feeling insecure about the actions and intentions of strangers, jobs providing private security in gated communities and elsewhere will decline. Such insecurity underpins a great deal of service employment in the United States.

Widespread insecurity in a different sense provides other kinds of service employment. As the gap between the rich and the rest widens, we've seen, it's increasingly important to be among the winners in the contest for professional and financial success. This creates what I've called "compulsory consumption," as people seek positional goods needed for success. Much of this consumption provides environmentally sustainable service employment. Many parents, for example, worry that their children will not compete successfully for positions in elite universities, which educate so many of our country's leaders in politics, science, and business. Others worry that their English isn't good enough to advance in their careers. Still others are competing to get into law school or med school. All of this insecurity creates a market for private test-preparation services. Kaplan, a leader in this area, introduces their test-preparation services this way,

> As the world leader in test preparation, we provide an edge for high-achieving students seeking competitive academic and professional opportunities. Middle schoolers, college-bound teens, graduate school prospects, aspiring doctors and lawyers and English language learners rely on Kaplan to help them succeed on high-stakes exams. We offer preparation for more than 90 standardized tests for college and graduate school admissions, English language proficiency and professional licensing.[30]

Offering these services creates a host of jobs at Kaplan, more than thirty thousand in all, and not just for teachers. Besides teachers who actually tutor students part- or full-time, Kaplan employs people in operations and management, customer service, marketing and sales, academic administration, technological development, finance and accounting, publication, and human resources.[31] Many similar jobs are created by Kaplan's competitors.

Private lessons in various competitive sports, summer camps devoted to individual sports, and sports leagues for young children all provide services that are similarly geared to helping children achieve competitive success. Many parents who lack the time and expertise to coach their own children support an array of sports-related service industries. These parents are intent on giving their children a secure foundation of self-confidence, self-discipline, and athletic excellence, which tend to be assets in competitive scholastic, professional, and business contexts.

A larger number of service jobs are created by insecurity in other areas of life, including areas of intimacy. With approximately one in two marriages ending in divorce in the United States,[32] many couples are understandably insecure about their ability to sustain a successful marriage. Responding to consumer demand for help in establishing and maintaining healthy relationships are fifty thousand individuals certified as therapists by the American Association for Marriage and Family Therapy.[33] The basic message of this service industry is that leaving the initiation, care, and maintenance of your intimate relationships to the vagaries of your own untutored ideas and impulses courts disaster. People need professional advice and help in their love life just as they do when they learn to drive. This help is needed not just when a marriage is in difficulty, but when people first contemplate initiating a serious relationship. Licensed marriage and family counselor Jennine Estes writes on her website, "Similar to driving, many people grow up with the future plans of marriage, excited to find a life partner, and to be committed. The success rate of marriages continues to drop in our country, yet there is little encouragement to attend marriage classes. . . . Premarital therapy and marriage counseling are a few ways people use to build healthy relationships."[34] In a society with more social capital, this training may be available free from parents, aunts, uncles, older siblings, and friends.

Suppose an individual or couple is expecting a child. Insecurity about naming the child creates additional opportunities for service-sector employment. A "nameologist" helps people choose the best name for their child. Applying what nameologist Maryanna Korwitts calls "the energetic science of names" can stave off problems that the newborn might otherwise encounter. Korwitts supplies a service of two one-hour phone calls for a total of $350 to help prospective parents "find out which names encourage weight problems, attention deficit disorder, and fear of intimacy, poverty syndrome, and addiction. Also learn which names stimulate leadership ability, financial reward, creativity, and satisfying soul-mate connections."[35]

Other professional services available to prospective and new parents who are insecure about their own abilities to protect and raise a child include help in safety-proofing an apartment or house; teaching a baby sign language; training babies to sleep through the night; training toddlers to stop thumb sucking; potty training a child; teaching a child table manners; and teaching a child how to control his or her temper. Many parents paying for these services may be motivated not so much by insecurity about their own parenting skills as by work and other time commitments that leave them little time to spend with their children. Such time constraints are probably the main reason why parents hire people to shop for their child's birthday presents or organize their child's photo album. Another reason for parents to buy such services is the lack of social capital. In a society with a great deal of social capital, a relative or family friend can offer help, when parents lack time or insight, with a child's potty training, table manners, thumb sucking, bad temper, and so forth.

Lack of self-confidence, weakened social networks, and institutional complexity may all contribute to growth in the services provided by "life coaches." Typically, a life coach interacts with clients by phone, often on a weekly basis over several months, to help clients achieve defined goals, such as "launch a new career, finish a project, go through a divorce, resolve a dispute, vacate a house, [or] birth a child."[36] Life coaches are primarily sounding boards and motivators, but are also often considered friends by most clients, and in this respect resemble rent-a-friends.

Perhaps the ultimate sign of insufficient security and self-confidence is the emergence of a field called "wantology." Given the wide array of choices and lifestyles in our society, many people are unsure about the life path that's right for them. They're not sure what goals to pursue in part because they don't know what achievements will make them happy. Wantologists help people think through their desires and options so that they have better self-direction. Hochschild comments, "The mere existence of a paid 'wantologist' indicates just how far the market has penetrated our intimate lives. Can it be that we are no longer confident to identify even our most ordinary desires without a professional to guide us?"[37]

In a society with greater social capital, perhaps friends would help one another with these issues. So this may be an example of consumerism feeding upon itself. Consumerism induces people to work so hard and move so often to get the best paycheck that they don't have time to make or maintain personal ties. In the absence of such ties they feel like lonely corks bobbing in the sea, so they hire someone to advise them about what to do. This service is another consumption item, which therefore furthers the hold of consumerism on our lives. Such self-reinforcing consumerism may not be ideal for human happiness or wellbeing, a topic already broached and discussed again below, but the service of a wantologist is certainly eco-friendly and can therefore provide as much employment as people are willing to pay for.

*　*　*

Many additional services seem to attract customers largely because of **increased affluence**, although insecurity may also be a motivating factor. The service of party motivator, for example, may presuppose parental anxiety among affluent Americans about their own abilities to generate high enough levels of enjoyment at their children's parties to meet social expectations, but the cost would be prohibitive in the absence of increased affluence. Elissa Gootman reports in the *New York Times* on this growing field. Decades ago, party planners often hired DJs to entertain at celebrations for preteens and young teens. Increasingly now, however, party planners, parents, and young guests want more. They want someone who will interact with the guests, getting the guests, especially the shyest among them who might otherwise be wall flowers, involved in dancing and games. This business is growing, as well as "lucrative and competitive," Gootman writes. "Recruiters set up booths at college campuses and lurk around clubs, where they hand business cards to the best and most flamboyant dancers. . . . Motivators are generally paid between $100 and $300 an hour." But this is not a job for a lifetime. "Motivators must look young enough to enthrall a 13-year-old [typically at a bar or bat mitzvah], yet mature enough that when they dance suggestively with the parents, everything looks legal."[38]

Live-event painting is among other services that reflect increased affluence. Picture taking and sharing is pervasive in our society—digital cameras, cameras in cell telephones, professional photographers, pictures in email attachments,

Facebook, etc. Nevertheless, reports Gootman, "a small but growing collection of artists have started advertising their services as event painters, usually charging from $1,000 to $5,000 to capture on canvas not just weddings but also birthday parties, retirement celebrations, christenings, bar and bat mitzvahs, store openings and the occasional dinner party."[39] Some artists insist that the painting is finished when signed at the end of the event; others will take weeks or months touching it up. Some advantages of memorializing events in such paintings is that people can be depicted as a bit thinner that they really were; happier and more relaxed than they were; and in groupings that have emotional meaning but that didn't actually occur during the event.

Another service becoming more popular is professional still and video photography at childbirth. Increasingly, Gootman writes, "there is . . . interest in the experience of childbirth—not just as a means to a baby but also as a moment to be relished in its own right—and a greater desire to capture all of life's moments (and often share them on Facebook)." Many of these newborns have parents who will photograph "every bite of a mushed banana as if it were a historical event, [so] does it not make sense that his or her entrance into the world be photographed by a professional?"[40] I guess it's all a matter of taste and disposable income.

Concern about our collective effects on the environment has sparked a new industry, especially among the well-to-do, but not confined to the enormously rich: eco-concierge services. Many people want their consumption to be more eco-friendly but don't have the time to inform themselves sufficiently about the environmental impacts of alternate products. Eco-concierges can, for a fee as low as $25 to $50 an hour, instruct people on how to make their consumption patterns greener, telling them, for example, which cleaning products are least toxic; what brands of coffee are organic; where vegan dog food and vegan manicures can be found; and what lines of clothing are made with no chemical dyes or pesticides. For time-constrained people with a great deal of money and environmental zeal, the eco-concierge does more. According to Jennifer Kingson, writing in the *New York Times*, "They will run your errands by bicycle . . . or buy organic clothes for you and your dog. They will even book you a dream vacation and buy the appropriate carbon offsets."[41] Gernot Wagner of the Environmental Defense Fund doesn't think such individual actions make measurable impacts on the environment. Nevertheless, eco-concierge companies that regularly perform multiple tasks for wealthy families charge membership fees that range from $175 a month to $3,500 a year, and because this work is inherently labor intensive, we shouldn't dismiss the prospects for future employment in this area.

Yet another service that reflects our nation's increasing affluence is the application to pets of medical advances designed initially to restore human health. For example, when Mike Otworth's ten-year-old chow, Tina, was diagnosed with cancer of the lymph nodes in Florida, the prognosis was poor. Even with standard chemotherapy, cancer usually reappears and leads quickly to death. So Mr. Otworth took Tina to North Carolina State University in Raleigh where the Bone Marrow Transplant Unit at its College of Veterinary Medicine took some of Tina's blood, used radiation to cleanse it of cancer cells, and then injected the cleansed blood into Tina's bone marrow. This painless bone marrow transplant cleared Tina of cancer, but cost $15,000. Total costs for Tina's care were closer to $25,000 when all of her treatments in Florida and North Carolina are combined.

According to William Grimes, writing in the *New York Times*, "A long list of cancers, urinary-tract disorders, kidney ailments, joint failures and even canine dementia can now be diagnosed and treated, with the prospect of a cure or greatly improved health, thanks to imaging technology, better drugs, new surgical techniques and holistic approaches like acupuncture."[42] Improved imaging technology, for example, helped a Wisconsin couple get highly accurate image-guided radiation treatment for their twelve-year-old Maltese-poodle mix Chip, who suffered from an inoperable brain tumor. The cost was $10,000.

One indication of growth in this field is increase in the number of stents performed by the Animal Medical Center in Manhattan. Used primarily to open up clogged passages in a dog or cat's bladder or kidneys, the center performed 34 stent procedures in 2005, but 630 in 2011. (One of these procedures was performed on a cat that was already seventeen years old.) Another indication of growth in this service industry is total consumer spending, $13.4 billion in 2011 compared to $9.2 billion five years earlier. Only an affluent society could spend so much money to prolong the lives and ease the suffering of pets. And even at these prices, success is sometimes fleeting. Although the chow Tina was cured of cancer in North Carolina, she died nine months later of liver cancer back in Florida.

Some service jobs reflect the increased affluence of some people compared to others more than increased affluence in society generally. The service of waiting in line is one of these. Free tickets for performances at New York City's Shakespeare in the Park are available on a first-come, first-served basis, so people have to cue up, possibly for hours, to get tickets to popular plays or to see popular performers. Affluent people often have others stand in line for them, paying up to $125 dollars for their free tickets. A similar service thrives in Washington, DC, where there is often limited seating at important congressional hearings. Corporate lobbyists, writes philosopher Michael Sandel,

> loath to spend hours in line to assure themselves a seat . . . , pay thousands of dollars to professional line-standing companies that hire people to cue up for them.
>
> The line-standing companies recruit retirees, message couriers, and, increasingly, homeless people to brave the elements and hold a place in the cue. . . . Shortly before the hearing begins, the well-heeled lobbyists arrive, trade places with their scruffily attired stand-ins, and claim their seats in the hearing room.
>
> The line-standing companies charge the lobbyists $36 to $60 per hour for the queuing service, which means that getting a seat in a committee hearing can cost $1,000 or more. The line standers themselves are paid $10–$20 per hour.[43]

This service, like so many others, can increase almost indefinitely within environmental limits, thereby promoting economic growth that creates jobs and reduces unemployment. Other service jobs, by contrast—training people to be recreational pilots of their individually owned small aircraft has been mentioned already—are not so eco-friendly. Retail trade is expected to add more than 1.75 million service jobs between 2010 and 2020, going from 14.4 million to nearly 16.2 million.[44] But many of these jobs concern sales of manufactured items whose production and use may not be environmentally sustainable. In all, however, enough services can increase indefinitely within environmental limits that the economy can grow and create jobs without limit.

*   *   *

Is such economic growth fundamentally efficient? Some people worry that efficiency is impaired because concentration on such services will make society materially poorer. Human welfare will suffer, they think, because not enough people will be *making things*, consumer items that people want and need. But this concern is misplaced. Our current difficulties with unemployment stem precisely from the fact that *we don't need many people making things for consumers to have the items that they want and need*. Efficiency in the sense of realizing the population's potential in manufacturing, mining, and construction is environmentally unsustainable and economically ruinous. We will never have enough consumer demand to soak up all of the products, materials, and structures that our population could produce with today's technology if most people worked in manufacturing, mining, and construction, nor would our environment remain livable with so much disruption of the earth's crust, atmosphere, and oceans.

Another concern is that a society whose economy is centered around services will tend to become increasingly bifurcated between rich and poor because many of the service occupations likely to become more popular are poorly paid, such as dog walkers and home health aides, and many services, such as eco-concierge and party planner, cater only to the relatively rich. Thus, in a society with increased reliance on service work, there may be a tendency for a small minority to become very rich while the vast majority makes a living serving the "needs" of this minority. Our society could end up resembling Britain during their Gilded Age as depicted in such dramas as *Upstairs, Downstairs* and, more recently, *Downton Abbey*.

Such a result would engender fundamental inefficiency. We saw in chapter 10 that inequality in society spurs people to work longer hours to make money, rather than embrace leisure or drop willingly out of the labor force. They work more hours because they become discontented with the material conditions of their lives, as they see other people—the rich and the famous who are covered assiduously by the major media—with levels of affluence that they want to imitate. This is why, as we saw in chapter 9, most Harvard students rejected a doubling of their income if the general level of income in society were quadrupled. Other things being equal, increased disparities between rich and poor are fundamentally inefficient because they reduce satisfaction among a majority of the population without compensating advantages.

Economist Tyler Cowen, who describes himself as leaning toward libertarianism, expects exactly this outcome, but doesn't see it as dystopic. He imagines that our increasingly service-oriented economy will become more socioeconomically bifurcated, where "10 or 15 percent of the citizenry is very wealthy and has fantastically comfortable and stimulating lives, the equivalent of current-day millionaires, albeit with better health care. Much of the rest of the country will have stagnant or maybe even falling wages in dollar terms, but a lot more opportunities for cheap fun and also cheap education."[45] Cowen justifies this prediction by observing what he calls a "still underappreciated lesson: *People really like extra cash in their pocket*."[46] In particular, "Americans would rather have more cash than better public services."[47] Accordingly, he holds up Texas as the model of the future for the rest of the country in spite of, or perhaps because of the fact that "Texas is skimpy on welfare benefits and Medicaid coverage, and 27 percent of the state has no health insurance coverage. Texas has one of America's poorest performing educational systems, at least as measured by high school graduation rates, which in Texas are below 70 percent."[48] Cowen imagines such conditions proliferating around the country in what he nevertheless characterizes as the successful, low-tax American economy of the future.

Cowen's work is instructive because its depiction of a successful, functioning twenty-first century economy with reduced public investment and enormous inequality is so unrealistic. We saw in chapter 12 that Cowen unrealistically counts on MOOCs for cheap higher education. He ignores the need for professors to answer student questions and grade student essays. It's not clear how he imagines preschool and K–12 education becoming cheap, except by making them less effective, in imitation of Texas. But then how are we supposed to have more college graduates when earlier academic preparation is essential to success in higher education? How can our economy thrive in a high-tech world with fewer rather than more college graduates? How will we transport people to work and products to market with a transportation infrastructure that is already crumbling and that will crumble further without massive public investments? How can our manufacturing compete internationally (to avoid balance of payment problems) without increased efficiency through additional public investments not only in education and transportation, but also in energy generation and consumption?

The unreality of Cowen's vision of an unequal society suggests that the realistic proposals made here for an economy that grows indefinitely within environmental limits through increases in service employment need not be afflicted with gross inequalities that impair fundamental efficiency. In fact, the general tendency of these proposals is to produce greater equality of opportunity, income, and wealth and thereby improve fundamental efficiency. We saw in chapter 12, for example, that the economy grows and incomes increase when more well-paying service-sector jobs for credentialed professionals are created to meet the educational needs of children from birth to kindergarten. The result will be not only a cohort of young people who are better able to take advantage of K–12 education and later educational and career opportunities, but also a cohort of young people for whom there is greater equality of opportunity and outcomes because everyone has a more equal start in life.

In general, increasing the number of people for whom higher education is affordable tends to reduce inequality, as more poor people are able to qualify for better-paying jobs. In *Capitalism in the Twenty-First Century*, French economist Thomas Picketty discusses reasons for long-term trends toward greater inequality of wealth. Although he introduces many complexities, he takes pains to affirm as well the standard economic view that increased public investment in higher education is necessary and effective in lifting the wages of average workers while improving efficiency.[49] Other studies also show that people with a college degree earn much more money than their contemporaries with only a high school diploma. MIT economist David Autor calculates that even after subtracting the high cost of a college education, college graduates end up gaining on average an additional $500,000 over their lifetimes for having attended and completed college. What is more, unemployment among college graduates was only three percent in April 2014.[50]

What kinds of work do all of these college-educated individuals have that earns them so much additional money? Steven Rattner reports in the *New York Times* that technological advances often create the need for more highly paid service providers and less need for jobs that typically command lower wages.

Many service jobs that became less available between 2000 and 2013, such as word processor/typist, telephone operator, and computer operator, pay much less than jobs that became more numerous, such as physical therapist, computer software engineer, financial advisor, and registered nurse.[51]

Research conducted by MIT business professor Zeynep Ton also bodes well for better pay in service employment. She has shown that retailers make more money by paying a higher salary to better-educated sales people because better-educated workers can engage customers and find out what they really want. They can also reconfigure displays to maximize appeal to the local audience. Thus, to cite just one example among the many in Ton's study, Costco does well paying average workers $21 an hour as compared to $13 at Walmart.[52] (I assume that these figures represent total compensation—payroll amounts plus employer contributions to healthcare plans, unemployment insurance, social security, etc.)

Another way that the service economy envisioned here contributes to improved fundamental efficiency through greater equality is that many improvements in our physical infrastructure, discussed in chapter 11, tend to reduce inequality. Efficiency improvements in energy generation, for example, will reduce its total social cost. At present, health impairment stemming from pollution related to energy generation is a social cost that falls disproportionately on poor people. Reducing this cost will therefore help poor people most, thereby reducing inequality. Efficiency improvements in transportation will also help the poor most because they are currently burdened most by the need to own and maintain a car to get to work. Increased availability of more efficient public transportation will therefore benefit the poor the most.

Thus, the main strategy of decreasing unemployment through increasing concentration on the provision of environmentally friendly services doesn't rely on the perpetuation or increase of inequality. On the contrary, its general tendency is to improve fundamental efficiency through greater equality.

❋   ❋   ❋

However, significant fundamental inefficiency and functional inefficiency remain in the service economy envisioned here because economic growth relies on ever-increasing consumer demand. Consumer demand increases indefinitely fast enough to promote the economic growth needed to reduce unemployment only under the sway of consumerism, and consumerism tends to impair human welfare, all things considered. Consumerism is thus functionally inefficient.

The fundamental inefficiency associated with consumerism doesn't diminish when consumers desire and purchase more services instead of more goods. Services that respond to time constraints, declining social capital, and increased insecurity depend on the perpetuation of social contexts that reduce human wellbeing rather than advance it in the long run. It would seem that people would generally be better off if prospective parents felt secure enough to name their own children; if there was enough social capital so that friends could help people with important decisions without need of a paid life coach; if people had real friends instead of rent-a-friends and could interact with older people from their own ethnic background instead of renting a grandma; if people had enough time to walk their own dogs; and if they felt safe enough to walk in ungated communities without a private security service keeping strangers at bay.

These are just particular examples illustrating general points made in chapters 8 and 9 about consumerism. Consumerism creates jobs; it's functional. But it's probably not otherwise good for people. As Hochschild writes, "The more anxious and isolated we are and the less help we receive from non-market sources, the more we feel tempted to fill the void with market offerings. . . . Greater isolation results in greater demand for market services and professionals—life coaches, party planners, photograph-album assemblers to fill in for what's missing."[53] Isolation, loneliness, distrust, and disconnection enable our economy to grow by creating environmentally friendly service jobs, but they detract from human wellbeing.

More generally, consumerism thrives on the perpetuation of individual discontent and on the widespread belief, contrary to fact in most cases, that buying something will improve one's life. Thus, in a service-oriented consumer society, people have to feel that they *need* the expensive designer haircut; they have to be *ashamed* to plan a wedding by themselves; they have to consider it *unacceptably negligent* to forego professional couples counseling before marriage and individualized tutoring for their school-age children regardless of their children's grades. They must be just as discontented without the services of a personal trainer as many are currently without new Corian or granite kitchen countertops to replace Formica. After they've paid for the personal trainer, they must be discontented without professional grooming for their dog. Individual discontent is like social isolation insofar as it degrades human welfare but is required for consumerism to flourish. Thus, an ever-expanding service economy is functional, but because it's consumerist, it's fundamentally inefficient.

This judgment doesn't cover all service work, of course. Doctors, dentists, plumbers, and people who repair washing machines, computers, and cars are more often than not providing services that add to human wellbeing, all things considered, even if the *systems* in which many of them work, such as the healthcare and transportation systems, are themselves functionally inefficient at present. In addition, much of the service work that responds to time constraints may contribute to human wellbeing, all things considered, even though it furthers consumerism by enabling people to work outside the home to earn money to buy more consumer items. Such service work helps millions of women to work outside the home, which may improve human wellbeing, all things considered, by giving women more opportunities and independence. Thus, it may be functionally efficient. But such efficient uses of service work aren't sufficient to keep the economy growing indefinitely, which is required to combat unemployment. A continuously growing economy requires a welfare-impairing consumerist attitude toward services.

CHAPTER 14
SUMMARY AND CONCLUSION

Keeping people working is a problem endemic to advanced industrial economies because, as a result of increasing efficiency in mining, agriculture, manufacturing, and many services, ever fewer people are needed to provide the commodities, goods, and services that people need and want. When domestic demand for commodities and goods is insufficient to keep unemployment low, production for export is not a long-term solution because other industrial countries are doing the same thing as a result of their own insufficient domestic demand, and because selling products by raising consumption levels around the world to the American standard would be environmentally ruinous and therefore ultimately counterproductive.

The inability of mining, agriculture, and manufacturing to employ all who want to work doesn't make us a postindustrial society. Quite the contrary, our employment problems results from our being a hyperindustrial society, so industrially efficient that we don't need many people working with materials to maintain our high standard of living. We must remain hyperindustrial because without our own base of material production we'd be more dependent on other countries to maintain our way of life, and our economy would suffer from increased balance of payment problems. In addition, without our own manufacturing base we'd be at the mercy of other countries for national defense, which relies heavily on manufactured items. All told, the United States needs continually to improve the efficiency of its mining, agriculture, and manufacture to remain internationally competitive. But such efficiency won't solve our endemic problem of unemployment. If anything, it tends to make the problem worse in the long run.

So how do we keep people working? In contrast to efficient mining, agriculture, and manufacture, we currently rely in part on inefficient systems to underpin a great deal of employment, such as inefficient systems in transportation and healthcare. However, inefficient transportation is environmentally destructive and inefficient healthcare is life-threatening and deprives many people of the healthcare that they need. For these reasons we look to other methods of maintaining employment.

One of these other methods is spreading the work around. Instead of a full-time job requiring sixty hours of work per week, as it did in the nineteenth century, it now requires only forty hours—and even less in France. Idling workers in this way and through more years spent on education, more time given for family leave and yearly vacations, and earlier retirement helps more workers find jobs. Such idling is efficient if the activities of the idled workers improve human wellbeing more than wellbeing could be improved through devotion of the same time and effort to productive activities in the monetary economy. Some of these activities, such as those associated with family leave and higher education, clearly contribute to overall human wellbeing, but the association in the United States of vacations and retirement with additional television watching casts doubt on the contribution to human welfare of these forms of idling.

Increased efficiency through a more highly educated workforce is mandatory in the present world. We can't maintain indefinitely our manufacturing base, our international competitiveness, or our stature as a world power militarily or financially without an increasingly educated populace. Just as many consumer items, such as cell phones, are positional goods or items of compulsory consumption that have become necessary to individuals largely because others have and use them, so an increasingly educated populace is necessary largely because standards of education have risen around the world, especially among our global competitors. If no society had raised its general level of education, innovation and technological change would be slower (for better or worse) and promoting additional higher education would be optional for the United States. As matters stand, however, it isn't at all optional.

The good news about education is, as we saw in chapter 12, that preparation for higher education properly begins shortly after birth. There is almost no end to employment possibilities in educational services for infants, toddlers, children in pre-k programs, children in K–12, and young adults in college. Even though the efficiency improvements that result from better-educated individuals in the labor force tend to exacerbate the problem of overproduction, one way that society can stay ahead of the game, perhaps indefinitely, is by employing ever more people in educational services of various kinds.

Healthcare is another area where indefinitely increasing employment is a possibility. We saw in chapter 6 that healthcare currently employs many people in the United States as a result of its inefficient organization. The good news is that healthcare doesn't have to be poorly organized to grow indefinitely. The vast majority of people want to live long and health lives. Scientific discoveries and technological innovations allow for at least marginal and sometimes spectacular improvements in the length and quality of many people's lives, but new medications and treatments are costly. This is why healthcare expenditures as a percentage of GDP have gone up dramatically since World War II in all industrial countries, including those with relatively efficient healthcare systems. Sonograms, MRIs, myriad blood tests, prostheses for the injured, sophisticated treatments for cancer based on DNA profiles, as well as pills and ointments to relieve psychological stress and reduce the symptoms of aging are all in great consumer demand. When a totally implantable human heart becomes available or when organs can be grown in vitro from one's own stem cells to replace an organ that is failing, these extremely expensive items will also be demanded by the consuming public, most of whom have religious faith in life after death for other people and yet will pay nearly anything to prolong their own lives.

Healthcare advocate Ezekiel Emanuel, writing in the *New York Times*, claims to the contrary that healthcare spending must come down for our economy to thrive. He notes that reduced expenditures for food resulting from mechanized agriculture improved human wellbeing by giving people the chance to spend more money on items other than food. Emanuel suggests that reduced spending on healthcare is needed similarly to allow for "other purchases, often ones that are more valuable, like higher education or rapid transit," which will create many jobs.[1] He fails to realize that the twenty-first century problem of unemployment is so extreme that to keep people working we must expand employment opportunities in healthcare as well as in higher education, rapid transit, and other items of physical and human infrastructure.

Updating our physical infrastructure in transportation, energy production, and energy consumption will create many jobs while improving efficiency. However, as with efficiency improvements from a more educated workforce, increased efficiency in these areas means that ever fewer hours of work will be needed to produce what people want and need, thereby exacerbating the problem of long-term endemic unemployment. Worse yet, building the new infrastructure will take more workers than maintaining it, so it's possible that the extra jobs created in the development of physical infrastructure will last only a generation or so. Nevertheless, as with improvement of our human infrastructure through better education and healthcare, improvement of our physical infrastructure is required by international competition.

One bit of good news on the employment front is that massive projects related to our physical infrastructure may be needed over the next few hundred years, not just over the next generation or so, providing many construction and related jobs. As noted in chapter 4, the concentration of carbon dioxide in the earth's atmosphere is increasing, the earth is getting warmer, and polar ice caps and glaciers are melting. Sea levels are therefore expected to rise considerably over the next few hundred years.

As we saw in chapter 11, expensive projects are already being proposed to protect New York City and other metropolitan areas from rising seas. One project will follow another in the same cities over the next few or several centuries as rising seawater makes successive projects obsolete. In a sense, the use of fossil fuels may be an extraordinary, long-term case of functional inefficiency. A quick response to scientific evidence of climate change would have required massive retooling to replace the use of fossil fuels with renewable sources of energy, and this would have required a lot of money and work. However, it may have cost less money and required less work than the additional adaptation to global warming that will be necessary as a result of the world's slow response to information about climate change. In that case, the slow response was inefficient (long-term costs are greater than short-term savings) but functional insofar as it creates a lot of additional jobs.

However, adaptation to climate change will not replace increased consumerism as a major sink for our society's productivity. The acceleration of consumerism coincided with accelerated development of urban and suburban infrastructure since World War II. If increased consumerism was needed since World War II to keep people working in spite of massive infrastructure projects, we can expect that consumerism will still be needed to keep people working when the massive infrastructure projects are largely responses to global warming.

As we saw in chapters 4 and 5, consumption of material items tends to be environmentally harmful and should therefore be discouraged in favor of consumption of services that have less environmental impact. However, a more service-oriented economy will provide enough economic growth and decent jobs in the future only so long as we remain a consumer-oriented society, and we have seen that consumerism is inherently inefficient insofar as it thrives and creates the greatest number of jobs only when people are isolated, discontented, insecure, and fearful. Consumerism is thus functional but fundamentally inefficient because human resources are used without improvements in human wellbeing.

*   *   *

A theoretically attractive alternative to such inefficiency is provided by the simplicity movement. This movement suggests that we consume less, pay less, repair things rather than replace them, do more things for ourselves rather than purchase goods and services from others, and rely more on informal exchanges with others when we need help. In these ways we can increase social capital, reduce our burden on the environment, spend less money, spend less time working for money, and improve the quality of our lives.

Ferenc Máté gives examples of items he thinks we could all forego, thereby allowing our houses to be smaller and our housing costs to be lower:

> Much of our must-have gear defies common sense. . . . There's the dishwasher. We had one once and I could never figure out why, if we had a machine that washed dishes, *I* had to wash each dish first by hand. . . .
>
> And the electric can opener. Was the old one too taxing because you had to use two hands? Or were the ten seconds of manual labor too demeaning?
>
> Forget the hundred other gadgets: electric knives, choppers, grinders, pulpers and slashers, most of which sit long-forgotten in some hard-to-get-at cupboard. . . .

The laundry room. . . . Why do dirty socks and undies need a room of their own? Some claim it's so you can iron there, but ironing boards are portable; you can iron anywhere, and who wants to iron shut away with a machine?

Then there's the dryer.

Not long ago our back yards were alive with clean laundry dancing in the breeze. And hanging out the laundry was not only a bit of exercise but also a social act, a time for a backyard chat with neighbors. It also worked in the city—the narrow streets of Naples and Venice still fly their colored banners on laundry day. So why are our clotheslines gone? And not only forgotten but in some places *forbidden*.[2]

Máté questions also the need for a garage to park the car. In Tuscany, where Máté lived for over twenty years, most people get along without a garage and seem no worse for it.

When people buy less of what they don't need, they need less money and can therefore work fewer hours for money. Having more free time allows them to save additional money. They can, for example, use more public transportation instead of their own cars.[3] Additional free time allows people to save money also when they use their extra time to do things for themselves instead of hiring other people to do things for them. Máté found that in Tuscany people quickly acquire whatever skills they need because they have self-confidence; they believe that they can quickly learn to do whatever others can do already. He writes, "I have seen Lamberto without having ever lifted a mason's trowel build a perfectly fitted hundred-foot-long stone wall. Pasquino, a truck driver by trade, has no fear of butchering and dressing his and the neighbors' pigs."[4] Máté suggests building your own house as he did his, working alongside professionals as they are needed. No one will care about the quality of the workmanship more than you will, and the professionals will go out of their way to do a good job when you've established rapport with them by working together. Perhaps best of all, having put the house together, you'll have confidence that you can fix whatever goes wrong with it in the future, which gives you peace of mind. Finally, you'll save a lot of money doing it yourself and that reduces your need to pursue work that you dislike just to get a bigger paycheck.

Sociologist Juliet Schor also favors this approach. She endorses what she calls "self-provisioning," which includes "producing for oneself, making items that may be sold or bartered for other things, and engaging in activities that are meaningful, skill-building, and contribute to one's standard of living." She recognizes that some such activities have long been popular—knitting and home repair, for example—but she sees opportunities for and a trend toward significant increase in self-provisioning activities which include "woodworking, quilting, brewing beer, and canning and preserving. Gardening, hunting, and fishing are other examples, as are sewing clothing . . . and building a computer from components." Benefits of self-provisioning include doing work that you enjoy and ending up with high-quality products at low cost. "Producing artisanal jams, sauces, and smoked meats, or hand-made sweaters, quilts, and clothing, makes these pricey items affordable."[5]

People can save money, and therefore afford to work fewer hours, Schor maintains, if they buy high-quality items and then extend their usable life through repair and restoration. When products are well made they also become available for sale in secondary markets, where the resale prices of high-quality products are typically far below the original cost.[6] These activities reduce environmental degradation as they save money and improve human wellbeing by allowing people, yet again, to live more cheaply so they have less need to work for money.

But what will happen to the economy if the simple lifestyle becomes the norm? What will professional dog walkers do when dog owners have enough time to walk their own dogs? What will professional daycares do when people have enough time to take care of their own children or when social capital improves and neighbors watch one another's children free of charge, as was common in generations past? What will all the retail clerks do when people shop less often and spend less at the store when they do shop? From the employment perspective, the perspective of this book, simplicity seems like a disaster.

However, Schor has a solution to the problem of unemployment in a society that embraces simplicity. She suggests what I've called idling workers through shorter work weeks and job sharing. She thinks this will actually improve efficiency and therefore international competitiveness, which is determined by "labor costs per unit of production, not the total number of hours worked by each person."[7] She notes that Germany and Sweden have some of the shortest work weeks and yet very high productivity per hour worked. "In fact," she writes, "long hours can be a sign of inefficiency. Typically, reductions in daily hours are associated with a rise in productivity per hour, as work is done more intensively and intelligently. So shorter hours are also a wealth-creating, as well as a wealth-sharing, solution."[8]

We saw earlier that shorter work hours have been accompanied in recent decades in the United States with the welfare-reducing practice of increased television viewing. However, this would not be a problem in a society dominated by the culture of simplicity because people would be busy walking and grooming their own dogs, minding their own and other people's children, making jams, wine, and beer, building and repairing their own houses, and helping their neighbors do the same. What's not to like? In principle it's an excellent solution to the problem of avoiding unemployment in environmentally responsible ways. It passes the tests of lowering unemployment, being efficient, and being environmentally responsible. But does it pass the fourth test that we've been using. Is it politically acceptable? I have my doubts.

Schor writes as if simplicity is a wave that's currently taking the country by storm. She cites increases in many of the self-provisioning activities that she endorses. "We . . . know that vegetable gardening has exploded. In April 2009, a national survey found that one in five Americans said they were making plans to plant a garden that year."[9] Call me cynical, but I wonder how many people would have said that they planned to lose weight that year.

The problem is that calls for and prognostications of declines in consumerism have been made for decades, during which consumerism has accelerated. The hippies of the late 1960s supposedly rejected the materialism of their parent's generation, but as a whole their age cohort fostered the increased materialism of today. Joe Dominguez and Vicki Robin report in their excellent book *Your Money or Your Life* on a joint survey of five hundred adults by *Time* magazine and CNN. The survey found that 69 percent of respondents preferred to "slow down and live a more relaxed life;" 61 percent thought that "earning a living today requires so much effort that it's difficult to find time to enjoy life;" 56 percent wanted to spend more time on personal interests and hobbies; and an amazing 89 percent wanted to spend more time with their families. Only 7 percent considered it worth the time and money to shop for status symbols, and just 13 percent wanted to keep up with fashions and trends. In the same vein, *Fortune* magazine reported an American return to frugality based on a poll done for Chivas Regal. The poll found that only 10 percent of respondents considered "earning a lot of money" to be a sign of success, whereas 62 percent thought "a happy family" was the most important status symbol. An impressive 75 percent of respondents between the ages of twenty-five and forty-nine wanted "to see our country return to a simpler life-style, with less emphasis on material success."[10]

This is all good news for the simplicity movement. The bad news is that the joint *Time* magazine/CNN poll was conducted in 1991, and the *Fortune* magazine article appeared in 1989. We now know that the purchase of clothing has doubled since 1991; that the size of new housing has continued to increase; and that the storage industry has blossomed. Consumerism may eventually fade, but I see no indications that simplicity is taking over at present.

Obstacles to widespread adoption of simplicity are formidable. Perhaps most significant is that widespread adoption of simplicity implies contraction of the monetary economy. As more people do things for themselves, help their neighbors without charge, and spend less time working for money, the monetary economy will necessarily contract, or at least fail to grow.

We saw in chapter 1 that economist Benjamin Friedman believes that social and political progress requires economic growth. Whether he's right about that or not, Derek Bok points out that a growing economy is needed to fund the improvements in our physical and human infrastructures required for international competitiveness. These are the kinds of projects discussed in chapters 11 and 12 that improve efficiency and create myriad jobs. Bok writes,

> The most determined opponents of growth would probably favor extending health insurance to every American, providing better schooling in the inner cities, expanding Head Start, and would probably acknowledge that health care costs for programs such as Medicare and Medicaid will have to continue rising faster than the cost of living because of persistent increases in the elderly population and the mounting costs of medical technology. Most people would also support increased funding for biomedical research to encourage discoveries that will prolong human life and bring relief to sufferers from cancer, AIDS, Alzheimer's, and other debilitating diseases.[11]

Even environmentalists who are generally opposed to growth favor basic research in such areas as hydrogen-powered automobiles and alternative sources of electricity. "Finally," Bok notes, "however much opponents of growth may protest, large majorities of Americans will doubtless want to keep spending more on defense as long as other major powers continue to improve their military capabilities and terrorist activities require expensive efforts to counter that threat."[12]

None of this seems practical without continued, robust economic growth in the monetary economy. Most of the items just listed are completely or largely public goods, goods that it's not in the interest of any private parties to create or maintain at the level that society needs. Public money drawn from tax receipts is needed for this purpose—a lot of public money. Federal tax receipts are generally a percentage of GDP, usually 20 percent or less. If the economy contracts or just fails to grow, tax receipts will diminish or remain stable even as educators are telling us that we should increase dramatically what we spend on education, and engineers are telling us that we must increase dramatically what we spend on physical infrastructure maintenance and development. To fund such infrastructural programs needed for competitiveness we'd have to increase the percentage of GDP paid in taxes if the size of the monetary economy was stable or shrinking. This means we'd have to increase tax rates. Raising tax rates in the United States is almost always a tough sell. Would it really be politically acceptable to raise tax rates when people are earning less money because they have fewer hours of paid employment? I don't think you need a professional political consultant to answer this one. Thus, the general expansion of the lifestyle of simplicity is not only unlikely given the current American culture, it would also be economically ruinous because we'd be unable to afford the public goods that we need. Thus, growth in the American economy is essential now and for the foreseeable future.

It sum, fundamental inefficiencies in transportation, healthcare, and crime control can be reduced drastically and efficiency can be improved, while jobs are created through development of our physical and human infrastructure. We can also reduce unemployment through some additional idling of workers, which is fundamentally efficient when concentrated on giving people leave to pursue education and take care of their families. Perhaps most important, we can have unlimited economic growth and job creation through concentration on the provision of (relatively) environmentally benign services combined with infrastructural developments that reduce our environmental impact. But it seems that for now and for the foreseeable future the functional inefficiency of consumerism is ineradicable. We need consumerism to underpin growth in the service sector and thereby growth in the economy as a whole. In addition, consumerism is so popular in the United States that no political candidate calling for its reduction has a serious chance of being elected and no program designed to reduce consumerism has a serious chance of being implemented. For the foreseeable future, our society and economy will host a great deal of functional inefficiency.

NOTES

CHAPTER 1: INTRODUCTION: HOW INEFFICIENCY CAN BE BENEFICIAL

1. Hsin-pao Chang, *Commissioner Lin and the Opium War* (Cambridge, MA: Harvard University Press, 1964), p. 17.

2. Ibid., p. 135.

3. Ibid., p. 137.

4. Peter N. Stearns, *The Industrial Revolution in World History*, 3rd edition (Boulder, CO: Westview Press, 2007), pp. 28–29.

5. Natalie McPherson, *Machines and Economic Growth: The Implications for Growth Theory of the History of the Industrial Revolution* (Westport, CN: Greenwood Press, 1994), p. 14.

6. Ibid., p. 17.

7. Ibid., p. 26.

8. Jack Beeching, *The Chinese Opium Wars* (New York: Harcourt Brace Jovanovich, 1975), p. 33.

9. Tan Chung, *China and the Brave New World* (Durham, NC: Carolina Academic Press, 1978), p. 82.

10. McPherson, *Machines and Economic Growth*, p. 18.

11. Tan, *China and the Brave New World*, p. 83.

12. Ibid., p. 148.

13. Beeching, *Chinese Opium Wars*, p. 17.

14. Ibid., p. 42.

15. Tan, *China and the Brave New World*, p. 83.

16. William Rosen, *The Most Powerful Idea in the World: A Story of Steam, Industry, and Invention* (New York: Random House, 2010), p. 240.

17. Ibid., pp. 242–43.

18. Ibid., p. 246.

19. McPherson, *Machines and Economic Growth*, p. 1.

20. Adam Davidson, "Making It in America," *Atlantic*, January/February 2012, p. 70.

21. Rosen, *Most Powerful Idea in the World*, p. xviii.

22. William Baxter, "People or Penguins," in *People, Penguins, and Plastic Trees*, 2nd edition, ed. Christine Pierce and Donald VanDeVeer (Belmont, CA: Wadsworth Publishing

Co., 1995), p. 381. Reprinted from William Baxter, *People or Penguins: The Case for Optimal Pollution* (New York: Columbia University Press, 1974). I disagree with Baxter that *human* wellbeing is the only proper concern and have argued elsewhere that human welfare is tied inextricably to direct concern for individual animals, animal species, and ecosystems as important in their own right, independent of any known connection to human flourishing. I call this position "environmental synergism." See Peter S. Wenz, *Environmental Ethics Today* (New York: Oxford University Press, 2001).

23. Paul Krugman, "The Capitalist; Viagra and the Wealth of Nations," *New York Times*, August 23, 1998, http://www.nytimes.com/1998/08/23/magazine/the-capitalist-viagra-and -the-wealth-of-nations.html (accessed June 13, 2012).

24. James Howard Kunstler, *The Geography of Nowhere* (New York: Touchstone, 1993), p. 93.

25. Carol Dimitri, Anne Effland, and Neilson Conklin, "The 20th Century Transformation of U.S. Agriculture and Farm Policy," The United States Department of Agriculture Economic Research Service, http://www.ers.usda.gov/publications/EIB3/eib3.pdf, p. 5 (accessed June 10, 2012).

26. Kunstler, *Geography of Nowhere*, p. 95.

27. David Kocieniewski, "A Shuffle of Aluminum, But to Banks, Pure Gold," *New York Times*, July 21, 2013, pp. 1, 14–15.

28. Paul Krugman, "The Jobless Trap," *New York Times*, April 22, 2013, p. A19.

29. Catherine Rampell, "For Millions, Part-Time Work is Full-Time Wait for a Better Job," *New York Times*, April 20, 2013, p. A1.

30. "Unemployment Rate: Labor Force Statistics from the Current Population Survey," Bureau of Labor Statistics, http://data.bls.gov/timeseries/LNS14000000 (accessed May 3, 2014).

31. "The Employment Situation—2014," Bureau of Labor Statistics, http://www.bls .gov/news.release/pdf/empsit.pdf, p. 1 (accessed May 10, 2014).

32. "Labor Force Participation Rate: Labor Force Statistics," Bureau of Labor Statistics, http://data.bls.gov/timeseries/LNS11300000 (accessed June 2, 2014).

33. Nelson D. Schwartz, "Amidst Gains in Jobs and Pay, Americans Rejoin the Workforce," *New York Times*, February 7, 2015, pp. A1, A3.

34. Christopher Flavin, "Preface," *State of the World 2008* (New York: W. W. Norton, 2008), p. xix.

35. Alan Thein Durning, *How Much Is Enough?* (New York: W. W. Norton, 1992), pp. 50–52.

36. Herman Daly, *Steady-State Economics* (Washington, DC: Island Press, 1991).

37. Benjamin M. Friedman, *The Moral Consequences of Economic Growth* (New York: Vintage Books, 2005), p. 17.

38. Ibid., p. 214.

39. Ibid., p. 16. Emphasis in original.

40. Jeff Sommer, "The War against Too Much of Everything," *New York Times*, Sunday Business, December 23, 2012, p. 1.

CHAPTER 2: IDLING WORKERS I: CONVICTS AND WOMEN

1. Benjamin M. Friedman, *The Moral Consequences of Economic Growth* (New York: Vintage Books, 2005), p. 177.

2. Joseph E. Stiglitz, *The Roaring Nineties* (New York: W. W. Norton, 2003), p. 293.

3. James W. Russell, *Double Standard*, 2nd edition (Lanham, MD: Rowman and Littlefield, 2011), p. 95.

4. DW Gibson, *Not Working: People Talk about Losing a Job and Finding Their Way in Today's Changing Economy* (New York: Penguin Books, 2012), p. 14.

5. Ibid., p. 16.

6. Ibid., pp. 18–19.

7. Richard Layard, *Happiness: Lessons from a New Science* (New York: Penguin Books, 2006), p. 64.

8. Ibid., p. 67.

9. Liliana Winkelmann and Rainer Winkelmann, "Why Are the Unemployed So Unhappy? Evidence from Panel Data," *Economica* 65, Issue 257 (1998): 3–4.

10. Layard, *Happiness*, p. 67.

11. Seymour Melman, *Profits without Production* (Philadelphia, PA: University of Pennsylvania Press, 1987), p. 239.

12. Benedict Carey, "Increase Seen in U.S. Suicide Rate Since Recession," *New York Times*, November 4, 2012, http://www.nytimes.com/2012/11/05/health/us-suicide-rate-rose-during-recession-study-finds.html (accessed January 4, 2013).

13. Zebulon Brockway, *Fifty Years of Prison Service* (Montclair, NJ: Patterson Smith, 1969), pp. 404–405. Emphasis in original.

14. Ibid., p. 80.

15. Charles Dickens, *American Notes* (New York: Modern Library, 1996), p. 252, quoted in Rebecca M. McLennan, *Crisis of Imprisonment: Protest, Politics, and the Making of the American Penal State, 1896–1941* (New York: Cambridge University Press, 2008), p. 66.

16. Glen A. Gildemeister, *Prison Labor and Convict Competition with Free Workers in Industrializing America, 1840–1890* (Dekalb: Northern Illinois University, 1987), pp. 156–57.

17. Ibid., p. 173. Emphasis in original.

18. Ibid., p. 174.

19. McLennan, *Crisis of Imprisonment*, p. 83.

20. Ibid., p. 172.

21. Blake McKelvey, *American Prisons: A History of Good Intentions* (Montclair, NJ: Patterson Smith, 1977), pp. 124–25.

22. McLennan, *Crisis of Imprisonment*, p. 97.

23. Warden Wright, *Proceedings of the Annual Congress of the National Prison Association of the United States*, 1894, pp. 141–42, quoted in McLennan, *Crisis of Imprisonment*, pp. 174–75. Emphasis in original.

24. Warden Patterson (New Jersey State Prison at Trenton), *Proceedings of the Annual Congress of the National Prison Association of the United States*, 1887, pp. 120–21, quoted in McLennan, *Crisis of Imprisonment*, p. 175.

25. McLennan, *Crisis of Imprisonment*, p. 210.

26. Senator Ahearn, "Resolution," *New York Times*, March 11, 1897, p. 5, quoted in McLennan, *Crisis of Imprisonment*, p. 265.

27. Commissioner of Charities and Corrections Burton, *New York Times*, October 9, 1897, p. 9, quoted in McLennan, *Crisis of Imprisonment*, p. 267.

28. "LSSI's Building Homes: Rebuilding Lives," Lutheran Social Services of Illinois, Spring 2005, http://www.lssi.org/Full%20Articles/LSSIsBHRL.aspx (accessed January 8, 2013).

29. "The Price of Prisons: What Incarceration Costs Taxpayers," Vera Institute of Justice, July 20, 2012, http://www.vera.org/download?file=3542/Price%2520of%2520Prisons_updated%2520version_072512.pdf, p. 10 (accessed January 14, 2013).

30. "Criminal Justice and Judiciary: How Much Does It Cost to Incarcerate an Inmate in Prison?" Legislative Analyst's Office, The California Legislature's Nonpartisan Fiscal and Policy Advisor, http://www.lao.ca.gov/laoapp/laomenus/sections/crim_justice/6_cj_inmatecost.aspx?catid=3 (accessed February 2, 2013).

31. John Schmitt, Kris Warner, and Sarika Gupta, "The High Budgetary Cost of Incarceration," Center for Economic and Policy Research, June 2010. http://www.cepr.net/documents/publications/incarceration-2010-06.pdf, p. 10 (accessed January 8, 2013).

32. Martha Teichner, "The Cost of a Nation of Incarceration," *CBS News*, April 22, 2012. http://www.cbsnews.com/2102-3445_162-57418495.html?tag=contentMain;contentBody (accessed February 12, 2013).

33. Adam Gopnik, "The Caging of America," *New Yorker*, January 30, 2012, p. 73.

34. Schmitt, Warner, and Gupta, "High Budgetary Cost," p. 4.

35. "Occupational Employment and Wages—May 2011," Bureau of Labor Statistics, http://www.bls.gov/news.release/pdf/ocwage.pdf (accessed March 27, 2012).

36. Emily Yellin, *Our Mother's War: American Women at Home and at the Front During World War II* (New York: Free Press, 2004), p. 40.

37. Chester W. Gregory, *Women in Defense Work during World War II: An Analysis of the Labor Problem and Women's Rights* (New York: Exposition Press, 1974), p. 33.

38. Amy Kesselman, *Fleeting Opportunities: Women Shipyard Workers in Portland and*

Vancouver during World War II and Reconversion (Albany: State University of New York Press, 1990), p. 6.

39. Gregory, *Women in Defense Work*, p. 33.

40. Karen Anderson, *Wartime Women: Sex Roles, Family Relations, and the Status of Women During World War II* (Westport, CN: Greenwood Press, 1981), pp. 61–62.

41. Ibid., p. 62.

42. Yellin, *Our Mother's War*, p. 41.

43. Anderson, *Wartime Women*, p. 29.

44. Yellin, *Our Mother's War*, p. 45.

45. Ibid., p. 47.

46. Gregory, *Women in Defense Work*, p. 156.

47. Ibid., p. 157.

48. Ibid., pp. 162–63.

49. Ibid., p. 161.

50. Laurence Hammond, "Kitchen Lore Speeds War Production," *Independent Woman*, December 1943, p. 362, quoted in Doris Weatherford, *American Women and World War II* (New York: Facts On File, 1990), pp. 184–185.

51. Kesselman, *Fleeting Opportunities*, pp. 13–14.

52. Anderson, *Wartime Women*, p. 63.

53. Weatherford, *American Women and World War II*, p. 189.

54. Kesselman, *Fleeting Opportunities*, p. 92.

55. Ibid., p. 98.

56. Ibid., p. 100.

57. Ibid.

58. Ibid., pp. 94–95.

59. Bernard M. Baruch and John M. Hancock, *War and Postwar Adjustment Policies* (Washington, DC: American Council on Public Affairs, 1944), p. 3.

60. Kesselman, *Fleeting Opportunities*, p. 97.

61. Anderson, *Wartime Women*, p. 168.

62. Kesselman, *Fleeting Opportunities*, p. 22.

63. Anderson, *Wartime Women*, pp. 170–71.

64. Ibid., p. 170.

65. Yellin, *Our Mother's War*, p. 68.

CHAPTER 3: MANUFACTURING FOR INTERNATIONAL MARKETS

1. Karl Marx and Friedrich Engels, *Communist Manifesto*, trans. Samuel Moore (New York: Penguin Books, 1967), p. 85.

2. Ibid., p. 83.

3. Ibid., p. 84.

4. H. W. Brands, *American Colossus: The Triumph of Capitalism, 1865–1900* (New York: Anchor Books, 2010), pp. 585–86.

5. Freda Kirchwey, "Marketing the Plan," *Nation*, June 28, 1947, p. 759.

6. John Gimbel, *Origins of the Marshall Plan* (Stanford, CA: Stanford University Press, 1976), p. 271.

7. Ibid.

8. The White House, Office of the Press Secretary, "President Obama Takes Actions to Promote American Manufacturing and Increase U.S. Exports at Boeing," press release, http://www.whitehouse.gov/the-press-office/2012/02/17/president-obama-takes-actions-promote-american-manufacturing-and-increas (accessed October 18, 2012). Another reason to manufacture for export is to improve our country's balance of payments, but that is not the focus of the present chapter.

9. Erika Bolstad, "Obama Administration to Promote Manufacturing and Exports in Miami," *Miami Herald* Blog, March 15, 2012, http://miamiherald.typepad.com/naked politics/2012/03/obama-administration-to-promote-manufacturing-and-exports-in-miami .html (accessed October 18, 2012).

10. Ibid.

11. William Rosen, *The Most Powerful Idea in the World: A Story of Steam, Industry, and Invention* (New York: Random House, 2010), p. 316.

12. Johan Norberg, *In Defense of Global Capitalism* (Washington, DC: Cato Institute, 2003), p. 117.

13. Ibid., p. 118. Emphasis in original.

14. Peter Singer, *One World: The Ethics of Globalization* (New Haven, CT: Yale University Press, 2002), p. 56.

15. Alexandra Harney, "Bye Bye Cheap Labor," *Far Eastern Economic Review*, March 2008, in Zhiqun Zhu, ed., *Global Studies: China*, 13th edition (New York: McGraw-Hill, 2010), p. 121.

16. Ibid., p. 122.

17. Dexter Roberts, "China's Factory Blues," *Business Week*, April 7, 2008, in Zhu, *Global Studies: China*, p. 119.

18. Harney, "Bye Bye Cheap Labor," p. 122.

19. Roberts, "China's Factory Blues," p. 119.

20. Harney, "Bye Bye Cheap Labor," p. 122.

21. Ibid.

22. Jeffrey D. Sachs, *The End of Poverty: Economic Possibilities for Our Time* (New York: Penguin Press, 2005), p. 12.

23. Ibid., p. 14.

24. Ibid.

25. Thomas L. Friedman, *The Lexus and the Olive Tree* (New York: Farrar, Straus and Giroux, 1999), p. 56.

26. Ibid., p. 285.

27. Ibid., p. 287.

28. Ibid., p. 167.

29. Thomas L. Friedman, *The World Is Flat: A Brief History of the Twenty-First Century* (New York: Farrar, Straus and Giroux, 2005), pp. 262–263. Emphasis in original.

30. Ibid., p. 231. Emphasis in original.

31. Ibid.

32. Erik Brynjolfsson and Andrew McAfee, *Race against the Machine* (Lexington, MA: Digital Frontier Press, 2011), p. 49.

33. Friedman, *World Is Flat*, p. 233. Emphasis in original.

34. Ibid., p. 234.

35. Elizabeth C. Economy, "The Great Leap Backward?" *Foreign Affairs*, September/October 2007, http://www.foreignaffairs.com/articles/62827/elizabeth-c-economy/the-great-leap-backward (accessed February 19, 2015).

36. Ted C. Fishman, "The Chinese Century," *New York Times Magazine*, July 4, 2004, p. 28.

37. Ibid.

38. Charles Duhigg and Keith Bradsher, "How the U.S. Lost Out on iPhone Work," *New York Times*, January 21, 2012, http://www.nytimes.com/2012/01/22/business/apple-america-and-a-squeezed-middle-class.html (accessed October 12, 2012).

39. Charles Duhigg and David Barboza, "In China, the Human Costs That Are Built Into an iPad," *New York Times,* January 26, 2012, pp. A1, B10.

40. Ibid., p. B10.

41. Duhigg and Bradsher, "How the U.S. Lost Out."

42. Fishman, "Chinese Century," p. 28.

43. Ibid., p. 31.

44. Duhigg and Bradsher, "How the U.S. Lost Out."

45. Fishman, "Chinese Century," p. 31.

46. Duhigg and Bradsher, "How the U.S. Lost Out."

47. Fishman, "Chinese Century," p. 46.

48. Ibid.

49. Ibid.

50. "The Third Industrial Revolution: Special Report— Manufacturing and Innovation," *Economist*, April 21, 2012, p. 5.

51. Adam Davidson, "Making It in America," *Atlantic*, January/February 2012, p. 60.

52. "Third Industrial Revolution," p. 4.

53. John Markoff, "Skilled Work, Without the Worker," *New York Times*, Sunday, August 19, 2012, p. 19.

54. Ibid.

55. "Third Industrial Revolution," p. 19.

56. Ibid., p. 6.

57. Jana Winter, "Homeland Security Bulletin Warns 3D Guns May Be 'Impossible' to Stop," *Fox News*, May 23, 2013, http://www.foxnews.com/us/2013/05/23/govt-memo-warns -3d-printed-guns-may-be-impossible-to-stop/ (accessed June 2, 2013).

58. "Third Industrial Revolution," p. 19.

59. Ibid., p. 20.

60. Markoff, "Skilled Work," p. 19.

61. Ibid.

62. "Third Industrial Revolution," p. 5.

63. Brynjolfsson and McAfee, "Race Against the Machine," p. 49.

64. Markoff, "Skilled Work," p. 19.

65. Kurt Brouwer, "Food Costs Decline vs. Personal Income," *Fundmastery Blog*, July 27, 2009, http://www.fundmasteryblog.com/2009/07/27/food-costs-decline-vs-personal-income/ (accessed October 25, 2012).

66. Duhigg and Bradsher, "How the U.S. Lost Out."

67. Ibid.

68. Davidson, "Making It in America," p. 62.

69. Ibid., p. 64.

70. Ibid., pp. 64–65.

71. Wendy Wang, Kim Parker, and Paul Taylor, "Breadwinner Moms," Pew Research Center: Social & Demographic Trends, May 29, 2013, http://www.pewsocialtrends.org/ 2013/05/29/breadwinner-moms/ (accessed July 25, 2013).

72. Lois M. Collins, "1 in 12 Households Headed by Single Dad, Pew Study Finds," *Deseret News*, July 4, 2013, http://www.deseretnews.com/article/865582639/1-in-12-households -headed-by-single-dad-Pew-study-finds.html?pg=all (accessed July 25, 2013).

73. Bill Vlasic, "To Make Tiny American Car, G.M. Also Shrinks Plant and Wages," *New York Times*, July 13, 2011, pp. A1, A19.

74. Brynjolfsson and McAfee, *Race Against the Machine*, p. 45.

75. Fishman, "Chinese Century," p. 46. Emphasis in original.

76. Ibid.

77. Ibid.

78. Markoff, "Skilled Work," p. 1.

79. Guillaume Grallet, "De Foxconn au 'made in France,'" *Le Point*, October 11, 2012, p. 15.

80. Fishman, "Chinese Century," p. 27.

81. Catherine Rampell, "Manufacturing Around the World," *New York Times*, November 16, 2009, http://economix.blogs.nytimes.com/2009/11/16/manufacturing-around-the-world/ (accessed October 22, 2012).

82. Shaila Dewan, Nelson D. Schwartz and Llicia Parlapiano, "How the Recession Reshaped the Economy," *New York Times*, Sunday Review, June 15, 2014, p. 6.

83. Davidson, "Making It in America," p. 60.

84. Thomas L. Friedman, *Hot, Flat, and Crowded* (New York: Farrar, Straus and Giroux, 2008), p. 56.

85. Ibid., p. 58.

CHAPTER 4: ENVIRONMENTAL LIMITS: FOOD AND WATER

1. Thomas L. Friedman, *The World Is Flat* (New York: Farrar, Straus and Giroux, 2005), p. 108.

2. Ibid.

3. Ibid., pp. 1–2.

4. Ibid., p. 2.

5. Thomas L. Friedman, *Hot, Flat, and Crowded* (New York: Farrar, Straus and Giroux, 2008), p. 67.

6. Lester R. Brown, *Eco-Economy: Building an Economy for the Earth* (New York: W. W. Norton, 2001), pp. 7–11. Emphasis in original.

7. Ibid., p. 5.

8. Jared Diamond, "What's Your Consumption Factor?" *New York Times*, January 2, 2008. http://www.nytimes.com/2008/01/02opinion/02diamond.html?_r=1&ref=&pagewanted=print (accessed November 8, 2012).

9. Ibid. Data in the "International Energy Outlook 2011" published by the US Energy Information Administration suggest figures about half of those presented by Diamond. [See DOE/EIA-0484, 2011, http://large.stanford.edu/courses/2011/ph240/nagasawa2/docs/0484-2011.pdf (accessed November 15, 2012).] However, even if we accept these lower figures, everyone on earth living as Americans do today would suggest consumption equivalent to that of thirty-six billion people living as the Chinese did in 2007. But we shouldn't accept these lower figures completely, because the data from the EIA is about five years more current than that in Diamond's work. Chinese consumption and energy use increased considerably during these five years. Perhaps the equivalent of everyone living as Americans do today would be the equivalent of fifty or so billion people living as the Chinese did in 2007.

10. Paul R. Ehrlich, prologue to *The Population Bomb* (New York: Ballantine Books, 1968).

11. Bjorn Lomborg, *The Skeptical Environmentalist: Measuring the Real State of the World* (New York: Cambridge University Press, 2001), p. 61.

12. Ibid., pp. 63–66.

13. Ehrlich, *Population Bomb*, p. 62.

14. Ibid., p. 57.

15. Donella H. Meadows, Jorgan Randers, Dennis L. Meadows, and William H. Behrens, *The Limits to Growth*, 2nd edition, revised (New York: Signet, 1974), p. 66.

16. Jad Mouawad, "Fuel to Burn: Now What?" *New York Times*, April 11, 2012, pp. F1, F8; Mark Scott, "Out of Africa (and Elsewhere): More Fossil Fuels," *New York Times*, April 11, 2012, p. F2.

17. Julian Simon, *The Ultimate Resource* (Princeton: Princeton University Press, 1981), pp. 43–44.

18. Clifford Krauss and Eric Lipton, "U.S. Inches Toward Goal of Energy Independence," *New York Times*, March 23, 2012, p. A1.

19. Elizabeth C. Economy, "The Great Leap Backward?" *Foreign Affairs*, September/October 2007, p. 2, http://www.foreignaffairs.com/articles/62827/elizabeth-c-economy/the-great-leap-backward (accessed February 19, 2015).

20. Edward Wong, "Pollution Leads to Drop in Life Span in Northern China, Research Finds," *New York Times,* July 9, 2013, p. A6.

21. Alexandra Harney, "Bye Bye Cheap Labor," *Far Eastern Economic Review*, March 2008, in Zhiqun Zhu, ed., *Global Studies: China*, 13th edition (New York: McGraw-Hill, 2010), p. 122.

22. Edward Wong, "China's Plan to Curb Air Pollution Sets Limits on Coal Use and Vehicles," *New York Times*, September 13, 2013, p. A4.

23. "Global Water Security," Intelligence Community Assessment, February 2, 2012, http://www.dni.gov/nic/ICA_Global%20Water%20Security.pdf, p. iii (accessed November 11, 2012).

24. Steven Solomon, *Water: The Epic Struggle for Wealth, Power, and Civilization* (New York: HarperCollins, 2010), p. 12.

25. Justin Gillis and Celia W. Dugger, "U.N. Sees Rise for the World to 10.1 Billion," *New York Times,* May 4, 2011, p. A1.

26. Solomon, *Water*, p. 228.

27. Ibid., pp. 368–69.

28. Vandana Shiva, *The Violence of the Green Revolution: Third World Agriculture, Ecology and Politics* (London: Zed Books, 1991), pp. 31–32.

29. Solomon, *Water*, p. 423.

30. Shiva, *Violence of the Green Revolution*, p. 125.

31. Ibid., p. 128.

32. Solomon, *Water*, p. 423.

33. Lester R. Brown, *Plan B 3.0: Mobilizing to Save Civilization* (New York: W. W. Norton, 2008), p. 71.

34. Ibid., p. 73.

35. Thomas Erdbrink, "Its Great Lake Shriveled, Iran Confronts Crisis of Water Supply," *New York Times,* January 31, 2014, pp. A1, A9.

36. Brown, *Plan B*, p. 70.

37. Solomon, *Water*, p. 430.

38. Economy, "Great Leap Backward?"

39. Ibid.

40. Edward Wong, "Plan for China's Water Crisis Spurs Concern," *New York Times*, June 1, 2011, http://www.thehindu.com/news/international/article2866492.ece?css=print (accessed November 20, 2012).

41. Ibid.

42. Ibid.

43. Gary Gardner, "Shrinking Fields: Cropland Loss in a World of Eight Billion," *Worldwatch Paper* 131 (July 1996): 40.

44. Lester R. Brown, *Who Will Feed China?* (New York: W. W. Norton, 1995), p. 14.

45. Brown, *Plan B*, p. 71.

46. Alan Durning and Holly Brough, "Taking Stock: Animal Farming and the Environment," *Worldwatch Paper* 103 (July 1991): 18.

47. Tim Lang, "Food Insecurity," *Ecologist* 38, no. 2 (March 2008): 33. Emphasis in original.

48. UN Commission on Sustainable Development, "Water—More Nutritious Per Drop," in *Worldwatch* 17, no. 4 (July/August 2004): 14.

49. Lester R. Brown, *Eco-Economy: Building an Economy for the Earth* (New York: W. W. Norton, 2001), p. 48.

50. Economy, "Great Leap Backward?"

51. Paul Hawkin, Amory Lovins, and L. Hunter Lovins, *Natural Capitalism: Creating the Next Industrial Revolution* (New York: Little, Brown and Company, 1999), p. 171.

52. Elizabeth L. Cline, *Over-Dressed: The Shockingly High Cost of Cheap Fashion* (New York: Portfolio/Penguin, 2012), p. 32.

53. Juliet B. Schor, *True Wealth* (New York: Penguin Books, 2010/2011), p. 29.

54. Ibid., p. 31.

55. Cline, *Over-Dressed*, p. 122.

56. Hawkins, Lovins, and Lovins, *Natural Capitalism*, p. 171.

57. Brown, *Eco-Economy*, p. 61.

58. Ibid., p. 60.

59. Michael J. de la Merced and David Barboza, "China, in Need of Pork, to Buy U.S. Supplier," *New York Times*, May 30, 2013, p. B6.

60. Marc Reisner, *Cadillac Desert: The American West and Its Disappearing Water* (New York: Viking Penguin, 1986), pp. 437–438.

61. Ibid., p. 459.

62. Ibid.

63. Solomon, *Water*, p. 42–43.

64. Reisner, *Cadillac Desert*, p. 460.

65. Felicity Barringer, "In California, What Price Water?" *New York Times*, March 1, 2013, pp. B1, B4.

66. "Selected Water Prices in California," California Water Plan Update 2005, http://www.waterplan.water.ca.gov/docs/cwpu2005/vol4/vol4-background-selectedwaterprices.pdf (accessed December 4, 2012).

67. "Central Valley Project," Bureau of Reclamation, http://www.usbr.gov/projects/Project.jsp?proj_Name=Central+Valley+Project (accessed December 4, 2012).

68. "Total Water Use in the United States, 2005," United States Geological Survey, http://ga.water.usgs.gov/edu/wateruse-total.html (accessed December 4, 2012). California statistics found at http://ga.water.usgs.gov/edu/wateruse/pdf/wutotal-2005.pdf (accessed December 4, 2012).

69. "Food as a Percent of Total Household Budget by Country," *Big Picture Agriculture*, September 28, 2011, http://bigpictureagriculture.blogspot.com/2011/09/food-as-percent-of-total-household.html (accessed December 4, 2012).

70. Joel Greenberg, "Israel No Longer Worried about Its Water Supply, Thanks to Desalination Plants," *McClatchy DC*, March 20, 2014, http://www.mcclatchydc.com/2014/03/20/221880/israel-no-longer-worried-about.html (accessed May 2, 2014).

71. Index Mundi (May 28, 2013), http://www.indexmundi.com/commodities/?commodity=wheat (accessed May 2, 2014).

72. Jeneen Interlandi, "The Race to Buy Up the World's Water," *Newsweek*, October 8, 2010, http://www.thedailybeast.com/newsweek/2010/10/08/the-race-to-buy-up-the-world-s-water.html (accessed December 4, 2012).

CHAPTER 5: ENVIRONMENTAL LIMITS: FOOD AND WARMING

1. "IPPC Fourth Assessment Report: Climate Change 2007," Intergovernmental Panel on Climate Change, http://www.ipcc.ch/publications_and_data/ar4/wg1/en/spmsspm-human-and.html (accessed May 10, 2014).

2. Justin Gillis, "Heat-Trapping Gas Passes Milestone, Raising Fears," *New York Times*, May 10, 2013, http://www.nytimes.com/2013/05/11/science/earth/carbon-dioxide-level-passes-long-feared-milestone.html?pagewanted=print (accessed May 15, 2013).

3. Rajendra K. Pachauri, Leo Meyer, and the Core Writing Team, eds, *Climate Change 2014, Synthesis Report: Summary for Policy Makers*, http://www.ipcc.ch/pdf/assessment-report/ar5/syr/SYR_AR5_SPMcorr2.pdf (accessed February 20, 2015).

4. "Fewer Americans See Solid Evidence of Global Warming," Pew Research Center, October 22, 2009, http://www.people-press.org/2009/10/22/fewer-americans-see-solid -evidence-of-global-warming/1/ (accessed December 15, 2012).

5. Coral Davenport, "Miami Finds Itself Ankle-Deep in Climate Change Debate," *New York Times*, May 8, 2014, p. A15.

6. "Global Summary Information—2014," National Climatic Data Center, http://www .ncdc.noaa.gov/sotc/summary-info/global/2014/12 (accessed February 21, 2015).

7. Orrin H. Pilkey and Rob Young, "Doubt Global Warming? The Planet Won't Tell a Lie," *USA Today*, January 7, 2010, p. 7A.

8. Andrew C. Revkin, "On Climate Issue, Industry Ignored Its Scientists," *New York Times*, April 24, 2009, p. A1.

9. Ibid., p. A14.

10. Saskia de Melker, "Two Texas Towns Run Out of Water," *PBS Newshour*, March 20, 2012, http://www.pbs.org/newshour/updates/science/jan-june12/texaswater_03-20.html (accessed December 15, 2012).

11. Ibid.

12. Michael Wines, "West's Drought and Growth Intensify Conflict Over Water Rights," *New York Times*, March 17, 2014, pp. A1, A14.

13. Saskia de Melker, "In Drought-Stricken Texas, Hunt for Water Heads Deeper Underground," *PBS Newshour*, March 20, 2012, http://www.pbs.org/newshour/ rundown/2012/03/in-drought-stricken-texas-hunt-for-water-heads-deeper-underground.html (accessed December 15, 2012).

14. Michael Wines, "Wells Dry, Fertile Plains Steadily Turn to Dust," *New York Times*, May 20, 2013, pp. A1, A13.

15. Michael Wines, "Colorado River Drought Forces a Painful Reckoning for States," *New York Times*, January 6, 2014, pp. A1, A10.

16. Marc Reisner, *Cadillac Desert: The American West and Its Disappearing Water* (New York: Viking Penguin, 1986), p. 332.

17. Jim Tankersley, "California Farms, Vineyards in Peril from Warming, U.S. Energy Secretary Warns," *Los Angeles Times*, February 4, 2009, http://articles.latimes.com/print/2009/ feb/04/local/me-warming4 (accessed December 16, 2012).

18. California Cooperative Snow Surveys, Department of Water Resources, http://cdec .water.ca.gov/snow/ (accessed May 14, 2014).

19. Ray Smith, "Alpine Glacier Retreat Pushing Europe Closer to Water Crisis," *Guardian*, July 22, 2011, http://www.guardian.co.uk/environment/2011/jul/22/glacier-europe -water-crisis/print (accessed December 15, 2012).

20. Ibid.

21. Ibid.

22. Pallava Bagla, "Most Himalayan Glaciers Retreating; 21% Stable or Expanding,

Survey Finds," *ScienceInsider*, August 10, 2011, http://news.sciencemag.org/scienceinsider/2011/08/most-himalayan-glaciers-retreati.html (accessed December 11, 2012).

23. Reisner, *Cadillac Desert*, p. 438.

24. Jeneen Interlandi, "The Race to Buy Up the World's Water," *Newsweek*, October 8, 2010, p. 44.

25. Steven Solomon, *Water: The Epic Struggle for Wealth, Power, and Civilization* (New York: HarperCollins, 2010), pp. 477–78.

26. David S. Battisti and Rosamond L. Naylor, "Historic Warnings of Future Food Insecurity with Unprecedented Seasonal Heat," *Science* 322 (January 9, 2009): 243.

27. Ibid.

28. Justin Gillis, "Climate Change Seen Posing Risk to Food Supplies," *New York Times*, November 2, 2013, pp. A1, A8.

29. Christopher B. Field et al., "IPCC, 2014: Summary for Policymakers," *Climate Change 2014: Impacts, Adaptation, and Vulnerability. Part A: Global and Sectoral Aspects*, http://ipcc-wg2.gov/AR5/images/uploads/WG2AR5_SPM_FINAL.pdf, pp. 17–18 (accessed May 14, 2014).

30. Justin Gillis, "How High Could the Tide Go?" *New York Times*, January 22, 2013, pp. D1, D6.

31. Field et al., "IPCC, 2014," p. 17.

32. Gillis, "Heat-Trapping Gas."

33. Field et al., "IPCC, 2014," p. 14.

34. Thomas L. Friedman, *Hot, Flat, and Crowded* (New York: Farrar, Straus and Giroux, 2008), pp. 119–24.

35. Gillis, "How High Could the Tide Go?"

36. Nick Nuttall, "Overfishing: A Threat to Marine Diversity," *10 Stories the World Should Hear More About*, http://www.un.org/events/tenstories/06/story.asp?storyID=800 (accessed December 8, 2012).

37. Randolph E. Schmid, "Ocean 'Dead Zones' Spreading Worldwide," *Sacramento Bee*, August 15, 2008, in *Annual Editions: Global Issues 09/10*, ed. Robert M. Jackson (New York: McGraw-Hill, 2010), p. 60.

38. VIMS Staff, "New Web-Based Map Tracks Marine 'Dead Zones' Worldwide," William and Mary, January 20, 2011, http://www.wm.edu/news/stories/2011/new-web-based-map-tracks-marine-dead-zones-worldwide-123.php (accessed February 26, 2015).

39. NOAA National Marine Fisheries Service, "Expanding Dead Zones Are Shrinking Tropical Blue Marlin Habitat," *ScienceDaily*, December 12, 2011, http://www.sciencedaily.com/releases/2011/12/111209150200.htm (accessed December 8, 2012).

40. Field et al., "IPCC, 2014," p. 17.

41. "Ocean Acidification," Natural Resources Defense Council, http://www.nrdc.org/oceans/acidification/ (accessed December 10, 2012).

42. Lester R. Brown, *Eco-Economy: Building an Economy for the Earth* (New York: W. W. Norton, 2001), p. 53.

43. Jenny Higgins, "Fisheries and Environment," Newfoundland and Labrador Heritage Web Site, 2011, http://www.heritage.nf.ca/society/env_fisheries.html (accessed December 18, 2012).

44. Nuttall, "Overfishing."

45. Jim Yardley, "Two Hungry Nations Collide Over Fishing," *New York Times*, September 5, 2012, pp. A4, A11.

46. Nuttall, "Overfishing."

47. Jenny Higgins, "Cod Moratorium," Newfoundland and Labrador Heritage Web Site, 2009, http://www.heritage.nf.ca/society/moratorium.html (accessed December 13, 2013).

48. Ibid.

49. Katharine Q. Seelye and Jess Bidgood, "Officials Back Deep Cuts in Atlantic Cod Harvest to Save Industry," *New York Times*, January 31, 2013, pp. A10, A13.

50. Higgins, "Fisheries and Environment."

51. Donella Meadows, Jorgen Randers, and Dennis Meadows, *Limits to Growth: The 30-Year Update* (White River Junction, VT: Chelsea Green Publishing Company, 2004), p. 229.

52. Ellen Pikitch et al., "Little Fish, Big Impact," the Lenfest Forage Fish Task Force, April 2012, http://www.oceanconservationscience.org/foragefish/files/Little%20Fish,%20Impact.pdf, pp. 2, 4 (accessed December 18, 2012).

53. Henry Fountain, "Too Many Small Fish Are Caught, Report Says," *New York Times*, April 2, 2012, p. A9.

54. Pikitch et al., p. 2.

55. Ibid. p. 4.

56. Meadows, Randers, and Meadows, *Limits to Growth*, p. 231.

57. Ed Hamer and Mark Anslow, "10 Reasons Why Organic Can Feed the World," *Ecologist* 38, no. 2 (March 2008): 44.

58. Paul Hawkin, Amory Lovins, and L. Hunter Lovins, *Natural Capitalism: Creating the Next Industrial Revolution* (New York: Little, Brown and Company, 1999), pp. 204–205.

59. Tim Lang, "Food Insecurity," *Ecologist* 38, no. 2 (March 2008): 34.

60. Brian Halweil and Danielle Neirenberg, "Watching What We Eat," *State of the World 2004* (New York: W. W. Norton, 2004), p. 74.

61. The Editors, "Meat: Now, It's Not Personal," *Worldwatch* 17, no. 4 (July/August 2004): 16.

62. Hamer and Anslow, "10 Reasons," p. 44.

63. Editors, "Meat," p. 15.

64. Elisabeth Rosenthal, "In Brazil, Paying Farmers to Let the Trees Stand," *New York Times*, August 22, 2009, p. A6.

65. Ibid., p. A1.

66. Elizabeth C. Economy, "The Great Leap Backward?" *Foreign Affairs*, September/October 2007, http://www.foreignaffairs.com/articles/62827/elizabeth-c-economy/the-great-leap-backward (accessed February 20, 2015).

67. "Air-conditioning," Department of Energy, July 1, 2012, http://energy.gov/energysaver/articles/air-conditioning (accessed December 22, 2012).

68. Elisabeth Rosenthal, "The Cost of Cool," *New York Times*, Sunday Review, August 19, 2012, p. 7.

69. Ibid., pp. 1, 7.

70. Ibid., p. 7.

71. "Air-conditioning."

72. Friedman, *Hot, Flat, and Crowded*, p. 60.

73. EarthTalk "Flying vs Driving: Which Is Better for the Environment?" About.com: Environmental Issues, http://environment.about.com/od/greenlivingdesign/a/fly_vs_drive.htm (accessed January 4, 2013).

74. Douglas G. Tiffany, "Economic and Environmental Impacts of U.S. Corn Ethanol Production and Use," *Regional Economic Development* 5, no. 1 (2009): 45, http://research.stlouis fed.org/publications/red/2009/01/Tiffany.pdf (accessed January 4, 2013).

75. Clifford Krauss, "Ethanol Subsidy Besieged," *New York Times*, July 8, 2011, p. B2.

76. Elisabeth Rosenthal, "Rush to Use Crops as Fuel Raises Food Prices and Hunger Fears," *New York Times*, April 7, 2011, pp. A1, A3.

77. Jad Mouawad, "Fuel to Burn: Now What?" *New York Times*, Special Section: Energy, April 11, 2012, p. F1.

78. See Illinois Clean Coal Institute (ICCI) for some current projects, http://www.icci .org/projects.php (January 15, 2013).

79. Elizabeth Kolbert, "Unconventional Crude: Canada's Synthetic-Fuels Boom," *New Yorker*, November 12, 2007, p. 50.

CHAPTER 6: FUNCTIONAL INEFFICIENCY IN TRANSPORTATION

1. "Passenger Miles: 1990–2005," RITA: Research and Innovative Technology Administration, http://www.rita.dot.gov/bts/sites/rita.dot.gov.bts/files/publications/pocket_guide _to_transportation/2008/pdf/entire.pdf, p. 19 (accessed February 25, 2015).

2. "Trucking and the Economy," American Trucking Associations, http://www.trucking. org/Newsroom/Trucks%20Are/Trucking%20and%20the%20Economy.pdf, p. 5 (accessed January 13, 2013). Article no longer on website.

3. Shira Ovide and Mike Spector, "GM IPO: Auto Bailout Saved More than 1 Million Jobs, Study Says," *Deal Journal*, WSJ Blogs, November 17, 2010, http://blogs.wsj.com/deals/2010/11/17/ gm-ipo-auto-bailout-saved-more-than-1-million-jobs-study-says/ (accessed January 15, 2013).

4. David Welch, "Doing the Math on Obama's Detroit Bailout," *The AutoBeat*, Bloomberg Business, August 2, 2010, http://www.businessweek.com/autos/autobeat/archives/2010/08/ doing_the_math_on_obamas_detroit_bailout.html (January 15, 2013).

5. Kim Hill, Debra Menk, and Adam Cooper, "Contribution of the Automotive Industry to the Economies of All Fifty States and the United States," Center for Automotive Research, April 2010, http://www.cargroup.org/?module=Publications&event=View&pubID=16 (accessed February 21, 2015).

6. Ibid.

7. Michaela D. Platzer and Glennon J. Harrison, "The U.S. Automotive Industry: National and State Trends in Manufacturing Employment," Cornell University ILR School, August 3, 2009, http://digitalcommons.ilr.cornell.edu/cgi/viewcontent.cgi?article=1671&context=key _workplace (accessed January 4, 2013).

8. Hill, Menk, and Cooper, "Contributions of the Automotive Industry."

9. Ibid.

10. Ibid.

11. "Auto Manufacturing: Driving America Forward," Auto Alliance, http://jobsfrom autos.com/autos-economy/ (accessed January 10, 2013). Site discontinued.

12. Trucking and the Economy, p. 3.

13. PriceWaterhouseCooper, "The Economic Impacts of the Oil and Natural Gas Industry on the U.S. Economy: Employment, Labor Income and Value Added," September 8, 2009, http://www.api.org/~/media/files/policy/taxes/economic_impacts_on_industry _report_09082009.pdf (accessed February 26, 2015).

14. Stephen Lacey, "Oil and Gas Jobs Increase by 75,000 Under Obama—69,000 More Than Would Be Created by Keystone XL," Center for American Progress, http://thinkprogress .org/climate/2012/01/18/406314/oil-and-gas-jobs-increase-by-75000-under-obama-69000 -more-than-would-be-created-by-keystone-xl/ (January 8, 2013).

15. Advertisement on NPR's *Morning Edition*, June 25, 2012.

16. "President Signs Jobs Bill, Extending Highway Trust Fund," Fast Lane: The Official Blog of the U.S. Secretary of Transportation, March 18, 2010, http://usdotblog.typepad.com/ secretarysblog/2010/03/president-signs-jobs-bill-extending-highway-trust-fund.html (accessed March 2, 2015).

17. "Politicizing the Highway Bill: Bad for America," LiUNA! Fact Sheet, http://www .liunabuildsamerica.org/files/Factsheet-PoliticizingHighwayBill.pdf (accessed January 9, 2013). Article no longer on website.

18. Dennis Slater, "Highway Bill Equals Jobs, Better Roads, Bridges," Construction EquipmentGuide.com, http://www.constructionequipmentguide.com/Highway-Bill-Equals -Jobs-Better-Roads-Bridges/13658/ (accessed January 9, 2013).

19. Jane Holtz Kay, *Asphalt Nation* (Berkeley, CA: University of California Press, 1997), pp. 198–199.

20. Jonathan Weisman, "Congress Approves a $127 Billion Transportation and Student Loan Package," *New York Times*, June 30, 2012, p. A14.

21. Marcia D. Lowe, "Back on Track: The Global Rail Revival," *Worldwatch Paper* 118 (April 1994): 10.

22. Jim Mele, "Truck Efficiency: More than MPG," *Fleet Owner*, May 2009, http://fleet owner.com/management/editorspage/more-than-mpg-0509 (accessed January 18, 2013).

23. Holly Arthur, "The Nation's Freight Railroads Now Average 480 Ton-Miles-Per-Gallon," Association of American Railroads, April 22, 2010, http://www.aar.org/NewsAnd Events/Press-Releases/2010-04-21-EarthDay.aspx (accessed January 18, 2013).

24. Lowe, "Back on Track," p. 11.

25. Deborah Gordon, *Steering a New Course: Transportation, Energy, and the Environment* (Washington, DC: Island Press, 1991), p. 131.

26. Lowe, "Back on Track," p. 11.

27. Yonah Freemark, "Why Do We Subsidize Transit? Is Skewing the Market Acceptable?" *Transport Politic*, September 21, 2011, http://www.thetransportpolitic.com/2011/09/21/a-note -on-transportation-subsidies/ (accessed January 19, 2013).

28. Ibid. Emphasis in original.

29. Kay, *Asphalt Nation*, p. 255.

30. Missouri-Kansas Passenger Rail Coalition and the Ohio Association of Rail Passengers, "America's Long History of Subsidizing Transportation," *TrainWeb*, http://www.trainweb.org/ moksrail/advocacy/resources/subsidies/transport.htm (accessed January 25, 2013).

31. Ibid.

32. Ibid.

33. Ibid.

34. Donald C. Shoup, *The High Cost of Free Parking* (Chicago, IL: Planners Press, 2005), p. 1.

35. Centers for Medicare & Medicaid Services, "National Health Expenditure Projections 2010–2020," https://www.cms.gov/Research-Statistics-Data-and-Systems/Statistics-Trends -and-Reports/NationalHealthExpendData/downloads/proj2010.pdf, p. 1 (accessed January 24, 2013).

36. Shoup, *High Cost of Free Parking*, p. 207. I have adjusted Shoup's figures for inflation between 2002 and 2010.

37. Ibid., p. 210. I have adjusted Shoup's figures for inflation between 2002 and 2012.

38. Bradley W. Lane, "A Time-Series Analysis of Gasoline Prices and Public Transportation in US Metropolitan Areas," *Journal of Transport Geography* 22 (May 2012): 221–235; http:// www.sciencedirect.com/science/article/pii/S0966692311001578 (accessed January 26, 2013).

39. Michael Cooper, "Use of Public Transit Grew in 2011, Report Indicates," *New York Times*, March 12, 2012, p. A13.

40. Shoup, *High Cost of Free Parking*, p. 2.

41. Ibid., p. 31.

42. Ibid., p. 90.

43. Ibid., p. 31.

44. Ibid., p. 131.

45. Ibid., p. 93.

46. Kay, *Asphalt Nation*, pp. 304–305.

47. Shoup, *High Cost of Free Parking*, p. 280.

48. Ibid., p. 284.

49. Ibid., p. 14. Emphasis in original.

50. Ibid., p. 282.

51. "Congested Corridors Report—Chicago," Texas A&M Transportation Institute: Urban Mobility Information, http://mobility.tamu.edu/ums/congestion_data/tables/chica.pdf, p. 2 (accessed May 5, 2011). No longer available on website.

52. Jonathan I. Levy, Jonathan J. Buonocore, and Katherine von Stackelberg, "The Public Health Costs of Traffic Congestion: A Health Risk Assessment," Harvard Center for Risk Analysis, Harvard School of Public Health, http://ibtta.org/sites/default/files/The%20Public%20Health%20Costs%20of%20Traffic%20Congestion.pdf, p. 2 (accessed February 26, 2015).

53. David Schrank, Tim Lomax, and Bill Eisele, "TTI's 2011 Urban Mobility Report," September 2011, http://tti.tamu.edu/documents/mobility-report-2011-wappx.pdf, p. 1 (accessed January 22, 2013).

54. Shoup, *High Cost of Free Parking*, pp. 496–500.

55. Ibid., pp. 380–85, 397–99, 529–41.

56. "Table 1105: Fatal Motor Vehicle Accidents—National Summary: 1990-2009," U.S. Census Bureau, http://www.census.gov/compendia/statab/2012/tables/12s1105.pdf (accessed January 20, 2013).

57. National Safety Council, "Frequently Asked Questions," http://www.nsc.org/news _resources/Resources/res_stats_services/Pages/FrequentlyAskedQuestions.aspx (accessed January 20, 2013). No longer available on website.

58. Binyamin Appelbaum, "As U.S. Agencies Put More Value on a Life, Businesses Fret," *New York Times*, February 16, 2011, http://www.nytimes.com/2011/02/17/business/ economy/17regulation.html?_r=1&pagewanted=print (accessed January 25, 2013).

59. "Gasoline Cost Externalities: Security and Protection Services," International Center for Technology Assessment, January 25, 2005, https://grist.files.wordpress.com/2006/11/rpg _security_update.pdf, p. 2 (accessed February 26, 2015).

60. Jenny B. Wahl, "Oil Slickers: How Petroleum Benefits at the Taxpayer's Expense," http://www.ilsr.org/wp-content/uploads/2012/05/Oil-Slickers.pdf, pp. 9, 16n44 (accessed January 30, 2013).

61. FY11 Federal Budget Spending Estimates, http://www.usfederalbudget.us/defense _budget_2011_3.html (accessed January 28, 2013).

62. "Gasoline Cost Externalities," pp. 5–6.

63. Earl Swift, *The Big Roads* (New York: Houghton Mifflin Harcourt, 2011), p. 317.

64. Ibid., p. 318.

65. Weisman, "Congress Approves a $127 Billion Transportation and Student Loan Package," p. A14.

66. Joshua L. Schank, "America's Highways, Running on Empty," *New York Times*, June 2, 2014, p. A17.

67. National Surface Transportation Infrastructure Financing Commission, *Paying Our Way: A New Framework for Transportation Finance*, February 2009, http://financecommission .dot.gov/Documents/NSTIF_Commission_Final_Report_Mar09FNL.pdf (accessed January 30, 2013).

68. "2010 Gasoline Consumption," *American Fuels: Alternate Fuels News and Commentary*, February 26, 2011, http://americanfuels.blogspot.com/2011/02/2010-gasoline-consumption .html (accessed May 6, 2011).

69. US General Accounting Office, "Excessive Truck Weight: An Expensive Burden We Can No Longer Support," Comptroller General's Report to Congress, http://archive.gao.gov/ f0302/109884.pdf, pp. 23–24 (accessed May 6, 2011).

70. See Illinois License Services, http://www.illinoislicenseservices.com/Truck_Auto _Licensing_.html, and Internal Revenue Service, "Form 2290: Heavy Highway Vehicle Use Tax Return," http://www.irs.gov/pub/irs-pdf/f2290.pdf (accessed May 15, 2011).

71. "Gasoline Taxes by State," GasPriceWatch.com, http://www.gaspricewatch.com/ usgastaxes.asp (accessed January 23, 2012).

72. Kenworth Truck Corporation, *White Paper on Fuel Economy*, August 2008, http:// www.kenworth.com/FuelEconomyWhitePaper.pdf, p. 2 (accessed January 23, 2012). No longer available on website.

73. Illinois License Services and Internal Revenue Service.

74. Schank, "America's Highways," p. A17.

75. Chris Isidore, "America's Vanishing Cars," *CNN Money*, March 13, 2009, http:// money.cnn.com/2009/03/13/news/companies/vanishing_cars/index.htm (accessed January 22, 2012).

76. "Class 8 Trucks: 'On the Road Again' a Matter of Debate," *Accuval*, May 2009, http:// www.accuval.net/insights/industryinsights/detail.php?ID=97 (accessed January 28, 2013).

77. National Surface Transportation Infrastructure Financing Commission, "Paying Our Way."

78. Arthur, "Nation's Freight Railroads," p. 23.

79. Lowe, *Back on Track*, p. 7.

80. American Public Transportation Association, "Transit Savings Report," Public Transportation.org, http://www.publictransportation.org/tools/transitsavings/Pages/default .aspx (accessed January 15, 2013).

81. Van Jones, *The Green Collar Economy*, with Ariane Conrad (New York: HarperCollins, 2008), p. 142. See also, Peter S. Wenz, "Environmental Justice through Improved Efficiency," *Environmental Values* 9, no. 2 (May 2000): 173–188.

CHAPTER 7: FUNCTIONAL INEFFICIENCY IN HEALTHCARE

1. Bureau of Labor Statistics, "Occupational Employment and Wages—May 2012," US Department of Labor, May 29, 2012, news release, http://www.bls.gov/news.release/pdf/ocwage.pdf (accessed February 5, 2013).

2. Ibid., p. 4.

3. Ibid.

4. Bureau of Labor Statistics, "Spotlight on Statistics: Health Care," US Department of Labor, November 2009, http://www.bls.gov/spotlight/2009/health_care/ (accessed February 5, 2013).

5. Anthony P. Carnevale, Nicole Smith, Artem Gulish, and Bennett H. Beach, *Healthcare: Executive Summary*, Georgetown Public Policy Institute, June 2012, https://cew.georgetown.edu/wp-content/uploads/2014/11/Healthcare.ExecutiveSummary.090712.pdf, p. 2 (accessed February 26, 2015).

6. Ken Terry, "Health Spending Hits 17.3 Percent of GDP in Largest Annual Jump," February 4, 2010, http://www.cbsnews.com/2102-505123_162-43841117.html?tag=contentMain;contentBody (accessed February 3, 2013).

7. Carnevale et al., *Healthcare*, p. 3.

8. James V. DeLong, "Maybe We Should Spend More on Healthcare," *American: The Journal of the American Enterprise Institute*, August 26, 2009, http://american.com/archive/2009/august/maybe-we-should-spend-more-on-healthcare (accessed February 5, 2013).

9. Bureau of Labor Statistics, "Spotlight on Statistics: Health Care."

10. Carnevale et al., *Healthcare*, p. 4.

11. Ibid., p. 7.

12. Annie Lowrey and Robert Pear, "Doctor Shortage Likely to Worsen with Health Law," *New York Times*, July 29, 2012, p. 1.

13. Carnevale et al., *Healthcare*, p. 5.

14. DeLong, "Maybe We Should Spend More on Healthcare."

15. OECD (2011), *Health at a Glance 2011: OECD Indicators*, OECD Publishing, http://www.oecd.org/health/healthpoliciesanddata/49105858.pdf, p. 7 (accessed February 10, 2013).

16. DeLong, "Maybe We Should Spend More on Healthcare."

17. Carnevale et al., *Healthcare*, pp. 3–4.

18. Douglas McCarthy, Sabrina K. H. How, Ashley-Kay Fryer, David Radley, and Cathy Schoen, "Why Not the Best? Results from the National Scorecard on U.S. Health System Performance, 2011," *The Commonwealth Fund*, October 18, 2011, http://www.commonwealthfund.org/Publications/Fund-Reports/2011/Oct/Why-Not-the-Best-2011.aspx?view=print&page=1 (accessed February 2, 2013).

19. Annie Lowrey, "Study of U.S. Health Care System Finds Both Waste and Opportunity to Improve," *New York Times*, September 12, 2012, p. A20.

20. OECD, *Health at a Glance 2011*, p. 149.

21. Ibid., p. 151.

22. Ibid., p. 29.

23. Ibid., p. 31.

24. Ibid., p. 29.

25. Ibid., p. 7.

26. Ibid.

27. Gerard F. Anderson and David A. Squires, "Measuring the U.S. Health Care System: A Cross-National Comparison," *Issues in International Health Policy*, June 2010, p. 8, http://www.commonwealthfund.org/~/media/Files/Publications/Issue%20Brief/2010/Jun/1412_Anderson_measuring_US_hlt_care_sys_intl_ib.pdf (accessed February 2, 2013).

28. OECD, *Health at a Glance 2011*, p. 29.

29. Ibid., p. 163.

30. John Wennberg and Alan Gittelsohn, "Small Area Variations in Health Care Delivery: A Population-Based Health Information System Can Guide Planning and Regulatory Decision-Making," *Science* 182 (1973): 1102–1108.

31. John E. Wennberg, *Tracking Medicine: A Researcher's Quest to Understand Health Care* (New York: Oxford University Press, 2010), p. 18.

32. Ibid.

33. Ibid., p. 32.

34. Ibid., pp. 39–40.

35. Ibid., p. 18.

36. David Rieff, "Illness as More than Metaphor," *New York Times Magazine*, December 4, 2005, http://www.nytimes.com/2005/12/04/magazine/04sontag.html?_r=1&pagewanted=print (accessed February 25, 2013).

37. Sabrina Tavernise, "Caesarean Deliveries Vary Widely, Study Finds," *New York Times*, March 5, 2013, p. A16.

38. Wennberg, *Tracking Medicine*, p. 19.

39. Ibid., p. 130.

40. Ibid., p. 131.

41. Ibid., p. 132.

42. OECD, *Health at a Glance 2011*, p. 63.

43. Ibid., p. 85.

44. Wennberg, *Tracking Medicine*, p. 128.

45. Ibid., p. 75.

46. Ibid.

47. Ibid., p. 77. Emphasis in original.

48. Ibid., p. 162.

49. Rita F. Redberg and Rebecca Smith-Bindman, "We Are Giving Ourselves Cancer," *New York Times*, January 31, 2014, p. A21.

50. Sanjay Gupta, "More Treatment, More Mistakes," *New York Times*, August 1, 2012, p. A21.

51. J. Gilbert Welch, *Overdiagnosed: Making People Sick in the Pursuit of Health* (Boston, Beacon Press, 2011), p. 177.

52. Gupta, "More Treatment, More Mistakes," p. A21.

53. Ibid.

54. Ibid.

55. Tara Parker-Pope, "Study Questions Need for Prostate Cancer Surgery," *New York Times*, July 19, 2012, p. A3.

56. Denise Grady, "Ovarian Cancer Screenings Have No Benefit, Panel Says, and Some Risks," *New York Times*, September 11, 2012, p. A13.

57. Roni Caryn Rabin, "Doctor Panels Recommend Fewer Tests for Patients," *New York Times*, April 4, 2012, p. A10.

58. Peggy Orenstein, "The Problem with Pink," *New York Times Magazine*, April 25, 2013, p. 39.

59. Jane E. Brody, "An Exam with Poor Results," *New York Times*, April 30, 2013, p. D4.

60. Jane E. Brody, "A Check on Physicals," *New York Times*, January 22, 2013, p. D5.

61. Rabin, "Doctor Panels Recommend Fewer Tests," p. A14.

62. Elisabeth Rosenthal, "The $2.7 Trillion Medical Bill," *New York Times*, Sunday, June 2, 2013, pp. 1, 18.

63. Amanda Bennett, *The Cost of Hope: The Story of a Marriage, a Family, and the Quest for Life* (New York: Random House, 2012), p. 64.

64. Ibid., p. 139.

65. Ibid., p. 124.

66. Haider Javed Warraich, "The Cancer of Optimism," *New York Times*, Sunday, May 5, 2013, p. 9.

67. Bennett, *Cost of Hope*, pp. 222–223.

68. Wennberg, *Tracking Medicine*, p. 64. Emphasis in original.

69. Ibid., pp. 79–80.

70. Ibid., pp. 103–104.

71. Ibid., pp. 235–237, 246.

72. Ibid., p. 246.

73. Ibid., p. 152.

74. Ibid., p. 165.

75. Ibid., p. 249.

76. Ibid., p. 250.

77. Ibid., pp. 220–221.

78. Neil Irwin, "G.D.P. Began Year 2.9% in the Hole," *New York Times*, June 26, 2014, pp. B1, B6.

79. Bennett, *Cost of Hope*, p. 70.

80. Melody Petersen, *Our Daily Meds* (New York: Farrar, Straus and Giroux, 2008), pp. 18–19.

81. Duff Wilson, "Drug Companies Increase Prices in Face of Change," *New York Times*, November 16, 2009, pp. A1, A16.

82. Katie Thomas, "Generic, but Not Cheap," *New York Times*, August 10, 2012, pp. B1–B2.

83. Petersen, *Our Daily Meds*, pp. 268–269.

84. Ibid., p. 270.

85. Laura Beil, "How Much Would You Pay for Three More Months of Life?" *Newsweek*, September 3, 2012, p. 42.

86. Peterson, *Our Daily Meds*, p. 270.

87. Beil, "How Much Would You Pay?" p. 42.

88. John McKenzie, "Critical Condition: Cheaper in Canada," ABCNews.go.com, October 22, 2011, http://abcnews.go.com/WNT/story?id=129359&page=1 (accessed February 2, 2013).

89. "Pharmaceutical Company Expenses: Cost of Sales, Marketing, R&D Compared," Consumer Project on Technology (CPT), April 19, 2000, http://www.cptech.org/ip/health/econ/allocation.html (accessed February 2, 2013).

90. Rosenthal, "$2.7 Trillion Medical Bill," pp. 1, 18.

91. T. R. Reid, *The Healing of America: A Global Quest for Better, Cheaper, and Fairer Health Care* (New York: Penguin Press, 2009), pp. 37–38.

92. McCarthy et al., "Why Not the Best?" p. 1.

93. Bureau of Labor Statistics, "Occupational Employment and Wages—May 2012."

94. Ian Urbina, "In the Treatment of Diabetes, Success Often Does Not Pay," *New York Times*, January 11, 2006, http://www.nytimes.com/2006/01/11/nyregion/nyregionspecial5/11diabetes.html?_r=1&pagewanted=print (accessed February 13, 2013).

95. Urbina, "In the Treatment of Diabetes."

96. Susan Starr Sered and Rushika Fernandopulle, *Uninsured in America: Life and Death in the Land of Opportunity* (Berkeley: University of California Press, 2007), p. 11.

97. Ibid., p. 18.

98. Robert Pear, "Court's Ruling May Blunt Reach of the Health Law," *New York Times*, July 25, 2012, p. A16.

99. Ezekiel J. Emanuel, "What We Give Up for Health Care," *New York Times*, Weekly Review, January 22, 2012, p. 4.

100. Ken Silverstein, "Can Ethanol Cut Foreign Oil Imports?" *Forbes*, August 26, 2012, http://www.forbes.com/sites/kensilverstein/2012/08/26/can-ethanol-cut-foreign-oil-imports-2/ (accessed November 8, 2012). For a more positive view see Douglas G. Tiffany, "Economic and Environmental Impacts of U.S. Corn Ethanol Production and Use," *Federal Reserve Bank of*

St. Louis Regional Economic Development 5, no. 1 (2009): 42–59, which gives a positive spin on ethanol, including its positive effects on employment and profit.

CHAPTER 8: CONSUMERISM AND INDIVIDUAL DISCONTENT

1. David Leonhardt, "We're Spent," *New York Times*, Sunday Review, July 17, 2011, p. 1.

2. Ibid., p. 6.

3. Jeff Sommer, "The War Against Too Much of Everything," *New York Times*, Sunday Business, December 23, 2012, p. 1.

4. Daniel Gross, "Stop Saving Now!" *Newsweek*, March 23, 2009, p. 28.

5. Victor Lebow, "Price Competition in 1955," *Journal of Retailing* (Spring 1955), http://ablemesh.co.uk/PDFs/journal-of-retailing1955.pdf, p. 3 (accessed December 9, 2010).

6. Rebecca Leung, "France: Less Work, More Time Off," CBS, February 11, 2009, http://www.cbsnews.com/2100-500164_162-704571.html?pageNum=1&tag=page (accessed December 9, 2010).

7. Lebow, "Price Competition in 1955," p. 3.

8. Benjamin M. Friedman, *The Moral Consequences of Economic Growth* (New York: Vintage Books, 2005), p. 82.

9. Ibid.

10. Ibid., pp. 91–92.

11. Adam Smith, *The Wealth of Nations*, ed. Edwin Cannan (New York: Modern Library, 1994), p. 93.

12. Adam Smith, *The Theory of Moral Sentiments*, ed. D. D. Raphael and A. L. MacFie (Oxford: Oxford University Press, 1976), p. 205. Cited in Friedman, *Moral Consequences*, pp. 49–50.

13. John Miller, *The Origin of Ranks* (1771). Cited in Friedman, *Moral Consequences*, p. 49.

14. Friedman, *Moral Consequences*, p. 96.

15. Ibid., p. 97.

16. Ibid., p. 214. Emphasis in original.

17. Ibid., pp. 124–128.

18. Ibid., pp. 132–143.

19. Ibid., p. 152.

20. Ibid., p. 243.

21. Ibid., p. 265.

22. Ibid., p. 294.

23. Ibid., p. 178.

24. "U.S. Federal Government Debt as a Percent of GDP Over Time," *Supporting Evidence*,

http://www.supportingevidence.com/Government/fed_debt_as_percent_GDP_over_time
.html (accessed March 3, 2003).

25. Sommers, "War Against Too Much," p. 1.

26. Richard Layard, *Happiness: Lessons from a New Science* (New York: Penguin Books,
2005), pp. 29–34.

27. Ibid., pp. 33–34.

28. Robert H. Frank, *Falling Behind: How Rising Inequality Hurts the Middle Class*
(Berkeley: University of California Press, 2007), p. 18.

29. Ibid., pp. 18–19.

30. Layard, *Happiness*, pp. 35–36.

31. Robert D. Putnam, *Bowling Alone* (New York: Simon and Schuster, 2000), p. 261.
Emphasis in original.

32. Ibid.

33. Tara Parker-Poe, "Suicide Rates in Middle Age Soared in U.S.," *New York Times*, May
3, 2013, pp. A1, A12.

34. Putnam, *Bowling Alone*, p. 263.

35. Layard, *Happiness*, pp. 36–37.

36. Ibid., p. 37.

37. Daniel Gilbert, *Stumbling on Happiness* (New York: Vintage Books, 2005, 2007), pp.
167–168.

38. Layard, *Happiness*, p. 48. Emphasis in original.

39. Gilbert, *Stumbling on Happiness*, p. 55. Emphasis in original.

40. Layard, *Happiness*, pp. 167–168.

41. Charles F. Kettering, "Keep the Consumer Dissatisfied," *Nation's Business* 17, no.
1 (January 1929): 30–31, 79, http://www.wwnorton.com/college/history/archive/resources/
documents/ch27_02.htm (accessed December 5, 2010).

42. Lebow, "Price Competition in 1955," p. 5.

43. Ibid., p. 6. Emphasis in original.

44. Layard, *Happiness*, p. 89.

45. Ibid., pp. 89–90.

46. Lebow, "Price Competition in 1955," p. 4.

47. Ibid., p. 3.

48. Christopher Lasch, *The Culture of Narcissism: American Life in an Age of Diminishing
Expectations* (New York: Warner Books, 1979), p. 521.

49. Layard, *Happiness*, p. 154.

50. Lasch, *Culture of Narcissism*, pp. 137–138.

51. Ibid.

52. Christopher Lane, *Shyness: How Normal Behavior Became a Sickness* (New Haven: Yale
University Press, 2007), pp. 120–121.

53. Harriet Fraad, "American Depressions," *Tikkun*, January/February 2010, p. 21.

54. Mary Carmichael, "When Medicine Meets Marketing," *Newsweek*, December 22, 2008, p. 51.

55. Melody Petersen, *Our Daily Meds* (New York: Farrar, Straus and Giroux, 2008), p. 16.

56. Ibid., p. 21.

57. Ibid., p. 22.

58. Prescription Access Litigation (PAL), "Direct-to-Consumer-Advertising (DTCA) of Prescription Drugs, http://www.prescriptionaccess.org/learnmore?id=0003 (accessed March 8, 2013). Website no longer available.

59. Tim Kasser and Richard M. Ryan, "A Dark Side of the American Dream: Correlates of Financial Success as a Central Life Aspiration," *Journal of Personality and Social Psychology* 65, no. 2 (1993): 420.

60. "United States GDP," *Trading Economics*, http://www.tradingeconomics.com/united-states/gdp (March 8, 2013).

61. Juliet B. Schor, *Born to Buy* (New York: Scribner, 2004), p. 27.

62. Ibid., p. 37.

63. Ibid., p. 13.

64. Ibid., p. 143.

65. Ibid., p. 167.

66. Ibid., p. 169.

67. Ibid., p. 170.

68. Ibid., p. 174.

69. Ibid., p. 174.

70. John Helliwell, Richard Layard, and Jeffrey Sachs, eds., *World Happiness Report* (New York: The Earth Institute, Columbia University, 2012), Figure 2.9, http://www.earth.columbia.edu/sitefiles/file/Sachs%20Writing/2012/World%20Happiness%20Report.pdf, p. 43 (accessed March 11, 2013).

71. Charles I. Jones and Peter J. Klenow, "Beyond GDP? Welfare across Countries and Time," September 1, 2010, Paper (version 2.0), http://www.stanford.edu/~chadj/rawls200.pdf, p. 3 (accessed March 11, 2013).

72. The general idea stems from the observation that more than 46 percent of French GDP is spent by the government, leaving only 54 percent of GDP for investment and consumption and making consumption about 50 percent of GDP. But the French government provides many goods and services that are most often consumer items in the United States, most notably, but not only, healthcare. When these items are classified as French consumption, their consumption as a percentage of GDP is 61.5. See Mark Deen, "Holland Economic Recovery Elusive as French Face Taxes, Cuts," *Bloomberg Business Week*, May 13, 2014.

73. Here's the math: Divide 70.5 percent by 61.5 percent to find out in percentage terms how much less French households spend on consumer items than American households spend.

French household spending on consumer items as a proportion of GDP is 87 percent as great as American household spending on consumer items as a proportion of GDP. Now multiply this 87 percent by 70 percent because the French GDP is only 70 percent as large as American GDP. The result is that French households spend about 61 percent of what American households spend on consumer items. Because happiness in France is nearly as great as happiness in the United States (97 or 98 percent), it takes only 63 percent as much household expenditure in France as in the United States to yield the same level of human satisfaction. Divide 100 by 63 to get the figure of 1.59, which indicates that in the United States, 59 percent more spending on household consumption is needed to reach equivalent levels of satisfaction found in France.

74. OECD, "How Does the U.S. Compare," OECD Health Data 2012, http://www.oecd.org/unitedstates/BriefingNoteUSA2012.pdf. (No longer available on website.) See also, "Countries That Spend the Most on Healthcare," 24/7 Wall St.—Insightful Analysis for U.S. and Global Equity Investors, March 29, 2012, http://247wallst.com/2012/03/29/countries-that-spend-the-most-on-health-care/2/ (accessed February 8, 2013).

CHAPTER 9: CONSUMERISM, COMPETITION, AND SOCIAL DISAFFECTION

1. Adam Smith, *The Wealth of Nations*, ed. Edwin Cannan (New York: Modern Library, 1994), p. 198.

2. Richard B. Lee, *The Dobe Ju/'hoansi*, 3rd edition (Glendale, CA: Thompson Learning, 2003).

3. Richard Wilkinson and Kate Pickett, *The Spirit Level: Why Greater Equality Makes Societies Stronger* (New York: Bloomsbury Press, 2009), p. 44.

4. Thorsten Veblen, *The Theory of the Leisure Class* (New York: Modern Library, 1934).

5. Richard Layard, *Happiness: Lessons from a New Science* (New York: Penguin Books, 2005), p. 31.

6. Robert Skidelsky and Edward Skidelsky, *How Much Is Enough? Money and the Good Life* (New York: Other Press, 2012), p. 104.

7. Layard, *Happiness*, pp. 41–42. See p. 47 for different results concerning time off.

8. Joel Magnuson, *Mindful Economics* (New York: Seven Stories Press, 2008), p. 275.

9. US Central Intelligence Agency, "Country Comparison: Distribution of Family Income—Gini Index," *The World Factbook*, https://www.cia.gov/library/publications/the-world-factbook/rankorder/2172rank.html (accessed March 29, 2013).

10. Paul Krugman, "The Tax-Cut Con," in *Annual Editions: American Government 06/07* (36th ed.), ed. Bruce Stinebrickner (Dubuque IA: McGraw-Hill, 2007), p. 186.

11. Hear it on YouTube at http://www.youtube.com/watch?v=yYtfejT4QgM (accessed March 29, 2013).

12. Robert H. Frank and Philip J. Cook, *Winner-Take-All Society: Why the Few at the Top Get So Much More Than the Rest of Us* (New York: Penguin Books, 1996), p. 144.

13. Ibid., p. 177.

14. Juliet B. Schor, *The Overspent American: Why We Want What We Don't Need* (New York: HarperPerennial, 1998, 1999), p. 101.

15. Dov Fox, "Human Growth Hormone and the Measure of Man," *New Atlantis*, Fall 2004/Winter 2005, pp. 75- 87, http://www.thenewatlantis.com/publications/article_detail .asp?id=245&css=print (accessed April 3. 2013).

16. Ibid.

17. Schor, *Overspent American*, p. 102.

18. Robert H. Frank, *Falling Behind: How Rising Inequality Harms the Middle Class* (Berkeley: University of California Press, 2007), p. 44; and Ferenc Máté, *The Wisdom of Tuscany: Simplicity, Security & the Good Life—Making the Tuscan Lifestyle Your Own* (New York: W. W. Norton, 2009), p. 60.

19. Robert D. Putnam, *Bowling Alone* (New York: Simon and Schuster, 2000), pp. 487–88n4.

20. Elizabeth Warren and Amelia Warren Tyagi, "What's Hurting the Middle Class," *Boston Review*, September/October 2005, http://bostonreview.net/BR30.5/warrentyagi.php (accessed April 5, 2013).

21. Ibid.

22. Frank, *Falling Behind*, p. 47.

23. Putnam, *Bowling Alone*, p. 19.

24. Ibid.

25. Ibid., p. 20.

26. Ibid., pp. 36–45.

27. Judith Shulevitz, "The Lethality of Loneliness," *New Republic*, May 13, 2013, http://www.newrepublic.com/article/113176/science-loneliness-how-isolation-can-kill-you#   (accessed June 15, 2013).

28. Putnam, *Bowling Alone*, p. 326.

29. Ibid., p. 327.

30. Ibid., p. 332.

31. Ibid., p. 193.

32. Frank, *Falling Behind*, p. 44; and Máté, *Wisdom of Tuscany*, p. 60.

33. Putnam, *Bowling Alone*, p. 223.

34. Ibid., p. 231. Emphasis in original.

35. Ibid., p. 241.

36. Benjamin M. Friedman, *The Moral Consequences of Economic Growth* (New York: Vintage Books, 2005), p. 214.

37. Putnam, *Bowling Alone*, p. 38.

38. Ibid., p. 40.

39. Ibid., p. 343.

40. Ibid., p. 36.

41. The Campaign Finance Institute, http://www.cfinst.org/data/historicalstats.aspx (accessed April 15, 2013).

42. Putnam, *Bowling Alone*, p. 342.

43. Ibid.

44. Ibid.

45. William Kornhauser, *The Politics of Mass Society* (Glencoe, IL: Free Press, 1959), p. 73.

46. Putnam, *Bowling Alone*, p 355.

47. Ibid., p. 356.

48. Ibid., p. 359.

49. Paul Krugman, *The Conscience of a Liberal* (New York: W. W. Norton, 2007), p. 69.

50. Steven Greenhouse, "Share of the Work Force in a Union Falls to a 97-Year Low, 11.3%," *New York Times*, January 24, 2013, pp. B1, B2.

51. Jeff Kolnick and Doug Anderson, "Examining 'Redistribution of Wealth,'" *National Voter*, February 2009, p. 5.

52. Putnam, *Bowling Alone*, p. 344.

53. Ibid., p. 298.

54. Ibid., p. 299.

CHAPTER 10: IDLING WORKERS II: MORE VACATIONS AND PAID LEAVES, FEWER HOURS, AND EARLY RETIREMENT

1. John Maynard Keynes, "Economic Possibilities for Our Grandchildren," *Essays in Persuasion* (New York: W. W. Norton & Co., 1963), http://www.econ.yale.edu/smith/econ116a/keynes1.pdf, p. 3(accessed May 2, 2013). Emphasis in original.

2. Ibid., p. 4.

3. Ibid., p. 5.

4. Michael Huberman and Chris Minns, "The Times They Are Not Changin': Days and Hours of Work in Old and New Worlds, 1870-2000," *Explorations in Economic History* 44 (2007): 542.

5. Ibid., p. 548.

6. Ibid., p. 546.

7. Marcello Estevao and Filipa Sa, "The 35-Hour Workweek in France: Straight Jacket or Welfare Improvement?" *Center for Economic Policy Research* (CEPR), 2007, pp. 6–7.

8. Kim Willsher, "Sarkozy Party Leader Vows to End France's 35-Hour Week," *Guardian*, November 23, 2011, http://www.guardian.co.uk/world/2011/nov/23/sarkozy-party-end-35-hour-week (accessed April 18, 2013).

9. David Jolly, "In France, an Effort to Compete," *New York Times*, November 7, 2012, pp. B1, B5.

10. Estevao and Sa, "35-Hour Workweek in France," p. 17.

11. "France Unemployment Rate," Trading Economics, http://www.tradingeconomics.com/france/unemployment-rate (accessed April 18 2013).

12. Daniel Flynn, "French Unemployment Hits 13-Year High," *Reuters*, September 6, 2012. http://www.reuters.com/article/2012/09/06/us-france-economy-unemployment-idUSBRE8850AQ20120906 (accessed April 18, 2013).

13. Estevao and Sa, "35-Hour Workweek in France," p. 7.

14. John Carney and Vincent Fernando, "French: The Most Productive People in the World," Business Insider, August 20, 2009, http://www.businessinsider.com/are-the-french-the-most-productive-people-in-the-world-2009-8 (accessed February 27, 2015).

15. "French PM Stirs Controversy over 35-Hour Work Week," France 24: International News 24/7, October 30, 2012, http://www.france24.com/en/print/5365255?print=now (accessed April 18, 2013).

16. Jolly, "In France, an Effort to Compete," pp. B1, B5.

17. "French PM Stirs Controversy."

18. "Changes in Net Reserves (BoP–US Dollar) in France," Trading Economics, http://www.tradingeconomics.com/france/changes-in-net-reserves-bop-us-dollar-wb-data.html (accessed April 20, 2013).

19. Rebecca Leung, "France: Less Work, More Time Off," CBS, February 11, 2009, http://www.cbsnews.com/2100-500164_162-704571.html?pageNum=1&tag=page (accessed April 20, 2013).

20. Willsher, "Sarkozy Party Leader."

21. "French PM Stirs Controversy."

22. Leung, "France: Less Work, More Time Off."

23. Ibid.

24. She was likely referring to the Energizer Bunny.

25. James W. Russell, *Double Standard: Social Policy in Europe and the United States*, 2nd edition (New York: Rowman and Littlefield, 2011), pp. 107–108.

26. US Department of Labor, "Use of the FMLA [Family and Medical Leave Act]," *Wage and Hour Division (WHD)*, chapter 3, http://www.dol.gov/whd/fmla/chapter3.htm (accessed May 8, 2013).

27. Human Rights Watch, "Failing Its Families," February 23, 2011, http://www.hrw.org/node/96432 (accessed May 8, 2013).

28. Human Rights Watch, *Failing Its Families: Lack of Paid Leave and Work-Family Supports in the US*, February 23, 2011, http://www.hrw.org/sites/default/files/reports/us0211webwcover.pdf, pp. 37–38 (accessed May 8, 2013).

29. Ibid.

30. Derek Bok, *The Politics of Happiness: What Government Can Learn from the New Research on Well-Being* (Princeton, NJ: Princeton University Press: 2010), p. 169.

31. Richard B. Freeman, *America Works: Critical Thoughts on the Exceptional U.S. Labor Market* (New York: Russell Sage Foundation, 2007), p. 60.

32. Paul Geitner, "On Vacation and Sick? A Court Says Take Another," *New York Times*, June 21, 2012, http://www.nytimes.com/2012/06/22/world/europe/europe-court-says-sick -workers-can-retake-vacations.html?pagewanted=print (accessed July 2, 2013).

33. Freeman, *America Works*, p. 60.

34. "The French Social Security System: IV—Family Benefits," CLEISS [Centre des Liaisons Européennes et Internationales de Sécurité Sociale], http://www.cleiss.fr/docs/regimes/ regime_france/an_4.html (accessed July 2, 2013).

35. "The French Social Security System: Schedule 1: Summary of Family Benefits Provided under Section L511–1 of the French Social Security Code," CLEISS, http://www.cleiss.fr/docs/ regimes/regime_france/an_a1.html (accessed July 2, 2013).

36. Jeremy Reynolds, "When Too Much Is Not Enough: Actual and Preferred Work Hours in the United States and Abroad," *Sociological Forum* 19, no. 1 (March 2004): 102.

37. Robert Skidelsky and Edward Skidelsky, *How Much Is Enough? Money and the Good Life* (New York: Other Press, 2012), p. 198.

38. "Retirement Planner: Benefits by Year of Birth," Social Security, http://www.social security.gov/retire2/agereduction.htm (accessed July 6, 2012).

39. "Retirement Planner: Delayed Retirement Credits," Social Security, http://www .socialsecurity.gov/retire2/delayret.htm (accessed May 20, 2013).

40. Christian Plumb and Patrick Vignal, "French PM Says Pension Reform to Keep Retirement Age at 62: Paper," *Reuters*, March 30, 2013, http://www.reuters.com/ article/2013/03/30/us-france-pensions-idUSBRE92T0C420130330 (accessed April 18, 2013).

41. "Retirement Ages across the OECD," *Guardian*, June 24, 2010, http://www .guardian.co.uk/news/datablog/2010/jun/24/retirement-ages-oecd-countries#data   (accessed May 2, 2013).

42. Russell, *Double Standard*, p. 11.

43. Ibid., pp. 47–50.

44. Juliet B. Schor, *The Overworked American: The Unexpected Decline of Leisure* (New York: Basic Books, 1992), pp. 81–82.

45. Malcolm Pearce and Geoffrey Stewart, *British Political History 1867–1990: Democracy and Decline* (New York: Routledge, 1992), p. 432.

46. Russell Shorto, "No Babies?" *New York Times Magazine*, June 29, 2008, p. 39.

47. Ibid., p. 36.

48. Wojciech Kopczuk, Emmanuel Saez, and Jae Song, "Earnings Inequality and Mobility in the United States: Evidence from Social Security Data Since 1937," *Quarterly Journal of Economics* 125, Issue 1 (February 2010): 104.

49. Joel Magnuson, *Mindful Economics* (New York: Seven Stories Press, 2008), pp. 274–275.

50. Joseph E. Stiglitz, *The Price of Inequality: How Today's Divided Society Endangers our Future* (New York: W. W. Norton, 2012), p. 2. Emphasis in original.

51. Ibid., p. 3.

52. Magnuson, *Mindful Economics*, p. 275; US Central Intelligence Agency, "Country Comparison: Distribution of Family Income—Gini Index." *The World Factbook*, https://www.cia.gov/library/publications/the-world-factbook/rankorder/2172rank.html (accessed May 8, 2013).

53. Thorsten Veblen, *The Theory of the Leisure Class* (New York: Modern Library, 1934), p. 81.

54. Samuel Bowles and Yongjin Park, "Emulation, Inequality, and Work Hours: Was Thorsten Veblen Right?" *Economic Journal* 115 (November 2005): F397–F412.

55. Richard Wilkinson and Kate Pickett, *The Spirit Level: Why Greater Equality Makes Societies Stronger* (New York: Bloomsbury Press, 2009), p. 224.

56. Schor, *Overworked American*, p. 81. Emphasis in original.

57. Freeman, *America Works*, pp. 34–36.

58. Schor, *Overworked American*, pp. 67–68.

59. Freeman, *America Works*, pp. 57–58.

60. Paul Krugman, *The Conscience of a Liberal* (New York: W. W. Norton, 2007), p. 69.

61. Magnuson, *Mindful Economics*, p. 275.

62. Bureau of Labor Statistics, "Union Members–2012," news release, January 13, 2013, http://www.bls.gov/news.release/pdf/union2.pdf (accessed May 2, 2013).

63. Magnuson, *Mindful Economics*, p. 275.

64. Freeman, *America Works*, pp. 12, 70.

65. Russell, *Double Standard*, p. 74.

66. Paul Krugman, "Health, Work, Lies," *New York Times*, February 7, 2014, p. A21.

67. Reynolds, "When Too Much Is Not Enough," p. 104.

68. Bok, *Politics of Happiness*, pp. 28–29.

69. Schor, *Overworked American*, p. 126. Scare quotes in original.

70. Ibid., 129. Emphasis in original.

71. Robert H. Frank, *Falling Behind: How Rising Inequality Harms the Middle Class* (Berkeley: University of California Press, 2007), p. 62.

72. Catherine Rampell, "Coveting Not a Corner Office, but Time at Home," *New York Times*, July 8, 2013, p. A12.

73. Richard Layard, *Happiness: Lessons from a New Science* (New York: Penguin Books, 2005), p. 47.

74. Fredrik Carlsson, Olof Hohansson-Stenman, and Peter Martinsson, "Do You Enjoy More than Others? Survey Evidence of Positional Goods," *Economica* 74 (2007): 586–98.

75. Mark Aguiar and Erik Hurst, "Measuring Trends in Leisure: The Allocation of Time over Five Decades," *Quarterly Journal of Economics* 122, no. 3 (August 2007): 972.

76. Ibid., p. 971.

77. The increase of French participation in civic organizations is documented in Nonna Mayer, "Social Capital, Trust, and Civicness," Cevipof, http://www.cevipof.com/fichier/p _publication/871/publication_pdf_n05_exeter2.pdf (accessed August 18, 2013).

Francesca Vasallo, *France, Social Capital and Political Participation* (Basingstoke: Palgrave Macmillan, 2010) argues that France has notably high individual political participation compared to the United States.

Robert Roy Britt, "France Beats U.S. at Eating and Sleeping," *Livescience*, May 4, 2009, indicates that the French spend twice as much time eating, which is generally a social activity in France, as do people in the United States (http://www.livescience.com/3540-france-beats -eating-sleeping.html [accessed February 27, 2015).

The OECD Better Life Index shows that a larger percentage of French than of American citizens voted in recent elections. See http://www.oecdbetterlifeindex.org/countries/france/ for information on France, and http://www.oecdbetterlifeindex.org/countries/united-states/ for information on the United States (accessed August 18, 2013).

Merle Patrick and Weiwu Zhang, "France and the United States: A Comparative Analysis of Social Capital on Both Sides of the Pond," *French Politics* 10: 3 (2012): 286. Television watching doesn't have the same negative impact on interpersonal trust in France as in the United States.

78. Monica Prasad, "Land of Plenty (of Government)," *New York Times*, Sunday, March 13, 2013, p. 8.

79. Aguiar and Hurst, "Measuring Trends in Leisure," p. 971.

80. Ibid., p. 987.

81. It is uncertain if this effect is reduced by time-switching technologies that enable television viewers to avoid many commercials. With all the ads on the Internet, it may be that time spent on the Internet has some of the same tendencies to promote consumerism that Putnam found in time spent watching television.

82. Keith A. Bender and Natalia A Jivan, "What Makes Retirees Happy?" *Center for Retirement Research* brief 28, February 2005, p. 3, http://crr.bc.edu/briefs/what-makes-retirees -happy/ (accessed May 15, 2013).

83. Ibid.

84. Ibid., p. 5.

85. Bok, *Politics of Happiness*, p. 102.

86. "American Time Use Survey–2012 Results," Bureau of Labor Statistics, June 20, 2013, table 11, http://www.bls.gov/news.release/pdf/atus.pdf (accessed July 2, 2013).

87. Rachel Krantz-Kent and Jay Stewart, "How Do Older Americans Spend Their Time?" *Monthly Labor Review*, May 2007, table 1, http://www.bls.gov/opub/mlr/2007/05/art2full.pdf (accessed July 2, 2013).

CHAPTER 11: PHYSICAL INFRASTRUCTURE AND PUBLIC GOODS

1. American Society of Civil Engineers, "Failure to Act: The Impact of Current Infrastructure Investment on America's Economic Future" (Boston: Economic Development Research Group, 2013), http://www.asce.org/uploadedFiles/Issues_and_Advocacy/Our _Initiatives/Infrastructure/Content_Pieces/failure-to-act-economic-impact-summary-report. pdf, p. 4 (accessed March 2, 2015).

2. Adam Smith, *The Wealth of Nations* (New York: Modern Library, 1994), p. 745.

3. Friedrich A. Hayek, *The Road to Serfdom* (Chicago: University of Chicago Press, 1944), pp. 38–39.

4. American Society of Civil Engineers, "Failure to Act," p. 4.

5. Ibid., p. 7.

6. Ibid.

7. Ibid., p 6.

8. Ibid., p. 9.

9. Ibid., pp. 7–8.

10. Ibid., p. 12.

11. Ibid.

12. Ibid., p. 17.

13. Ibid.

14. Ibid., p. 23.

15. Ibid., p. 9.

16. James Heintz, Robert Pollin, and Heidi Garrett-Peltier, *How Infrastructure Investments Support the U.S. Economy: Employment, Productivity and Growth*, Political Economy Research Institute, January 2009, http://www.peri.umass.edu/fileadmin/pdf/other_publication_types/ green_economics/PERI_Infrastructure_Investments, p. 2 (accessed March 2, 2015).

17. Ibid., p. 22.

18. Ibid., p. 30.

19. Ibid., pp. 25–26.

20. Ibid., p. 38.

21. Robert Pollin and Heidi Garrett-Peltier, "The US Employment Effects of Military and Domestic Spending Priorities," *International Journal of Health Services* 39, no. 3 (2009): 444.

22. Ibid., pp. 448–50.

23. Thomas R. Casten, *Turning Off the Heat: Why America Must Double Energy Efficiency to Save Money and Reduce Global Warming* (Amherst, NY: Prometheus Books, 1998), pp. 47–48.

24. Salman Zafar, "Introduction to Trigeneration," EcoMENA, January 19, 2013, http:// www.ecomena.org/tag/difference-between-cogeneration-and-trigeneration/ (accessed June 8, 2013).

25. Michael E. Webber, "Will Drought Cause the Next Blackout?" *New York Times*, July 24, 2012, p. A19.

26. David Leonhardt, "There's Still Hope for the Planet," *New York Times*, Sunday Review, July 22, 2012, p. 7.

27. Clifford Kraus, "U.S. Coal Companies Scale Back Export Goals," *New York Times*, September 14, 2013, pp. B1, B6.

28. John M. Broder, "New Rule Requires Disclosure of Drilling Chemicals, but Only after Their Use," *New York Times*, May 5, 2012, p. A13.

29. Ian Urbina, "Pressure Limits Efforts to Police Drilling for Gas," *New York Times*, March 4, 2011, pp. A1, A14.

30. Webber, "Will Drought Cause the Next Blackout?"; Kate Galbraith, "As Fracking Increases, So Do Fears about Water Supply," *New York Times*, March 7, 2013, http://www.nytimes.com/2013/03/08/us/as-fracking-in-texas-increases-so-do-water-supply-fears.html?pagewanted=all&pagewanted=print (accessed June 10, 2013); and Felicity Barringer, "Spread of Hydrofracking Could Strain Water Resources in West, Study Finds," *New York Times*, May 2, 2013, p. A12.

31. Henry Fountain, "Experts Eye Oil and Gas Industry as Quakes Shake Oklahoma," *New York Times*, December 13, 2013, pp. A16, A25.

32. Eduardo Porter, "Another Look at Natural Gas," *New York Times*, March 22, 2013. http://economix.blogs.nytimes.com/2013/03/22/another-look-at-natural-gas/?ref=naturalgas&pagewanted=print (accessed June 10, 2013).

33. Anthony R. Ingraffea, "Gangplank to a Warm Future," *New York Times*, July 29, 2013, p. A15.

34. Porter, "Another Look at Natural Gas."

35. Ingraffea, "Gangplank to a Warm Future," p. A15.

36. Joe Nocera, "How to Frack Responsibly," *New York Times*, February 28, 2012, p. A23.

37. Coral Davenport, "Study Finds Methane Leaks Negate Benefits of Natural Gas as a Fuel for Vehicles," *New York Times*, February 14, 2014, p. A12.

38. "Levelized Cost of New Generation Resources in the Annual Energy Outlook 2013," US Energy Information Administration (EIA), January 2013, http://www.eia.gov/forecasts/aeo/er/pdf/electricity_generation.pdf, p. 5 (accessed February 28, 2015).

39. Ibid.

40. "Levelized Cost and Levelized Avoided Cost of New Generation Resources in the Annual Energy Outlook 2014," US Energy Information Agency (EIA), April 17, 2014, http://www.eia.gov/forecasts/aeo/electricity_generation.cfm, p. 3 (accessed February 28, 2015).

41. Edward Humes, "Anywhere It Blows," *Sierra*, March/April 2013, p. 36.

42. William D. Nordhaus, "Energy: Friend or Enemy?" *New York Review of Books*, October 27, 2011, p. 29.

43. "Levelized Cost of New Electricity Generating Technologies," Institute for Energy Research, http://instituteforenergyresearch.org/wp-content/uploads/2009/05/Levelized-Cost-of-New-Electricity-Generating-Technologies.pdf (accessed February 28, 2015).

44. "Mining Coal, Mounting Costs: The Life Cycle Consequences of Coal," Center for Health and the Global Environment, Harvard Medical School, January 3, 2011, http://chge .med.harvard.edu/resource/mining-coal-mounting-costs-life-cycle-consequences-coal (accessed March 10, 2013).

45. Ryan Tracy "Sun Peeks Through in Solar," *Wall Street Journal*, September 10, 2012, pp. B1, B6.

46. "Levelized Cost of New Generation Resources in the Annual Energy Outlook 2011," US Energy Information Agency, November 2010, http://www.eia.gov/oiaf/aeo/electricity _generation.html (accessed February 28, 2015).

47. EIA Annual Energy Outlook 2013.

48. EIA Annual Energy Outlook 2014.

49. Marissa N. Newhall, "Harnessing the Wind Off the Atlantic Coast," *Regional Energy, National Solutions: A Real Energy Vision for America*, ed. Kate Gordon and Kiley Kroh, October 2012, http://www.americanprogress.org/wp-content/uploads/2012/10/RER_full.pdf, pp. 7–8 (accessed August 2, 2013).

50. Ibid., p. 9.

51. Catherine Bowes and Justin Allegro, "The Turning Point for Atlantic Offshore Wind Energy," National Wildlife Federation, September 13, 2012, http://www.nwf.org/News-and -Magazines/Media-Center/Reports/Archive/2012/09-13-12-The-Turning-Point-for-Atlantic -Offshore-Wind-Energy.aspx (accessed August 2, 2013).

52. Rob Jordan, "Stanford Researcher Maps Out an Alternative Energy Future for New York," *Stanford Report*, March 12, 2013, http://news.stanford.edu/news/2013/march/new-york -energy-031213.html (accessed August 3, 2013).

53. Paul Rauber, "Solar for All," *Sierra*, January/February 2013, p. 40.

54. Jordan, "Stanford Researcher Maps Out an Alternative Energy Future."

55. Marilyn A. Brown, Etan Gumerman, Xiaojing Sun, Youngsun Baek, Joy Wang, Rodrigo Cortes, and Diran Soumonni, *Energy Efficiency in the South* (Atlanta: Southeast Energy Efficiency Alliance, 2010), http://www.aaec.arkansas.gov/Solutions/Documents/ ReportEfficiencyInTheSouth.pdf, pp. xiv–xv (accessed June 10, 2013).

56. Ibid., p. xii.

57. Ibid., p. xv.

58. Michael Conathan and Kiley Kroh, "The Foundations of a Blue Economy," Center for American Progress, June 27, 2012, http://www.americanprogress.org/issues/green/ report/2012/06/27/11794/the-foundations-of-a-blue-economy/ (accessed August 2, 2013).

59. "Texas, Oklahoma, Kansas Look to Seize the Day with Passenger Rail Symposium," Fast Lane: The Official Blog of the U.S. Secretary of Transportation, April 6, 2012, http:// usdotblog.typepad.com/secretarysblog/2012/04/passenger-rail-symposium-in-kansas-city. html (accessed March 2, 2015).

60. Ibid.

61. "Illinois Workers Powering Revitalized Rail Industry," Fast Lane: The Official Blog of the U.S. Secretary of Transportation, November 20, 2012, http://usdotblog.typepad.com/secretarys blog/2012/11/illinois-workers-to-power-revitalized-rail-industry.html (accessed January 9, 2013).

62. "Texas, Oklahoma, Kansas Look to Seize the Day."

63. "Sleeper Sell," *Ecologist*, March 2009, p. 22.

64. "Texas, Oklahoma, Kansas Look to Seize the Day."

65. Ron Pernick and Clint Wilder, *Clean Tech Nation: How the U.S. Can Lead in the New Global Economy* (New York: HarperCollins, 2012), p. 75.

66. David Cay Johnston, "Danger! Exploding Pipelines. Bursting Dams. Massive Blackouts: This Is What Awaits America in the Coming Infrastructure Crisis," *Newsweek*, September 10, 2012, pp. 38–43.

67. John Schwartz, "Led by Youth, Americans Are Seen Driving Less," *New York Times*, May 14, 2013, p. A12.

68. Elisabeth Rosenthal, "The End of Car Culture," *New York Times*, Sunday, June 30, 2013, p. 3.

69. Jon Hurdle, "Use of Public Transit in U.S. Reaches Highest Level Since 1956, Advocates Report," *New York Times*, March 10, 2014, p. A15.

70. Katharine Q. Seelye, "Revived Train Service to Cape Cod Offers Travelers an Alternative to Road Rage," *New York Times*, May 27, 2013, p. A10.

71. Ross Ramsey, "On Matters of Transportation, Some Dare to Bring Up Taxes, Tolls and Debt," *Texas Tribune*, April 6, 2013, http://www.nytimes.com/2013/04/07/us/texans-dare-to -talk-tax-debt-and-tolls-for-highway-spending.html (accessed August 5, 2013).

72. Nicholas Confessore "Lobbyists Fighting Spending Cuts Find Ally in Group That Usually Backs Them," *New York Times*, April 10, 2013, p. A12.

73. Kia Gregory and Marc Santora, "Bloomberg Offers $20 Billion Plan to Protect City as the Climate Changes," *New York Times*, June 12, 2013, p. A22.

74. McKenzie Funk, "Deciding Where Future Disasters Will Strike," *New York Times*, November 4, 2012, p. A9; Mireya Navarro, "Weighing Sea Barriers as Protection for New York," *New York Times*, November 8, 2012, p. A18; and Cornelia Dean, "Costs of Shoring Up Coastal Communities," *New York Times*, November 6, 2012, p. D1.

75. Eduardo Porter, "For Insurers, No Doubts on Climate Change," *New York Times*, May 15, 2013, pp. B1–B2.

76. William D. Ruckelshaus, Lee M. Thomas, William K. Reilly, and Christine Todd Whitman, "A Republican Case for Climate Action," *New York Times*, August 2, 2013, p. A19.

77. Coral Davenport, "Large Companies Prepared to Pay Price on Carbon," *New York Times*, December 5, 2013, p. A1.

78. Coral Davenport, "Threat to Bottom Line Spurs Action on Climate," *New York Times*, January 24, 2014, pp. A1, A21.

79. Winston Churchill, http://www.brainyquote.com/quotes/quotes/w/winstonchu135 259.html (accessed January 4, 2013). The attribution of this quote to Churchill is in dispute.

80. Coral Davenport, "Obama to Take Action to Slash Coal Pollution," *New York Times*, June 2, 2014, pp. A1, A12.

81. Paul Krugman, "Cutting Back on Carbon," *New York Times*, May 30, 2014, p. A25.

82. Paul Krugman, "Interests, Ideology, and Climate Change," *New York Times*, June 9, 2014, p. A17.

CHAPTER 12: HUMAN INFRASTRUCTURE

1. William T. Dickens, Isabel Sawhill, and Jeffrey Tebbs, "The Effects of Investing in Early Education on Economic Growth," The Brookings Institution, April 2006, http://www.brookings.edu/~/media/research/files/papers/2006/4/education%20dickens/200604dickenssawhill.pdf, p. 1 (accessed March 2, 2015).

2. Ibid.

3. "Employment Projections: Education Pays in Higher Earnings and Lower Unemployment Rates," Bureau of Labor Statistics, http://www.bls.gov/emp/ep_chart_001.htm (accessed August 25, 2013).

4. Martin Carnoy and Richard Rothstein, "What Do International Tests Really Show about U.S. Student Performance?" Economic Policy Institute, January 28, 2013, http://www.epi.org/publication/us-student-performance-testing/ (accessed August 3, 2013).

5. Ibid.

6. Diane Ravitch, "The Myth of Charter Schools," *New York Review of Books*, November 11, 2010, p. 23.

7. Thomas L. Friedman, "How About Better Parents?" *New York Times*, Sunday, November 20, 2011, p. 11.

8. Carnoy and Rothstein, "What Do International Tests Really Show about U.S. Student Performance?"

9. Diane Ravitch, "School Reform: A Failing Grade," *New York Review of Books*, September 29, 2011, p. 32.

10. David Denby, "Public Defender: Diane Ravitch Takes on a Movement," *New Yorker*, November, 19, 2012, p. 75.

11. Sabrina Tavernise, "Rich and Poor Further Apart in Education," *New York Times*, February 10, 2012, pp. A1, A3; Sean F. Reardon, "No Rich Child Left Behind," *New York Times*, Sunday Review, April 26, 2013, pp. 1, 4.

12. Diane Ravitch, "Do Our Public Schools Threaten National Security?" *New York Review of Books*, June 7, 2012, p. 45.

13. Diane Ravitch, "How, and How Not, to Improve the Schools," *New York Review of Books*, March 22, 2012, p. 18; Denby, "Public Defender," p. 74.

14. Susan Wolf, "New Stanford Report Finds Serious Quality Challenge in National

Charter School Sector," press release for Stanford University, June 15, 2009, http://credo.stanford.edu/reports/National_Release.pdf, p.1 (accessed August, 10, 2013).

15. Ravitch, "Myth of Charter Schools," p. 24.

16. Sam Dillon, "Study Says Charter Network Has Financial Advantages Over Public Schools," *New York Times*, March 31, 2011, p. A15.

17. Ravitch, "Do Our Public Schools Threaten National Security?" p. 46.

18. Byron Auguste, Paul Kihn, and Matt Miller, *Closing the Talent Gap: Attracting and Retaining Top-Third Graduates to Careers in Teaching: An International and Market Research-based Perspective*, September 2010, https://mckinseyonsociety.com/downloads/reports/Education/Closing_the_talent_gap.pdf, p. 5 (accessed August 2, 2013).

19. Ibid., p. 7.

20. Dave Eggers and Ninive Clements Caligari, "The High Cost of Low Teacher Salaries," *New York Times*, Sunday, May 1, 2011, p. 12.

21. Raj Chetty, John N. Friedman, Nathaniel Hilger, Emmanuel Saez, Diane Schanzenbach, and Danny Yagan, *How Does Your Kindergarten Classroom Affect Your Earnings? Evidence from Project STAR*, February 2011, http://obs.rc.fas.harvard.edu/chetty/STAR_slides.pdf, p. 58 (accessed August 18, 2013).

22. Jal Mehta, "Teachers: Will We Ever Learn?" *New York Times*, April 13, 2013, p. A19.

23. Ibid.

24. Motoko Rich, "Intensive Tutoring and Counseling Found to Help Struggling Teenagers," *New York Times*, January 27, 2014, p. A13.

25. Robert Pollin and Heidi Garrett-Peltier, "The US Employment Effects of Military and Domestic Spending Priorities," *International Journal of Health Services* 39, no. 3 (2009): 444.

26. Ravitch, "Myth of Charter Schools," p. 24.

27. James Heintz, Robert Pollin, and Heidi Garrett-Peltier, *How Infrastructure Investments Support the U.S. Economy: Employment, Productivity and Growth*, Political Economy Research Institute, January 2009, http://www.peri.umass.edu/fileadmin/pdf/other_publication_types/green_economics/PERI_Infrastructure_Investments (accessed March 2, 2015).

28. Catherine Rampell, "Where the Jobs Are, the Training May Not Be," *New York Times*, March 2, 2012, p. A3.

29. Ibid., p. A1.

30. Another way to look at it is this: The total cost of two years of study for the master's degree would be about $186,000, which includes two years of study at $40,000 a year and $106,000 in foregone earnings during the two years (assuming, unrealistically, that the master's candidate earns no money at all during those two years). Assuming that the real monetary value of the master's degree remains as great as at present when compared to the bachelor's degree, the total benefit in real dollars will be $321,000 if the person works for thirty years with the master's degree and $428,000 if she works for forty years with the master's degree. The benefits (adjusted for inflation) are about double the costs, making this a good investment.

31. "Employment Projections."

32. "OECD Report: Education at a Glance 2012: *EI Summary of Key Findings*," http://download.ei-ie.org/Docs/WebDepot/EI_Analysis_EAG2012_non-official.pdf, p. 5 (accessed August 15, 2013).

33. Charles M. Blow, "A Dangerous 'New Normal' in College Debt," *New York Times*, March 9, 2013, p. A17.

34. Eric Kelderman, "State Spending on Higher Education Rebounds in Most States after Years of Decline," *Chronicle of Higher Education*, January 21, 2013, http://chronicle.com/article/State-Spending-on-Higher/136745/ (accessed August 12, 2013).

35. Rampell, "Where the Jobs Are," p. A3.

36. Blow, "A Dangerous 'New Normal,'" p. A17.

37. Peter Brooks, "Our Universities: How Bad? How Good?" *New York Review of Books*, March 24, 2011, p. 12.

38. Tamar Lewin, "College Loans Weigh Heavier on Graduates," *New York Times*, April 12, 2011, p. A3.

39. Phyllis Korkki, "Ripple Effects from Rising Student Debt," *New York Times*, Sunday, May 25, 2014, p. 6.

40. "Student Loan Debt by Age Group," Federal Reserve Bank of New York, March 29, 2013, http://www.newyorkfed.org/studentloandebt/index.html (accessed August 18, 2013).

41. Lewin, "College Loans Weigh Heavier on Graduates," p. A3.

42. Ibid.

43. Korkki, "Ripple Effects from Rising Student Debt," p. 6.

44. Hans Johnson, "Defunding Higher Education: What Are the Effects on College Enrollment?" Public Policy Institute of California, May 2012, http://www.ppic.org/content/pubs/rb/RB_512HJRB.pdf, p. 1 (accessed August 18, 2013).

45. Advisory Committee on Student Financial Assistance, "Condition of Access and Persistence Study," US Department of Education, July 13, 2011, http://www2.ed.gov/about/bdscomm/list/acsfa/edlite-caps.html (accessed July 29 2013). Emphasis in original.

46. Katherine Long, "Online Classes May Worsen Educational Achievement Gap, Study Shows," *Seattle Times*, March 16, 2013, http://seattletimes.com/html/localnews/2020577099_onlinecollegexml.html (accessed July 29, 2013).

47. Tyler Cowen, *Average is Over: Powering America Beyond the Age of the Great Stagnation* (New York: Dutton, 2013), p. 182.

48. A. J. Jacobs, "Two Cheers for Web U!" *New York Times*, Sunday Review, April 21, 2013, pp. 1, 6, 7.

49. Ryan Brown, "Community-College Students Perform Worse Online than Face to Face," *Chronicle of Higher Education*, July 18, 2011, http://chronicle.com/article/Community-College-Students/128281/ (accessed August 20, 2013). See also, Katherine Long "Online Classes May Worsen Educational Achievement Gap"; Tamar Lewin, "Colleges Adapt Online

Courses to Ease Burden," *New York Times*, April 30, 2013, pp. A1, A3; and Tamar Lewin, "After Setbacks, Online Courses Are Rethought," *New York Times*, December 11, 2013, pp. A1, A20.

50. Tamar Lewin, "Scrutiny and Suits Take Toll on For-Profit College Company," *New York Times*, November 10, 2010, p. A22.

51. Tamar Lewin, "For-Profit College Group Sued as U.S. Portrays Wide Fraud," *New York Times*, August 9, 2011, p. A3.

52. Lewin, "Scrutiny and Suits," p. A22.

53. Lewin, "College Loans Weigh Heavier on Graduates," p. A3.

54. *Managing Our Future: How Financial Barriers to College Undercut America's Global Competitiveness*, Advisory Committee on Student Financial Assistance, September 2006, http://www2.ed.gov/about/bdscomm/list/acsfa/mof.pdf, p. 1 (accessed August 15, 2013).

55. "OECD Report: Education at a Glance 2012," p. 2.

56. Steven Greenhouse, "Paycheck 101," *New York Times*, March 1, 2012, p. F1.

57. Robert Kuttner, "Economic Recovery and Social Investment: A Strategy to Create Good Jobs in the Service Sector," *New American Foundation*, November 2012, http://nsc.newamerica.net/sites/newamerica.net/files/policydocs/Kuttner_Robert_Service_Sector_Recovery_November_2012.pdf, p. 9 (accessed February 13, 2013).

58. Rampell, "Where the Jobs Are," p. A3.

59. Kuttner, "Economic Recovery and Social Investment," p. 6.

60. Ibid., p. 5.

61. Ibid., p. 7.

62. Ibid., p. 10.

63. *Why Business Should Support Early Childhood Education*, Institute for a Competitive Workforce, 2010, http://uschamberfoundation.org/sites/default/files/publication/edu/ICW_EarlyChildhoodReport_2010.pdf, p. 8 (accessed August 22, 2013).

64. Ginia Bellafante, "Before a Test, a Poverty of Words," *New York Times*, October 5, 2012, http://www.nytimes.com/2012/10/07/nyregion/for-poor-schoolchildren-a-poverty-of-words.html?_r=0&pagewanted=print (accessed August 2, 2013).

65. Sean F. Reardon, "No Rich Child Left Behind," *New York Times*, Sunday Review, April 26, 2013, p. 4. See also, Flavio Cuhna and James J. Heckman, "Investing in Our Young People," Working paper 16201, National Bureau of Economic Research (Cambridge, MA, 2010), published in *Rivista Internazionale di Scienze Sociali, Vita e Pensiero, Pubblicazioni dell'Universita' Cattolica del Sacro Cuore*, vol. 117(3): 387–418.

66. Sarah Jane Glynn, "The New Breadwinners: 2010 Update," Center for American Progress, April 16, 2012, http://www.americanprogress.org/issues/labor/report/2012/04/16/11377/the-new-breadwinners-2010-update/ (accessed August 28, 2013).

67. Dickens, Sawhill, and Tebbs, "Effects of Investing in Early Education," p. 3.

68. *The Economic Promise of Investing in High-Quality Preschool: Using Early Education to Improve Economic Growth and the Fiscal Sustainability of States and the Nation*, Committee for

Economic Development (CED), http://www.ced.org/pdf/Economic-Promise-of-Investing-in
-High-Quality-Preschool.pdf, p. 3 (accessed March 2, 2015).

69. Ibid., p. 4.

70. Ibid., p. 1.

71. Programme for International Student Assessment (PISA), "FAQ," OECD, http://
www.oecd.org/pisa/pisafaq/ (accessed March 2, 2015).

72. OECD (2012), *Education at a Glance 2012—Highlights*, OECD Publishing, http://
www.oecd.org/edu/highlights.pdf, p. 75 (accessed August 15, 2013).

73. *Economic Promise of Investing in High-Quality*, p. 4.

74. Kuttner, "Economic Recovery and Social Investment," p. 8.

75. *Economic Promise of Investing in High-Quality*, p. 3.

76. Mike Ramsey, "'Preschool for All' Law Signed," *State Journal-Register* (Springfield,
Illinois), July 26, 2006, pp. 1, 5.

77. W. Steven Barnett, Megan E. Carolan, Jen Fitzgerald, and James H. Squires, "The
State of Preschool 2012—Executive Summary," The National Institute for Early Education
Research (NIEER), April 29, 2013, http://nieer.org/sites/nieer/files/yearbook2012.pdf, p. 5
(accessed August 15, 2013).

78. Dickens, Sawhill, and Tebbs, "Effects of Investing in Early Education," p. 7.

79. Bruce Bartlett, *The Benefit and the Burden: Tax Reform—Why We Need It and What It
Will Take* (New York: Simon & Schuster, 2012), Appendix I.

80. Bill McBride, "The Rapidly Shrinking Federal Deficit," *Calculated Risk: Finance and
Economics*, April 11, 2013, http://www.calculatedriskblog.com/2013/04/the-rapidly-shrinking
-federal-deficit.html (accessed June 5, 2013).

81. *Why Business Should Support Early Childhood Education*.

82. Adam Davidson, "Boom, Bust or What?" *New York Times Magazine*, May 2, 2013, p. 32.

83. Richard Perez-Pena and Motoko Rich, "Preschool Push Moving Ahead in Many
States," *New York Times*, January 4, 2014, p. A3.

84. Ibid.

85. Kelderman, "State Spending on Higher Education Rebounds."

86. The Editorial Board, "Resurrecting California's Public Universities," *New York
Times*, March 30, 2013, http://www.nytimes.com/2013/03/31/opinion/sunday/resurrecting
-californias-public-universities.html (accessed August 20, 2013).

87. Jane Nho, "Governor Brown Signs 2013–14 State Budget, Increases Funds for UC
and USC Systems," *Daily Californian*, June 28, 2013, http://www.dailycal.org/2013/06/28/
gov-brown-signs-2013-14-state-budget/ (accessed June 28, 2014).

88. Kate Murphy, "Higher Education: Brown's Budget Proposal Calls for Funding
Increase, Tuition Freeze," *San Jose Mercury News*, May 13, 2014, http://www.mercurynews.com/
education/ci_25753843/higher-education-browns-budget-proposal-calls-funding-increase
(accessed June 28, 2014).

89. Derek Bok, *The Politics of Happiness: What Government Can Learn from the New Research on Well-Being* (Princeton, NJ: Princeton University Press, 2010), p. 94.

CHAPTER 13: THE SERVICE SECTOR AND INDEFINITE ECONOMIC GROWTH

1. "Occupational Employment and Wages—May 2011," Bureau of Labor Statistics, http://www.bls.gov/news.release/archives/ocwage_03272012.pdf, p. 2, chart 1 (accessed March 27, 2012).

2. "Employment Projections—2010–20," Bureau of Labor Statistics, http://www.bls.gov/news.release/pdf/ecopro.pdf, table 2 (accessed March 27, 2012).

3. Ibid., p. 1.

4. Ibid., table 2.

5. "China's Achilles Heel," *Economist*, April 21, 2012, p. 53.

6. "U.S. Census Bureau Projections Show a Slower Growing, Older, More Diverse Nation a Half Century from Now," United States Census Bureau, http://www.census.gov/newsroom/releases/archives/population/cb12-243.html (accessed June 8, 2013).

7. Buttonwood, "Demography: Swallowing the Python," Buttonwood's Notebook, *Economist*, January 22, 2013, http://www.economist.com/blogs/buttonwood/2013/01/demography (accessed June 8, 2013).

8. Janice Lloyd, "Alzheimer's 'Epidemic' Could Hit USA by 2050," *USA Today*, February 7, 2013, p. 5A.

9. "Employment Projections," table 6.

10. Theresa Brown, "When No One Is on Call," *New York Times*, Sunday, August 18, 2013, p. 12.

11. Arlie Russell Hochschild, *The Outsourced Self: Intimate Life in Market Times* (New York: Metropolitan Books, 2012), pp. 84–85.

12. Ibid., pp. 88–91, 101.

13. Ibid., pp. 7–8.

14. Richard B. Freeman, *America Works: Critical Thoughts on the Exceptional U.S. Labor Market* (New York: Russell Sage Foundation, 2007), pp. 25–26. Emphasis in original.

15. Hochschild, *Outsourced Self*, p. 44.

16. Ibid.

17. Patricia Marx, "Outsource Yourself," *New Yorker*, January 14, 2013, p. 33.

18. Hochschild, *Outsourced Self*, p. 10.

19. Ibid., p. 195.

20. Ibid. Emphasis in original.

21. Ibid., p. 11.

22. Ibid., p. 196.

23. Ibid., p. 11.

24. Ibid., p. 124.

25. "Employment Projections," table 5.

26. Rich Benjamin, "The Gated Community Mentality," *New York Times*, March 29, 2012, http://www.nytimes.com/2012/03/30/opinion/the-gated-community-mentality.html?_r=0 (accessed August 28, 2013).

27. John Schmitt, Kris Warner, and Sarika Gupta, *The High Budgetary Cost of Incarceration*, Center for Economic and Policy Research, June 2010, http://www.cepr.net/documents/publications/incarceration-2010-06.pdf, p. 4 (accessed August 28, 2013).

28. "Occupational Employment and Wages," table 1.

29. Adam Gopnik, "The Caging of America," *New Yorker*, January 30, 2012, p. 74.

30. "Our Programs: Test Preparation," Kaplan, http://www.kaplan.com/our-programs/test-preparation (accessed August 30, 2013).

31. "Career Areas," Kaplan, http://www.kaplan.com/careers-at-kaplan/career-areas (accessed August 30, 2013).

32. Hochschild, *Outsourced Self*, p. 67.

33. Ibid., pp. 57–58.

34. Jennine Estes, "Premarital Therapy: Great Start for Marriage," http://estestherapy.com/relationshiptips/2009/04/20/the-training-wheels-for-marriage/ (accessed August 28, 2013).

35. Hochschild, pp. 108–109.

36. Ibid., p. 189.

37. Ibid., p. 222.

38. Elissa Gootman, "Job Description: Life of the Party; The Proper Motivator Ensures That the Bar Mitzvah Celebration Boogies," *New York Times*, May 30, 2003, http://www.nytimes.com/2003/05/30/nyregion/job-description-life-party-proper-motivator-ensures-that-bar-mitzvah-celebration.html (accessed September 2, 2013).

39. Elissa Gootman, "Captured Live, on Canvas," *New York Times*, November 9, 2012, http://www.nytimes.com/2012/11/11/fashion/live-event-artists-paint-right-there.html?ref=elissagootman&pagewanted=print (accessed September 2, 2013).

40. Elissa Gootman, "Honey, the Baby Is Coming; Quick, Call the Photographer," *New York Times*, June 16, 2012, http://www.nytimes.com/2012/06/17/us/now-in-the-delivery-room-forceps-camera-action.html?ref=elissagootman&pagewanted=print (accessed September 2, 2013).

41. Jennifer A. Kingson, "Personal Eco-Concierges Ease Transition to Green: Paying a Price to Help the Planet," *New York Times*, October 24, 2011, p. A14.

42. William Grimes, "New Treatments to Save a Pet, but Questions About the Price," *New York Times*, April 6, 2012, p. A1.

43. Michael J. Sandel, *What Money Can't Buy: The Moral Limits of Markets* (New York: Farrar, Straus and Giroux, 2012), pp. 22–23.

44. "Employment Projections," table 2.

45. Tyler Cowen, *Average is Over: Powering America Beyond the Age of the Great Stagnation* (New York: Dutton, 2013), pp. 229–230.

46. Ibid., p. 240. Emphasis in original.

47. Ibid., p. 241.

48. Ibid., p. 239.

49. Thomas Picketty, *Capitalism in the Twenty-First Century* (Cambridge, MA: Belknap Press, 2014), pp. 314–15.

50. David Leonhardt, "Is College Worth It? Clearly Yes, New Data Says," *New York Times*, May 27, 2014, p. A3.

51. Steven Rattner, "Fear Not the Coming of the Robots," *New York Times*, June 22, 2014, Sunday, p. 4.

52. Adam Davidson, "A Ready-To-Assemble Business Plan," *New York Times Magazine*, January 5, 2014, pp. 12–13.

53. Hochschild, *Outsourced Self*, p. 222.

CHAPTER 14: SUMMARY AND CONCLUSION

1. Ezekiel J. Emanuel, "We Can Be Healthy and Rich," *New York Times*, Sunday, February 3, 2013, p. 13.

2. Ferenc Máté, *The Wisdom of Tuscany* (New York: W. W. Norton, 2009), pp. 166–167. Emphasis in original.

3. Juliet B. Schor, *True Wealth: How and Why Millions of Americans Are Creating a Time-Rich, Ecologically Light, Small-Scale, High-Satisfaction Economy* (New York: Penguin, 2010, 2011), p. 114.

4. Máté, *Wisdom of Tuscany*, pp. 171–172.

5. Schor, *True Wealth*, pp. 115.

6. Ibid., pp. 130–133.

7. Ibid., p. 166.

8. Ibid., p. 167.

9. Ibid., p. 116.

10. Joe Dominguez and Vicki Robin, *Your Money or Your Life: Transforming Your Relationship with Money and Achieving Financial Independence* (New York: Penguin Books, 1992), pp. 141–142.

11. Derek Bok, *The Politics of Happiness: What Government Can Learn from the New Research on Well-Being* (Princeton, NJ: Princeton University Press: 2010), p. 70.

12. Ibid., p. 71.

INDEX